APPLYING THE RASCH MODEL

Cited more than 1,900 times, this classic text facilitates a deep understanding of the Rasch model. The authors review the crucial properties of the model and demonstrate its use with a variety of examples from education, psychology, and health. A glossary and numerous illustrations aid the reader's understanding. Readers learn how to apply Rasch analysis so they can perform their own analyses and interpret the results. The authors present an accessible overview that does not require a mathematical background.

Highlights of the new edition include:

- More learning tools to strengthen readers' understanding, including chapter introductions, boldfaced key terms, chapter summaries, activities, and suggested readings.
- Divides chapters (4, 6, 7, and 8) into *basic* and *extended understanding* sections to allow readers to select the level most appropriate for their needs and to provide more in-depth investigations of key topics.
- A website at www.routledge.com/9780415833424 that features free Rasch software, data sets, an Invariance worksheet, detailed instructions for key analyses, and links to related sources.
- Greater emphasis on the role of Rasch measurement as *a priori* in the construction of scales and its use *post hoc* to reveal the extent to which interval scale measurement is instantiated in existing data sets.
- Emphasizes the importance of interval-level measurement data and demonstrates how Rasch measurement is used to examine measurement invariance.
- Insights from other Rasch scholars via innovative applications (Ch. 9).

- Extended discussion of invariance now reviews DIF, DPF, and anchoring (Ch. 5).
- Revised Rating Scale Model material now based on the analysis of the Children's Empathic Attitudes Questionnaire (CEAQ; Ch. 6).
- Clarifies the relationships among Rasch measurement, True Score Theory, and Item Response Theory by reviewing their commonalities and differences (Ch. 13).
- Provides more detail on how to conduct a Rasch analysis so readers can use the techniques on their own (Appendix A).

This book is intended as a text for graduate courses in measurement, Item Response Theory, (advanced) research methods, or quantitative analysis taught in psychology, education, human development, business, and other social and health sciences. Professionals in these areas also appreciate the book's accessible introduction.

Trevor G. Bond is Adjunct Professor at the College of Arts, Society and Education at James Cook University, Australia.

Christine M. Fox is Full Professor in Research and Measurement at the University of Toledo.

APPLYING THE RASCH MODEL

Fundamental Measurement in the Human Sciences

Third Edition

Trevor G. Bond
Christine M. Fox

Routledge
Taylor & Francis Group

NEW YORK AND LONDON

Third edition published 2015
by Routledge
711 Third Avenue, New York, NY 10017

and by Routledge
27 Church Road, Hove, East Sussex BN3 2FA

Routledge is an imprint of the Taylor & Francis Group, an informa business

© 2015 Taylor & Francis

The right of Trevor G. Bond and Christine M. Fox to be identified as
the authors of this work has been asserted by them in accordance with
sections 77 and 78 of the Copyright, Designs and Patents Act 1988.

First edition published by Lawrence Erlbaum Associates, Inc. 2001
Second edition published by Routledge 2007

Library of Congress Cataloging-in-Publication Data
Bond, Trevor G.
   Applying the Rasch model : fundamental measurement in the human
sciences / authored by Trevor G. Bond and Christine M. Fox. — Third
edition.
      pages cm
   Includes bibliographical references and index.
   1. Psychology—Statistical methods.   2. Social sciences—Statistical
methods.   3. Psychology—Research—Methodology.   4. Social
sciences—Research—Methodology.   I. Fox, Christine M.   II. Title.
   BF39.B678 2015
   150.72'7—dc23   2014049808

ISBN: 978-0-415-83341-7 (hbk)
ISBN: 978-0-415-83342-4 (pbk)
ISBN: 978-1-315-81469-8 (ebk)

Typeset in Bembo
by Apex CoVantage, LLC

Printed and bound in the United States of America by
Edwards Brothers Malloy on sustainably sourced paper

To Mike Linacre,
Cooperative, collegial, and collaborative.
TGB & CMF

CONTENTS

FOREWORD

It is not a mere coincidence that after my doctoral training in quantitative research methodology in Germany, I became more involved in Rasch measurement and that I met up with Trevor Bond while he was working in Hong Kong. Ironically, for me, the initial spark was the closing chapter "A Synthetic Overview" of the second edition of "Bond & Fox", which contains a whole bunch of illustrative examples and explanations about the importance of measurement invariance. It was actually because of this chapter in particular that I decided to dig deeper into the subject of Rasch measurement. I do know that some of my colleagues turn up their noses at this less formalized introduction to Rasch measurement, and I do agree that, if one wants to gain an increasingly deeper understanding of the Rasch model, mathematical formalization is unavoidable. However, if Rasch experts cannot communicate even the most fundamental aspects of their best ideas to those who did not have the magical handshake of mathematics, their ideas are likely to be damned to remain as the secret knowledge of a kind of secret society. Fortunately, communicating the principles of Rasch measurement by revealing the underlying conceptual ideas and practical implications runs like a golden thread through this book.

So, back to the Hong Kong Institute of Education, November 2006: After assisting Trevor with the setup of a workshop on Rasch measurement, I sat down and listened to his introductory part. I already was quite versatile in Rasch measurement, its mathematical rationale, and the principle of specific objectivity of comparisons in particular, but the following line from Trevor's talk was a flabbergasting eye-opener into the *meaning* of Rasch measurement: He asked, "If all items of a test are supposed to measure the same 'thing', why should it then make a difference which items we use when comparing persons?" In fact, I did know the mathematical principle of specific objectivity of comparisons between two arbitrarily chosen people, which can more formally expressed as follows:

Since, according to the equation of the Rasch model, the probability of solving an item depends only on the item's difficulty and the person's ability, or the difference between the person parameter and item parameter, it is possible to calculate the difference in solving probability of a person j and j as the difference between the person abilities: $\beta_j - \alpha_i - (\beta_{j'} - \alpha_i) = \beta_j - \beta_{j'}$ (with α_i: item difficulty parameter of an item i, and β_j: person parameter of a person j). A comparison of persons is therefore equal to the difference between their positions on the latent dimension. This is independent of the item i that has been used for the comparison.

While the latter is a perfectly correct description of the mathematical implication, Trevor's interpretation made meaning out of the numbers by relating it to everybody's (hopefully) sound implicit or perhaps even explicit understanding of the need for measurement invariance even in the social sciences.

I always had trouble communicating the property of invariant comparisons, and, admittedly, I did have trouble *understanding* the implications of this property. Trevor's illustration of the conceptual idea behind measurement invariance bridged my own gap between theory and practice—and between mathematical formalization and communication.

But, this new, third edition of Bond & Fox must not be regarded as a mere practical guideline of how to construct measurement scales according to the Rasch model. The critical scrutiny of common practices to assess model or item fit as discussed in the chapter "Rasch Model Requirements: Model Fit and Unidimensionality" leaves no doubt about the authors' deep doubts about many current practices. Unfortunately, there are too many Rasch model papers that carefully avoid focused model fit tests, and this suggests, in my view, that applied Rasch measurement is running the risk of damning itself to mediocre pragmatism. The book is thus exactly diametrically opposed to what Andreski (1972) described as ". . . the custom of refraining from mutual criticism (which) merely serves as a shield against responsibility for negligence". Bond and Fox, furthermore, leave no doubt that they regard Rasch scalability is as a *falsifiable* hypothesis (i.e., a hypothesis that needs not to be true for all attempts at scaling).

Throughout the book, the importance of proper substantive theory building *before* the Rasch model is applied is stressed. So, then, if Rasch measurement cannot be obtained, we should not blame the Rasch model. Instead, we should not delude ourselves but be honest by asking ourselves whether the theory under consideration is strong enough to lead to scales that satisfy the requirements of the Rasch model. I do not know whether we can develop theories about cognitive abilities or personality that lead to the Rasch model. But I know of no case of a method in the natural sciences—which psychologists tend to mimic—having been developed in a theoretical vacuum and then successfully used to make substantial or even groundbreaking discoveries. That's why I became increasingly suspicious about the blind application of the Rasch model in recent decades.

Many will know that I am not a "true believer" in Rasch measurement (e.g., Heene, 2013), and a foreword to this volume by a denigrator of some Rasch practices might appear misplaced. However, the fight for more rigorous standards of measurement in the social sciences, combined with scientific integrity and honesty, is a value that should always be appreciated, and I have, in fact, learned a great deal about it from this book.

Moritz Heene
Ludwig Maximilian University
Munich, Germany

References

Andreski, S. (1972). *Social sciences as sorcery*. London: Deutsch.

Heene, M. (2013). Additive conjoint measurement and the resistance toward falsifiability in psychology. *Frontiers in Quantitative Psychology and Measurement*, 246. doi:10.3389/fpsyg.2013.00246

PREFACE

We have always aimed to produce a book, written in an accessible style, that would facilitate a deep understanding of the Rasch model without requiring readers to have a sophisticated mathematical or statistical background. With over 3,000 citations to date, our readers have made this a classic text. The third edition of our book, often called just "Bond & Fox", reviews the crucial interval-level measurement properties of the Rasch model and demonstrates its use with examples across the human sciences, including educational achievement, human development, attitudes, and health outcomes. A comprehensive glossary and numerous illustrations further aid the reader's understanding. Readers learn how to apply Rasch analysis so they can perform their own analyses and interpret the results using the data sets that are used as in-text examples and those housed on the book's website.

We are always interested to hear the not-always-flattering views of our readers, our colleagues, book reviewers, and our critics. But, for all that, we have not heeded the advice of a few colleagues and one reviewer to soften our critique of True Score Theory (TST) and other Item Response Theory (IRT) methods. However, in this edition, we do reflect on some of the commonalities—as well as the distinctive differences—between these approaches to psychometrics. We are not conducting a 'religious war' for 'true believers', and we do not disparage or dismiss our colleagues with wider IRT interests and knowledge. We simply assert the cornerstones of the Rasch approach to constructing and monitoring variables and contrast the consequences of using data-driven and theory-driven approaches. Clearly, we commend the 'data fit the model' approach rather than the converse. In spite of the best the Rasch model has to offer, the choice of methodology is always in the hands of the analyst.

New to This Edition

In the third edition, we emphasize:

> Many statistical analyses used in the human sciences require the input of interval-level data; Rasch measurement focuses on providing interval-level measurement.
>
> The core role of Rasch measurement is, *a priori*, in the construction and monitoring (quality assurance) of scales.
>
> Rasch analysis techniques can also be used *post hoc* to reveal the extent to which interval-scale measurement can be instantiated in already-existing data sets.

To do this, we have clarified the relationship among Rasch measurement, TST, and IRT (esp. in closing Ch. 13).

From the premise that scientific measurements should remain invariant across time and place, we show how Rasch measurement provides the means for instantiating and examining measurement invariance.

We have invited three other Rasch scholars to contribute their own expertise in applying the Rasch model to the new Chapter 9: 'Making Measures, Setting Standards, and Rasch Regression'.

We have divided the substantive chapters (4, 6, 7 and 8) into two sections:

(a)   an introduction aimed at basic understanding, followed by
(b)   a section to develop Extended Understanding.

We did this by condensing the second-edition exposition in each chapter and then by extending that coverage with in-depth investigation and interpretation using a wider range of examples from the literature. We did this so readers can easily select the level of reading and activity most appropriate for their needs.

Chapter 6, based on the Rating Scale Model, has been rewritten based on the analysis of the CEAQ. (The CAIN data set and tutorial have been moved online.)

We have included a set of activities (readings and analyses) in boxed sections for each chapter. We invite our readers to take the time and opportunity to enhance their skills at actually applying the Rasch model rather than merely reading what we have to say about it.

In addition, we have included:

- More learning tools, including chapter introductions, boldfaced key terms, chapter summaries, activities, and suggested reading lists
- A wider range of examples from both established and emergent leaders in Rasch analysis
- A partial data set for the pathway analogy so readers can work through those concepts more easily

- More detail on how a set of items can be 'built' and understood using a combination of Rasch model diagnostics and substantive theory (Ch. 4)
- Extended discussion of invariance now reviews DIF, DPF, and anchoring (Ch. 5)
- New interpretations of other data sets on measuring facets (Ch. 8)
- A new chapter includes *post hoc* measure creation; Rasch regression addressing IV—DV relationships; and Objective Score Setting in simple as well as complex testing situations (Ch. 9)
- A wider range of Rasch measurement examples across the breadth of the human sciences (Ch. 10)
- Extended Appendix A 'Getting Started', to provide a step-by-step walkthrough of a Rasch analysis of .txt and SPSS data files shows readers how to conduct Rasch analyses on their own.

Website

On the book's website at www.routledge.com/9780415833424, we have provided:

Free Rasch analysis software, Bond&FoxSteps and Bond&FoxFacets, through the generosity of Mike Linacre (Winsteps). These are preloaded with the introductory data sets for Chapters 4, 6, 7, and 8 and step-by-step tutorial guides.
Data sets for other analyses described in the book.
The Invariance worksheet for Chapter 5 as an Excel file.
A folder of step-by-step instruction PDFs for each of those analyses. Many of those will be available in languages other than English for the benefit of our many ESL readers.
Links to key articles and websites for further reading on important Rasch measurement topics.
Other data sets with guidance for analyses.

Intended Audience

This approach reveals more clearly our pedagogical strategies to address the breadth of our intended audience.

For those who are *relatively new* to Rasch measurement and especially those who are learning without the guidance of an experienced Rasch colleague, we suggest approaching your reading in these steps:

1. Work from the Preface to the end of Chapter 13, completing the supplementary readings and the data analysis exercises for each chapter. On your first attempt, complete only the basic introduction sections (and corresponding activities) for Chapters 4, 6, 7, and 8.

2. Return to read the Extended Understanding sections of those four chapters and complete the remaining analyses for each section.
3. Complete the reading and activities described in Appendix A, 'Getting Started'. Online instructions will help you to become more independent with conducting your own Rasch analyses.

For those more familiar with Rasch methods, completing the *whole* chapters, readings, and analyses in the order we have written them is our general advice.

For those experienced teachers, especially those who have many students for whom the mathematics is an integral part of their understanding and who remained frustrated by the generality and lack of mathematics in our presentation, we urge you to use your superior knowledge of the Rasch model and that of your students to devise your own class-relevant reading and analysis sequence better to suit their needs.

Our book is often used as a text for graduate courses in (advanced) measurement, Item Response Theory, (advanced) research methods, or quantitative analysis taught in psychology, education, human development, health care, nursing, business, and other social and life sciences due to its accessible introduction to Rasch measurement.

Acknowledgments

We didn't actually leap to the task of writing a third edition of what has become the best-selling text on Rasch measurement when invited by our editor, Debra Riegert, to submit a proposal to Routledge/Taylor & Francis for consideration. Thanks to Debra and her team at T&F for bringing our ideas to publication. Part of that proposal process involved the editor soliciting reviews of the proposal in light of selected sections of the existing second edition, and we thank those reviewers for the time, thought, and effort that they contributed to that task.

We must thank you, our readers, for considering the value of the Rasch model as we presented it in the previous two editions. Thanks for the book sales and, more particularly, the citations. We trust you will find even more to think about and enjoy in this volume. Thanks to our Rasch measurement colleagues, who have provided us with many lessons to learn, along with their constructive critiques. To readers who emailed questions, comments, and corrections, thank you. It is always heartening to have communication with readers who have read the details so carefully. Chan Wai Fong taught herself Rasch measurement from the second edition; thank you, Wai Fong, for your similarly careful readings of every chapter of the third. Thanks to George Engelhard's grad students, who also provided feedback on drafts of Chapters 1 through 4.

A special thanks to our colleagues Svetlana Beltyukova, Gregory Stone, and Yan Zi, who wrote Chapter 9 between them:

Dr. Yan Zi is Assistant Professor in the Department of Curriculum and Instruction at the Hong Kong Institute of Education. He publishes in the areas of educational and psychological assessment, specializing in the application of Rasch analysis. He obtained a B.Sc. and an M.Ed. from the Wuhan Institute of Physical Education (China) and a Ph.D. from James Cook University (Australia). Dr. Yan chairs the group of scholars translating Bond & Fox into Chinese.

Dr. Gregory E. Stone serves as Professor of Research and Measurement at the University of Toledo (Ohio) and is a partner in the consulting firm MetriKs Amérique. He is widely published in North America, and his book *Applications of Rasch Measurement in Criterion-Referenced Testing* brings his Rasch expertise to bear on that important topic. In 2008, Dr. Stone was honored by the governor of the state of Veracruz, Mexico, as a Distinguished Visitor. He holds a B.A. from Shimer College, an M.A. from Loyola University Chicago, and a Ph.D. from the University of Chicago.

Dr. Svetlana Beltyukova is Associate Professor of Research and Measurement at the University of Toledo (Ohio). Her academic and consulting work focuses on creative applications of the Rasch model in student satisfaction research, health, and human services research, as well as the use of Rasch regression for identification of key drivers in health care. Dr. Beltyukova holds a Ph.D. from Kiev Linguistic University (Ukraine) and a Ph.D. from the University of Toledo.

And thanks to Yan Zi, Jason Fan, and the team of young postdocs from Hong Kong and China who recently completed a translation of Bond & Fox into Chinese. Well done.

In partial response to those critics who wonder aloud as to why we, authors and readers together, persist with advocating and using just one small niche of IRT and statistical theory, we quote from an Editorial in the *New York Times* written about a theory of corporate finance:

> *That is the true test of a brilliant theory*, says a member of the Nobel Economics committee. *What first is thought to be wrong is later shown to be obvious.* People see the world as they are trained to see it, and resist contrary explanations. That's what makes innovation unwelcome and discovery almost impossible.
>
> *An important scientific innovation rarely makes its way by gradually winning over and converting its opponents. . . . What does happen is that its opponents gradually die out and that the growing generation is familiarised with the (new) idea from the beginning.* No wonder that the most profound discoveries are often made by the young or the outsider, neither of whom has yet learned to ignore the obvious or live with the accepted wisdom.
>
> "Naked Orthodoxy" (October 17, 1985)

Trevor Bond & Christine Fox

ABOUT THE AUTHORS

Trevor G. Bond is currently Adjunct Professor at the College of Arts, Society and Education at James Cook University, Australia. He was recently an Adjunct Professor at the Faculty of Education at Universiti Kebangsaan Malaysia. Previous to that, he was Professor and Head of the Department of Educational Psychology, Counselling & Learning Needs at the Hong Kong Institute of Education and then a Visiting Scholar to HKIEd. He taught undergraduate and graduate courses based on developmental and educational psychology to teacher education students and continues to supervise doctoral students who use Rasch measurement approaches to research. In 2005, he instigated the annual PROMS—the Pacific Rim Objective Measurement Symposia—to support the development of measurement capacity in Southeast and Eastern Asia. Prof. Bond regularly conducts Rasch measurement workshops in countries where English is a second language.

Christine M. Fox is a Full Professor in Research and Measurement at the University of Toledo, Ohio, where she teaches graduate courses in statistics, measurement, and survey design. Her research focuses on constructing meaningful measures in the social sciences, with specific interest in developing new methodologies and measures for high-stakes decision making. Two of her major projects (in conjunction with Dr. Beltyukova) entail the measurement of perceptions for high-stakes decisions: developing passenger experience scales for Boeing Commercial Airplanes and serving as a core member of the research team for a project titled 'NATO Global Perceptions—Views from Asia-Pacific Region', funded by NATO's Science for Peace and Security Programme. Along with Dr. Beltyukova, she develops risk-assessment tools for insurance underwriting in the health care industry.

1

WHY MEASUREMENT IS FUNDAMENTAL

Doctoral students in Malaysia report about a group of rather hard-nosed social science professors, who, during dissertation defense, insist on cross-examining candidates on the nature of the data they are analyzing. In particular, they enquire as to whether the data are really interval or merely ordinal in nature. Apparently, this rather old-fashioned disposition has been the undoing of a number of doctoral defenses; candidates who could not argue for the interval nature of their data were required to redo their statistical analyses, replacing Pearson's *r* with Spearman's *rho* and so on. Most professors in the Western world, at least in education, psychology, and the other human sciences, seem to have given up quibbling about such niceties: Pearson's *r* seems to work just as well with all sorts of data—as SPSS doesn't know where the data come from, and apparently many of its users don't either. The upside of this difficulty is that many of these hard-nosed professors now realize that measures derived from Rasch analyses may be considered as interval and therefore permit the use of the wide array of statistical calculations that abound in the social sciences. Unfortunately, however, measurement is not routinely taught in standard curricula in the Western world, and the fallback position is to analyze ordinal data as if they were interval measures.

It seems, notwithstanding those old-fashioned professors and a small number of measurement theorists, that for more than half a century, social science researchers have managed to delude themselves about what measurement actually is. In our everyday lives, we rely both explicitly and implicitly on calibrated measurement systems to purchase gasoline, buy water, measure and cut timber, buy lengths of cloth, assemble the ingredients for cooking, and administer appropriate doses of medicine to ailing relatives. So how is it that when we go to university or the testing company to conduct social science research, undertake some psychological investigation, or implement a standardized survey, we then go about treating and analyzing those data as if the requirements for measurement that served us so well at home in the morning no longer apply in the afternoon? Why do we change our definition of and standards for measurement when the human condition is the focus of our attention?

Measurement systems are ignored when we routinely express the results of our research interventions in terms of either probability levels of $p < 0.01$ or $p < 0.05$, or—better yet—as effect sizes. Probability levels indicate only how un/likely it is that A is more than B or that C is different from B, and effect size is meant to tell us by how much the two samples under scrutiny differ. Instead of focusing on constructing measures of the human condition, psychologists and others in the human sciences have focused on applying sophisticated statistical procedures to their data. Although statistical analysis is a necessary and important part of the scientific process, and the authors in no way would ever wish to replace the role that statistics play in examining relations between **variables**, the argument throughout this book is that quantitative researchers in the human sciences are focused too narrowly on statistical analysis and not concerned nearly enough about the nature of the data on which they use these statistics. Therefore, it is not the authors' purpose to replace quantitative statistics with Rasch measurement but rather to refocus some of the time and energy used for data analysis on the prerequisite construction of quality scientific measures.

Those hard-nosed professors mentioned earlier, of course, recur to the guidelines learned from S.S. Stevens (1946). Every student of Psychometrics 101 or Quantitative Methods 101 has Stevens's lesson ingrained forever. In short, Stevens defined measurement as the assignment of numbers to objects or events according to a rule and, thereby, some form of measurement exists at each of four levels: **nominal, ordinal, interval**, and **ratio**. By now, most of us accept that ratio-level measurement is likely to remain beyond our capacity in the human sciences, yet most of us assume the data that we have collected belong to interval-level scales.

Still, it remains puzzling that those who set themselves up as scientists of the human condition, especially those in psychological, health, and educational research, would accept their ordinal-level 'measures' without any apparent critical reflection, when they are not really measures at all. Perhaps we should all read Stevens himself (1946) a little more closely. "As a matter of fact, most of the scales used widely and effectively by psychologists are ordinal scales" (p. 679). He then specified that the only statistics 'permissible' for ordinal data were medians and percentiles, leaving means, standard deviations, and correlations appropriate for interval or ratio data only. And, even more surprisingly, "The rank-order correlation coefficient is usually deemed appropriate to an ordinal scale, but actually this statistic assumes equal intervals between successive ranks and therefore calls for an interval scale" (p. 678). Can it be clearer than this: "With the interval scale we come to a form that is 'quantitative' in the ordinary sense of the word" (p. 679)? This is also our point: only with 'interval' do we get 'quantitative' in the ordinary sense, the sense in which we use scientific measures in our everyday lives. So why are social scientists left in a state of confusion?

Unfortunately, in this same seminal article, Stevens then blurred these ordinal/interval distinctions by allowing us to invoke "a kind of pragmatic sanction: In numerous instances it leads to fruitful results" (p. 679). He added a hint of a proviso: "When only rank order of data is known, we should proceed cautiously with our statistics, and especially with the conclusions we draw from them" (p. 679). It appears that his implicit 'permission' to treat ordinal data as if they were interval was the only conclusion to reach the social scientists, scientists who were so obviously desperate to use their sophisticated statistics on their profusion of attitude scales.

One reasonably might expect that those who see themselves as social scientists would aspire to be open-minded, reflective, and, most importantly, critical researchers. In empirical science, it would seem that this issue of measurement might be somewhat paramount. However, many attempts to raise these and "whether our data constitute measures" issues result in the abrupt termination of the opportunities for further discussion even in forums specifically identified as focusing on measurement, quantitative methods, or psychometrics. Is the attachment of our field to the (mis?)interpretation of Stevens—the blatant ignorance that ordinal data do not constitute measurement—merely another case of the emperor's new clothes? (Stone, 2002). Let's look at the individual components of that tradition: what is routine practice, what the definition of measurement implies, and the status of each of the ubiquitous four levels of measurement.

Under the pretense of measuring, the common practice has been for psychologists to *describe* the raw data at hand. They report how many people answered the item correctly (or agreed with the prompt), how highly related one response is to another, and what the correlation is between each item and total score. These mere descriptions have chained our thinking to the level of raw data, and raw data are *not* measures. Although psychologists generally accept **counts** as 'measurement' in the human sciences, this usage cannot replace measurement as it is known in the physical sciences. Instead, the flurry of activity and weight of scientific importance has been unduly assigned to statistical analyses instead of measurement. This misemphasis, coupled with unbounded faith in the attributions of numbers to events as sufficing for measurement, has blinded psychologists, in particular, to the inadequacy of these methods. Michell (1997) is quite blunt about this in his paper, titled 'Quantitative Science and the Definition of Measurement in Psychology', in which psychologists' "sustained failure to cognize relatively obvious methodological facts" is termed "methodological thought disorder" (p. 374). The question remains: Is it possible that as scientists specializing in the human sciences, we might open our minds to the possibility that we haven't been measuring anything at all? Or if we have, it has been due as much to good intentions and good fortune as to our invocation of appropriate measurement methodology?

Children Can Construct Measures

It is clear that in the social sciences, the term 'measurement' has a cachet not shared by the terms 'quantitative' or 'statistics'. Perhaps we could learn something about what measurement really entails if we could look at the development of measurement concepts among those in whom these developments are still taking place: children. Part of Jean Piaget's research agenda in Geneva was stimulated by discussions he had in Davos, Switzerland, with Albert Einstein during a meeting in 1928 (Ducret, 1990). Einstein counseled Piaget to examine the development of the concepts of speed, distance, and time in young children to see which of those concepts was logically primitive (i.e., if speed = distance/time, which of them could possibly develop before the others?). Piaget went on to examine the progressive construction of the concepts of length (and measurement) in children and reported those findings in 1948 (Piaget, Inhelder, & Szeminska, 1948/1960).

Piaget's assistants provided children with sets of materials to use in their investigations and, through a series of loosely structured questions, asked children to develop a rudimentary measurement system for the materials (usually wooden dowels) provided. The authors reported the following temporal and logical sequence in the acquisition of lineal measurement concepts in children:

1. Children classified (grouped) the supplied objects into a class with at least one common attribute suitable for measurement (e.g., wooden rods) and put aside the rest (e.g., tumbler, ball, etc.).
2. They then seriated (ordered) those selected objects according to the variation of that attribute (e.g., length).
3. Children then identified an arbitrary unit of difference between two successive lengths (e.g., a small piece of rod, A, such that rod C − rod B = rod A). Their iteration of that unit was used to calculate length relationships, so that rod B = 2 × rod A; and rod B + rod A = rod C, and so forth. Their measurement attempts revealed that the generalized difference between any two adjacent rods, X_n and the next largest $X_{(n+1)}$, was the arbitrary unit, A.
4. In time, each child realized that iterated unit of measurement must be standardized across all appropriate measurement contexts so all lengths could be measured against a common linear measurement scale.

Of course, it does not take Schopenhauer to detect the parallels between the outcomes of the investigations with young children and what we have learned about levels of measurement from Stevens in our introductory college classes. For Piaget and the children, the hierarchical developmental sequence is classification, seriation, iteration, and then standardization; for Stevens's levels, nominal, ordinal, interval, and ratio. The interesting but crucial difference—which is well known to mature grade school children and seems to be ignored by many in the human sciences—is that although classification and seriation are necessary precursors to the development of measurement systems, they, in and of themselves, are not sufficient for measurement. The distinctive attribute of the lineal measurement system is the requirement for an arbitrary unit of difference that can be iterated between successive lengths. School children are quick to insist that convenient lineal measurement units such as hand width and foot length are inadequate even for classroom projects; they demand the use of a standard length of stick, at least.

It is on this latter point that proponents of the Rasch models for measurement focus their attention: How do we develop units of measurement, which at first must be arbitrary but can be iterated along a scale of interest so the unit values remain the same? This is the prime focus for Rasch measurement. The cover of a handout from the Rasch measurement Special Interest Group of the American Educational Research Association bore the motto 'Making Measures'. Each cover of the *Journal of Applied Measurement* states the same objective in a different way: 'Constructing Variables'. It might be a very long time before those of us in the human sciences can happily adopt a genuine zero starting point for the measurement of math achievement or cognitive development or decide what zero introversion or quality of life looks like, but those who work painstakingly toward making measures so that the resultant scales have interval measurement properties are making an important contribution to scientific progress. In keeping with the development of instruments in the physical sciences, we need to spend more time investigating our scales than investigating *with* our scales. These attempts at the construction of measures go beyond merely naming and ordering indicators toward the perhaps unattainable Holy Grail of genuine ratio measures.

In terms of Stevens's levels, the authors then would conclude that the nominal and ordinal levels are NOT any form of measurement in and of themselves. Of course, we concur that his interval and ratio levels actually would constitute some form of genuine measurement. However, the scales to which we routinely ascribe that measurement status in the human sciences are often merely presumed to have interval-level measurement properties; those measurement properties are almost never tested empirically. It is not good enough to allocate numbers to human behaviors and then merely to assert that this is measurement in the social sciences.

Up to this point in the chapter, the authors have ignored a crucial aspect of Stevens's definition (because we want to direct particular attention to it). Stevens reminded us that the numerical allocations have to be made 'according to a rule', and therein lies the rub. What his definition fails to specify is that scientific measurement requires the allocations to be carried out according to a set of rules that will produce, at minimum, a resultant scale with a unit value that will maintain its value along the whole scale. Numerical allocations made 'according to just a(ny) rule' produce many of the very useful indicators of the human condition we habitually use in our research, but only some of those would qualify as 'measurement' so defined.

Statistics and/or Measurement

One regrettable consequence of the Stevens tradition, and the position of others on this matter, is that statistical analysis has dominated social sciences to the almost complete exclusion of the concept of measurement. Introductory texts and courses about social science measurement are, routinely, about statistical analysis; after a token rehearsal of Stevens's four levels, the matter is dropped. It does not follow that the aim of Rasch measurement proponents is to replace our use of conventional statistics. Rather, the aim is to provide social scientists with the means to produce genuine interval measures and to monitor the adherence of those scales to scientific measurement principles. In that way, the interval nature of data—a requirement for many of our most crucial and useful statistical analyses— is made explicit, not merely presumed. For example, many input their raw data into the SPSS or SEM software, assuming they are 'measures' for each variable, and then calculate the relationships between them. The alternative approach is to construct each variable from the relevant item responses, to check the measurement properties of each using the Rasch **model**, and then to impute those quality-controlled Rasch person measures into the software for the structural equation modeling or any other parametric analysis.

Why Fundamental Measurement?

Ben Wright (from the University of Chicago) would variously amuse, annoy, provoke, or enlighten members of his audience by taking a folding yard rule from his back pocket to illustrate the points he was making about using Rasch measurement. He would denounce scales in the human sciences as being like a yardstick made of elastic, as having segments made of rubber, having gaps, or not being straight, and the like. The physical measurement analogy was useful both as a model to strive toward and for exposing the weaknesses of inferior scale-building techniques. The yardstick (or meter stick) makes obvious to us the properties of a **fundamental measurement** scale that is based on the extensive attribute of length. As Piaget revealed, grade school kids soon discover that they can concatenate lengths to show the additive relations in the physical linear measurement scale; they can put arbitrary 'units' or rods together physically to add lengths.

This gives us great power when we match the properties of the system of natural numbers to reflect the iterative relations in adding unit lengths together (100 cm = 1 meter; 1,000 m = 1 kilometer, etc.). Consider how our predecessors used to line up locals to get lineal measures based on 'feet' (*pieds* in French) and 'thumbs' (imperial inches, or *pouces* in French). It is worth checking the human role in the development of physical measures (Stone, 1998); the inordinate political, scientific, and personal difficulties in establishing the basis for the meter (Alder, 2002); and how the process for estimating the height of something as obvious and solid as Mount Everest was hailed as "one of the most stupendous works in the whole history of science" even when the team had access to precisely calibrated measuring chains (Keay, 2000).

There are many lessons implied by reading the history behind Ben Wright's ruler. The first is that lots of arbitrary, local measures were used before they became standardized and interchangeable. The second is that even when measures are standardized and apparently sufficiently reliable and precise, iterating the units in context to make estimates of physical size can still be a daunting task. Moral: If we think that making scientific measures in the human sciences is too difficult for us to persist, perhaps we don't know the history of the development of something as simple as the meter stick and how difficult it is to use that simple device for seemingly straightforward measurement tasks. Even the exemplar model of the meter—two dots of gold on a platinum bar in a carefully controlled environment—is now merely of historical interest; today's definition of the meter is nothing as crude as that. Of course, the downside of Ben's ruler analogy, as his critics regularly argued, is that we cannot physically align bits of the human psyche together to produce measures, as we can with centimeters to make meters.

Derived Measures

Those in the physical sciences had already discovered that, although fundamental measurement is possible when units can be physically concatenated (as in weight, angles, time, etc.), these scales were in the minority, even in the physical sciences. The additive nature of other physical science measures—and density is an excellent exemplar—has to be discovered (or constructed) indirectly rather than demonstrated in repeated physical actions on concrete units. Adding one liter of water, mass one kilogram, and density of one to another identical amount of water will give two liters of water with a mass of two kilograms, but the density remains at just one. The units of volume and weight can be physically concatenated, but not the unit of density—even though we can be scientifically correct in referring to substances as having twice, three times, or even half or one third the density of water. The density scale is derived from the constant ratio between mass and volume for any substance: 1.0 for pure water, 19.3 for gold, 1.7 for magnesium, and so forth.

So, if density is a derived measure, how did we go about measuring density in our school science classes? Well, if the science curriculum, text, or teacher were sensitive to the developmental bases of children's understanding of science, these experiments would not have taken place until much later than those exercises based on just measuring length, weight, and time. (Piaget discovered that children's conception of volume is constructed later than that of length, weight, etc., and that density is not likely to be understood by children before the end of grade school or the start of high school. Furthermore, the conceptions of probability—which are central to Rasch measurement—are not constructed till late adolescence!)

So our high school science teacher gave us a collection of objects and had us measure the weight and the volume of each, then enter the values into the cells of a class table so we could calculate the relative densities: Density = Mass/Volume. And, if the teacher knew her job, she would have encouraged us to 'discover for ourselves that the density of any substance (e.g., copper) worked out to be consistently the same, even though the sizes and shapes of copper objects varied considerably from group to group in the classroom: Ah! The wonder of discovering not easily detected **invariance** (density) in the face of such obvious variation (weight and volume)! In this simple example, we have one of the cornerstones of our scientific endeavors: Our task is to find invariant measures, rules, and theories in the face of the variations that are obvious to all. Conversely, we are required to explain the unexpected variations we observe when applying those invariant measures, rules, and theories in a new situation. We search for constancy in the face of change and change where we hope for constancy. This part of the scientific enterprise is central to our consideration of measurement invariance in Chapter 5.

Table 1.1 reveals not only the increasing fundamental measurement scale values for weight from left to right in the top row (0.2, 0.4, 0.6, . . ., 1.2, etc.) and a similar additive scale for volume (0.5, 1.0, . . ., 3.0) going from top to bottom in the left-hand column but, as well, a derived measurement scale for density increasing diagonally (dotted line) from the lower left-hand corner of the table to the top right-hand corner.

So the physical scientists have fundamental (physically concatenating) measurement and derived (indirectly detected or constructed) measurement to cover the measurable physical attributes of objects. Importantly for social scientists, in 1940, the Ferguson Committee determined that nothing in the world of psychological quantification had properties of either fundamental or derived physical measurement scales (Ferguson, 1940). Our current dependence on Stevens's four levels is indirectly attributable to the critique of those on the committee, especially of prominent British physicist N.R. Campbell, who espoused the physical

TABLE 1.1 Calculations of Density of Materials in Classroom Science Exercise

Mass	0.2 k	0.4 k	0.6 k	0.8 k	1.0 k	1.2 k
Volume						
0.51	.4	.8	1.2	1.6	2.0	2.4
1.01	.2	.4	.6	.8	1.0	1.2
1.51	.13	.27	.4	.53	.67	.8
2.01	.1	.2	.3	.4	.5	.6
2.51	.08	.16	.24	.32	.4	.48
3.01	.07	.13	.2	.27	.33	.4

science ideas of measurement. Coincidentally and unfortunately, Stevens's own attempts at the measurement of the perception of loudness had attracted the negative attention of the Ferguson Committee, and the seminal work of Campbell was instrumental in dismissing out of hand the claims to scientific measurement of those involved in what we would loosely call psychometrics.

The response of Stevens was to redefine measurement for the benefit of psychologists: "Paraphrasing N.R. Campbell (Final Report, p. 340), we may say that measurement, in the broadest sense, is defined as the assignment of numerals to objects and events according to rules" (Stevens, 1946, p. 667). Stevens appealed to the authority of one of the sternest critics of his position, using what appeared, on the face of it, to be reasonable reworkings of Campbell's own quotations to justify Stevens's now-familiar four levels of measurement in psychology: nominal, ordinal, interval, and ratio—each of which constituted some form of measurement.

Conjoint Measurement

R. Duncan Luce and his colleagues have shown that both physicist Campbell and psychometrician Stevens were in error. Luce and Tukey (1964) argued that their concept of simultaneous conjoint measurement was a new type of fundamental measurement that subsumed both the existing categories of fundamental (e.g., weight, volume) and derived (e.g., density, temperature) measurement from the physical sciences and, more importantly for us, paved the way for detecting measurement structures in nonphysical attributes such as psychological **constructs.** Alluding back to the matrix of densities in Table 1.1, the key to measurement does not reside in the collusion of two fundamental measurement scales of weight and volume to produce a third, derived measurement scale for density that conserves the crucial properties of scientific measurement already inherent in weight and volume. According to Luce and Tukey, the crucial indicator of an additive measurement structure in the data (for density and, quite possibly, for some psychological attributes as well) is in the observable relationships between and among the matrix cells themselves.

Let's see the potential if we were able to apply some ideas from simultaneous conjoint measurement to an idea from educational or psychological testing. If we have some indicator of the two attributes (aspects or facets) of a testing situation that can be ordered from least to most—let's say, ability of the candidates from least able to most able and difficulty of the items from least to most difficult—we could try to check whether the Luce and Tukey interval-level scale measurement structures might exist in the ensuing data matrix.

Imagine that Table 1.2 is based on a relevant 100-item test given to a sample of 100 appropriate persons. Along the top row, we have ordered some of our items from the most difficult on the left (1 person correct/99 incorrect) to the easiest on the right (99 correct/1 incorrect), and down the left-hand column, we have ordered our persons from the most able (99 correct responses/1 incorrect) to

TABLE 1.2 Persons Ordered by Ability (Row) and Items Ordered by Facility (Column)

Items Persons	p	q	r	s	t	u	v	w	x	y	z	Ability
P												99/1
Q												90/10
R												80/20
S												70/30
T												60/40
U												50/50
V												40/60
W												30/70
X												20/80
Y												10/90
Z												1/99
Facility	1/99	10/90	20/80	30/70	40/60	50/50	60/40	70/30	80/20	90/10	99/1	

the least able (only 1 correct response/99 incorrect). In essence, what Luce and Tukey require of us is to search Table 1.2 for the patterns of relationships between the cells—the same sorts of relationships that are evident in the weight/volume/density matrix of results for the derived measurement scale example in Table 1.1.

The mathematical axioms by which a data matrix can be tested for satisfying the requirements of the simultaneous conjoint measurement structures are, as we might imagine, rather complex, but a basic illustration or two might suffice by way of a conceptual introduction. Please take a moment for a fresh look at the relationship between the cells in the density matrix in the earlier Table 1.1 to try to find:

(a) What is the relationship between any cell and the one to its right in any row?
(b) What is the relationship between any cell and the one above it in any column?
(c) What is the relationship between any cell and the one diagonally to the right and above it?

Each cell in the density table (Table 1.1 and see Figure 1.1) has a value that is *less* than:

(a) the value of the cell to its right in the row (i.e., A < B);
(b) the value of the cell above it in the column (i.e., C < A);
(c) the value of the cell diagonally to the right and above it (i.e., C < B).

A little template summarizing those between-cell relationships can be represented as in Figure 1.1.

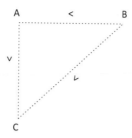

FIGURE 1.1 Relationships between adjacent cells in a matrix of measures.

Check back through Table 1.1 for density calculations to confirm that those 'less-than' relations hold between all adjacent pairs of cells as detailed in the template in Figure 1.1. Moreover, all those 'less-than' relations exist simultaneously. But be aware that the Luce and Tukey requirements (axioms) for measurement are much more comprehensive than this.

The Rasch Model for Measurement

Georg Rasch's formulation of his *Probabilistic models for some intelligence and attainment tests* (1960), quite independently of Luce and Tukey, saw the necessity for a similar set of relationships in the data matrix that ensued from using a well-constructed test. The principle he enunciated is delightfully straightforward:

> a person having a greater ability than another person should have the greater probability of solving any item of the type in question, and similarly, one item being more difficult than another means that for any person the probability of solving the second item is the greater one.
>
> *(Rasch, 1960, p. 117)*

A central feature of the **Rasch model** is a table of **expected response** probabilities designed to address the key question: When a person with this ability (number of test items correct) encounters an item of this difficulty (number of persons who succeeded on the item), what is the likelihood that this person gets this item correct? Answer: The probability of success depends on the difference between the ability of the person and the difficulty of the item.

And this is what makes some Rasch measurement folk really enthusiastic about the scientific measurement possibilities for the Rasch model: the table of expected probabilities (see Table 1.3 for a snippet) generated using Rasch's formulation has the same set of 'greater-than/less-than' relationships between the cells as does the density matrix in Table 1.1.

The Rasch model incorporates a method for ordering persons (e.g., from a sample of school children) according to their ability and ordering items (e.g., from

TABLE 1.3 Table of Probabilities of Success When Ability Confronts Difficulty

Items / Persons	p	q	r	s	t	u	v	w	x	y easy	z	Ability
P most	.500	.866	.924	.949	.963	.973	.980	.986	.991	.995	.999	99/1
Q able	.134	.500	.653	.741	.801	.847	.884	.915	.942	.968	.995	90/10
R	.076	.347	.500	.603	.682	.746	.801	.851	.896	.942	.991	80/20
S	.051	.259	.397	.500	.585	.659	.726	.789	.851	.915	.986	70/30
T	.037	.199	.318	.415	.500	.578	.653	.726	.801	.884	.980	60/40
U	.027	.153	.254	.341	.422	.500	.578	.659	.746	.847	.973	50/50
V	.020	.116	.199	.274	.347	.422	.500	.585	.682	.801	.963	40/60
W	.014	.085	.149	.211	.274	.341	.415	.500	.603	.741	.949	30/70
X	.009	.058	.104	.149	.199	.254	.318	.397	.500	.653	.924	20/80
Y	.005	.032	.058	.085	.116	.153	.199	.259	.347	.500	.866	10/90
Z	.001	.005	.009	.014	.020	.027	.037	.051	.076	.134	.500	1/99
Facility	1/99	10/90	20/80	30/70	40/60	50/50	60/40	70/30	80/20	90/10	99/1	

a diagnostic test of numerical computations) according to their difficulty. The Rasch principle is that interval-level measurement can be derived when the levels of some attribute increase along with increases in the values of two other attributes. We can see from the snippet in Table 1.3 that levels of one attribute (probability of correct response) increase with the values of the two other attributes: item difficulty (facility) and person ability. Then the purely ordinal relationships between the levels of probabilities are indicative of an interval-level quantitative measurement structure for all three. The template relationships from Figure 1.1 that held for the density table in Table 1.1 also apply for the Rasch expected response probabilities in Table 1.3. In fact, the required relationship is not quite so strict for Rasch; it is 'equal to or less than' (≤) rather than just 'less than' (<). The definitive exposition of the theory of simultaneous conjoint measurement is Krantz, Luce, Suppes, and Tversky (1971). While Narens and Luce (1986) and Michell (1990) provide simpler accounts, the most approachable is that of Michell (2003).

A Suitable Analogy for Measurement in the Human Sciences

We can readily see why Ben Wright used a simple ruler (linear measurement) for his measurement analogy rather than the derived density scale. While the measurement principles underlying the ruler are the ideal to which we researchers in the human sciences could aspire, using the ruler as the key analogy does have some drawbacks that are not so helpful for many in the field.

The ruler can be used as an analogy for fundamental measurement only in situations in which the actual objects can be physically concatenated. Not only does that seem a little far-fetched to apply to the study of human attributes, it is a principle that cannot work even with derived measures in the physical sciences such as density and temperature. The history of lineal physical measurement is so long, and measuring using a ruler is so ubiquitous that often we do not readily see the parallels between the problems that befell the scale developers and the measurement problems that we in the human sciences currently face. For example, we presume that the use of such standardized lineal measures is unproblematic and routinely 'error free', even though just a little reading and thought would reveal otherwise. With the exception of one major country, the use of the metric lineal measurement system is so routine that the progression in calibrations from millimeters through centimeters to meters and kilometers is taken for granted—all we need is a long enough ruler, or enough iterations of the shorter ruler.

Following on from and developing on the ideas of Bruce Choppin (1985), we ask, might thermometry—the measurement of temperature—be a more useful analogy for those of us who are trying to measure human attributes? The history of the thermometer is much more recent; there are written eye-witness accounts of the earliest efforts of Hookes, Galileo, and others. Chang's (2004) fascinating 300-page account, *Inventing Temperature: Measurement and Scientific Progress*, might be seen as definitive. Even the title sounds promising to social scientists: Was temperature invented rather than discovered? Do measurement and scientific progress go hand in hand? So what are the parallels for us? Keep your favorite human science measurement project in mind as you consider the following. Temperature is not measured directly but instead is estimated indirectly by recording its effects on other substances such as mercury, colored alcohol, and bimetallic strips. Scientists have theories about the way that certain substances behave in response to changes in temperature, and those theories have changed over time. We don't use just one prototypical thermometer across all (or even most) temperature-measuring situations. In fact, most common thermometers have quite a limited scale range and restricted applications: A medical mercury thermometer is next to useless in the kitchen, unless the cook is thought to be sick. We know we can readily move between degrees Celsius (°C) and degrees Fahrenheit (°F), while those with a smattering of high school physics can tell about the kelvin scale (K). We understand that 0°C and 100°C have been arbitrarily set by earlier scientists at the freezing and boiling points of pure water at sea level for our convenience, not because these are the scientific ends of the temperature scale. We could start measuring temperatures at 0°C, 0°F, or 0 K, depending on our purpose or on a whim. The theory that posits 0 K (−273°C) as absolute zero also suggests that actually measuring absolute zero temperature is itself impossible (Choppin, 1985).

We have no problems (other than feeling too cold) when negative temperatures are recorded: $-10°C$ or 'seven below' doesn't have us baffled about having a negative amount of temperature! No single principle of thermometer construction works across the temperature scale, that is, expanding liquids, bimetallic strips, and changes in electrical conductance; all have limited applications. We all can use some thermometers effectively. But others require specialist knowledge and are used only in specialist settings. Some quite functional thermometers are virtually given away; others are expensive, delicate, and rarely even imagined by us ordinary folks. We know that any collection of thermometers will vary in their readings, even in the same setting at the same time. In high-stakes situations, when our child is very ill, we check the child's temperature two or three times in a row to make sure we got it right, but driving back home from the hospital, we will rely on the car's thermostat to turn on and off at 'round about' the correct temperatures to keep the engine running smoothly. We expect that we will get what we pay for in a thermometer: a couple of bucks for the car engine or the temperature in the living room; a few more bucks to control the temperature in the wine cellar; and a lot more in the operating theater for monitoring core body temperature during major surgery. And what price should governments be willing to pay for measuring core temperature in a nuclear reactor?

Our measurement endeavors in the human sciences might fit better with the thermometry analogy. While the whole scale (cf. temperatures from 0 K to $+\infty$) might eventually represent development from before birth (even as far back as conception for some attributes) to death (even beyond for concepts of spirituality), each of us might work on just one small part of the total variable at a time. The tasks/tests/schedules we develop are likely to be as specialized and as different as an infrared medical thermometer and the thermostat in a 1965 Ford Mustang. Some will be quite inexpensive and have low-stakes consequences (just like the household thermometer); others will be high cost, high stakes, and high maintenance (like that required to monitor and control the core temperature of that nuclear reactor, perhaps). We will acknowledge immediately that the accuracy and the precision of the test are likely to be cost/effort dependent and that all estimates necessarily have error but that those qualities (accuracy/precision/error) will be appropriate to the decision-making requirements. The names and sizes of our measurement scale units might vary (as they do with degrees Celsius, Fahrenheit, and Kelvin). Yet while many of our indicators will appear remarkably different and function in obviously different ways in a variety of apparently unrelated contexts, the eventual aim will be the **calibration** of the test, checklist, and so forth on a single underlying interval-level measurement scale that has general applicability across a variety of human conditions (as for temperature). For those who need a boost in optimism and motivation to tackle the tasks in front of us, please take a look at 'Thermoscopes, Thermometers, and the Foundation of Measurement' (Sherry, 2011). Sherry spells out how those lessons derived from the history of thermometry might be garnered for guiding us through our measurement problems in the human sciences. He specifically addresses the claim that ordinal thermoscope scales moved to interval thermometer scales due to the experimental work of Joseph Black (*c.* 1760).

It seems that the problems we have in human sciences for developing, standardizing, and converting measurement scales could appear a lot more tractable when viewed from the perspective of the major advances in conceptualizing and measuring temperature in mere centuries. And the shortcomings of our attempts at scaling have obvious parallels in the variety of thermometers that are regularly in use even though many of them produce readings that are barely 'good enough for government work'!

And this brings us to another crucial philosophical issue for those involved in trying to measure those human strengths and weaknesses that fall under the general heading of '**latent traits**'. Remember the simple colored alcohol in a glass thermometer: We don't measure temperature directly, we measure its effect on other objects. We look at the length of the tube of red liquid and read off the temperature. We look at units of length and *infer* them to be units of temperature. Ben Wright's parallel claim would go something like this:

If I want to measure a child's math ability, all I have is the number of items he scored correctly. That's not what I want. So I have to *go from what I have and don't want* (a score) *to what I want and can't have* (his math ability). THAT is called 'inference'.

That is the principle underlying our attempts at the measurement of latent traits, and the Rasch model is the method we use to infer latent trait interval measures from raw counts of test items correct.

In Conclusion

Much is to be gained by learning about and reflecting on the problems that beset the development and scientific use of measurement scales in the physical sciences. Popular accounts by Alder (2002), Keay (2000), and Sobel (1996) are both readable and informative. Many of the chapters in Chang (2004) are accessible to the amateur metrologist; and Sherry (2011) might be just the object lesson we need. It's reassuring to know we are not alone in our problems. Moreover, it also helps to understand a little how we came to fall so short of our reasonable expectations for scientific measurement in the human sciences. Michell (1999) provides a very readable account of key players, events, and apparent motivations. He also gives a potted introduction to the relationship between scientific measurement and the ideas of Luce and Rasch (Michell, 2003). While many in Rasch measurement do not agree with all of Michell's prognostications about measurement in our field, he certainly addresses many important issues that we hold in common but are rarely considered in other forums in our discipline (see Bond, 2001).

In this chapter, the term 'fundamental' was used in two different but equally important ways. Measurement of the sort we use in our daily lives—scales with iterative unit values—is *fundamental* to logical, empirically based research in the human sciences. The properties of scientific measurement are most obvious in what is termed *fundamental measurement*, in which attributes such as weight and length can be physically concatenated along the measurement scale. Many measurement scales in the physical sciences are derived such that, although the measurement units can be iterated, the attribute itself (e.g., temperature and density) cannot be physically added together.

Luce and his colleagues have outlined the principles and properties of conjoint measurement that would bring the same sort of rigorous measurement to the human sciences as those in the physical sciences have enjoyed for a considerable time. Indeed, the fundamental and derived measurement systems of the physical sciences are special (restricted) cases of conjoint measurement; Luce termed conjoint measurement "a new type of fundamental measurement" (Luce & Tukey, 1964).

The Rasch models for measurement are currently the closest generally accessible approximation of these fundamental measurement principles for the human sciences. Of course, taking such an obviously chauvinistic approach risks alienating many of our colleagues in quantitative approaches to human sciences research. Even those completely dedicated to developing and using Rasch-calibrated scales sometimes implore us to tread more softly, to be more circumspect, to appear less assertive. The authors' championing of the Rasch model approach to measurement is not designed to be offensive; confronting, perhaps, but never offensive. It is encouraging that colleagues who have such high standards for measuring water, cloth, and flour will now have the tools to achieve those same standards with math achievement, introversion, cognitive development, or health-related quality of life.

This book is an invitation (exhortation?) to set impossibly high standards for measurement in human science research and to work incrementally toward achieving those standards. We must remember that landing on the moon was once too far a goal.

Summary

In this chapter, we laid the groundwork for understanding the crucial difference between measurement and statistics. We argued that social science's reliance on Stevens's framework for what constitutes measures and their corresponding statistical analyses has led to a widespread ignorance of measurement and an overreliance on statistical significance for interpreting research. This oversight, whether intentional or not, has had grave consequences for understanding our phenomena under investigation.

Suggested Readings

Introductory (You Should Read These)

Bond, T. G. (2001). Book review *Measurement in psychology: A critical history of a methodological concept. Journal of Applied Measurement, 2*(1), 96–100.

Choppin, B.H.L. (1985). Lessons for psychometrics from thermometry. *Evaluation in Education, 9*(1), 9–12.

Michell, J. (2003). Measurement: A beginner's guide. *Journal of Applied Measurement, 4*(4), 298–308.

Stevens, S.S. (1946). On the theory of scales of measurement. *Science, 103*, 677–680.

For the More Serious Student of Measurement

Michell, J. (1999). *Measurement in psychology: Critical history of a methodological concept.* New York, NY: Cambridge University Press.

Sherry, D. (2011). Thermoscopes, thermometers, and the foundation of measurement. *Studies in History and Philosophy of Science, 42*, 509–524.

ACTIVITIES

Read Stevens (1946), particularly his section on Ordinal Scales, and the cautions he advises about their statistical analyses. "As a matter of fact, most of the scales used widely and effectively by psychologists are ordinal scales" (p. 679).

Does this view of Stevens's ideas match with the version you understood before reading Stevens in his own words? Why? Why not?

Find an important research paper in your field and identify the ways in which it addresses the ideas of statistics, measurement, and Stevens's cautions.

Read Choppin (1985), noting the parallels and differences between principles of thermometry and measurement in the human sciences.

Complete a table like the one that follows summarizing the parallels and differences:

Thermometry	Human Sciences
Many thermometers	Many instruments
Mostly interval scales	Mostly ordinal scales
Some ratio scales	Some interval scales

References

Alder, K. (2002). *The measure of all things.* New York, NY: Free Press.

Bond, T. G. (2001). Book review *Measurement in psychology: A critical history of a methodological concept. Journal of Applied Measurement, 2*(1), 96–100.

Chang, H. (2004). *Inventing temperature: Measurement and scientific progress.* New York, NY: Oxford University Press.

Choppin, B. H. L. (1985). Lessons for psychometrics from thermometry. *Evaluation in Education, 9*(1), 9–12.

Ducret, J. J. (1990). *Jean Piaget: Biographie et parcours intellectuel* [Jean Piaget: Biography and intellectual development]. Neuchatel: Delachaux et Niestle.

Ferguson, A. (1940). Quantitative estimates of sensory events. The advancement of science. *Report of the British Association for the Advancement of Science, 2,* 331–349.

Keay, J. (2000). *The great arc: The dramatic tale of how India was mapped and Everest was named.* New York, NY: Harper Collins.

Krantz, D. H., Luce, R. D., Suppes, P., & Tversky, A. (1971). *Foundations of measurement, volume 1: Additive and polynomial representations.* New York, NY: Academic Press.

Luce, R. D., & Tukey, J. W. (1964). Simultaneous conjoint measurement: A new type of fundamental measurement. *Journal of Mathematical Psychology, 1*(1), 1–27.

Michell, J. (1990). *An introduction to the logic of psychological measurement.* Hillsdale, NJ: Lawrence Erlbaum Associates.

Michell, J. (1997). Quantitative science and the definition of measurement in psychology. *British Journal of Psychology, 88*(3), 355–383.

Michell, J. (1999). *Measurement in psychology: Critical history of a methodological concept.* New York, NY: Cambridge University Press.

Michell, J. (2003). Measurement: A beginner's guide. *Journal of Applied Measurement, 4*(4), 298–308.

Narens, L., & Luce, R. D. (1986). Measurement: The theory of numerical assignments. *Psychological Bulletin, 99*(2), 166–180.

Piaget, J., Inhelder, B., & Szeminska, A. (1960). *The child's conception of geometry.* London: Routledge and Kegan Paul. (Original work published 1948)

Rasch, G. (1960). *Probabilistic models for some intelligence and attainment tests.* Copenhagen: Danmarks Paedagogiske Institut.

Sherry, D. (2011). Thermoscopes, thermometers, and the foundations of measurement. *Studies in the History and Philosophy of Science, A, 42,* 509–524.

Sobel, D. (1996). *Longitude: The true story of a lone genius who solved the greatest scientific problem of his time.* Harmondsworth, UK: Penguin.

Stevens, S. S. (1946). On the theory of scales of measurement. *Science, 103,* 677–680.

Stone, G. E. (2002, April). *The emperor has no clothes: What makes a criterion-referenced standard valid?* Presented at the fifth annual International Objective Measurement Workshop, New Orleans, LA.

Stone, M. H. (1998). Man is the measure . . . the measurer. *Journal of Outcome Measurement, 2*(1), 25–32.

2

IMPORTANT PRINCIPLES OF MEASUREMENT MADE EXPLICIT

We introduce this chapter by using a sporting analogy. Imagine the competitors at an athletic meet as they ready themselves to participate in the high jump event for a national or international title or even the Olympic Games. The winner, of course, will be the person who clears the highest setting of the crossbar. The competition rules require the athletes to face a series of progressively higher settings of the crossbar until just the winner is left (with some special provisions if two or more competitors reach exactly the same height). This competition considers the difficulty of the jumps in terms of just *one quantifiable empirical variable*: the height of the bar above the ground. But that is a gross simplification; other variables (aspects, factors, **facets**, dimensions) invariably play a role: the competition surface, the air temperature, the prevailing wind (direction and strength), the relative humidity or rain, the lighting (brightness, natural, or artificial), even the support (or lack of it) from the audience. ("I would like to thank the spectators, today. They were marvelous! Without their support I could not have won!") What about the ability of the athletes? We take more notice of their latest competition results than of any other relevant but usually dismissed indicator: each athlete's health status, recent injuries, suppleness relative to that state in other competitions, motivation, confidence, family or other personal circumstances, and so forth. We ignore most of these influences on jump difficulty or athlete ability while we try to predict which of the contestants is likely to succeed at each of the jumps in turn; we consider just two key influences for each jump attempt. For the indicator of the relative difficulty of each jump, we use just the height of the bar; and for the ability of the athlete, we refer only to the most recent results in competition. Interestingly, both jump **difficulty** and athlete **ability** are expressed on the same scale in the same units: the meter scale of linear measure—and we typically ignore all other likely influences in predicting the athlete's probability of success.

If we could predict perfectly each outcome when a variety of athletes face a variety of jumps, we wouldn't even bother to hold the competition; we could award the medals on some summary of recent high jump performances. Given that we cannot predict perfectly each athlete's performance, we instead make probabilistic estimates based on past performance. As the athlete lines up to jump each time the bar is raised, a group of spectators in the grandstand or the TV commentators might estimate the chances each jumper has at being successful at each jump. They might consider all the variables mentioned in estimating the probability of success for each attempt, but it is most likely that they would use only a few pieces of information in order to ease their cognitive load. Most likely, they would express their predictions in terms of chances/odds/probabilities rather than just "definitely will/will not succeed". For example, they might make statements such as, "more than 50%"; "less than 50%"; "almost impossible to fail/succeed"; "ah, about 60:40, I think!"

We as researchers could make these predictions by making a simple calculation: Take the current jump height (jump difficulty, expressed in meters), the contestant's last competition result (athlete's ability, expressed on the same scale in meters) and compare the two. If jump difficulty and athlete ability (as estimated) were the same, we could predict success:fail odds at 50:50, or 50% probability of a successful attempt and equal (50%) odds of failure. As the ability of the jumper exceeds the difficulty of the jump by more and more (calculated on the simple meter scale alone), we would predict odds more and more in favor of athlete success (60%, 70%, 85%)—according how big the ability–difficulty distance is in favor of the athlete (e.g., 1 cm, 2 cm, 3 cm). If the calculation shows the athlete to be at a disadvantage in the ability–difficulty comparison (e.g., −1 cm, −2 cm, −3 cm, etc.), our predictions would decrease (40%, 30%, 15%, etc.). But few serious followers of the sport would predict 0% or 100% for any competitive athlete for any reasonable competition height: The world record holder fails to take an Olympic medal, and the competitor who just made the final eight upset our predictions often enough that we must make allowances for such human foibles.

Although this book emphasizes a particular version of one approach to the quantitative analyses of data from the human sciences, it raises a number of problems and principles endemic to the investigation of almost any human performance. The human abilities and task difficulties we observe in the human sciences cannot be reduced conveniently to locations on existing scientific measurement scales (such as the meter scale in the high jump example). Although, both qualitative and quantitative approaches to gathering data from human observations are designed to yield summaries of these observations, the aim is to communicate the essence of the data in a meaningful, useful, and valid way. As it is currently the fashion to criticize quantitative approaches to educational, psychological, health, and other human research for their reductionism, it is obvious that *all* summarizing methods do more or less injury to the phenomena under investigation, just as in the case of the high jump competition.

Admittedly, the summary of any complex human behavior in exclusively quantitative terms makes the reductionism obvious to all but the most hardened empiricist. The written summary of the same act in several sentences or even paragraphs also misses the mark in similar but perhaps less obvious ways. Neither *Wine Spectator*'s score of 93/100 nor its paragraph of suitably purple prose can capture adequately the experience of tasting an extraordinary wine. Each misses the point completely. But each summary (quantitative or qualitative) can summarize effectively aspects of the experience sufficiently for others to be tempted into purchasing and drinking a bottle of the same wine! We read the paragraph or look at the score or both; then we make a decision (purchase or not) and act upon that decision.

As we try to record any event to share with others, the original experience is damaged in a multitude of ways: via the orientation of the investigator, the adequacy of the observation schedule, the choice of the observations, and the completeness of the set of observations, and all this, before we look at the adequacy of the particular analytical devices along with the care and rigor of their use. When we focus on one attribute, we don't automatically ignore the other aspects altogether—but we do tend to do so more when we start at *quantifying* that attribute—the distinction being that when we move from observation to measurement, the focus narrows. The very act of quantifying any aspect of human experience immediately relegates all other aspects toward oblivion. The authors would argue that both quantitative and qualitative approaches have the same starting point: in observation. The extent of this common ground becomes evident in later chapters, where a synthesis of quantitative and qualitative approaches will be demonstrated.

"All that can be observed is whether or not the specified event occurs, and whether the data recorder (observer or respondent) nominates (any particular) category as their observation" (Wright, 1996, p. 3). This is the basis of the results for all our investigations. In the grandstand, we watch the athlete attempt the height of 1.75 meters and summarize all the drama, all the training, all the effort, as merely success or failure; green light/red light; ✓ or ✗. The test candidate might fill in the bubble for 'True' on a response sheet, write a paragraph, or produce a journal. The observer might record that an appropriate word was inserted into a space in a sentence, note that 'a' was the correct response to Item 17, or compose a particular phrase or statement to correspond to an identified segment of a video or journal record. In essence, all of our observations can be so depicted, mere summaries, whether qualitative or quantitative analyses are intended.

In the case of simple observations, the investigator might make a qualitative decision about whether the event was absent or present, whether it did or did not occur. As part of a more complex schedule, the investigator might decide whether a particular event was absent, whether it occurred to some extent or to a greater extent, or whether a complete display of the checklisted behavior was observed. In this way, all of our investigatory observations are qualitative, and the classification or identification of events deals with data at the nominal level.

Nominal-level data: We observe just those events that are the focus of our enquiry and not others—we classify observations into *types*.

Ordinal-level data: We record which of those observed events is better than another—we classify observations into *levels*.

When we start classifying or counting these observed events, we apply numerical values to them. This counting is the beginning (but not the completion) of an expressly quantitative approach. Even in the first instance, nominal data (presence/absence), can arguably be classified as ordinal data because we hold the presence of an event (a tick, a mark in the correct box, a 'yes') as more valuable than the absence of that event (a cross, a mark in the wrong box, or a 'no'). In the second instance (none/some/more/all), our data are much more evidently ordinal. Whether classified strictly as nominal or ordinal, our counting of observations or events always remains on those levels. It is only then in our successful attempt to make meaningful measures of those counted observations that constructs an **interval** scale, in which the distances between scale units are made equal and meaningful. Observations and counts are only ever ordinal; measures are interval. As a consequence, any analytical model that implicitly or explicitly makes assumptions about 'interval' or 'ratio' relations between data points that are nominal or ordinal does so unjustifiably. The hard-nosed professors were right in questioning the measurement level of the data.[1]

Recording the presence/absence of behavior and ordering observations along a none/some/more/all continuum should always be guided by some underlying theory for making and recording these observations. Unfortunately, for many researchers in the human sciences, that theory often remains implicit or doesn't exist at all. Theory about how the underlying human trait functions seems to be the exception rather than the rule in human science research. Indeed, what separates the work of the early thermometer builders from much of the work done in the human sciences—even in the Rasch measurement world—is that those early scientists were also working on their theories of temperature as they were trying to measure it. Thus, much of the research reported as exemplars in this volume shares common origins in expressly articulated explicit psychological theories. The researchers took to heart the advice of two of Piaget's closest collaborators:

> If you want to get ahead, get a theory.
>
> (Karmiloff-Smith & Inhelder, 1975)

Any investigator's record of qualitative observations represents nominal categories, focusing on some thing(s) and ignoring others. The investigator might then score these observations to organize them into a stepwise order of precedence according to the theoretical model used to generate the observational schedule. This presumption or expectation of meaningful ordering of data is at the very heart of any of those conceptions of humans that have developmental origins.

An example: "By how much?"

As a useful starting point, quantitative summarizing of qualitative observations can be achieved by simply assigning 1 (or ✓) for the presence of an occurrence and 0 (or ✗) for its absence so that the data summary for Person A across all items is recorded as a row:

A 111000011001 or ✓ ✓ ✓ ✗ ✗ ✗ ✗ ✓ ✓ ✗ ✗ ✓

The data summary for Item d across all persons is recorded as a column:

d		d
0	or	✗
1		✓
0		✗
1		✓
0		✗
1		✓
0		✗
0		✗
1		✓
1		✓
0		✗
0		✗
0		✗
0		✗

A teacher's record book or a complete record of a sample's performances on the items of a developmental math test could look just like this. Typically, our preference for focusing on the performance of the persons, rather than investigating the performance of the items, has us rushing to express the results of the investigation as a **raw score** total for each person. We often do not make even that same crude summary for items. We share with our schoolteachers an implicit but unjustifiable belief in our ability to write good items. Student answer writing is tested, but teacher item writing never is. So, in the matrix shown as Table 2.1, the last column entry for each person is the total raw score. This practice of using the raw score as the estimate of a person's ability on a test is ubiquitous in the human sciences.

In keeping with a guiding principle adopted for the writing of this book, the authors have selected from some data actually collected to answer substantive questions from different fields in the human sciences, often developmental or educational psychology. The data for Chapter 2 are taken from a classroom mathematics test generated by a group of primary school teachers (Bond, 1996; Bond & Parkinson, 2010; Parkinson, 1996). The test was designed to make explicit

TABLE 2.1 Data Matrix for 14 Selected Persons (A–N) on 12 Selected Items (*a–l*)

Persons	*a*	*b*	*c*	*d*	*e*	*f*	*g*	*h*	*i*	*j*	*k*	*l*	Raw Score
A	✔	✔	✔	✗	✗	✗	✗	✔	✔	✗	✗	✔	6
B	✔	✗	✔	✔	✗	✗	✗	✗	✔	✗	✗	✗	4
C	✔	✔	✔	✗	✔	✗	✗	✔	✔	✔	✔	✔	9
D	✔	✗	✔	✔	✗	✗	✗	✗	✔	✗	✗	✔	5
E	✗	✔	✔	✗	✗	✔	✗	✔	✔	✔	✔	✔	8
F	✔	✔	✔	✔	✔	✗	✗	✔	✔	✗	✗	✔	8
G	✔	✗	✔	✗	✗	✔	✗	✗	✔	✗	✔	✔	6
H	✔	✗	✔	✗	✗	✗	✗	✗	✗	✗	✗	✔	3
I	✔	✔	✔	✔	✗	✗	✗	✔	✔	✗	✗	✔	7
J	✔	✔	✔	✔	✔	✔	✔	✔	✔	✗	✔	✗	10
K	✔	✗	✔	✗	✗	✔	✗	✗	✔	✗	✔	✔	6
L	✗	✔	✔	✗	✗	✔	✗	✔	✔	✔	✔	✔	8
M	✗	✗	✗	✗	✗	✗	✗	✗	✗	✗	✗	✗	0
N	✔	✔	✔	✔	✗	✔	✔	✔	✔	✔	✔	✔	11

the school's mathematics syllabus requirements for dealing with area-based concepts. The school requirements are based directly on the state curriculum directives. (Interestingly, the sequence or ordering of these understandings was based originally on Piaget's work in the field.) Questions at the lower level required students to color the surface of, say, a square. Others required computations based on formulas such as area = length × width, and area = side.[2] Advanced skills were tested by questions requiring calculations based on several formulas, added or subtracted, to give area measures of complex figures.

What then might we infer from the data matrix shown in Table 2.1? Of course, we can see that quite a range of person performances, from 0/12 (all wrong, Person M) to 11/12 (almost all correct, Person N), is evident. However, from this information alone, we cannot immediately draw any conclusions about the items or about the interactions between the items and the persons.

Because the following steps (often implicit or omitted) can show us a lot about our data and introduce some crucial features of Rasch analysis, we should take each of them in turn. The authors would argue that researchers (and teachers) could learn a great deal about their testing procedures merely by taking time to inspect their raw data regularly in the following fashion. A simple spreadsheet on a laptop or tablet will do the job. The data matrix (i.e., the result of the theory-driven qualitative observations) can be arranged so that the items are ordered from least to most difficult, and the persons are ordered from most to least able (Table 2.2). This organized data table is termed a **Scalogram** (Guttman, 1944). The higher up the table one goes, the more able the persons (Person

TABLE 2.2 Selected Ordered Data Matrix With 14 Persons Arranged According to Ability (From Top to Bottom) and 12 Items Arranged by Facility (From Left to Right)

Persons	c	i	a	l	b	h	k	d	f	j	e	g	Ability
N	✔	✔	✔	✔	✔	✔	✔	✔	✔	✔	✗	✔	11
J	✔	✔	✔	✗	✔	✔	✔	✔	✔	✗	✔	✔	10
C	✔	✔	✔	✔	✔	✔	✔	✗	✗	✔	✔	✗	9
E	✔	✔	✗	✔	✔	✔	✔	✗	✔	✔	✗	✗	8
L	✔	✔	✗	✔	✔	✔	✔	✗	✔	✔	✗	✗	8
F	✔	✔	✔	✔	✔	✔	✗	✔	✗	✗	✔	✗	8
I	✔	✔	✔	✔	✔	✔	✗	✔	✗	✗	✗	✗	7
A	✔	✔	✔	✔	✔	✔	✗	✗	✗	✗	✗	✗	6
K	✔	✔	✔	✔	✗	✗	✔	✗	✔	✗	✗	✗	6
G	✔	✔	✔	✔	✗	✗	✔	✗	✔	✗	✗	✗	6
D	✔	✔	✔	✔	✗	✗	✗	✔	✗	✗	✗	✗	5
B	✔	✔	✔	✗	✗	✗	✗	✔	✗	✗	✗	✗	4
H	✔	✗	✔	✔	✗	✗	✗	✗	✗	✗	✗	✗	3
M	✗	✗	✗	✗	✗	✗	✗	✗	✗	✗	✗	✗	0
Facility	13	12	11	11	8	8	7	6	6	4	3	2	

N: 11/12). The farther right across the table one goes, the more difficult the items (Item *g*: only two persons are successful). The table then reveals some properties about the observations that will help to guide future data collection and the data analysis.

The simple task of ordering data from least to most occurrences (for persons and for items) is likely to show that the theoretical model used for the collection of the qualitative observations has not produced results entirely as anticipated. Usually, the first use of a test will not yield a complete set of distinctively useful observations. In the case of the observation schedule or items, some items might have no observations of presence (i.e., all zeroes were recorded, meaning every child 'failed' on that item). Other items might not discriminate between the persons in the sample observed (i.e., all ones were recorded, meaning every child 'passed' on that item). These items should be dropped temporarily from that data set because they are not useful discriminators of the substantive sequence under investigation with this particular sample. What a simple, meaningful check, more often omitted than observed. Subsequently, these items should be examined closely and perhaps improved, omitted, or used in other appropriate tests or with other samples.

Similarly, some persons might have no observations showing presence of the anticipated behaviors on this test (all zeroes, meaning they 'fail' all items; e.g., person M), or they might be more capable than this observation schedule predicted (all ones, meaning they 'pass' all items; but there are none of those here). The results for these persons should be dropped temporarily also as inadequate. It is not possible to make satisfactory descriptions showing the progress of these persons along the continuum revealed by this qualitative observation schedule, because they are not along the continuum. All we can conclude definitively is that person M had too little ability to score on this test;[2] but with our current system of recorded observations, we can never adequately answer the crucial measurement question, "By how much?"

This procedure is not meant to disregard our intention to record that one child got everything right or that another failed on all items for a particular sample or purpose. Rather, it reminds us that these results are quite insufficient for estimating ability. It should tell us that next time, when we construct subsequent versions of such a test, we will need to include some easier as well as some more difficult items of this sort to cover properly the range of abilities shown in a sample such as the one under investigation. This is related to the '**targeting**' concept.

The authors' claim is that qualitative inspection of the data is a necessary prerequisite to meaningful quantitative analysis and, hence, should always precede it. We have discovered already how valuable information about the match or mismatch between the persons observed and the items used to observe them could guide our next investigation of this ability. We have been cautioned about the inadequate information we have about persons (in this case, Person M). Strictly speaking, we should remove such cases from the data matrix temporarily and follow up with some extra data collection for M. It is now revealed that we have some less-than-useful items (in this case, Item c). With the nonscoring Person M removed from the matrix, Item c is correctly answered by all. It might be a useful item for less able children, but not for the 13 remaining children in this subsample. For our next use of this test, we also have a guide to the difficulty level of further useful items.

The next step is to calculate item difficulties and person abilities (expressed as the fraction n/N, the item or person raw score divided by the total possible score for each: $n/13$ for item difficulty; $n/11$ for person ability). These fractions show more readily the ordinal relations among abilities on the one hand and among difficulties on the other, allowing us to make crude comparisons between the dispersions of difficulties and abilities in the observations (Table 2.3). The routine procedure in education circles is to express each of these n/N fractions as a percentage and to use them directly in reporting students' results. We will soon see that this commonplace procedure is not justified. In keeping with the caveat we expressed earlier, these n/N fractions should be regarded as merely orderings of the nominal categories (i.e., ordinal data) and as insufficient for the inference of interval relations between the frequencies of observations.

Just as theories about humans would predict, the data displayed in Table 2.3 show substantial variation in the presence of the targeted ability in the sample observed. They also show considerable variation in the facility or difficulty of the items that represent the observation schedule. Indeed, the very concept of a **variable** has variation at its heart. Immediately, the developmental nature of these observations is obvious in the way the presence of the observations (1) changes to absence (0) in the direction of increasing difficulty of the items ($\rightarrow$) and in the direction of decreasing ability of the persons ($\downarrow$).

Even at this level, the arrangements of some data points should cause us to reflect on the nature of these children's development made evident by these empirical manifestations of the underlying theoretical ideas. We should focus now on the patterns of success and failure revealed in the data matrix. Typically, 1s do not change to 0s in a rigid, step-like (or **Guttman**) fashion, either for persons or for items. In Table 2.3, person A shows a Guttman pattern, with all items to

TABLE 2.3 Selected Ordered Data Matrix for Items (11) and Persons (13) With Sufficient Information

Persons	i	a	l	b	h	k	d	f	j	e	g	Ability	n/11 %
N	1	1	1	1	1	1	1	1	1	0	1	10	91
J	1	1	0	1	1	1	1	1	0	1	1	9	82
C	1	1	1	1	1	1	0	0	1	1	0	8	73
E	1	0	1	1	1	1	0	1	1	0	0	7	64
L	1	0	1	1	1	1	0	1	1	0	0	7	64
F	1	1	1	1	1	0	1	0	0	1	0	7	64
I	1	1	1	1	1	0	1	0	0	0	0	6	55
A	1	1	1	1	1	0	0	0	0	0	0	5	45
K	1	1	1	0	0	1	0	1	0	0	0	5	45
G	1	1	1	0	0	1	0	1	0	0	0	5	45
D	1	1	1	0	0	0	1	0	0	0	0	4	36
B	1	1	0	0	0	0	1	0	0	0	0	3	27
H	0	1	1	0	0	0	0	0	0	0	0	2	18
Facility	12	11	11	8	8	7	6	6	4	3	2		
n/13%	92	85	85	62	62	54	46	46	31	23	15		

Items $\rightarrow$ *difficulty*

increasing ability $\downarrow$

the left of the | correct and all items to the right of it incorrect. Only of passing concern is the evidence showing that the intersection of the patterns of 'success' and 'difficulty' has a small zone of unpredictability associated with it. It is reasonable to suggest that this pattern of responses reflects recently acquired or yet-to-be consolidated abilities that might not be fully reliable in their display. Therefore, the data contained in the shaded cells of Table 2.3 should delay us no further.

Unlike the data patterns that display small zones of unpredictability, 'unexpected' observations of presence (1) or absence (0) that seem more out of place (cells with dotted boxes) are of greater concern. These unexpected observations will be of greater or lesser concern depending on their number and their location in the data matrix. Persons who score well on difficult items despite low overall total scores (e.g., F, K, G, and B) might have done so by guessing or cheating. Similarly, poor scores on easy items despite high overall total scores (e.g., H, E, L, and J) might indicate lack of concentration or guessing. Of course, the presence of other unexpected idiosyncratic circumstances, including particular person–item interactions, is always a possibility. Think of the high jump competition again. When the champion misses an early, easy jump or two, we suspect that it is due to nerves or that the champ didn't take the jump seriously. For the past unknown who succeeds beyond all expectations, we might attribute that success to a new jumping technique, altered training regimens, or even chemical assistance. However unlikely such unexpected athletic performances are (based on the existing records), they are not impossible.

This brings to our attention an important principle guiding our use and interpretation of observational schedules and tests. Some students (see Student A) perform in a strictly orderly fashion: raw score of 5 for Student A means exactly the five easiest items correct and the six hardest items incorrect. This is known as a **Guttman pattern**, However, our observations of most human behaviors rarely show perfectly rigid, step-like patterns of progression. The vagaries of our observational abilities and those of human performance ensure that rigid adherence to even precisely defined developmental sequences is the exception rather than the rule.

Similarly, items that precisely separate more able from less able students, as Items *i* and *g* appear to do, also are rare. It is more plausible that the sequence will be more or less predictable: that the likelihood of getting any question correct increases in line with the person's raw score. Of course, the lower a person's raw score is, the lower the likelihood of the person getting any question correct or of meeting any of the observational criteria. Predicting success or failure is most hazardous where the 0s meet the 1s for any student. Obviously, in such cases, the response is almost equally likely to be successful or unsuccessful. Any prediction of success is determined by how far the item is embedded in the student's zone of success. The further the item is embedded in the student's zone of success (the 1s), the more likely it is that the student will succeed on that item. Conversely, the likelihood of failure increases the further the item is embedded in the student's zone of failure (the 0s).

The pattern for Person A is almost too good to be true, but a closer look at the response patterns of the students gaining raw scores of 6 or 7 is illuminating. The pattern for Person I is quite orderly enough according to the general principle of increased likelihood of success and failure just outlined. How could anyone who has taken a test quibble about the little reversal of Items *k* and *d*? Person F is just like Person I, but what is the source of F's unexpected success on very difficult Item *e*? Guessing? Cheating? Some special knowledge? The response patterns for Persons E and L, however, do not match our expectations as easily. Although the unexpected failure on moderately difficult Item *d* might be overlooked, the unexpected failure on very easy Item *a* starts us wondering whether Person E's and Person L's understandings of area as revealed by this test are directly comparable with those of C and I. The more circumspect teacher, noting the identical and unexpected patterns for E and L, might revisit the seating plan for test day; were E and L seated side by side? However, we are not likely to be so equivocal when we try to interpret the success/failure patterns of Person F. The responses of Person F are so erratic and unpredictable in comparison with the general orderliness that is evident in the rest of the data matrix that it would be unfair to say that a raw score of 7 is a good summary of Person F's ability to solve area problems.

The same argument can be applied just as readily to the performance patterns of items or observations. Responses to Items *i, b, h,* and *g* are Guttman-like (all answers correct down to the bar). It is possible to predict with a good deal of success any student's overall likelihood of doing well or poorly on the whole area test just by looking at that student's performance on Items *i, b, h,* and/or *g*. But in looking at Item *d*, we see that it is not only a more difficult item but that the responses to it are so erratic that it is practically impossible to predict who will be successful with it and who will not. Success on Item *d* should be highly predictable for about the most able one third of the group, but the response pattern tells us that the difficulty rating for this item (0.46) cannot be taken at face value: High scorers C, E, and L failed on Item *d*, whereas lower scorers B, D, F, and I were successful. Now, the failure by C, E, and L on Item *d* might be due to those persons, or due to Item *d*. The data themselves can't tell us. But since we note that *d* has more problems (unexpected performances on it) than do the persons, we would investigate Item *d* first. Something else is going on with this item, something different from the general response pattern that we see in the whole data matrix for area. Is the item content misspecified? Perhaps we don't write items as well as we thought we did?

The next part of this procedure shows the inadequacy of treating raw scores of ability and difficulty directly as measurement scales. To illustrate the point, the ability fractions have been taken from Table 2.3 and their locations plotted along a continuum to see how the items and persons disperse (Fig. 2.1). Of course, the raw score fraction (0.45) corresponds exactly to the same raw score expressed as a percentage (45%). Many teachers and university professors would recognize the pattern shown for person abilities. They regularly see their students' results in this format as they go through the process of assigning grades. Often, the raw score percentage is the grade and 50% is automatically the pass point. However, it is much less common for teachers or researchers to give even this very basic treatment to the test questions they use to produce these student grades.

The problem with using raw score fractions or percentages is that this procedure tends to clump students around the middle scores and does not adequately contrast the results of the more able and less able students. Earning a few extra marks near the midpoint of the test results, say from 48% to 55%, does not reflect the same ability leap required for a move from 88% to 95% at the top of the test or from 8% to 15% at the bottom. The real problem here is that we routinely mistake the distances between fraction or percentage scores as having direct interval-scale meaning, when all we really may infer from these data is the ordering of the persons or the items. We need a sound way of interpreting the size of the gaps between the scores so that we are able to say, for example, "Betty shows more ability than Bill on this test, *and* by this much."

Moving From Observations to Measures

A simple mathematical procedure for better representing the relative distances between the raw scores has been available since the work of Thurstone in the 1920s. This procedure involves converting a raw score summary to its natural logarithm. Although such mathematical transformations to produce linear measures abound in the physical sciences, we have tended to avoid them or even to be suspicious of them in the human sciences; for example, the pendulum swing (http://web.mit.edu/aa-math/www/modules/node8.html). In addition to transforming the score from a merely ordinal scale to a mathematically more useful interval scale, a log odds scale avoids the problem of compression at the ends of the raw score scale due to its restricted range, leading to floor and ceiling effects. (**Log odds**: a logarithmic transformation of the odds or probability of success.) Further, it makes the calculations independent of the actual number of items on the test.

The first step in this procedure is to convert the raw score percentage into its success-to-failure ratio or odds. A raw score of 60% becomes odds of 60 to 40; 90% becomes 90 to 10; 50% becomes 50 to 50; and so on. Then a spreadsheet command or a calculator app can perform the elementary function of converting scores to their natural log odds. For Person L (64% or odds of 64 to 36), we enter 64/36, push the log function, and read off the result (+0.58). Try a few of these to get the hang of it: Ability odds of 55 to 45 for Person I become a log value of +0.20, and the odds of 45 to 55 for Person A become a value of −0.20. Using the data from the matrix, try a few other values or use a more familiar set of results to

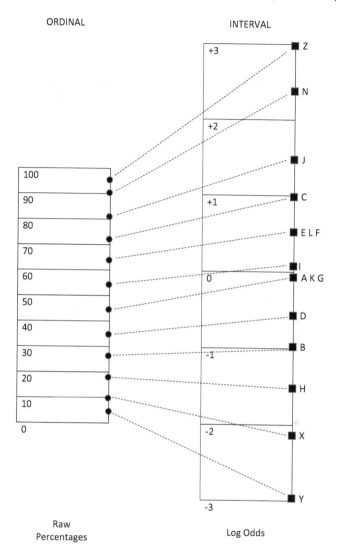

FIGURE 2.1 Relative abilities of persons A–K shown in raw percentages (left) and as log odds (right). More extreme persons' locations (X = 10%, Y = 5%, and Z = 95%) are added for purposes of illustration only.

see what happens. Georg Rasch based his own analytical work on just this type of approximation (e.g., Rasch, 1980, p. 97).

We have included the logarithmic transformation of the person data on the right-hand side of Figure 2.1. The relative placements (i.e., the ordinal relations) are, of course, the same as those on the left. The all-important order remains exactly the same. However, looking at the *positions* for the lower achievers on this test (those below the 50% level), we can observe that the distances between the person locations have been stretched out. Note that Rasch person estimates for those pairs of identical raw score totals (e.g., L & F; A & K) will also be identical; the differences in the response *patterns* will be revealed in the **fit statistics**.

The distances between Persons G, D, and B (each only one raw score apart) are now considerably larger than the gaps between Persons A, I, and F (each one raw score apart as well). Please check what the 1 raw score differences look like for Persons N, J, and C. Now the scale we have for plotting the person and item locations approximates an interval scale, whereby the value of the scale is maintained at any position along that scale. It is only with an interval scale that we can begin to say how much more able Betty is than Bill instead of merely saying that she is more able. Moreover, the effect becomes much more marked if we introduce some more extreme person abilities into these figures: A person with a 95% raw score becomes located at +2.94 on the log ability scale, whereas the low score of 10% translates as −2.2 and 5% becomes −2.94. The argument is that this wider distribution of person locations more fairly represents the increase in ability required to move from a score of 90% to a score of 95% as considerably greater than the ability difference between, say, a score of 50% and a score of 55%. This log-odds transformation of our raw data is a first approximation of the Rasch measurement scale that is the focus of this book. The Rasch model is an interesting model in that it follows from a small set of assumptions.

The basic Rasch assumptions are that:

(a) each person is characterized by an ability, and
(b) each item by a difficulty that
(c) can be expressed by numbers along one line. Finally,
(d) from the difference between the numbers (and nothing else), the probability of observing any particular scored response can be computed.

Up to this point, we have attempted to show that for a model to be useful for investigating aspects of the human condition represented in developmental and other theories, it needs to incorporate the following properties:

It should be sensitive to the ordered acquisition of the skills or abilities under investigation (i.e., it should aim at uncovering the order of development or acquisition).

It should be capable of estimating the developmental distances between the ordered skills or persons (i.e., it should tell us by how much Person T is more developed, more capable, more depressed, or more rehabilitated than is Person S).

It should allow us to determine whether the general developmental pattern shown among items and persons is sufficient to account for the pattern of development shown by every item and every person.

The reader will not be very much surprised if we now go on to demonstrate that analyses based on Rasch measurement are particularly suited to investigations in the wide range of human sciences on exactly these grounds.

Summary

In this chapter, we proceeded through the logical and practical steps necessary to construct interval-level measures from ordinal level observations. Using the high jump event as an example, we argued that, for all practical purposes, the probability of an athlete succeeding at any jump is dictated by just two aspects of the event: the ability of the athlete and the difficulty of the jump—both of which are measured on the same linear interval-level measurement scale. The probability of success increases as the athlete's ability exceeds the difficulty of the jump decreases; it's the difference between the two that is the key. If the two are nearly equal, then it is reasonable to predict the odds of success to failure at 50:50 or 50%.

In fact, this logic holds for any event/observation/response that can be summarized and recorded as a presence/occurrence/success, by simply assigning 1 (or ✓) for the presence of an occurrence and 0 (or ✗) for its absence. Thus, for a true/false test aimed at discriminating a group of persons on some underlying human ability, we need only to follow a few simple steps to construct a linear measure of that ability. Once we recognize that these true/false responses are merely qualitative observations and total 'number of correct' responses forms merely an ordinal level score, we can proceed to:

- Calculate item difficulties and person abilities (by expressing the item or person raw score as a percentage of the total possible score).
- Convert the raw score percentage into its success-to-failure ratio or odds. For example, a raw score of 60% becomes odds of 60 to 40.
- Calculate the natural log of the odds ratio.

These steps transform the ordinal-level data to interval-level measures and eliminate the compression at the ends of raw score scale. Using these measures (transformed raw counts), we can then proceed to examine a host of useful diagnostics to aid us in uncovering the extent to which the persons and items actually form an interval-scale linear measure.

Suggested Readings

Introductory

Wright, B.D., & Stone, M.H. (1979). Item calibration by hand. *Best Test Design: Rasch Measurement*. MESA Press, Chicago, IL.

Wright, B.D., & Linacre, J.M. (1989). Observations are always ordinal; measurements, however, must be interval. *Archives of Physical Measurement and Rehabilitation, 70*(12), 857–860.

Advanced

Applied

Karabatsos, G. (1997). The sexual experiences survey: Interpretation and validity. *Journal of Outcome Measurement, 1*(4), 305–328.

ACTIVITIES

Read

Wright, B.D., & Linacre, J.M. (1989). Observations are always ordinal; measurements, however, must be interval. *Archives of Physical Measurement and Rehabilitation, 70*(12), 857–860.

Activity

Use a calculator or spreadsheet to calculate the log odds intervals for each of the persons A–K in Table 2.3. Start with the *n/N*% for each (right-hand column); calculate the odds (e.g., Person L, 64% yields odds of 64:36, so input 64/36) and convert that to its natural logarithm (ln or $\log_e$) (+0.58). (e.g., the LN function in Excel "returns the natural logarithm of a number") Check your results against those in Figure 2.1. Calculate log odds values for more extreme persons, X, Y, and Z.

Notes

1 Wright and Linacre (1989) developed these points more fully.
2 When the items and persons do not share the same range on the continuum, they are considered 'mistargeted'. Good targeting helps to improve measurement. The concept of targeting is introduced in Chapter 3.

References

Bond, T. G. (1996, January). *Confirming ideas about development: Using the Rasch model in practice* [Videotape]. Invited address at the Human Development and Psychology Colloquium series, Graduate School of Education, Harvard University.

Bond, T. G., & Parkinson, K. (2010). Children's understanding of area concepts: Development, curriculum and educational achievement. *Journal of Applied Measurement, 11*(1), 60–77.

Guttman, L. (1944). A basis for scaling qualitative data. *American Sociological Review, 9*, 139–150.

Karmiloff-Smith, A., & Inhelder, B. (1975). If you want to get ahead, get a theory. *Cognition, 3*(3), 195–212.

Parkinson, K. (1996). *Children's understanding of area: A comparison between performance on Piagetian interview tasks and school-based written tasks.* Unpublished thesis, James Cook University, Townsville, Queensland, Australia.

Rasch, G. (1980). *Probabilistic models for some intelligence and attainment tests* (Expanded ed.). Chicago, IL: University of Chicago Press.

Wright, B. D. (1996). Comparing Rasch measurement and factor analysis. *Structural Equation Modeling, 3*(1), 3–24.

Wright, B. D., & Linacre, J. M. (1989). Observations are always ordinal; measurements, however, must be interval. *Archives of Physical Measurement and Rehabilitation, 70*(12), 857–860.

3

BASIC PRINCIPLES OF THE RASCH MODEL

This chapter presents the pathway analogy we originated in 2001 to explain the basic concepts of the Rasch model. The analogy is quite directly applicable to observations in many aspects of education and psychology, and its relevance for the other measurement situations in the human sciences in which the Rasch model should be used is detailed in the following chapters. The high jump exemplar from the previous chapter is used to introduce a formal statement of the Rasch model as well as basic ideas of the Rasch item characteristic curve (ICC).

The Pathway Analogy

Let us imagine a segment in children's development, such as the progressive attainment of the skills in drawing a reasonable human form or their progress toward understanding lineal measurement as revealed by Piaget in Chapter 1. Our underlying developmental *theory* for either of these two examples might define a single sequence of development that could be represented by the arrow in Figure 3.1, but we would not really expect our recorded observations of those developments to be as perfectly ordered or precise as the points on that straight line. In *practice*, what we need to be able to do is build a measurement tool (a set of tasks, a list of assessment criteria, or a series of questions) that will be empirically useful enough to make meaningful assessments of that ability.

What then will be good enough—good enough to support and defend the decisions we will make? Our theory-based tool must represent our best effort to acknowledge both the role of that straight line in measurement theory and the diversions from this straight path that exist in the empirical reality of practice. Only the user will be able to tell what is good enough by experience, but the criteria by which usefulness can be gauged are built into the Rasch model and demonstrated in our analogy.

The arrow represents the unattainable theoretical ideal, and the circular stepping-stones in Figure 3.1 represent a selection of the items (L, M, N, . . ., U) in our test or observation schedule. The steps at the bottom of the path will suit all children, even the beginners, and those steps at the top will be reached only by the most developed children. Therefore, the different intermediary stepping-stones along the way will be useful for the varied levels of development we expect among our varied sample of test takers. The distance of the step from the bottom of the path (A) represents its difficulty relative to the other items. This is our representation of item difficulty: Closer to the bottom is easier; further is more difficult.

The idea is that each child will progress along the steps as far as the child's ability (development) will carry him or her. The child will use (master) the steps until the steps become too difficult. How far any child moves along the pathway will be our estimate of the child's development or ability. We have used little squares to represent how far each of the children has moved along the pathway. This is our representation of person ability.

This map of item and person relationships we have used to represent the pathway analogy contains a lot of basic information that is central to Rasch measurement but can be gleaned readily by attending to the basic difficulty/ability concepts mentioned earlier. Please look carefully at Figure 3.1 and try to answer the following questions (with reasons). All the answers can be derived directly from the figure without any extra knowledge of Rasch modeling. And remember to keep in mind the 50:50 principle from the high jump analogy in Chapter 2. First, take a look at the positions of the round stepping-stones (item locations).

Is Item S (much) more difficult or (much) less difficult than Item N? Why?
Which item is the most likely to be failed by the students? Why?
Which item is the most likely to be passed by the students? Why?

Now take a look at the positions of the squares that represent the person locations on the pathway (it's an item-person map of abilities and difficulties). With the Rasch model, the principles about items work with exactly the same logic for persons. According to the pathway representation of these data in Figure 3.1,

Is Bill (much) more able or (much) less able than Bob? Why?
Which student is revealed as least able on this test? Why?
Is Bill likely to have answered Item U correctly? Why?
What would be more unexpected—that Bill will miss Item S or Item M? Why?
Mike scored 1 on the test. Which item is most likely to be the one he answered correctly? Why?

The vertical dotted lines in Figure 3.1, where white meets shaded, are meant to represent the edges of the pathway. Stepping-stones within these boundaries can

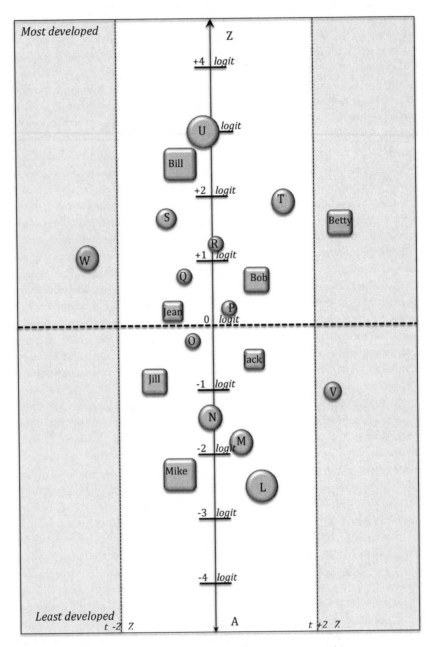

FIGURE 3.1 Developmental pathway for selected ersatz persons and items.

be seen as useful steps on this particular pathway. Locations outside the boundaries must be interpreted cautiously—just as we would when stepping off a pathway into rougher country. So, now,

> Which items are not usefully located on the pathway in their present forms? Why?
>
> Which person is not developing in the manner common to all others? Why?
>
> Is Bob's ability well measured by this test? Why?
>
> Jill scored 3 on the test. Which items did she most likely answer correctly? Why?

Just from the representation of persons and items on the map, Item S is much more difficult than Item N—it is much higher on the pathway. Item U— highest on the map—is the toughest on this test, and most of these children will not succeed on Item U. Item L is the very lowest on the map and is the easiest on this test. Most of these children will answer Item L correctly. The map shows that Bill is considerably more able than Bob on this test. Bill is higher up, and there is a fair-sized gap between the two. Bill is not likely to have succeeded on Item U—its difficulty exceeds his ability level. Persons who succeed on Item U usually need more ability than Bill shows. Bill has much more ability than required to succeed on Item M. For Bill, missing Item M would be a rare but not impossible event. However, because Item S is much tougher, much closer to Bill's ability level, we should not be so surprised if Bill misses items such as Item S from time to time.

Stepping-stones V and W are not located well enough on our pathway to be useful as they are, whereas Betty has not used the pathway in the same manner as the others. Bob's location fits well between the dotted quality-control lines, indicating he has performed according to the model's expectations, and thus Bob is well measured. Jill is most likely to have succeeded with Items L, M, and N. Her location shows that she is more able than necessary to answer Items L, M, and N correctly at most administrations of this test.

In developing any test, our aim would be to put enough stepping-stones along the path to represent all the points useful for our testing purposes, between little development (A) and much development (Z). Of course, to do that, we would need to collect observations from enough suitable persons. Good data analysis requires many more items and many more persons than we have included in our Figure 3.1. We have merely selected some illustrative examples here. Also, with our emphasis on building and defining a pathway, we have concentrated on items and (unforgivably) tended to ignore persons at this point. Let us now turn our attention to some specific Rasch measurement ideas and establish some guidelines that will aid us in accomplishing this task.

Unidimensionality

Underlying the ideas about measuring development that have been raised so far is an important implicit principle. Unfortunately, this principle is so taken for granted in our use of measurement tools for size, weight, temperature, and the like that when it is made explicit, it causes concern for researchers in the human sciences who perhaps have not thought the matter through. In attempting to measure the physical attributes of objects, people, or the weather, scientists and laypeople alike take care to measure just one attribute of the target at a time. A rectangular solid has many attributes (e.g., length, breadth, height, weight, volume, density, and even hardness, to name a few), but all attempts to make meaningful estimations of the particular block under scrutiny focus on only one attribute at a time. This focus on one attribute or dimension at a time is referred to as unidimensionality.

Surely we can learn something from Galileo's attempts to measure temperature mentioned in Chapter 1. His thermoscope—an early 'thermometer' designed to detect the hotter *versus* the cooler of different situations—was open to the atmosphere and therefore sensitive to changes in both temperature and atmospheric pressure at the same time. Sherry (2011) termed it a barothermoscope—both a baroscope (sensitive to the influence of atmospheric pressure) and a thermoscope (sensitive to the influence of temperature)—but because it was sensitive to both, it could not be relied on for either. Was the change in the result due to change in the temperature dimension, change in pressure dimension, or changes in both? Impossible to tell. Rasch himself was influenced by what we should learn from physical measurement, and Rasch measurement incorporates indicators to detect when extraneous influences degrade our efforts to measure our single variable of interest.

We all are aware that the complexity of human existence can never be satisfactorily expressed as one score on any one test. We can, however, develop some useful quantitative estimates of some human attributes, but we can do that only for one attribute or ability at a time. Confusing a number of attributes into a single generic score makes confident predictions from that score more hazardous and the score a less useful summary of ability or achievement. But carefully constructed tests that make good measurement estimates of single attributes might be sufficient for a number of thoughtfully decided purposes. For special or difficult situations, collecting additional estimates of other appropriate attributes is essential. Of course, qualitative data might be used to complement the quantitative results. Human beings are complex, multidimensional creatures to be sure. But whereas using height as a measure of a person is an obvious and convenient reductionism, in many cases useful predictions can be made about the suitability of doorway heights based on that just that one estimate alone. And we would be naïve to think that this would be sufficient for every person.

The meaning of the estimates of person ability and item difficulty in the data matrix we have used so far (see Chapter 2) will be meaningful only if each and every question contributes to the measure of a single underlying attribute (e.g., the ability to solve area problems). If the intention of teachers who test for this ability is not well implemented in each of the items, we might find that other attributes of the children's abilities are included in the measure and hence degrade the meaning of the test results. For example, one item might rely very heavily on language comprehension. Another item might focus too much on children's ability to interpret a complex geometrical drawing. Still another might be so poorly written that children find it difficult to understand the response options provided, and so on. Then, of course, the children must cooperate with the teachers' intention as expressed in the test. To the extent that the children replace strategies based on the understanding of area with other strategies based on, say, simple recall, guessing, cheating, carelessness, use of a calculator, and so forth, the estimate of that child's ability to solve area problems will be degraded by the influence of other attributes not intentionally targeted by the teachers. The resultant score then is uninterpretable to the extent that these other abilities, and not the understanding of area, are manifested in the children's responses. (Remember, from Chapter 2, how other variables disturbed the measurement process in the high jump: the competition surface, the air temperature, the prevailing wind—direction and strength—etc.) When those aspects overwhelm the role of the athletes' ability, the outcome will be unpredictable, just as we found with Galileo's attempt to measure only temperature. It is here that the principles of **unidimensionality** require that our analytical procedures must incorporate indicators of the extent to which the persons and items fit our concept of the ideal unidimensional line.

Item Fit

A good measurement process in education, psychology, and the other human sciences will provide for the estimation of just one ability at a time and will not, intentionally or unintentionally, confuse two or more human attributes into one measure or score. Each of the items should contribute in a meaningful way to the construct/concept being investigated. It will be helpful here to reflect explicitly on how the Rasch model focuses on the key ideas of 'construct validity' and 'order'. First, one aspect of **construct validity** focuses on the idea that the recorded performances are reflections of a single underlying construct: the theoretical construct that has been made explicit by the investigator's attempt to represent it in items or observations and by the human ability inferred to be responsible for those performances. The data matrix that relates the items and the persons together in a coherent, integrated way is more likely to represent (i.e., fit) the construct under examination satisfactorily than one in which the relations appear serendipitous.

Of course, detecting this confusion might not be an easy matter, but for teacher-made tests and early drafts of potentially large-scale tests, it is useful to sit down with a few selected examinees after the test marking has been done to work through the questions with each examinee in turn to help determine the extent to which the intentions of the test writer are revealed in the students' responses. Ask the children how they worked out the correct answer to some items; check to see how some of the smartest children missed one of the easier items. The ordered data matrix, as shown in Chapter 2, could be easily implemented using a spreadsheet, and that would be a very good device for deciding which students and which questions might be worth closer scrutiny. Items or persons that do not adhere to the expected ability/difficulty pattern would be good starting points. That way, the quantitative and qualitative aspects of investigation can work together to improve test design.

Because visual inspection of a data matrix typically is not practical for assessing the impact of individual items or persons, Rasch analysis provides fit statistics designed to aid the investigator in making a number of interrelated decisions about the data (Smith, 1991, 1992, 2000; Smith & Miao, 1994; Wright & Masters, 1982; Wright & Stone, 1979). Rasch analysis provides indicators of how well each item fits within the underlying test construct. Typical fit indicators use the *patterns* of responses to estimate how *much* misfit is evident, or, how *likely* that misfit is. In Rasch measurement, the concept of **fit** is as a 'quality-control mechanism' (akin to the use of fit in industrial statistics). Fit statistics provide one indication as to whether the researcher has completed a task of sufficient quality to allow that values for persons and items can be represented with interval-level measures. This is a crucial aid for the investigator assessing the meaning of the unidimensional construct. That is, fit indices help the investigator to ascertain whether the Rasch requirement for unidimensionality holds up empirically. Items that do not fit the unidimensional construct (the ideal straight line as shown in Fig. 3.1) are those that diverge unacceptably from the expected ability/difficulty pattern (see Chapter 2). Then, fit statistics help to determine whether the item estimations may be held as meaningful quantitative summaries of the observations (i.e., whether each item contributes to the measurement of only one construct).

Notice in Figure 3.1 that the steps (e.g., Items, L, M, N) do not lie precisely along the theoretical straight line. We might get some of our items or observations close to perfect, but our aim is to place them close enough to the theoretical straight line to be good practical indicators of the hypothetical path from A to Z. Suppose we are developing a test of basic math skills. Items such as L, M, and N (easy items) might be simple addition problems, whereas Items T and U (difficult items) might be long-division problems. Stepping-stone items that are not close enough to the centerline to be part of this path, such as Items V and W in our drawn example, most likely do not follow this pattern. Perhaps item V is a story problem that confounds reading ability with math ability; the correct answer for item W might be revealed in other items. The fit statistics then would indicate that these items might be included better in some other related pathway. They will not be a useful part of this A-to-Z pathway until they fit a bit better. Typical issues revealed by erratic fit statistics include 'double-barreled' attitude questions in which some respond to part a, some to part b, and some to both, or health-related items that apply to only some but not all patients. Perhaps we could try rewriting those items or expressing them some other way the next time we use this test. We could replace them or use them in some other test.

At this early stage, however, it could be more appropriate not to count the results of Items V and W in any child's test score. Our measure of children's math ability is likely to be more meaningful if these results were not counted. At this point, novices might be given to despair of writing enough 'good' items or collecting enough 'good' data; they tend to throw out far too much and finally decide to look for an analytical approach that is less demanding of them, their items, and their data. Often the flaws in items that behave as Items V and W have are too small to distort the measurement in any noticeable way. It is important to remember that the misfitting items (or persons) have different meanings, depending on the nature of their misfit. On the right of the pathway are located those items (e.g., V) that do not fit well enough—their performance is 'too erratic' to contribute to good measurement. We could investigate that by temporarily deleting a couple of unexpected observations in the response column for Item V; that might help reveal the nature of the problem. Removing the correct responses of a couple of low-ability 'guessers' or the incorrect responses of a few 'inattentive' high-ability persons might give some clues about the cause of item V's misfit.

On the left of the pathway are those items (e.g., W) that fit so well that we can think of them as 'too good to be true'. A small number of those 'too good to be true' items do not degrade measurement. Further, in this example, removing just one of those misfitting items, say, Item V (too erratic), will shift the pathway toward Item W, so that Item W will now be on the pathway. Removing **overfitting** item W might result in V falling on the useful pathway. Talk to the item writers about the relative qualities of V and W; quite likely they'll agree to put aside 'too erratic' item V in favor of keeping 'too good to be true' item W. In the end, those working assessments in high-stakes decision making in educational testing or health monitoring will be less tolerant of misfitting (i.e., erratic) item and person performances. For the rest of us, using Rasch fit indicators should be an iterative learning experience: uncovering more about the variable, how it is revealed in person and item performances, discovering how our data collection can be better controlled, and so forth. To understand fit statistics a little better, we could interactively delete subsets of persons or items and compare the diagnostics for each output. But we certainly do not recommend this procedure for 'tidying up' a misfitting data set.

To help us to decide which items are meaningfully included in our pathway, we could put a dotted line on each side of and parallel to our theoretical straight line as a check that the fit of our steps to the pathway is good enough for our intended purposes (e.g., something like **95% confidence** or quality-control lines). Indeed, some Rasch software outputs report item fit data in a graphical form in just this way.

In each case, the analytical output tables would provide greater detail on how each item or person performance met or failed to meet the model's expectations. Clearly, items whose **estimations** do not sufficiently 'fit' the model require further investigation. Presumably, then, as asserted in the previous chapter, there would always be sound theoretical grounds for including each of the items in an observation schedule and for using that schedule or checklist to make observations of any particular person. Given that test construction, testing, and data collection are usually done for some very good reasons, important insights into the *theory*—or its expression in *practice*—are likely outcomes of such deliberations. Our theories guide us in deciding what sort of items we should use and with whom we should use them. Thus, this Rasch-informed method, coupled with theory, can be contrasted with the often-used procedure of generating a huge net of possible items and then trawling through very large, supposedly **normally** distributed samples to find a subset of items with acceptable statistical characteristics, statistics that have precious little to do with the construction of measures.

> A good theory can be promptly compromised or greatly enhanced through this process. Also, the way in which measurement alternatives are identified and selected, and measurement problems anticipated and resolved, influences the development, choice, and use of frameworks that guide the researcher in deciding what strategies and techniques are most appropriate to those frameworks. In affecting the validity of research results, the measurement process has repercussions for the ongoing revision and improvement of theory.
>
> *(Blalock & Blalock, 1982, p. 37)*

The Rasch model incorporates a theoretical idealization of the data's interrelations, an unachievable perfect state that is mathematically represented as the ideal straight line shown in Figure 3.1. The Rasch model represents the concept of perfect 'one attribute at a time' measurement, and hence we want to see whether reality (our data) adheres to that concept of a straight measurement line (psychometricians also refer to this construct underlying their investigation as a **latent trait**). Conversely, if the chief contention of this volume is accepted, then the outcomes of Rasch modeling can also reveal the suitability of the observation schedule as an expression of the substantive human sciences theory in empirical practice. That is, we can take the conventional approach and see this as a test of whether our data correspond with our substantive theory. However, it is more useful if we complement this use with the idea of whether our construct, as expressed in developmental or other theory, fits with our data. Ideally, this is just one part of an epistemologically iterative research program in which theory informs practice and practice informs theory dialectically.

Difficulty/Ability Estimation and Error

In developing the mathematical representation of the straight line, the Rasch model specifically addresses the conception of order, an idea fundamental to any account of developing human ability or condition and basic to the idea of measuring more or less of any human condition. And the idea of measuring more or less is central to the idea of detecting and measuring *change*. Whereas order obviously is important in psychological theories of child development, it also is central to the arrangement of cells in a Likert-type response scale, is easily detected in medical rehabilitation settings, and is directly relevant to academic achievement when the difficulty of test questions varies. Specifically, in the Rasch model, performances are attributed relative importance in correspondence to the position they hold on the measurement continuum. For example, correctly worked-through long-division problems are attributed more importance in the assessment of advanced mathematical skill than correctly worked-through simple addition problems. The Rasch model thus incorporates an algorithm that expresses the probabilistic expectations of item and person performances when one and only one construct is held to underlie the sequence represented by the observation schedule (Wright & Stone, 1979).

When a data matrix reflects a successful attempt to implement a theoretically guided line of inquiry with a sample for whom that inquiry was appropriate, then a number of propositions are supportable. Two key propositions drawn directly from Rasch's basic principle quoted in Chapter 1 are as follows:

> Persons who are more able, more developed, or more agreeable have a greater likelihood of correctly answering/endorsing all the items in the observation schedule (e.g., in Figure 3.1, Bill is more likely than Bob to answer all the items correctly).
>
> Easier/more agreeable items are more likely to be endorsed/answered or reached correctly by all persons (e.g., both Bob and Bill are more likely to answer Item L correctly than Item P and more likely to answer P correctly than S).

These propositions are necessary for expressing the unidimensionality of data, and they explicitly illustrate the concept of order in establishing that unidimensionality. Based on this logic of order, as an initial approximation, the Rasch analysis software programs perform a logarithmic transformation of the item and person data to convert those ordinal data to yield interval data (see, e.g., Fischer & Molenaar, 1995). These transformations represent the estimation of person ability and item difficulty detected in the data set (i.e., item and person placement along the single line of inquiry). Actual item and person performance probabilities determine the interval sizes. They are not introduced as *a priori* assumptions of the investigator or of the analytical algorithm. To the extent that the set of observations adheres sufficiently to Rasch's mathematical model of expectations, it is held to be unidimensional (i.e., the single difficulty/ability continuum is sufficient to explain the actual patterns of item/person performances). A common misunderstanding is that misfit makes the Rasch estimates nonlinear. This is not the case. Most estimation algorithms used in Rasch analysis produce linear estimates on the basis that the data are unidimensional. The estimates themselves are forced to be unidimensional and linear, as the Rasch model requires. But the Rasch estimates produced by the software's estimation procedure might not match the data in the matrix very well at all. Misfit means that the actual collected data in the matrix are not a good match to the calculated Rasch estimates, not that the estimates are nonlinear; they are linear, but they are not a good summary of the data—the data do not fit the model.

These person ability and item difficulty estimates, having been subjected to a log transformation (and many **iterations** of the estimation procedure), are displayed in computer output along a **logit (log odds** unit) scale. The logit scale is an interval scale in which the unit intervals between the locations on that item-person map have a consistent value or meaning. The Rasch model routinely sets at 50% the probability of success for any person on an item located at the same point on the item–person logit scale. Because Bob's logit ability estimate is equal to Item Q's difficulty estimate, Bob has a 50% chance of passing this item, for which he is equally matched. The probability of Bob's success increases to almost 75% for a dichotomous item that is 1 logit easier (perhaps Item O) or decreases to about 25% for a dichotomous item that is 1 logit harder (perhaps Item T). The investigator now has more detailed information than that provided by just the data matrix alone on which to make judgments concerning the items, the persons, and the substantive human sciences theory that guided the investigation.

But how do we interpret the precision of these estimates? What is the use of item and person estimates if we do not know how good they are? Often our best intentions to realize our theoretical ideas as observation schedules or items go astray. Yes, the stepping-stones along the pathway might be located at an exact point (at the Rasch estimate) along the pathway, but our Figure 3.1 gives each one a size as well. The difficulty location of any test item (stepping-stone) is located at a point but always has a zone of imprecision, or error, associated with it. Small stepping-stones (small **errors**) suggest that we can locate their difficulty rather precisely. With the larger stepping-stones (larger errors), the item locations are not as precise. Figure 3.1 shows that some of the items overlap, particularly at the extremes of the path, where errors of location tend to be larger. Collecting more data is usually the easy remedy for item imprecision—find more appropriate persons to test. Reducing error in person estimates is more problematic, especially when we want to separate persons into mutually exclusive groups like 'not yet ready to leave hospital' and 'ready to go home'. In that case, we have to develop more of these appropriate items in order to improve precision of person estimates so we can make the high-stakes decision with more confidence and fewer mistakes.

Figure 3.1 shows that Items O, P, Q, R, and S have relatively little error associated with their difficulty estimates, because ability estimates for a number of our test candidates (Jill, Jack, Jean, Bob, and Bill) are close to or *targeted* near the same level as those items. Thus, if Items Q, R, and S are, say, multiplication problems, this means that the ability of both Bill and Bob includes capabilities at or near the ability to solve multiplication problems. Hence, their responses provide us with enough information to estimate the difficulty of those items more precisely. Items L, M, N, and U, on the other hand, have relatively large errors associated with their estimates. Very few persons in our sample have ability levels equal to the difficulty estimates of these items (i.e., the bulk of our sample is too competent for the simple addition problems but not up to the demands of long-division Item U), so estimating the difficulty of such items involves somewhat less statistical information, so we are left with more imprecision.

Each person's ability location on the map has an error estimate as well. Note that Bill's square is a bit larger (less precise) than is Bob's. Bill's ability estimate contains more uncertainty because there are not as many items in our observation schedule *targeted* at his level of ability. Bob, on the other hand, has more items close to his ability level, thereby providing more detailed information to estimate his ability level accurately. Mike has only one or perhaps two items directly relevant to him, so his ability estimate will be clouded by a larger error estimate.

We do not mean that the stepping-stones provided to measure some human ability along some pathway under investigation represent all or the only steps along that path. Development occurs, attitudes change, or ability develops independently of our observing it in some organized manner via a test or observation schedule. The items we use are a sample of items chosen for any one of a number of pragmatic or theoretical reasons from the almost endless population of possible relevant items. Therefore, a child's progress along the pathway can be imagined in any reasonable way: as little steps, large steps, skipping, or a mixture of these. However, the record of development produced by our observation of it, via a test or checklist, will depend on which stepping-stones the child succeeded in using and which the child did not use on the day of the test to progress as far as possible along the pathway. In that sense, it is a record of what the child actually did rather than what the child could do.

Measurement of any human performance and the estimation of any ability depend on the cooperation of the subject being tested. We tend to assume that the person being examined cooperates with our intention, as revealed by the test instructions and items. However, we all know about some notorious practices of test takers that subvert our measurement intentions. Sometimes respondents just guess at some or all of the answers. Sometimes they copy from neighbors. Sometimes they even bring notes to crib. They also have been known to have lapses in concentration, give up partway through the testing, try to remember formulaic responses to problem-solving tests, and so on. Some even appear less than entirely motivated to complete our clever tasks or do not speak the test language well enough.

Despite all these well-known problems, we as psychologists, teachers, health professionals, and examiners tend to ignore those problems and just count the number of correct steps taken on the pathway (i.e., the raw score) as the indicator of ability. This is a time-honored strategy, but it could stand some serious reconsideration, such as by including some quality-control processes. A pathway is useful only to the extent that the vast majority of respondents use it in demonstrably similar ways. Betty, who scores 6/10 (getting Items L, O, R, S, T, and U correct on our test in Fig. 3.1), is not showing the same development as Bob, who scores a raw score of 5/10 by using Steps L, M, N, O, and Q. Therefore, if we want to plot Bob and Betty somewhere on the pathway, we must credit Bob with five and Betty with six answers correct. We can locate Bob on the pathway well within the dotted lines, showing that his performance pattern fits our developmental expectations sufficiently well. Betty is located outside the pathway's dotted lines (i.e., her erratic response pattern does not fit the model). That is a warning to us: Even though Betty scores 6/10, her pattern for scoring those six marks was not orderly enough for us to claim that her performance fits our Rasch-generated expectations. Something else—other than just the underlying latent trait—has contributed to Betty's score. We should not take 6/10 at face value as an indicator of Betty's development. If our path is set up according to Rasch's specifications, then we will want to check out Betty's result: Is she a guesser (item U unexpectedly correct)? Were the items she missed somehow unfair to her? Did she lose concentration on easy items (say, item V) that did not engage her? Of course, we cannot tell that from her score alone; we can tell it from the *erratic pattern* of her successes and failures: her misfitting location off the pathway suggests that 6/10 is not a representative score for her and that we need to find out more. Remember our problem with misfitting item V? Removing Betty's row of responses could see item V become useful enough for measuring the rest of the sample; item misfit is due to unexpected person behavior.

Reliability

Suppose the investigator did not provide enough steps along the pathway (items on the test). The first consequence would be that the locations of the persons along the pathway would be less precise. More good items give more precise person locations than do fewer good items. Because we do not have many steps to separate the varying levels of development in our example, the children would tend to be distributed along the steps in clumps. This would not be a problem if the test were designed to provide merely a coarse-grained group-level picture of the ability or attitude being recorded. However, if we are involved in high-stakes testing to certify the sufficient development of skills for working in a critical medical setting or to allow just certain schoolchildren to move on in a particular educational direction as the result of some testing or recording procedure, then coarse-grained measures will not suffice. The representation of the pathway as test items or tasks would require many more stepping-stones (items), each with a quite precise location, so that any person's location on the path could be located precisely. This would be of utmost importance at the point along the pathway where the 'able enough/not able enough' decision is to be made (i.e., at the high-stakes cutoff score).

The Rasch measurement model provides indices that help the investigator to determine whether there are enough items spread along the continuum, as opposed to clumps of them, and enough spread of ability among persons to make those decisions. The **person reliability index** indicates the replicability of person ordering we could expect if this sample of persons were given another a parallel set of items measuring the same construct (Wright & Masters, 1982).

That is, given another set of the same number and distribution of items purported to measure the same construct, will Bill still be estimated as being more able than Bob and Bob more able than Jean? Person **reliability** is enhanced by small errors in ability estimates, which in turn is affected by the number of targeted items. Then, in the make-believe example represented in Figure 3.1, we would expect person reliability to be fairly low (too few items). What we do have working for us in terms of person reliability is that our items are targeted at the ability level of our sample. This helps to give us confidence in our ability estimates. However, the shortcoming with this pathway example is the lack of many additional items and persons spread along the ability continuum. Person reliability requires not only ability estimates well targeted by a suitable pool of items but also a large enough spread of ability across the sample so that the measures demonstrate a hierarchy of ability/development (person separation) on this construct (Fox & Jones, 1998). Therefore, high person reliability means that we have developed a line of inquiry in which some persons score higher and some score lower and that we could expect consistency of these inferences.

The **item reliability index** indicates the replicability of item placements along the pathway if these same items were given to another same-sized sample of persons who behaved in the same way. For example, if other persons were given these same items, would the item estimates remain stable? For example, would Item P still be more difficult than Item N? In Figure 3.1, we would expect a very low item reliability index because there are not enough people in the example at the lower ability levels. Therefore, Items L through P, for example, do not have enough information (and hence have large errors) to pinpoint their difficulty levels more precisely. We would need more children with lower math ability in the sample to estimate better the location of these easier items. Therefore, from high item reliability, we can infer that we have developed a line of inquiry in which some items are more difficult and some items are easier and that we could expect consistency of these inferences. In summary, low item (person) reliability directs us to collect more data in order to reduce the error or imprecision of the estimates. However, achieving high item (person) reliability does not signal the end of the task. Having satisfied this criterion allows us to look elsewhere for additional evidence that the measures are valid.

A Basic Framework for Measurement

The Rasch model provides a mathematical framework against which test developers can compare their data. The model is based on the idea that useful measurement involves examination of only one human attribute at a time (unidimensionality) on a hierarchical 'more than/less than' line of inquiry. This line of inquiry is a theoretical idealization against which we can compare patterns of responses that do not coincide with this ideal. Person and item performance deviations from that line (fit) can be assessed, alerting the investigator to reconsider item wording and score interpretations from these data.

Each item difficulty and person ability is estimated on a common logit scale, and each of these estimates has a degree of error associated with it. Estimation error decreases as information about difficulty and ability increases (i.e., when items and persons are appropriately targeted with the sample of items and persons at hand). These error estimates, coupled with item and person reliability estimates, indicate the stability and replicability (i.e., invariance) of the item and person estimates. This information then guides the researcher in knowing how better to interpret and modify measures in the human sciences. We will develop the concept of measurement invariance more thoroughly in Chapter 5.

How then would these pathway features be represented in a Rasch analysis?

Most Rasch software output includes a form of item–person map in which person ability and item difficulty relations are easily seen. However, representing all the Rasch concepts on one variable map as we have in Figure 3.1 can be very

TABLE 3.1 Ersatz Item Statistics for the Pathway in Figure 3.1

Item Name	Difficulty Estimate	Error of Estimate	Fit Estimate as t
U	+3.0	0.60	−0.3
T	+1.9	0.43	+1.3
S	+1.6	0.33	−0.9
R	+1.2	0.28	+0.2
W	+0.9	0.43	−2.6
Q	+0.8	0.30	−0.6
P	+0.2	0.30	+0.4
O	−0.3	0.28	−0.4
V	−1.1	0.30	+2.4
N	−1.5	0.43	−0.2
M	−1.8	0.45	+0.6
L	−2.5	0.60	+1.0

difficult, so estimates for fit and error usually are included in tables along with ability and difficulty estimates, as shown in Table 3.1. The depiction of estimate, error, and fit on one Pathway map, now included in Winsteps software, was original with Bond and Fox (2001).

Item difficulty estimates are expressed in logits, in which a logit value of 0 is arbitrarily set as the average, or mean, of the item difficulty estimates. Thus, item O is near the average on the scale; Items L and N are easier, having negative logit scores; whereas Items R, S, and T have positive logit estimates, meaning that they are progressively more difficult. Those who are put off a little by negative logit values could refer to estimates of temperature. The 0 of the Celsius scale has been arbitrarily set at the freezing point of water, and values below 0 are routine, depending on the climate in which you live. Seven degrees below 0, $-7°C$, easily carries the message of just how cold it is. We address the issue of scale conversion in Chapter 10.

Person ability is estimated in relation to the item difficulty estimates (e.g., the more negative the value, the lower the child's ability on this test). Bill's ability estimate of +2.3 logits makes him clearly 'top of the class' on this test, even with the relatively imprecise nature of his estimate. Please take a few minutes to examine how each of the estimates in Tables 3.1 and 3.2 has been represented diagrammatically in Figure 3.1. It is the item–person map representation of Rasch modeling that is very attractive to both new and experienced users. The values of the key attributes being measured can be meaningfully interpreted at a glance. A picture paints a thousand words.

SO FAR . . .

Figure 3.2 is included to clarify the principles that we will use to construct the **pathway variable maps** and that readers will need to understand to interpret these maps in Chapters 3 through 8.

Estimation (Difficulty, Ability, and Precision)

Both items (as circles) and persons (as squares) are located on the same map. The logit scale is an interval-level measurement scale in which all logit units are of the same size. The highest values are located at the top of the map, and the lowest values are located at the bottom.

TABLE 3.2 Ersatz Person Statistics for the Pathway in Figure 3.1

Person Name	Ability Estimate	Error of Estimate	Fit Estimate as t
Bill	+2.3	0.45	−0.6
Betty	+1.2	0.36	+2.8
Bob	+0.8	0.36	+0.8
Jean	+0.2	0.30	−0.8
Jack	−0.7	0.30	+0.5
Jill	−1.0	0.36	−1.6
Mike	−2.4	0.50	−1.0

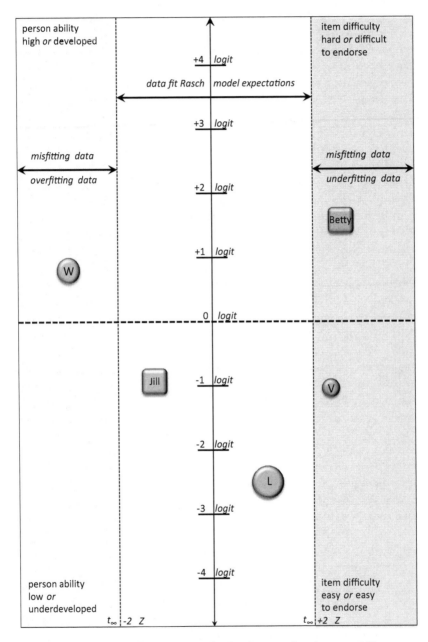

FIGURE 3.2 Principles used to construct the developmental pathway variable maps.

Each item and person is located along the **logit scale** according to its estimated value: More positive (higher) persons are more able, and more positive (higher) items are more difficult.

The measurement error of the item and person estimates is indicated by the vertical size of the symbol: Larger symbols indicate greater error (in logits—along the vertical logit scale).

Estimated values are read vertically (only) on the logit scale for both estimates and errors.

Fit (Quality Control)

Items and persons that fit the model's expectations are located in the white zone.

Items and persons that do not fit the model are located in the shaded zones. Fit values are read horizontally (only) on a standardized **Zstd** or t_∞ scale.

Acceptable values (white) fall between −2.0 and +2.0 with sample sizes between about 30 and 300. Locations on the right (> +2.0) are too erratic to be useful. Locations on the left (< −2.0) are too good to be true.

The Rasch Model

While the Rasch model provides a mathematical framework against which researchers in the human sciences should compare their data, readers will not be surprised to learn that the formulations and calculations of the model are both more detailed and more exact than portrayed in the Pathway analogy. While the Rasch model guides us in doing exactly the sorts of things we have discussed in the previous two chapters, it is not simply a matter of setting up a **Scalogram** matrix for our data and then adding the raw scores for items and persons and hitting the '**natural logarithm**' button (ln or $\log_e$) on a calculator app. The authors deliberately have kept the mathematical/technical details of the Rasch model to Appendix B so that readers are faced with understanding the concepts (of scientific measurement and the Rasch model) before they are confronted with the mathematical formulations. This approach seems to be just as bewildering for our mathematically sophisticated colleagues as it appreciated by newcomers to the field. The psychometricians see the mathematics-free approach as self-evidently inferior; the novices see it as obviously user friendly. There are trade-offs in adopting that approach.

So, let us return to the high jump example. The spectators in the grandstand had decided that, although there were potentially many, many variables involved in any and every high jump attempt during the competition, the most parsimonious and effective predictor of success or failure at each attempt was the relationship between the difficulty of the particular jump (expressed as height of the bar in meters) and the ability of the particular athlete faced with the jump (expressed as previous best competition jump, also in meters). Then the best indicator of the likely success of any athlete at any jump is athlete ability minus jump difficulty difference; the probability of any athlete's success is a function of the difference between the two key facets in the jumping equation:

Probability (conventionally written as *P*) of *success* (i.e., a result of $x = 1$ rather than $x = 0$) for athlete *n* facing jump *i* is a *function* of the *difference* between the athlete's *ability* (*B*, so we use B_n for the ability of athlete *n*) and the jump's *difficulty* (*D*, so we adopt D_i for the difficulty of jump *i*); or

$$P_{ni}(x = 1) = f(B_n - D_i) \tag{1}$$

In English: The probability, when athlete *n* faces jump *i*, of a successful jump 1, is a mathematical function *f* of the difference between the ability of that athlete B_n and the difficulty of the jump D_i.

We can then imagine some possible outcomes of our mental calculations:

Where the ability–difficulty difference favored the athlete ($B_n > D_i$), the athlete would be more likely to make the jump (i.e., more than 50:50); and

where the ability–difficulty difference favored the jump ($B_n < D_i$), the athlete would be likely to fail the attempt (i.e., success less than 50:50).

The greater the ability–difficulty difference in favor of the athlete ($B_n \gg D_i$), the more and more likely the athlete would be to succeed (i.e., much more than 50:50);

the greater the ability–difficulty difference in favor of the high jump bar ($B_n \ll D_i$), the more and more likely the athlete would be to fail at that attempt (i.e., success much less than 50:50); and

where the ability–difficulty difference favored neither the athlete or the bar ($B_n = D_i$), the athlete would have a 50:50 probability of success or failure.

So far, we haven't specified the exact nature of the mathematical function *f*. We could ask some statisticians for a bit of guidance there, but we have already reduced their options somewhat because we have estimated both athlete ability and jump difficulty as points along the same meter measurement scale.

A little table of some observed values as we are about start the high jump competition might help. We could then develop a little look-up table that would be independent of any particular bar heights or athlete record; for any difference between bar height and athlete record, the function would yield the same probability of success or failure. In Figure 3.3, we have a graph based on that table to help with our predictions.

To make the chart in Figure 3.3 useful in predicting the likely success of all athletes at all high jump attempts, we have plotted θ, the $B_n - D_i$ differences in centimeters on the horizontal axis. As one moves to the right along the horizontal axis, the advantage is more and more in favor of the athlete (positive difference: $B_n > D_i$). As one moves to the left, the athlete is more and more disadvantaged

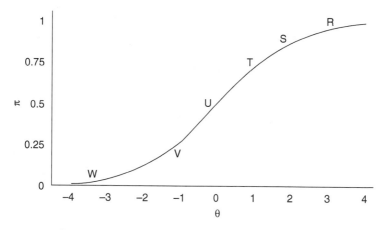

FIGURE 3.3 Predicting the likely success of all athletes at all high jump attempts.

(negative difference: $B_n < D_i$). The vertical axis shows π, the probability of success for any $B_n - D_i$ difference. When the ability of the athlete matches exactly the height of the bar ($B_n - D_i = 0$), the graph predicts success for the athlete half (0.5) of the time. Athlete U from Table 3.3 would have that 50% prediction at height (c): no difference between the previous best competition jump and the height to be faced (both at 1.85 m). Athletes R and S from Table 3.3 provide an instructive comparison: Each is facing a jump (e), difficulty of 1.84 m. Athlete R has an ability estimated at 1.87 m (previous competition best), while Athlete S's ability is recorded at 1.86 m. Might Athlete S beat Athlete R today? It is certainly possible. But who would have the higher probability of success? Our model tells us that Athlete S has a better than 75% prediction: Athlete S's best jump is 2 cm better than the height being faced. For Athlete R, whose $B_R - D_e$ difference is +3 cm, the probability of success can be read from the y-axis as at well over 90%. For Athlete W from Table 3.3, the prospects of succeeding at even the lowest jump

TABLE 3.3 Some Ersatz Observed Values for High Jumpers

n	B	D	i	$B_n - D_i$
R	1.87 m	1.84 m	e	3 cm
S	1.86 m	1.84 m	e	2 cm
T	1.84 m	1.83 m	c	1 cm
U	1.85 m	1.85 m	f	0 cm
V	1.76 m	1.77 m	b	−1 cm
W	1.70 m	1.73 m	a	−3 cm

seem a little grim; $B_W - D_a$ difference is −3 cm, so much less than a 10% probability of jumping the bar set 3 cm higher than Athlete W's previous competition best. Of course, it has been done—but not often. That is what the low probability (< 10%) is communicating; not zero chance—some—but not much. Note that it did not matter that the spectators were predicting the probable success for three different athletes for three different jumps: it is not raw ability or mere bar difficulty that is important but the *difference* between the two. Then, for the subjects for whom this model is meant to hold (coached high jumpers) and the task for which it is relevant (important high jump competitions), this graph represents the relationship between odds of success on the one hand and the ability–difficulty difference on the other.

This logistic curve just presented is known as the response expectation curve of the Rasch model for **dichotomous** items (usually called the **item characteristic curve** or ICC). With logits (log odds units) rather than centimeters on the x-axis, to summarize the $B_n - D_i$ differences from any person–item pair from the pathway analogy (Fig. 3.1), we can read the predicted success probabilities when any person meets any dichotomous item on a Rasch-modeled scale, simply by knowing the $B_n - D_i$ difference between ability and difficulty. The measurement theorem for the Rasch model requires that a data matrix from a test, and so forth, meet the probability expectations from the two formal statements of the Rasch model: the first as the formula (1), the second in the ICC graphical form (Fig. 3.3).

A third summary of the probabilistic relationships between items and persons is provided as Table 3.4. These are the P_{ni} values calculated by using different values for B_n and D_i in formula (1). This set of probability-of-success relationships between ability (in logits) and difficulty (in logits) is part of the Rasch

TABLE 3.4 Rasch Probabilities of a Correct Response for a Range of Ability/Difficulty Combinations From −3 to +3 Logits

	Item Difficulty in Logits *Increasing >>*												
	−3.00	−2.50	−2.00	−1.50	−1.00	−0.50	0.00	0.50	1.00	1.50	2.00	2.50	3.00
3.00	0.99	0.99	0.99	0.99	0.98	0.97	0.95	0.92	0.88	0.82	0.73	0.62	0.50
2.50	0.99	0.99	0.99	0.98	0.97	0.95	0.92	0.88	0.82	0.73	0.62	0.50	0.38
2.00	0.99	0.99	0.98	0.97	0.95	0.92	0.88	0.82	0.73	0.62	0.50	0.38	0.27
1.50	0.99	0.98	0.97	0.95	0.92	0.88	0.82	0.73	0.62	0.50	0.38	0.27	0.18
1.00	0.98	0.97	0.95	0.92	0.88	0.82	0.73	0.62	0.50	0.38	0.27	0.18	0.12
0.50	0.97	0.95	0.92	0.88	0.82	0.73	0.62	0.50	0.38	0.27	0.18	0.12	0.08
0.00	0.95	0.92	0.88	0.82	0.73	0.62	0.50	0.38	0.27	0.18	0.12	0.08	0.05
−0.50	0.92	0.88	0.82	0.73	0.62	0.50	0.38	0.27	0.18	0.12	0.08	0.05	0.03
−1.00	0.88	0.82	0.73	0.62	0.50	0.38	0.27	0.18	0.12	0.08	0.05	0.03	0.02
−1.50	0.82	0.73	0.62	0.50	0.38	0.27	0.18	0.12	0.08	0.05	0.03	0.02	0.01
−2.00	0.73	0.62	0.50	0.38	0.27	0.18	0.12	0.08	0.05	0.03	0.02	0.01	0.01
−2.50	0.62	0.50	0.38	0.27	0.18	0.12	0.08	0.05	0.03	0.02	0.01	0.01	0.01
−3.00	0.50	0.38	0.27	0.18	0.12	0.08	0.05	0.03	0.02	0.01	0.01	0.01	0.01

Person Ability in Logits Increasing >> (row axis label)

model—independent of any test content. In Table 3.4, B_n and D_i values vary between −3 to +3 logits. Any $B_n - D_i$ difference of zero yields a P_{ni} value of .50, *anywhere* in the table. Similarly, $B_n - D_i = 1$ logit always yields a success probability of .73; $B_n - D_i = 2$ logits always yields .88, and so on.

For Georg Rasch, in his quest to develop measurement scales that generalized across all relevant persons meeting all appropriate items of the type under investigation, this is his summary of how items and persons should behave when they meet in a testing situation. This is not an assumption of the Rasch model but a requirement. For measurement along an interval scale, where estimates of person abilities and item difficulties remain invariant, this is the elegant mathematical expression of the impossible-to-achieve-in-practice gold standard. Just as the theorem of Pythagoras states a perfect but impossible-to-achieve relationship between the lengths of the sides of right-angled triangles, so Rasch's theorem states how persons and items should perform in concert in the perfect measurement world.

Summary

An unidimensional *interval*-level measurement scale can be constructed when *ordinal* relationships between two aspects of a human performance (say, person ability and item difficulty) are preserved in the third aspect (say, response probabilities);

Ability of any person is estimated conveniently from the total number of correct responses by calculating each person's success:failure odds;

Difficulty of any item is estimated conveniently from the total number of correct responses by calculating each item's success:failure odds;

The ordered item/person data matrix from any unidimensional test should reveal strong ordering of response probabilities between all pairs of adjacent cells;

The response probability for any person n attempting any item i is a function f of the difference between the ability of the person (B_n) and the difficulty of the item (D_i);

Fit is a quality-control principle used to help decide whether the actual item and person performances are close enough to the Rasch model's requirements to be counted as linear interval scale measures;

Differences between persons, between items, and between persons and items can be read directly from the interval level scale to make comparisons interpreted as 'how much difference' exits between any two locations in probabilistic terms.

When you read, as you often will, that *unidimensionality* is a Rasch model *assumption* and that *misfitting* items should be *deleted*, you'll be warned that the author, perhaps, has not understood the crucial Rasch measurement principles contained in this chapter.

ACTIVITIES

Read: "Chapter One: What Is Measurement?" from Wu & Adams (2007).

Refer to Figure 3.1: Developmental pathway for selected ersatz persons and items to answer the following questions:

Items

Is Item S (much) more difficult or (much) less difficult than Item N? Why?
Which item is the most likely to be failed by the students? Why?
Which item is the most likely to be passed by the students? Why?

Persons

Is Bill (much) more able or (much) less able than Bob? Why?
Which student is revealed as least able on this test? Why?

Person/Item Interactions

Is Bill likely to have answered Item U correctly? Why?
What would be more unexpected, that Bill will miss Item S or Item M? Why?
Mike scored 1 on the test. Which item is most likely to be the one he answered
    correctly? Why?

Fit

Which items are not usefully located on the pathway in their present forms? Why?
Which person is not developing in the manner common to all others? Why?
Is Bob's ability well measured by this test? Why?
Jill scored 3 on the test. Which items did she most likely answer correctly? Why?

Go to Figure 3.3: Predict the likely success of all athletes at all high jump attempts and draw vertical lines from each of the athletes' locations on the ICC logistic curve to the horizontal axis. (That should show the $B_n - D_i$ differences in Table 3.3.) Now draw horizontal lines from each of the athletes' locations on the ICC logistic curve to the vertical axis. (That should show the probability of success of each athlete for the nominated jumps, a, b, c, e, & f.)

Go to Table 3.4: Check the probability of correct response values in Table 3.4. Do they follow the greater-than, less-than principles illustrated in Figure 1.1? What is the probability of success at each intersection when difficulty and ability are *equal*?

Now look back at Figure 3.3 for high jumpers. You should be able to check the 'successful jump' probabilities (in Table 3.4) for R, S, T, U, V, and W by setting the item (jump) difficulty at 0.0 logits and then using the jumpers' abilities from the horizontal axis of Figure 3.3. Remember that the ICC in Figure 3.3 summarizes all possible relationships by plotting probability against the $B_n - D_i$ differences from *any* person–item pair.

References

Blalock, A. B., & Blalock, H. M. (1982). *Introduction to social research* (2nd ed.). Englewood Cliffs, NJ: Prentice-Hall.

Bond, T. G., & Fox, C. M. (2001). *Applying the Rasch model: Fundamental measurement in the human sciences.* Mahwah, NJ: Lawrence Erlbaum Associates.

Fischer, G. H., & Molenaar, I. W. (Eds.). (1995). *Rasch models: Foundations, recent developments, and applications.* New York, NY: Springer-Verlag.

Fox, C. M., & Jones, J. A. (1998). Uses of Rasch modeling in counseling psychology research. *Journal of Counseling Psychology, 45*(1), 30–45.

Sherry, D. (2011). Thermoscopes, thermometers, and the foundations of measurement. *Studies in the History and Philosophy of Science, A, 42,* 509–524.

Smith, R. M. (1991). The distributional properties of Rasch item fit statistics. *Educational and Psychological Measurement, 51,* 541–565.

Smith, R. M. (1992). *Applications of Rasch measurement.* Chicago, IL: MESA Press.

Smith, R. M. (2000). Fit analysis in latent trait measurement models. *Journal of Applied Measurement, 1*(2), 199–218.

Smith, R. M., & Miao, C. Y. (1994). Assessing unidimensionality for Rasch measurement. In M. Wilson (Ed.), *Objective measurement: Theory into practice* (Vol. 2, pp. 316–327). Norwood, NJ: Ablex.

Wright, B. D., & Masters, G. N. (1982). *Rating scale analysis.* Chicago, IL: MESA Press.

Wright, B. D., & Stone, M. H. (1979). *Best test design.* Chicago, IL: MESA Press.

Wu, M., & Adams, R. (2007). *Applying the Rasch model to psycho-social measurement: A practical approach.* Melbourne: EdMeasurement.

4

BUILDING A SET OF ITEMS FOR MEASUREMENT

The Nature of the Data

At the basis of all Rasch modeling is the model developed first: the model for analyzing dichotomous data, which are data that have simply two values, usually 0 and 1. It is easy to mistake this level of data as being 'nominal', the sort of data we get when we categorize hair color as being brunette or blonde or when we categorize a subject's sex as male or female. However, there is an important distinction concerning the data that are appropriate for analysis with the Rasch dichotomous model: The value of 1 is meaningfully greater than the value of 0, not merely different from 0. This might sound pedantic, but it is a very important point. If we allocate the code of 0 for the females in a sample and 1 for the males, we intend just to differentiate them in terms of sex, showing that the sex of one group of respondents is different from that of the other group. However, when we use the code 1 to indicate the correct answer to a math problem and 0 as the code for the incorrect answer, we are saying something very different: Not only is the correct answer different from the incorrect answer, it also is better than the incorrect answer in a crucially important way. We regard the correct answer as superior to the incorrect answer, and we routinely regard children who give the correct answer as showing more ability than those who do not. Note, then, that Rasch modeling is appropriate only when we can impute some order in the allocation of scores such that 1 represents more of the attribute than does 0 (as in a correct response versus an incorrect response). In a scale designed to measure rehabilitation after surgery, allocating 1 = pain free and 0 = some pain develops an index of improved health status, whereas for an index of the progression of arthritis, the same indicators would be given the reverse values: 0 = pain free and 1 = some pain. So 1 = better health in the first example, but 1 = more arthritis in the second. Order does not apply to the case in which 1 (e.g., male) is merely different from 0 (e.g., female), but certainly not better.

Researchers can save themselves a bit of hair tearing in the future by remembering always to use the lower/lowest code to record the lower/lowest level of performance on any test item so that increasing values represent increasing amount of the underlying latent variable. Although this is obvious in the 0 = wrong and 1 = right format, so 1 = more language ability, it is not as obvious in coding a **rating scale** (see Chapter 6). One routinely used format for the collection of dichotomous data is the multiple-choice test. Such a test should have only one 'completely correct' or 'best' answer that would receive the score of 1 for that item, with all the other distractors or alternative answers receiving the score of 0, although a **partial credit** scoring and model might also be arranged for multiple-choice data (see Chapter 7).

Analyzing Dichotomous Data: The BLOT

In keeping with an important premise of this volume, that the key worked examples will be derived from the research of developmentalists, educators, and others trying to solve actual measurement problems, the dichotomous data discussed in this chapter come from a test of cognitive development for adolescents: Bond's Logical Operations Test (BLOT; Bond, 1976/1995). The BLOT was developed to provide a test suitable for administration to whole class groups at a time, as a partial replacement for the individual interview technique developed and used by Jean Piaget and his colleagues in Geneva. The idea was to develop a multiple-choice test with response sheets that could be computer scored so that a child's cognitive development could be categorized as more or less developed according to the total number of test items the child answered correctly. Of course, this general principle applies to most educational and psychological tests, as well as to health status checklists, so the principles outlined in the following discussion have far wider application than just to those interested in Piaget's idea of formal operational thinking.

One theme reiterated throughout this volume is that good tests have, as their basis, a very clear and explicit understanding concerning the line of inquiry the test is trying to put into practice—what was once termed construct validity. Of course, this understanding might be revealed in a number of different ways. It could be part of a general psychological theory explained in one or more textbooks by some renowned guru or part of a treatise on the exact sequence of development during a certain period of life. It might derive from a set of curriculum statements in a particular subject area at the grade school or high school level, or it might just as easily be taken from detailed theoretical or conceptual analysis of a field of knowledge being tested (e.g., math or spelling). In medical settings, it might be the understanding of rehabilitation progress after stroke, gleaned by health professionals who reflect on the effects of their practice. A more encompassing concept of validity introduced by Messick (1995) and developed in a pair of articles by Wolfe and Smith (2007a, 2007b) is reviewed in relation to Rasch measurement in Chapter 13.

In the case of the BLOT, the specifications for the items were taken one by one from chapter 17 of the textbook titled *The Growth of Logical Thinking* (Inhelder & Piaget, 1958). In this chapter, Piaget spelled out in detail each of the logical operations that he thought were central to mature thought. The test developer's task, then, was to represent each of these logical specifications as accurately as possible in multiple-choice test items that would make sense to preadolescents and adolescents without requiring any specific background knowledge. As can be imagined, some items were rewritten several times as a result of trials with high school students.

Here, the key role of the test developer in putting the substantive theory into measurement practice is clear. In this case, it might have been handy to have Professor Piaget write the items, but then he was not interested in this aspect of group assessment at all. In all test development, the success of the enterprise will be determined largely by how well the intentions of the theory writer, the classroom teacher, or the health specialist have been converted into items, not merely any items, but items such that the performances of the target audience will reveal exactly those intentions and not some other sort of ability. Clearly, then, the test developer needs some detailed understanding of the substantive area of inquiry as well as a great deal of commitment to the implementing of that theoretical understanding into measurement practice.

The BLOT is a 35-item multiple-choice test that operationalizes, item by item, each of the schemas of the formal operational stages identified by Inhelder and Piaget (1958). Each item comprises an item stem of two to four short sentences followed by a set of four or five alternative responses. The students' responses are collected on computer scan sheets and computer scored. The following interpretation shows us the sense that Rasch modeling can make of the BLOT and allows us to determine how much faith we can place in the idea that adolescents' cognitive development can be represented by the total raw score on the BLOT.

Using the BLOT generates a data file that looks like the following sample:

```
111111111011010101101011111011111
111111111111111111111111101111111
110101111111111011111011111101011111
111111111111111111111011111111111
111111111110111111011111111111111
111111111111011110101111111111111
111111111110111111011111111111111
111111111111111111111111101011111
111111111111111111111111101111111111
```

```
11011111011111101111101111000110111
11111110111111111111011011111101111
11111110111111111111111111101001111
11111111111111101111101011101111111
11111111111110111110111111111111111
11111111111110111110111111111111111
11111111111110111111101111101110111
And so forth.
```

Each row represents the performances of one student on the 35 BLOT items. Given the principle of dichotomous scoring, the 1s represent the correct answers and the 0s represent the incorrect answers: The score for Item 1 is in Column 1, for Item 2 in Column 2, and so on up to Item 35 in column 35. With this example, there is no student ID. The file is set up in the input order of the students' results. Although the BLOT can be computer scored, this file was typed in as a WordPerfect (.txt) file by the investigator.

A Simple Rasch Summary: The Item Pathway

For the first part of the interpretation of the Rasch analysis of these dichotomous data, we have included the results of the item analysis only as Figure 4.1. This pathway is in exactly the same format as that described for the developmental pathway analogy introduced in Chapter 3: Easy items are located at the bottom of the map and difficult items at the top. The precision of the item estimates is indicated by the vertical size of each item marker (larger markers indicate larger standard errors of measurement—SEs). BLOT items that fit the Rasch model (using **infit** *t*) are located on the white pathway between the parallel dotted lines.

A number of ideas can be appreciated immediately as a result of trying to find meaning in Figure 4.1. First, it is intended to represent the developmental acquisition of cognitive reasoning ability: There are easy items, moderately difficult items, and difficult items. For example, Items 6 and 12 are the easiest BLOT items, and Items 21 and 28 are very difficult in comparison with the others, whereas Item 4 sits right near the midpoint (0 logits) on the (vertical) item difficulty scale. Given that the BLOT items reveal a range of varying difficulties, we reasonably might expect that a group of suitable students would show a range of developmental abilities on this test. It is worth noting that the extremely easy items (6 and 12) have the least precise estimates (largest SEs), whereas the error estimates for the remaining 33 items are comparatively quite small.

A glance at the pathway between the dotted lines reveals that the fit of the BLOT to the Rasch model's expectations is quite good. Locations for just two of the 35 items (i.e., Items 21 and 30) do not seem to fit to the same developmental pathway as well as the remaining items. Items 21 and 30, therefore, should be candidates for further consideration before they are included routinely in students'

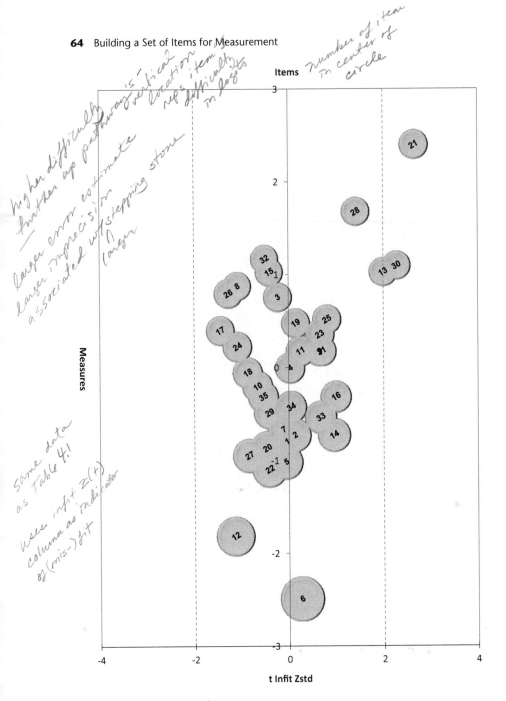

Handwritten annotations:

higher difficulty is' further up pathway vertication location item

rep's item difficulty in logits

number of item in center of circle

larger error estimate imprecision

associated w/ stepping stone larger

Some data as Table 4.1

Uses infit Z(t) column as indicator of (mis-) fit

FIGURE 4.1 BLOT item pathway.

BLOT scores in the future. This is good initial evidence for reasonably inferring that the ability underlying the BLOT items follows a single line of inquiry. The Piagetian conception of cognitive development seems to be a reasonable description of that line of inquiry, given its explicit use in the BLOT development phase.

It is rather artificial to consider item performance separately from person performance, but the primary purpose of this chapter is to demonstrate the development of a dichotomous test. Although the item difficulties span five complete units on the logit scale, Figure 4.1 shows that more than two logits of that development are represented by merely four items: Items 6 and 12 at the bottom of the vertical logit scale and Items 21 and 28 at the top. However, from below −1 logits to above +1 logits, we have approximately 30 closely packed and overlapping items. The consequence of this is that we would find it very hard to locate persons precisely at the extreme ends of the scale represented by the BLOT items, but we could have a great deal of confidence (due to the small standard errors) if we had to make important decisions relating to students who perform in the −1 to +1 logits zone.

Item Statistics

Table 4.1 includes the item statistics from a Rasch analysis of dichotomous BLOT data using Winsteps. For each item number, the estimate of item difficulty and its accompanying error estimate in logits are given. These should correspond in a one-to-one way with the pictorial representation in Figure 4.1 (and, later, in Fig. 4.2): the higher the difficulty estimate, the further up the pathway; the larger the error estimate, the larger the imprecision associated with the stepping-stone. The output in Table 4.1 has been ordered in terms of descending item difficulty, so the direct correspondences between estimate values (and errors) and map locations for items are more readily appreciated. The point-measure (point-biserial) correlation statistic is the first check that we have that all items are working in the one direction as intended. Positive statistics are acceptable for this check: negative or close-to-zero values would indicate items that were not working well with the others. Point measure correlations for BLOT items vary from +0.2 to +0.55. However, the columns that contain the fit statistics are not so easily interpreted.

Item Fit

The concept of fit and its relationship to unidimensionality is the subject of Chapter 12. Fit is at the core of Rasch measurement. The beautiful properties of Rasch measurement (e.g., invariant measurement on an interval scale) exist only to the extent that the data fit the Rasch model. In the Figure 4.1 item pathway, only one of the fit statistics (from the infit Z (t) column from Table 4.1) is used as the indicator of (mis-)fit. Note that the infit Z value for each item is located in relation to the horizontal axis of the map; the vertical location represents the item difficulty in logits. The usually reported fit statistics focus on two aspects of fit (infit and outfit), each of which is routinely reported in both an unstandardized form (mean squares) and a standardized form (t_∞ or Z). In Table 4.1, the two aspects of fit reported are item infit and outfit. The 'mean squares' is the unstandardized form of the fit statistic, and is merely the mean, or average value,

TABLE 4.1 BLOT Item Difficulty Estimates With Associated Error Estimates for Each Item

Item #	Difficulty	Error	Outfit Mean Square	Infit Mean Square	Infit t (z)	Outfit t	Pt /Meas Corr.
21	2.33	0.2	1.27	1.75	2.6	3.4	.32
28	1.63	0.19	1.12	1.23	1.4	1.4	.43
32	1.14	0.19	0.96	0.85	−0.5	−0.9	.53
30	1.07	0.19	1.19	1.15	2.3	0.9	.38
13	1.00	0.19	1.16	1.32	2.0	1.8	.37
15	1.00	0.19	0.96	0.84	−0.4	−0.9	.52
8	0.85	0.19	0.91	1.00	−1.1	0.1	.52
26	0.78	0.2	0.89	0.75	−1.3	−1.4	.55
3	0.74	0.2	0.98	0.9	−0.2	−0.5	.49
25	0.51	0.2	1.07	1.26	0.8	1.2	.40
19	0.47	0.2	1.01	1.05	0.1	0.3	.44
17	0.39	0.2	0.87	0.75	−1.4	−1.2	.54
23	0.35	0.21	1.06	0.92	0.7	−0.3	.42
24	0.22	0.21	0.89	1.03	−1.1	0.2	.49
9	0.18	0.21	1.07	0.97	0.7	0.0	.40
11	0.18	0.21	1.02	0.96	0.2	−0.1	.42
31	0.18	0.21	1.07	1.55	0.7	2.0	.36
4	0.00	0.22	1.00	0.88	0.0	−0.4	.43
18	−0.05	0.22	0.9	0.74	−0.9	−1.0	.49
10	−0.19	0.23	0.92	0.68	−0.7	−1.1	.47
16	−0.30	0.23	1.13	1.03	1.0	0.2	.33
35	−0.30	0.23	0.93	0.73	−0.5	−0.9	.45
34	−0.41	0.24	1	0.79	0.1	−0.6	.41
29	−0.46	0.24	0.94	0.71	−0.4	−0.8	.43
33	−0.52	0.25	1.1	0.93	0.7	−0.1	.33
7	−0.64	0.25	0.97	0.65	−0.1	−1.0	.41
2	−0.70	0.26	1.01	0.75	0.1	−0.6	.37
14	−0.70	0.26	1.15	1.32	1.0	0.9	.25
1	−0.77	0.26	0.98	0.69	0.0	−0.8	.39
20	−0.84	0.27	0.91	0.81	−0.5	−0.4	.40
27	−0.91	0.27	0.85	0.62	−0.8	−0.9	.43
5	−0.98	0.28	0.98	0.76	−0.1	−0.5	.35
22	−1.06	0.29	0.91	1.69	−0.4	1.4	.35
12	−1.76	0.36	0.69	0.24	−1.1	−1.5	.46
6	−2.42	0.47	1.06	0.83	0.3	0.1	.20

of the squared residuals for any item. The residuals represent the differences (i.e., the amount left over) between the Rasch model's theoretical expectation of item performance and the performance actually encountered for that item in the data matrix. Larger residuals indicate an item with larger differences between how the item should have performed (i.e., Rasch model expectations) and how it actually performed (i.e., when the children took the test). Residuals are squared, following the usual statistical convention, to make all 'actual minus expected' differences positive so they can be added to give a sum of differences. Mean square fit statistics indicate the size of (how much) misfit is revealed in the actual data. (Step-by-step detail is given in Chapter 12.)

In the standardized versions of fit statistics, the mean square value is transformed, with the sample size kept in mind, to produce a statistic with a distribution just like *t* or *Z* in which acceptable values are those routinely accepted for *t* (i.e., −2 to +2). The **standardized fit statistic** indicates 'how likely' is that amount of misfit. So, for (mis)fit: Mean squares indicate 'how *much* misfit'; *Z* or *t*, however, indicate 'how *likely* is the misfit'.

Infit and **outfit statistics** adopt slightly different techniques for assessing an item's fit to the Rasch model. To calculate infit statistics, relatively more weight is given to the performances of those persons located closer to the item's difficulty value. The argument is that the performance of persons whose ability is close to the item's difficulty should give a more sensitive insight into that item's performance. Infit is an information-**weighted** indicator of misfit. The outfit statistic is not weighted and therefore remains relatively more sensitive to the influence of outlying scores: the performances of persons distant from the item's location. It is for this reason that many users of the Rasch model tend to pay more attention to infit values than to outfit values. Aberrant infit statistics usually cause more concern than do large outfit statistics. Of course, outfit statistics do have meaning (ignore them at your peril). Indeed, making 'fit' decisions based on considering these four indices is quite a balancing act; it might be easy to accept one of these indicators as more important for a particular purpose, but none is unimportant. The fit statistics used for describing person performances work identically to those just outlined for items. We return to the issues involved in interpreting infit and outfit statistics in Chapter 12. The 'fit' issue will be raised again and again in this volume and everywhere that Rasch analysts gather to chat (e.g., see Smith, 2000).

The Wright Map

Many versions of Rasch analysis software produce some form of the map shown as Figure 4.2, in which the items are indicated by the item number, and each individual person's performance is represented by an 'X'. This item–person map or 'variable' map is often called a Wright map (e.g., Wilson, 2005) to honor Ben Wright's seminal influence on its development and use. One delightful aspect of this Rasch representation of data analysis is that many of the person and item relations are shown in meaningful pictorial, or 'map' form.

The logit scale, which is the measurement unit common to both person ability and item difficulty, is displayed down the middle of the map in Figure 4.2.

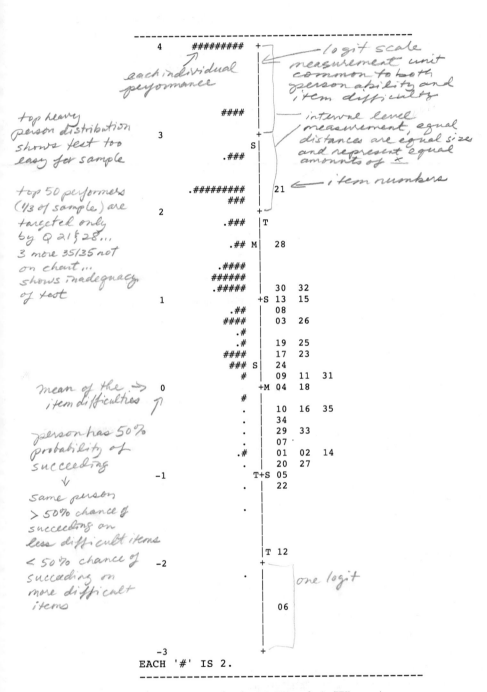

FIGURE 4.2 Item–person map for the BLOT analysis (Winsteps).

Because the logit scale is an interval-level measurement scale, the equal distances at any point on that vertical scale are of equal size, that is, they represent equal amounts of cognitive development. Therefore, Item 15 is as much more difficult than Item 4 as Item 4 is more difficult than Item 5. The distances between are equal (1 logit). Of course, the same equal-value principle applies to differences in person locations as well. Persons and items are located on the map according to their ability and difficulty estimates, respectively.

As a convenient starting point for the mapping process, the mean of the item difficulties is adopted by default as the 0 point. In this case, ignoring the error of measurement for a moment, Item 4 is calculated as being at the mean of the item difficulty estimates, so it is ascribed an estimate of 0.0 logits and is located at the 0 point on the item–person map. The rest of the items are spread above and below 0 to represent their difficulties relative to Item 4's 0. Remember that interval level measurement scales (e.g., °C) have their origin points assigned arbitrarily (e.g., freezing point of water); for Rasch interval scales, the mean of the item difficulties is usually adopted as the zero scale origin. Person locations are then plotted so that any person has a 50% probability of succeeding with an item located at the same point on the logit scale. For example, a person with an ability estimate of 0 logits has a 50% probability of succeeding (or failing) on Item 4. That same person would have a greater than 50% chance of succeeding on items less difficult than Item 4 (say, Items 10, 29, and 5) and less than a 50% probability of succeeding on items that are more difficult than Item 4 (say, Items 17, 25, and 26). The 50% **limen**, or threshold, is adopted routinely in Rasch analysis, although some Rasch software allows for variations from this value to be specified. For example, those committed to the concept of mastery learning might want to use the 80% threshold that is used routinely in that field to indicate mastery.

Targeting

With those basic principles in mind, we now can tell immediately from the **Wright map** in Figure 4.2 that the BLOT is too easy for a sample like this one. Just look where the persons are located in comparison with the items. First, the *inter-* person distribution is top heavy in comparison with the item distribution. Sec- *preta-* ond, the top 50 BLOT performers (one third of this sample) are targeted by only *tion* two questions: Items 21 and 28. The Rasch output tells us as well that three more candidates topped out on the BLOT with a perfect score of 35 of 35; they do not even appear on the variable map. From a general test-development perspective, this would be regarded as a serious inadequacy in a test. If this is the usual sort of target group for this test, then the test needs some more questions with difficulties like those of Items 21 and 28 so the abilities of the high fliers can be estimated more precisely. As well, we would need some even more difficult questions to raise the 'ceiling' of the test.

A key point to remember, however, is that Wright maps report the relations between only the two key aspects of the variable: the item difficulty estimates and person ability estimates. Other key parts of the analysis—the precision of those person and item estimates (error), the fit of the items, the fit of the persons, the reliabilities of the person and item estimates—are reported in detail in the output tables. The pathway variable map (e.g., Figure 4.1), which presents estimates (ability or difficulty) and their errors as well as a fit indicator is original with the authors (Bond & Fox, 2001), and is now implemented in Winsteps (Linacre, 2006). However, it represents only one aspect of the results, persons or items, at a time.

Usual output includes some summary of the analysis results (see Table 4.2), which includes some useful information about the items.

[handwritten: ITEMS)]
[handwritten: standardized fit scores — mean of Ø SD of 1]
[handwritten: ability of test to define a distinct heirarchy of items along measured variables, the higher the # the more confidence we can place in replicability of item placement across samples]

TABLE 4.2 Summary of the BLOT Analysis Results—Items

[handwritten: unstandardized fit estimate]
[handwritten: mean squares / expected]

```
SUMMARY OF 35 MEASURED (NON-EXTREME) Items
INPUT: 150 Persons   35 Items   MEASURED: 150 Persons  35 Items
+-----------------------------------------------------------------------+
|          RAW                          MODEL    INFIT     OUTFIT        |
|          SCORE     COUNT    MEASURE   ERROR  MNSQ ZSTD  MNSQ  ZSTD     |
|-----------------------------------------------------------------------|
| MEAN   109.9      147.0      .00      .24   1.00   1    .95    0       |
| S.D.    19.5        .0       .97      .05    .11  1.0   .31   1.2      |
| MAX.   142.0      147.0     2.40      .47   1.27  2.7  1.76   3.7      |
| MIN.    51.0      147.0    -2.50      .19    .70 -1.4   .24  -1.6      |
|-----------------------------------------------------------------------|
| REAL RMSE .25 ADJ.SD .93 SEPARATION 3.79 Item RELIABILITY .93         |
|MODEL RMSE .24 ADJ.SD .94 SEPARATION 3.86 Item RELIABILITY .94         |
| S.E. OF Item MEAN = .17                                               |
+-----------------------------------------------------------------------+
```

[handwritten annotations around table: "0 logits is default"; "scale 12 to +2 across"; "+2"; "Confirm by looking at maps—items located btw +1 and -1"; "Reliability calculated as the # of standard errors of spread among items"; "0-1 scale interpret like Cron ∝"]

We already know that the mean of item estimates (measure) will be located at 0 logits (by default) and can see that the standard deviation for item estimates (i.e., their spread) is nearly 1 logit. We can confirm the latter by referring to the maps (Figures 4.1 and 4.2): The vast majority of items are located in a narrow band between +1 and −1 logits. The reliability of the item difficulty estimates is 0.93 on a 0-to-1 scale. Item reliability can be interpreted on this 0-to-1 scale, in much the same way as Cronbach's alpha is interpreted. More usefully, it can be transformed to an item separation index (3.79), wherein the reliability is calculated as the number of standard errors of spread among the items (see Wright & Masters, 1982, or Appendix B of this text for an explanation).

Item reliability and item separation refer to the ability of the test to define a distinct hierarchy of items along the measured variable. The higher the number, the more confidence we can place in the replicability of item placement across other samples. Then the item reliability index of .93 suggests that we can quite readily rely on this order of item estimates to be replicated when we give the BLOT to other samples for whom it is suitable. But take care not to over interpret the Rasch reliability index for items. In the majority of cases, high item reliability is merely an artifact of large sample size; **item separation index** and number of **item strata** are much more telling (Appendix B). Furthermore, a look at the

[handwritten margin notes: "interpretation of analysis of results"; "in most cases high reliability is artifact of sample & sizes"]

targeting on the map will help us to tell where separation is or is not working along the linear variable.

The summary of fit statistics can also provide a few useful hints but similarly risks overinterpretation. Unstandardized fit estimates (i.e., **mean squares**) are modeled by the Rasch algorithm to have a mean of 1. The actual unstandardized item fit statistics for the BLOT have their means (infit mean squares = 1.0; outfit mean squares = 0.95) very close to the expected 1, with the infit mean squares showing little spread ($SD = 0.11$) from that ideal and the outfit mean squares show greater variation ($SD = 0.31$).

In the standardization of fit scores, the mean square values are transformed so they are distributed as Z or t_∞, with a mean of 0 and a standard deviation of 1. Therefore, we should not be surprised to see the preceding item mean squares of around 1 transformed into near 0 values (in fact, .1 and 0). Beware, however: Rasch software calculates those fit means to be as close as possible to the ideal values—it's the spread (SDs) that will be telling for misfit. In other words, while the mean fit statistics might look very close to what we are aiming for, it is the item-by-item and person-by-person fit statistics that tell us how successful our attempts at measurement have been. For how many of the BLOT items is this summary table information applicable? A note on the output reminds us that all the BLOT items (35 input; 35 measured) were useful for this sample. An item would not be useful for discriminating ability among members of this group if everyone were successful with it (item too easy) or everyone failed (item too hard).

Comparing Persons and Items

When we turn our focus on Table 4.3 toward the summary of person performances, we find that Rasch modeling has the distinct advantage of applying the same analytical logic, and therefore the same logic of interpretation, to persons as it does to items.

PERSONS

TABLE 4.3 Summary of the BLOT Analysis Results—Persons

```
    SUMMARY OF 147 MEASURED (NON-EXTREME) Persons
+----------------------------------------------------------------+
|        RAW                     MODEL    INFIT     OUTFIT       |
|        SCORE  COUNT  MEASURE   ERROR  MNSQ  ZSTD  MNSQ  ZSTD   |
|----------------------------------------------------------------|
| MEAN   26.2   35.0    1.57      .52   .99    .1   .95    .1    |
| S.D.    6.2    .0     1.30      .20   .13    .6   .46    .7    |
| MAX.   34.0   35.0    3.96     1.04  1.31   1.6  4.50   2.7    |
| MIN.    5.0   35.0   -2.09      .37   .70  -1.5   .16  -1.4    |
|----------------------------------------------------------------|
| REAL RMSE .57 ADJ.SD 1.17 SEPARATION 2.04 Person RELIABILITY .81|
|MODEL RMSE .56 ADJ.SD 1.17 SEPARATION 2.09 Person RELIABILITY .81|
| S.E. OF Person MEAN = .11                                      |
+----------------------------------------------------------------+
  MAXIMUM EXTREME SCORE:        3 Persons
```

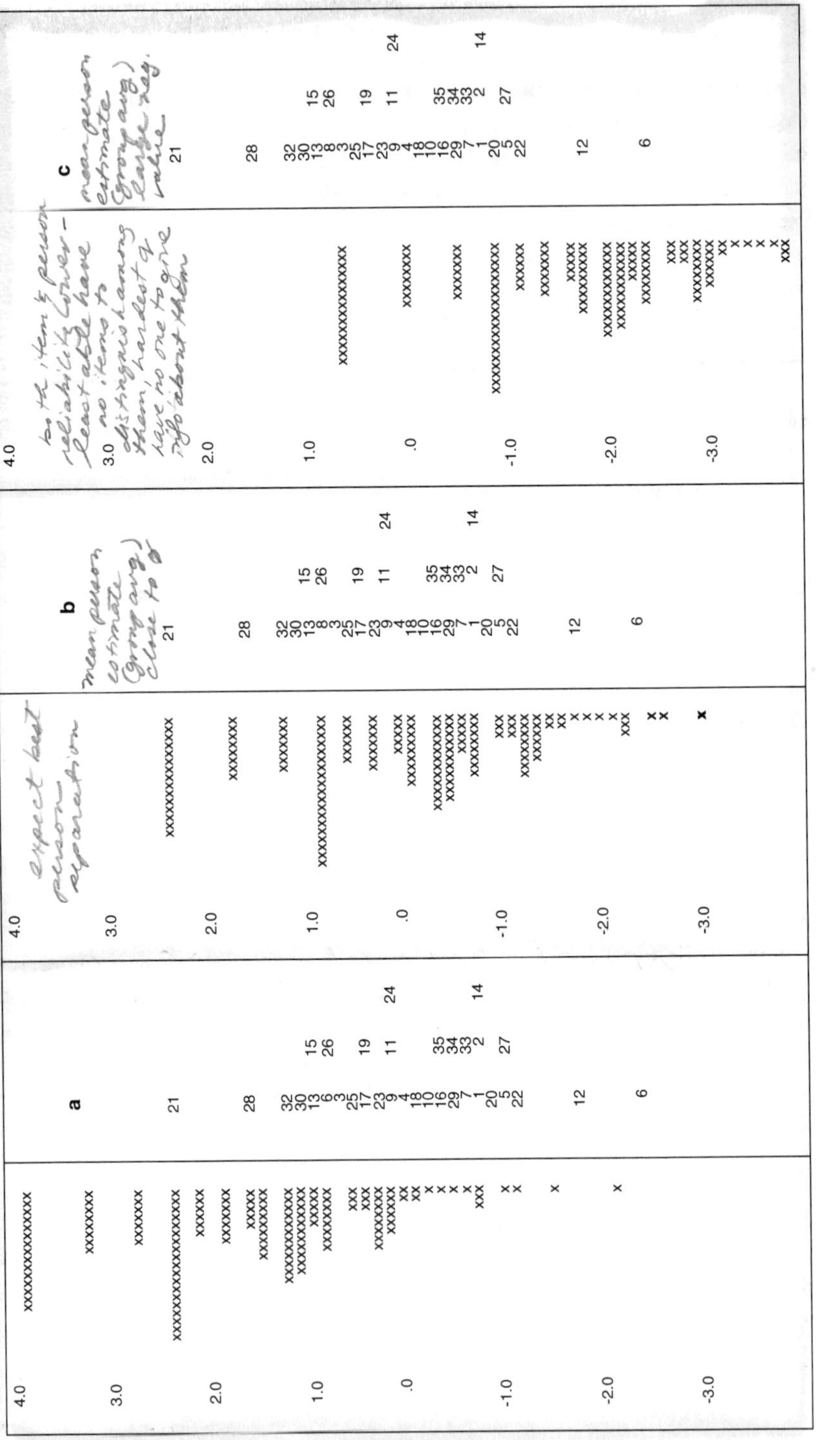

FIGURE 4.3 Item–person maps showing a test as (a) relatively easy for the sample, (b) well matched to the sample, and (c) relatively difficult for the sample.

The person ability estimate mean of +1.57 logits is the first result in this table to indicate that this sample finds this BLOT test comparatively easy. The standard deviation of 1.30 logits for person estimates indicates greater spread of person measures or variation in those measures than evident in the item measures. The reliability of the person ability estimates is 0.81 (person separation = 2.04), which is not as high as the item reliability but more than acceptable nonetheless.

This corroborates, in part, the targeting problem we identified from the Wright map. Although we can rely on this order of person estimates to be replicated when we give these persons another test like the BLOT, in the current analysis, we have better information about the items than we do about the persons, so the item estimates are more reliable. All other things being equal (and they never are), reliability is driven primarily by N: In other words, the performances of 150 persons give us more good information about the 35 BLOT items than the 35 BLOT items give about the 150 persons.

Now, Figure 4.3 is included to show three possible relations between the distributions of item difficulty and person ability; two of those maps are merely hypothetical. Given that the mean item difficulty is arbitrarily set at 0 logits, the mean person estimate (i.e., the group average) would be closer to 0 for a well-targeted test (Fig. 4.3b). A tough test would yield a mean person estimate with a large negative value (Fig. 4.3c). From consideration of the three distributions in the item–person maps of Figure 4.3, where the N of items and persons remain the same, we could expect the best person separation index in Case 4.3b, where the targeting of items and persons is the best. In Case 4.3c, the difficult test, both item and person reliability would be lower: The least able persons have no items to distinguish among them, whereas the toughest questions have no persons sufficiently able to provide good information about them.

Going back to Table 4.3, we can see that the summary statistics for person fit are equally good as those for items in Table 4.2. The mean of the infit mean squares at 0.99 and the outfit mean squares at 0.95 are very close to the Rasch-modeled expectations of 1. Consequently, they produce standardized fit Z values around zero (infit Z = 0.1; outfit Z = 0.1). The spread in, or variation of, modeled fit scores for persons (infit Z SD = 0.6 and outfit Z SD = 0.7) suggests that the vast majority of person ability estimates will have transformed fit statistics well inside the conventionally acceptable range of −2 to +2. Often, mean square and Z fit statistics will have quite comparable values, as we have seen in the person and item summary tables; it is when those values (person by person and item by item) don't correspond, that 'on balance' interpretations of fit need to be made.

Summary

The BLOT is a multiple-choice test that has dichotomous scoring: 1 = correct response; 0 = incorrect response.

The BLOT pathway shows items distributed by difficulty (vertically), by fit (horizontally), with *SE* shown by size of the stepping-stone. Item 6 is easiest and fits well but has large *SE*; Item 21 is hardest, with small *SE*, but does not fit well.

The item–person Wright map shows person and item distributions but not *SE* or fit.

Tests that are well targeted on the sample yield better estimates.

Reliability is driven primarily by *N*; so 150 person will produce better item reliability and 35 items will produce lower person reliability.

ACTIVITIES

Download the free copy of Bond&FoxSteps from the book website. Open and read the ReadMe file. Make sure you have Excel and Adobe Reader already installed on your PC.

Install and run Bond&FoxSteps. Open the Bond Fox Chapter 4.pdf file from the Tutorial pull-down menu.

Follow the step-by-step instructions and analyze the BLOT data set pre-loaded into the software.

Check your results and interpretations at each stage by referring to the Tutorial file and this chapter.

If this is your introduction to Rasch measurement, we would advise you to continue with Chapter 5 and to return here after you have finished all chapters. If you already have a sound grasp of Rasch measurement principles, we invite you to go further.

Extended Understanding—Chapter 4

The logistic curve introduced in Chapter 3 to summarize the prospects of high jumpers is extended in Figure 4.4 to represent some key aspects of the Rasch expectations of performances on the BLOT test. Figure 4.4 shows the theoretical item characteristic curves (or ICCs) for three BLOT items: Item 6, the easiest BLOT item, to the left; Item 21, the most difficult BLOT item, to the right; and Item 4, which it so happens is conveniently located at the origin point of the BLOT item and person calibrations. You can check the location of the response expectation curves against the estimations in Table 4.1: The 0.50 expected score point (limen) on each curve should locate on the horizontal logit scale directly above the item estimate value from Table 4.1 (Item 6 at *c*. −2.5 logits, Item 21 at *c*. +2.4 logits and Item 4 at 0.00 logits).

So Alain (A: ability −2.5 logits) has a 0.5 probability of selecting the correct answer on easiest Item 6 (also −2.5). From that point, it looks like it's going to

Item Characteristic Curves

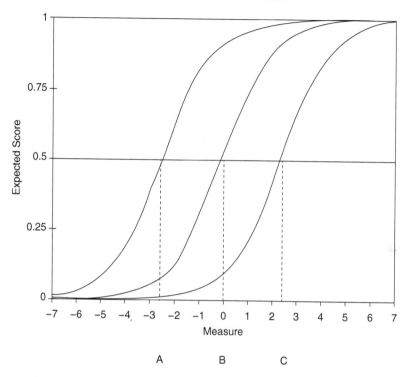

FIGURE 4.4 The theoretical ICCs for three BLOT items: 6 (easiest), 4 (0.0 logits), and 21 (hardest).

be more and more challenging for Alain as he faces the more difficult BLOT questions. Chrissie (C: ability = 2.4 logits) has a 50% probability of success on the toughest BLOT item (Item 21); for the other BLOT items, her probability of selecting the correct answer will increase as she meets easier and easier items. Bob (B: ability = 0.00 logits) has a 0.5 expectation of success on Item 4 (at the same location 0.0 logits) and much higher probability on easy Item 6 but much lower on difficult Item 21. Table 4.4 provides a helpful summary of the theoretical expectations of success for Alain, Bob, and Chrissie on dichotomous BLOT Items, 6, 4, and 21 based on the Rasch-modeled relationships between the person abilities and the item difficulties (only). Table 4.5 reports those expectations in terms of likely pass or fail by each student on each item. It's worth taking some time to check out your understanding of those expectations. You can see the graphical representation of those relationships in the plot of ICCs in Figure 4.4, the Wright map in Figure 4.2, and the pathway map in Figure 4.1. (We'll return to the actual performance plots of BLOT items in Chapter 5 when we discuss DIF and in Chapter 12 on fit.)

TABLE 4.4 Rasch-Modeled Expectations of Performances of Three Persons on Three BLOT Items

Person	Alain (−2.5)		Bob (0.00)		Chrissie (+2.4)	
Item	B − D logits	P Success	B − D logits	P Success	B − D logits	P Success
6 (−2.5)	0.00	0.50	2.5	0.91	4.9	0.99
4 (0.00)	−2.5	0.08	0.00	0.50	2.4	0.91
21 (+2.4)	−4.9	0.01	−2.4	0.09	0.00	0.50

TABLE 4.5 Success Expectations of Performances of Three Persons on Three BLOT Items

Person	Alain (Low)	Bob (Average)	Chrissie (High)
Item	Pass/Fail Likely	Pass/Fail Likely	Pass/Fail Likely
6 (Easy)	50:50	Pass	Pass
4 (Ave)	Fail	50:50	Pass
21 (Hard)	Fail	Fail	50:50

Item estimates have been rounded up for convenience.

The Problem of Guessing

It takes very little imagination to realize that some children faced with completing the BLOT during a high school science class might resort to strategies not based on the underlying latent variable of Piagetian cognitive development to solve BLOT items; for example, they might try guessing answers to the items.

We would be naïve to presume that test performances, especially those involving multiple-choice questions (MCQs) such as the BLOT, were free of such candidate behavior. It is much more reasonable to presume that where the student is required to choose the correct answer from alternatives (rather than to compose a response), the possibility of guessing always exists. Indeed, some data analysis models (including some **IRT models**) are touted as superior to the Rasch model explicitly because they are claimed to account for guessing behavior with their model parameters. Even accidental marks on a scan sheet might later be marked as 'correct' by the computer. Children faced with many demands to respond to MCQs as part of regular school assessments might not always remain completely on task or fully motivated to work out every answer fully. The dichotomous Rasch model, on the other hand, models the relationship between two aspects of the testing situation—the abilities of the candidates and the difficulties of the items. What's left over (the **residuals**) is counted toward misfit. In contrast to models in which a guessing parameter is included as an attribute of items, no such allowance is included in the Rasch model.

Now, the problem with random guessing is that it tells us nothing about the ability of the candidate, and random answers might be mistaken as indicators of the ability being tested. However, research shows that random guessing is not ubiquitous and should be examined in context. Some candidates proceed by eliminating the alternative answers that are obviously wrong in their eyes and then guess among the possibly correct alternatives not so eliminated. At least that sort of informed guessing does contain some information about candidate ability and item difficulty. Some candidates do not guess at all—they always try to work out the right answer. Others try to work out the answer when they feel they have the ability to do so but resort to random (or pattern) guessing when they feel they do not. In that light, guessing is not merely an item property that is invoked of respondents by all or some (difficult) items, nor is it just a person property invoked by tests. More likely, guessing is one of a number of possible measurement disturbances that should not go undetected. Although we worry about the possibility of unearned success by lucky guessing, the reflective measurement practitioner should be also concerned with other possible candidate behaviors such as 'sleeping' through the easy or early test items (thereby getting them wrong) or 'plodding' slowly through the test (and not reaching, or merely guessing at the items near the end of the test). Thus, the Rasch model provides a set of diagnostics for detecting these types of respondent (or off-variable) behaviors and informs the researcher as to the type of disturbance as well as the severity and effect of it. In fact, other measurement disturbances such as 'cheating' on high-stakes tests are routinely detected by using Rasch diagnostics.

Difficulty, Ability, and Fit

A(n) unique strength of the Rasch model is its requirement that the outcome of any interaction between person and item be solely determined by just two parameters, the ability of the person and the difficulty of the item. This requirement establishes a strong framework against which to test data for the presence of anomalous behavior that may influence the estimation of item and person parameters. The identification of anomalies is not restricted to guessing, but addresses any potential measurement disturbance.

(Smith, 1992)

We could hypothesize, as did Waller (1973), "that when a guesser engages in random guessing, it is only on items that are too difficult for him" (see Gershon, 1992). Now, that implies the importance of the relationship already at the center of the Rasch model—the relationship between person ability (B_n) and item difficulty (D_i), that is, guessing is more likely when $B_n - D_i$ is large and negative. It also suggests something else about another key Rasch concept: fit. When $B_n - D_i$ is large and negative for any person × item combination, the expected probability of success is very low; an unexpected success (unearned success by random guessing) would result in large misfit (esp. outfit) for that item–person combination. We will return to the guessing/ability/difficulty issue in the chapter on fit, but two clarifications are worth reiterating: Under the Rasch model, estimates of ability and difficulty are based on the total number of correct responses (only), while the pattern of those responses is revealed in the indicators of fit. When guessing occurs, the patterns of success will not likely accord with expectations based on ability and difficulty alone—we will have detected an important indicator of a measurement disturbance.

Our inspection of the ICC and fit statistics will reveal how measurement disturbances such as guessing might be detected in practice. Here is a snippet of the Item 21 output from Table 4.1: *persons targeted by item 21 fit the model more or less okay*

Item	Estimate	Error	Infit MnSq	Outfit MnSq	Infit Z *list of persons outlying item is poor*	Outfit Z
21	2.33	0.2	1.27	1.75	2.6	3.4

<1.33 ok   >>1.33 high   >2.0 little high   >>2.0 high

At first pass, infit mean squares value for the item looks okay (< 1.33); infit Z, a little high (> 2.0); but the outfit indicators are really erratic (outfit mean squares >> 1.33 and outfit Z >> 2.0). So, we should eliminate Item 21 from our test? No! Let's try to diagnose what has gone wrong. We should try to find out where the misfitting responses occur and further investigate the reasons for these occurrences. For example, these indices (i.e., the INFIT indices) mean that persons *targeted* by Item 21 fit the model more or less okay (Infit MnSq 1.27; Infit Z 2.6). But fit of persons outlying from Item 21 is poor (Outfit MnSq 1.75; Outfit Z 3.4). Now, Item 21 is the *most difficult* BLOT item; so the persons targeted by Item 21 (both at the top of the Wright map in Figure 4.2) are the most able of the 150 (and they fit comparatively well). The outlying persons (far away from Item 21) are the least able persons on the BLOT (the ones at the bottom of Figure 4.2). Q: What is the improbable response of least able persons on any most difficult item? A: Unexpected success on the difficult item, when the predicted response would have been failure on Item 21. Their erratic (improbable/unexpected) performances, then, are likely due to some common strategies used by teenagers in classroom tests (perhaps cheating, copying, or guessing). The BLOT testing was low stakes and well supervised, so we suspect no cheating/copying. Guessing, then? Perhaps ...Any more evidence?

We return to the issues of guessing and fit in Chapter 12, so Figure 12.2 in that chapter can help. That graph shows the *actual* person performances on Item 21 (grouped into 15 ordered slices of ability with $n = 10$ at each plotted point)

[handwritten margin note:] Process used to identify cause of measurement disturbance

against the Rasch *expected* ICC for that same item. For the seven plot points (7 × 10 = 70 students) on the right (where students' abilities are well targeted: near to or above the item location), students perform more or less as predicted by the model (the *actual* plots follow the *expected* curve). For the next six plotted groups (60 students with BLOT abilities 1.5 to 3.5 logits *below* Item 21's difficulty), they *actually* do much better on Item 21 than the Rasch model *predicts*, given their overall BLOT measures. Eyeballing those six plotted points suggests an *actual* average success rate of about 0.25 or 25% instead of rates in the teens or lower. By the way, there are four alternative multiple-choice answers to Item 21, so complete random guessing from among them would produce a success rate of 1 in 4, 1/4, or 25%.

Three points are worth reiterating: Misfit does not mean 'throw it away'; it means 'find out why'. Guessing is a measurement disturbance, for which Rasch analysis produces empirical evidence. Guessing is not an item parameter or a person parameter but occurs in particular item × person interactions, especially when students do not feel capable of solving the question by using the ability they have.

The Theory–Practice Dialogue

Of course, every test developer and user should try to discern what the results from the performance of the items and persons in practice have to say about the substantive theory being investigated and should try to decide what the theory tells about the persons and items under investigation. This should always be seen as an ongoing dialectical process. As it is not the authors' intention to bore the reader with mini-lectures on the detail of Piagetian theory but to guide the reflective measurement practitioner, we have included just a little consideration of it here to indicate the sort of meanings that might be attributed to the results of the BLOT analysis shown earlier. (Please see Bond & Tryphon, 2009, for discussion of Piagetian method and psychometric research.)

The analysis so far provides quite good evidence that the items work well together to represent a single underlying path of inquiry or ability. Given that the specifications for the logical structure of each and every item in the BLOT were lifted directly from the Inhelder and Piaget (1958) text, this could be seen to confirm the idea that Piaget's model for adolescent intelligence is coherent in itself. At least the psychometric evidence points to 'a single something' and not 'many things' as the object of inquiry. Moreover, whatever this ability is, it also is evident in the BLOT–answering behavior of a bunch of suitable subjects: 150 adolescent schoolchildren.

Because both the items and the persons were shown to behave in sufficiently lawful and predictable ways, it is reasonable to infer that this part of Piaget's theory and its instantiation in the BLOT are certainly worth the effort of continued refinement and investigation. Moreover, the measurement invariance tests performed for Chapter 5 show that BLOT person and item measures are sufficiently invariant to support claims that BLOT Rasch estimates are interval-level measures. From a validity perspective, BLOT and the PRTIII produce person measures that are invariant within the limits of measurement error.

Practically, the ceiling effect on the BLOT continues to be an ongoing problem in some research contexts: The most cognitively developed kids top out on the test. Although the summary table shows that amounts to only 3 of the 150 tested for this chapter (at age 15), we reasonably could expect that more and more of these students would 'hit the ceiling' as we tracked their development over time (e.g., Endler & Bond, 2001, 2006, 2008). Clearly, the BLOT needs more difficult items based on Piaget's specifications if we intend to use it to estimate accurately the cognitive development of our more intellectually able teenagers. If, however, its purpose is merely to separate those high school students with less cognitive development from those with more in order to provide developmentally appropriate learning experiences in, say, science and math, then adding more difficult items would not serve that end.

The spread of items, or the lack of spread, on the item–person map suggests that some of the BLOT items are psychometrically redundant: The area from 0 to −1 logits is saturated with items. It seems that a number of the particular intellectual skills incorporated into BLOT items are very much like other skills (items) and that it would not be necessary to include them all in a parsimonious test. Indeed, dropping some of the psychometrically redundant items in favor of more difficult items would remedy two of the apparent measurement deficiencies of the BLOT.

Of course, psychometrically redundant and theoretically redundant are two different but related perspectives on the theory–practice nexus; the BLOT was constructed, in the first place, as a sort of test of Piagetian theory (or at least of the author's understanding of it), not to test children. In the first round, the practice tells us that the conceptualization of the theory has a lot going for it but that a more useful test could be developed by going back to the theory to find specifications for further item development and rationalization.

Summary

Substantive (content) theory and Rasch (measurement) theory should work hand in hand for the construction and monitoring of a set of items for measurement.

Fit statistics are quality-control devices that should be used in concert.

Guessing is an off-trait behavior that might be prevalent in multiple-choice testing in particular.

Guessing is not an item property but, more likely, a property of particular item difficulty–person ability combinations.

Fit statistics and ICCs can be used diagnostically to investigate the existence and potential impact of guessing.

ACTIVITIES—EXTENDED UNDERSTANDING

Read: Gershon, R. (1992). Guessing and measurement. *Rasch Measurement Transactions, 6*(2), 209–210.

Rerun the BLOT analysis for Chapter 4 on Bond&FoxSteps.

Use the 'Graphs'. Click on 'Category Probability Curves' and follow the Chapter 4 tutorial instructions to build multiple ICCs for BLOT Items 4, 6 and 21.

Use the 'Graphs'. Click on 'Expected Score ICC' and compare the actual empirical curves (Blue x) with the Rasch-modeled expected ICCs for some well-fitting items (e.g., 4, 5, 10, 11) and then do the same for misfitting Item 21. Go back to the 'The Problem of Guessing' section in this chapter and reread the relationships between Rasch indicators and guessing.

Create Table 23 Principal Components Analysis and check 'Variance explained by measures' and 'Unexplained variance' in the various contrasts and use the dimensionality discussion in Chapter 12 to establish your own case for the extent to which these BLOT data meet those Rasch requirements for good measurement.

References

Bond, T. G. (1995). *BLOT—Bond's logical operations test.* Townsville, Queensland, Australia: James Cook University. (Original work published 1976)

Bond, T. G., & Fox, C. M. (2001). *Applying the Rasch model: Fundamental measurement in the human sciences.* Mahwah, NJ: Lawrence Erlbaum Associates.

Bond, T., & Tryphon, A. (2009). Piaget and method. In U. Mueller, J. Carpendale, & L. Smith (Eds.), *The Cambridge companion to Piaget* (chapter 8). Cambridge: Cambridge University Press.

Endler, L. C., & Bond, T. G. (2001). Cognitive development in a secondary science setting. *Research in Science Education, 30*(4), 403–416.

Endler, L., & Bond, T. (2006). Tracking science achievement and cognitive development with the Rasch model: Empirical evidence of growth and heterogeneity, In X. Liu & W. J. Boone (Eds.), *Rasch measurement in science education* (pp. 74–110). Maple Grove, MN: JAM Press.

Endler, L. C., & Bond, T. G. (2008). Changing science outcomes: Cognitive acceleration in a US setting. *Research in Science Education, 38,* 149–166.

Gershon, R. (1992). Guessing and measurement. *Rasch Measurement Transactions, 6*(2), 209–210.

Inhelder, B., & Piaget, J. (1958). *The growth of logical thinking from childhood to adolescence* (A. Parsons & S. Milgram, Trans.). London: Routledge & Kegan Paul. (Original work published 1955)

Linacre, J. M. (2006). Winsteps (Version 3.61.2) [Computer Software]. Chicago, IL: Winsteps.com.

Messick, S. (1995). Validity of psychological assessment. *American Psychologist, 50*(9), 74–149.

Smith, R. M. (1992). *Applications of Rasch measurement*. Chicago, IL: MESA Press.

Smith, R. M. (2000). Fit analysis in latent trait measurement models. *Journal of Applied Measurement, 1*(2), 199–218.

Waller, M. (1973). *Removing the effects of random guessing from latent ability estimates*. (Doctoral dissertation). University of Chicago, IL.

Wilson, M. (2005). *Constructing measures: An item response modeling approach*. Mahwah, NJ. Lawrence Erlbaum Associates.

Wolfe, E., & Smith, E. (2007a). Instrument development tools and activities for measure validation using Rasch models: Part I—Instrument development tools. *Journal of Applied Measurement, 8*(1), 97–123.

Wolfe, E., & Smith, E. (2007b). Instrument development tools and activities for measure validation using Rasch models: Part II—Validation activities. *Journal of Applied Measurement, 8*(2), 204–234.

Wright, B. D., & Masters, G. N. (1982). *Rating scale analysis*. Chicago, IL: MESA Press.

5

INVARIANCE

A Crucial Property of Scientific Measurement

They do not understand the thrill of discovering an invariance of some kind which never covers the totality of any situation. Social studies will not become science until students of social phenomena learn to appreciate this essential aspect of science.

— *L.L. Thurstone (1952)*

"You can't measure change with a measure that changes" is an oft-cited truism—at least, amongst psychometricians. But what does that mean? And how is that related to the quest for measurement invariance? And why is that important?

We all know that the freezing and boiling points of pure water have a special significance in the measurement of temperature: They now represent 0°, and 100°, respectively on the Celsius scale, or 32° and 212° Fahrenheit. And every time we measure the temperature of water in those two conditions (freezing/boiling) with good-quality thermometers, we'd expect results to be extremely close to those given values. But it wasn't always so. Early temperature instruments such as Galileo's were open to the atmosphere, not sealed as are modern liquid-in-glass thermometers. The relative temperatures indicated by such instruments, could be wildly inaccurate, depending on where (e.g., at what altitude) they were used. Researchers concluded that, in fact, the open-to-the-atmosphere instruments were sensitive to two variables at the same time: the expansion of the liquid in the tube was sensitive not only to temperature of the water, as expected, but also, unexpectedly, to atmospheric pressure. Moreover, they could not tell how much of the expansion was due to temperature and how much was due to pressure. Sealing the instrument and using mercury in the tube eliminated the pressure effect and meant that the readings became far more consistent.

In this analogy, we have two mutually supportive examples of measurement invariance: All suitable thermometers plunged into any one vat of boiling water should register (more or less) 100°C (or 212°F); and any one thermometer should always read 100°C, regardless of which vat of boiling water is measured. The measurement function of the instrument is invariant (constant) across all suitable uses; any one use will reveal an invariant (constant) measure across all suitable instruments. In the human sciences, we might study different variables of interest (e.g., empathy, math achievement, health-related quality of life), but the principle of measurement invariance should apply.

So the invariance requirement is that the values (measures) attributed to variables by any measurement system should be independent of the particular measurement instrument used (as long as the instrument is appropriate to the purpose), that is, the values should be invariant. Moreover, the calibrations of the measurement instrument should also remain invariant across any of its intended purposes. By reflecting on the earlier thermometry analogy, we would see it as crucial that any one thermometer would give useful indications of the temperature across any number of contexts for which the particular thermometer was appropriate—in terms of its construction and the part of the temperature scale for which it was calibrated. One example might be that it would give accurate enough readings of atmospheric temperature at any place on earth where humans can live outdoors. We would also expect that any number of appropriate thermometers will yield usefully equivalent temperature readings in that same outdoors context. *Thus, for any one device, the readings will remain invariant across all suitable contexts, and for any one context, all suitably calibrated devices will yield invariant readings.*

Note that within our conception of invariance is the expectation that thermometers will be more or less *accurate*: The reading will provide a good match with the actual temperature, and any thermometer's reading will have precision suitable to its purpose. So two properties of measuring devices will impact the invariance we routinely expect from scientific measurement. Does the estimate provided more or less match the actual state of affairs, that is, is it accurate? You may prefer the language, 'Is it valid? Does it actually detect what it claims to detect?' And does the estimate have a margin for error that is small enough for the intended purpose? That is, is it sufficiently precise?

Invariance is directly related to the *first* idea we claim to be central to the concept of measurement: unidimensionality—that is, we must attempt to measure one single construct at a time. Galileo's instrument to detect differences in the variable temperature is more accurately called a barothermoscope (Sherry, 2011) because it was sensitive to *two variables* at the same time: temperature and atmospheric pressure. His instrument did not actually measure temperature (it was not valid), so it is no wonder his estimates varied wildly. But his instrument paved the way for other eventually successful thermometers. Given Galileo's undoubted brilliance, his difficulty at operationalizing just *one* of these unobservable constructs at a time, should be of some comfort to human scientists, who have often combined two or more constructs into a single data collection instrument.

Throughout this book, we have established the importance of measuring one single construct at a time, and in Chapter 4, using the BLOT, we demonstrated how this might be achieved in practice. A detailed theoretical description was taken as the starting point, and we used Rasch methodology as the technique to examine how successful our attempt had been to implement that construct into measurement practice. Now, in terms of our claim that *invariance* is the second requirement of scientific measurement, two questions immediately arise from our work so far: Does the BLOT yield invariant measures? And, more importantly: *How could we know that?*

> Measurement is the process of converting observations (e.g. counts) into measures (quantities) via a construct theory. The Rasch Model states a requirement for the way observations and construct theory combine in a probability model to make measures. There is no other combination of observation and theory that produces sufficiency, invariance and objectivity in the resultant measures.
>
> *(Stenner, 2001, p. 804)*

Given our own relatively brief history of attempting genuine measurement in the human sciences, it must be expected that our measurement attempts should fall somewhat short of those based on the physical sciences model. But if measurement, rather than mere quantification, is going to be the hallmark of our research, then we are bound to attempt to overcome the obvious difficulties that lie in store.

However, in the human sciences, invariance of item and person measures remains the exception rather than the rule. Interpretations of results from many tests of common human abilities must be made exactly in terms of which sample was used to norm the test, and candidates' results for those tests depend on which test was actually used. This context-dependent nature of estimates in human science research, both in terms of who was tested and what test was used, seems to be the complete antithesis of the invariance we expect across thermometers and temperatures.

An important goal of early research in any of the human sciences should be the establishment of item difficulty values for important testing devices such that those values are sufficiently invariant—for their intended purposes. (No reasonable user expects every thermometer to give readings that are both perfectly accurate and infinitely precise.) Further investigations then would involve the anchoring of the new results to the item values derived from that earlier research.

> We construct measures, but we must also monitor the measuring process. To make accurate measures we require a unit whose own error is under

control. In this sense, the history of science can be said to be a history of measurement precision.

(Stone, 2001, p. 793)

It would be naïve, however, to expect that our early attempts will satisfy even the relative invariance principle on all appropriate occasions. In the same way as the Inspector of Weights and Measures should monitor the scales used by the local greengrocer or the gasoline bowsers, we should monitor continually that the item values continue to behave as expected, taking into account the error of measurement. Where the invariance principle is not instantiated in practice, we should be motivated to examine the reason for that inadequate behavior and avoid using any such item in the measure in its current form. "This is the main reason that validity is an evolving property and validation is a continuing process" (Messick, 1995, p. 741).

A test which is to have continued usefulness must have a scale which does not change with the times, which will permit acquaintance and familiarity with the system of units, and which will permit and accumulation of data for historical comparisons.

(Angoff, 1960, p. 815)

In practice, this monitoring is accomplished by collecting data at regular intervals and comparing the item estimates and errors across different subsamples of respondents. For example, in health care, patient satisfaction responses drive government reimbursement for patient care. Rasch practitioners who construct measures for high-stakes decisions regularly monitor the stability (i.e., invariance) of their patient satisfaction 'rulers'. Likewise, measures of passenger preference for different aircraft features can determine, in large part, what features will be added to the next round of aircraft design. Then, hospitals and aircraft designers pay close attention to monitoring measure invariance—data are collected semi-annually to detect item 'drift'. How could we have evidence of construct validity if the item locations drift or change unpredictably? Thus, our attention to the validity of our measures should derive from the principle of invariance of Rasch measures and is checked in practice by estimates of item difficulty on the one hand and estimates of person ability on the other.

Person and Item Invariance

While we readily see that the group of persons who took the test is a sample of the population of all possible test candidates, we often less readily realize that the group of test items themselves is merely a sample of all possible test items. This is due, in no small part, to the relative ease of capturing a new sample of suitable test candidates and the relative difficulty of constructing a new sample of suitable test items. Further, we might painstakingly develop a set of appropriate items but in that process become 'wed' to these items simply due to the amount of time and thought invested in developing and/or choosing them. However, in Rasch measurement, as we have already seen, the principles and logic of analysis and interpretation for persons completely mirror the analytical principles for items.

Ben Wright's persistent challenge to those claiming to have a good test was rather forthright and based on the simple requirement for invariance of estimates—an important measurement principle for any testing situation and quite easy to implement: Simply divide your sample of persons in two according to their ability and estimate the item difficulties for each half of the test. The invariance principle requires that the difficulties of the items relative to each should remain stable across the two substantially different subsamples (within the constraints of the requirement for targeting items and persons). The corollary is also true: Simply divide your test into two and estimate the person abilities for each half of the test: Person ability estimates should remain invariant relative to each other regardless of which half of the sample test items is used for the person estimation (an example follows).

Rasch measurement instantiates interval-level measurement, so it is the size of the intervals which must remain invariant (constant). In Chapter 10, we will introduce the feature of parameter separation (see also Smith, 2001). This is the property of the Rasch model that supports direct comparisons of person ability and item difficulty estimates, that is, independently of the distribution of those abilities and difficulties in the particular samples of persons and items under examination. "An acceptable method of scaling must result in a derived scale which is independent of the original scale and of the original group tested" (Loevinger, 1947, p. 46).

Common Item Linking

Figure 5.1, then, represents the results of finally taking up Wright's challenge, rather than merely paying lip service to it, as the advice was passed on to others. The data from the 150 students who took the BLOT (the bond87.txt data set from Chapter 4) were divided into two *equal-sized* subsamples. The first ($n = 75$) contained those with higher scores of 27 to 35 (Higher), and the second ($n = 75$) contained those who had raw scores of 5 to 26 (Lower). Data from each subsample were analyzed separately, and the 35 item estimates (and SEs) for each group were imported into an Excel spreadsheet (Bond & Fox, 2001, pp. 62–65). The plot of item values (in Figure 5.1) shows that, with the notable exception of Item 21, the item estimates of the BLOT items are invariant (within error); the dotted line is not a regression line but the Rasch-modeled relationship required for invariance (the 95% control lines are based on the SEs for each of the item pairs).

The simple first step is to plot the pair of calibrations for each item onto a simple scatter plot, using the pair of Rasch-modeled ability estimate measures

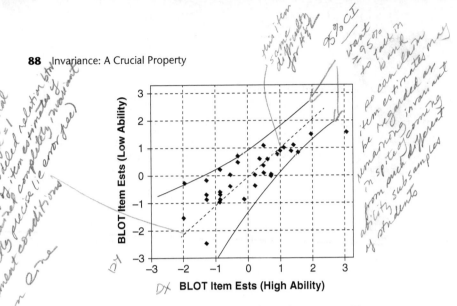

FIGURE 5.1 Item difficulty invariance—Bond's Logical Operations Test.

(in logits) for each item. Although the Rasch item measures are based exactly on the raw score totals for each half of the sample (High and Low), these modeled ability estimates contain much more information about the interval scale and the measurement errors associated with each of the measures. If we draw a diagonal line (45° or slope = 1) through the point representing the calibration means of Dx and Dy (0.0 logits), we would construct a line that represented the exact modeled relation between the two sets of item estimates if they remained completely invariant under perfectly precise (i.e., error-free) measurement conditions. In such a situation (unachievable in practice), all the plotted points (i.e., the Dx/Dy location for each of the 35 BLOT item pairs) should lie exactly along this diagonal line. Usefully and realistically, Rasch modeling provides us with error estimates for each and every item difficulty estimate, and we can use these to construct quality-control lines (shown in Figure 5.1) to see whether the distribution of the plotted ability points is close enough to the modeled relationship diagonal line for the measures to be regarded as sufficiently invariant (i.e., constant within the limits of measurement error).

The formula for constructing the control lines for a 95% confidence band around the diagonal through the mean estimates, derived originally from Wright and Stone (1979, pp. 94–95), is given as an Excel spreadsheet on the book website. Some Rasch analysis software (e.g., Winsteps) will produce a graph of such comparisons on demand, but anyone familiar with the graphing procedures in a spreadsheet can develop a worksheet that will import Rasch analysis output and use the pairs of item difficulty estimates to plot the locations and the associated pairs of error estimates to plot the control lines. Simple visual inspection will reveal whether enough of the points (i.e., 95% or more of them) lie within the control band. With only 1/35 BLOT item locations outside the control lines (i.e., 2.9%), it seems reasonable to claim that the item estimates may be regarded as remaining *invariant* in spite of coming from such different ability subsamples of students.

Now, Item 21 is, by far, the most difficult BLOT item (see Figures 4.1 and 4.2). The High-ability subsample allows us to gauge the difficulty difference between Items 21 and 28 quite well; the most difficult BLOT items are well targeted by the students in the High ability subsample. However, the 21 to 28 gap is well out of the range of (i.e., poorly targeted by) the BLOT abilities shown by the Low-ability half of the sample. This results in the 21 to 28 interval being *underestimated* with the Low-ability group (the targeting problem). Given that 26/35 correct has been estimated as the bound between concrete operational and formal operational performance on the BLOT, the invariance of the item estimates (within error) helps affirm the integrity of the BLOT under Rasch analysis procedures and demonstrates that the BLOT Rasch interval scale maintains its measurement properties across quite disparate subsamples (after Bond, 2004).

Key Points to Keep in Mind

Those working in the application of fundamental measurement principles take care to distinguish between raw scores, usually regarded as *counts*, and Rasch-modeled ability estimates, which satisfy the requirements necessary to be regarded and used as measures. If you want to proceed to other analyses (e.g., SEM), then use the Rasch *measures* and errors as input—not the *counts* or *raw scores*. The difficulty estimates of items from each of the analyses with the High-ability and Low-ability subsamples of students are plotted on the corresponding x and y axes in Figure 5.1. Recall that each of the calibrations is centered, by default, on the mean of the BLOT item values at 0.0 logits and that each item now has two item estimates (Dx from the High-ability estimation and Dy from the Low-ability estimation) and corresponding error terms (shown in Table 5.1).

The invariance principle should also apply when the same test (e.g., BLOT) is used in two unconnected testing situations (e.g., the BLOT has been used as a measure of cognitive development research projects in Australia and the United States, as well as in the UK). Then, the measurement requirement is that the BLOT item estimates should remain invariant across analyses conducted in different countries. In Figure 5.2, the Dx values came from the research conducted in Australia (Stanbridge, 2001), and Dy are the BLOT values from Chapter 4 collected from high school children in the UK, and each item estimate is tied to its corresponding error term. Again, just one item out of 35—one of the very easiest BLOT items—fails the invariance requirement. This should be regarded as a particularly rigorous internal validation technique, especially in comparison with, say, calculating test–retest correlations.

Having established the invariance of the test item values under such circumstances as those listed, researchers might then capitalize on that invariant measurement property by treating the item difficulty estimates as known calibrated

TABLE 5.1 BLOT Item Estimates and Errors Based on Split Half Subsamples. Errors Increase Dramatically With Off-Target (High-Ability) Respondents.

BLOT item #	High-Ability Subsample Estimate	Error	Low-Ability Subsample Estimate	Error
1	−0.85	0.6	−0.74	0.29
2	−0.85	0.6	−0.65	0.29
3	0.93	0.31	0.73	0.25
4	0.23	0.39	−0.01	0.26
5	−1.27	0.73	−0.91	0.31
6	−1.27	0.73	−2.5	0.53
7	−1.98	1.01	−0.35	0.27
8	1.02	0.3	0.85	0.25
9	0.73	0.33	−0.01	0.26
10	−0.54	0.53	−0.01	0.26
11	0.73	0.33	−0.08	0.26
12	−1.98	1.01	−1.57	0.37
13	1.35	0.28	0.85	0.25
14	−0.1	0.44	−0.91	0.31
15	1.11	0.3	0.97	0.25
16	0.23	0.39	−0.42	0.28
17	−0.3	0.48	0.67	0.25
18	−0.85	0.6	0.18	0.25
19	0.37	0.37	0.55	0.25
20	−1.27	0.73	−0.74	0.29
21	3.08	0.25	1.5	0.27
22	−0.85	0.6	−1	0.31
23	0.5	0.36	0.31	0.25
24	−0.3	0.48	0.43	0.25
25	0.62	0.34	0.55	0.25
26	0.5	0.36	1.04	0.25
27	−0.85	0.6	−0.91	0.31
28	1.98	0.26	1.43	0.27
29	−0.54	0.53	−0.42	0.28
30	1.57	0.27	0.79	0.25
31	0.5	0.36	0.05	0.26
32	1.43	0.28	1.04	0.25
33	−0.54	0.53	−0.42	0.28
34	−1.27	0.73	−0.21	0.26
35	−1.27	0.73	−0.08	0.26

values: a sort of within-laboratory decision to anchor the measurement scale so comparisons of person and group ability estimates taken in different research contexts might be facilitated. Early development and refinement of thermometers underwent such procedures.

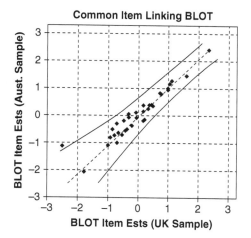

FIGURE 5.2 Item difficulty invariance—BLOT UK vs. Australia.

Anchoring Item Values

Based on the evidence to date (e.g., Endler & Bond, 2001), it seemed reasonable to expect changes in the BLOT estimates of cognitive development for cohorts of adolescents as they undertook classroom interventions designed to impact the understanding of science (Adey & Shayer, 1994). Indeed, even without such a science intervention program, it would be reasonable to expect that BLOT scores would change during the period in which this development has been specifically theorized—adolescence (Inhelder & Piaget, 1955/1958). While many children's scores might be expected to rise over 2 or 3 years, those of others might remain rather flat; and some, might, indeed, decline. Failure to establish 'known values' for the cognitive development scale (e.g., *invariant* BLOT item estimates) could yield confounded results.

In order to track the cognitive development of middle school and high school students over the 3 years of the CASE (Cognitive Acceleration through Science Education) intervention in an Oregon school district (Endler & Bond, 2006, 2008), the BLOT item difficulties were *anchored* on those resulting from the pre-intervention BLOT testing of a cross-sectional sample of 658 students from 6th through 10th grades. Rasch analysis software such as Winsteps allows the user to input known values (e.g., as **anchored** item values) so output (e.g., person values) might be more validly compared across different research contexts. *Anchoring* item values maintains their *invariance*; those values are imported into all the analyses over the term of a project.

The item difficulty estimates calculated during that ($N = 658$) analysis were then used as anchored known values, so that any child's BLOT estimate taken at any time during the 3-year CASE intervention would be calibrated against

[handwritten marginalia: tracking for longitudinal studies]

that invariant item difficulty ruler, one that was fixed for the life of the project. While this allowed for valid comparisons between the estimates for children across year levels, cohorts, and time, it was *essential* for tracking the changes for any one child over the course of the longitudinal study. The tracking of changes in cognitive development for cohorts of students tested at least twice (2006, Fig. 3; 2008, Fig. 2), as well as individual change graphs for 'Vicky' and 'Arthur' (2008, Figs. 6 & 7) *require* changes to be calculated against anchored (invariant) item values. "You can't measure change with a measure that changes."

These exemplars might best be termed **common–item linking**: What **links** the data sets together are items that the data sets have in common. The High- and Low-ability students in Figure 5.1 and the UK and the Australian sample in Figure 5.2 all have performances on the same 35 BLOT items in common. Showing these item values to be invariant allows comparisons between samples to be made directly. Given that the common items formed a complete test, the procedure might be termed common-test linking: two samples having one test in common. This procedure could then form the basis for, say, measurement of scholastic performance across years: The Year 3 and Year 5 math tests each have 10 of the 50 math items in common—presumably they would be among the more difficult items on the Year 3 test and the easier items on the Year 5 test. The items for which invariance of item difficulties can be established empirically are then used as common items for linking the performance estimates for the Year 3 and Year 5 samples. Those link values might also be anchored so that comparisons can be made over time.

Ingebo (1997) describes in detail how the crucial scientific principle of invariance of measures guided the use of the Rasch model in Oregon. They calibrated the large item banks for mandated assessment by using the principles of common-item linking and anchoring described. While Endler took the appropriate precaution of anchoring the BLOT item values to those calculated in the pre-intervention analysis, for the cohort-by-cohort analysis, this ultimately proved unnecessary. As it happened, because of the adequately representational size of the cohorts, the BLOT item values actually showed no meaningful variations across the annual estimations (Endler, 2004).

Returning to the temperature analogy: 100°C on the Celsius temperature scale was calibrated to indicate the boiling point of pure water at sea level. Failure to fix that indicated position on the thermometer's scale before climbing Mont Blanc or Mount Everest would confound the effect of a crucial contextual variable (lower atmospheric pressure) if a new boiling point were independently calibrated in the new context alone.

Common-Person Linking

The converse of Ben Wright's challenge (invariance of item calibrations derived from splitting the person sample in two) should also hold true: Splitting a sample of items (the test) into two and calculating person ability estimates for each half test should yield person estimates that are invariant for all practical purposes (identical within error). That realization prompted further analyses of the BLOT data from Chapter 4, the results of which are reported as a graph in Figure 5.3. The steps of the analysis remain the same as before, but some procedural and interpretative modifications are needed because of the asymmetry of the BLOT data matrix. The earlier split person-sample comparison yields two subsets of data for analysis: Each subset contained 75 person performances across 35 items. The current split-test comparison is based on two subsets of data each with 150 person performances on just 17 (or 18) items.

For the investigation of the invariance of person estimates reported in Figure 5.3, the odd-numbered items (1, 3, 5 . . . 35) provided the person estimates plotted on the y-axis, and the even-numbered items (2, 4, 6, . . . 34) were used to estimate person abilities on the x-axis. Again, the line (slope = 1) represents the error-free Rasch-modeled perfect equivalence between the person estimates, but there is considerable dispersion away from that line. Has the investigation failed? Are Rasch person estimates not invariant even when drawn from two halves of the same test?

The answer to both questions is no. The most important difference between the BLOT *person* invariance graph in Figure 5.3 and the BLOT *item* invariance graph in Figure 5.1 is the *imprecision* of these new estimates. When the BLOT test is divided in two (odd numbered questions and even numbered questions), the person estimates so calculated plummet in precision: No SE is below 0.50, and

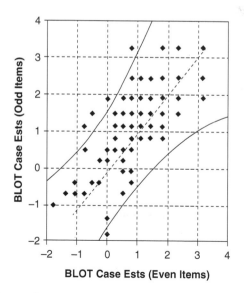

FIGURE 5.3 Invariance of BLOT person abilities, each estimated with half the items (odd vs. even).

many approach or exceed 1.0 logit. You can see in Figure 5.3 that the 95% control lines are widest apart at the top of the graph, where BLOT person estimates are the least precise (larger SEs). Figure 5.3 plots the 122 cases (from a total of 150) that had estimates calculated from both half tests. The usual Rasch estimation procedures do not calculate item or person estimates for cases with perfect scores: 18/18 on the 'odds' or 17/17 on the 'evens' did not have two Rasch person ability estimates to plot. Still, very few of the person locations fall outside those control lines: The person estimates remain invariant (identical allowing for error) when each person's ability is estimated twice, once from each half of the BLOT. Note that the correlation between person performances is $r = 0.71$ (explaining 50% of the variance in the person data).

How can the Rasch measurement evidence be so strong while the correlation seems so modest? The Rasch model provides us with more statistical information (estimated score + standard error) than used by a true score correlation calculations. For the true score model, all we ever have is X (observed score), and that is all that can be used for calculating correlations, factors, and so forth. In Rasch measurement, a person's performance is represented by a number of components relating to quantity and quality (the person estimate and its error term). The linking graphs in this chapter incorporate both components (estimate and error) to monitor invariance. Correlation calculations do not take SE into account, so the ensuing r values are *attenuated* because they must ignore the (unknowable) errors. Seeing how error terms increase in size as the number of items decreases should encourage all those in Rasch measurement to be more circumspect about hard-and-fast interpretations based on just counts or estimates alone. If there is a single failing common to many scales, it is that the number of items is too small to support the decisions made by the test users —because of the large SEs of the person estimates (see person separation in Appendix B).

Invariance of Person Estimates Across Tests: Concurrent Validity

We should expect that when one latent trait or underlying construct is the subject of a variety of tests, person measures should remain invariant (within error) across those different testing conditions. This is the idea that (loosely) underlies the almost routine demonstration of **concurrent validity** undertaken when a sample of candidates is given two tests and the resulting scores are correlated (notwithstanding the problems with correlations noted). The long-term aim of a genuine measurement system in the human sciences should be access to a series of cocalibrated testing situations, such that the raw score or locally calculated person measure could be expressed on the single scale used worldwide. That might remind us of the analogy drawn from thermometry. Thermometers are used to estimate temperature indirectly, by observation of the effect of temperature on some testing variable: the length of an enclosed column of colored alcohol, the electrical resistance of a metal wire, the straightening of a bimetallic strip, and so forth. The units of temperature are not physically additive in the fundamental measurement sense, and there are almost as many types of thermometers as there are temperatures to estimate. No single thermometer type is useful for more than a few selective applications, and no thermometer measures over the full range of the temperature variable. Certainly, none measures without error. Temperatures are measured internationally, translations from °F to °C are routine, and temperature estimations are understood and compared after the most elementary sort of training in 'test administration'.

So the next step in achieving this end (after establishing the invariance of item and person performances as before) is addressed by one of the questions continually asked in psychological and other human sciences research: "Does this test measure the same construct as this other test?" This is *one* important technique in helping to establish the validity of a test. Suffice it to say, here, that, *a priori*, the researcher must first be satisfied by an elaboration of the theoretical construct under examination in a pair of tests that they purport to measure the same construct. Of course, the answer to the question "Do two tests measure the same construct?" involves another issue, "How could we tell if test A measures the same construct as test B?"

One purpose of a test A versus test B comparison might be to develop two forms of the same test so that we can use them validly as equally useful alternatives in a test–retest format. Why else would we want to develop a test that measures the same construct as an already existing test? Of course, there are a number of very pragmatic reasons. The new test might be shorter, offer a new format, or allow greater ease of administration, scoring, or interpretation. It might be more suitable to a particular target population or a particular testing context; it might be written in another language. It might provide greater precision around important high-stakes decision points, or it might help to prevent cheating, or to avoid the learning effect when tests are used more than once. On the other hand, it might just provide a useful, low-cost, quick-to-use screening device when the high cost of high-power testing of all potential subjects is not warranted. For example, while the Family Strain Questionnaire (FSQ, Rossi Ferrario, Baiardi, & Zotti, 2004) is a structured interview administered, after referral, by qualified psychologists to caregivers of chronically ill patients, the short form of the Family Strain Questionnaire (FSQ-SF; Bond, Rossi Ferrario, & Zotti, 2005; Vidotto, Ferrario, Bond, & Zotti, 2010) was developed using Rasch analysis principles so that it could be used routinely as a 10-minute screening device for signs of caregiver stress administered by home-care nurses or medical practitioners (see Chapter 10).

Although the core validity issue in test development revolves around the crucial question of construct validity (see Messick, 1995), test developers legitimately appeal to the psychometric overlap between a new test and an established and recognized test to claim that the new test has concurrent validity. It is, indeed, unfortunate that a combination of concurrent and face or content validity often is held as the only sufficient prerequisite for test development. Almost total reliance on the results of empirical data analysis techniques to resolve issues of validity have obscured the central role of construct validity in the human sciences. The authors return to this important issue in the closing chapter.

Inherent in all these possibilities is the theory–practice dialogue that is the important focus of all good measurement. Tests apparently quite dissimilar in format that measure the same construct will inform us about the theoretical construct we are investigating, as will apparently similar tests that cannot be accepted as measuring the same underlying trait. To illustrate a Rasch measurement approach to examining concurrent validity, we investigate the properties of another classroom test of formal operational thinking—this time, one developed in the United Kingdom. Then we use the linking procedures from Rasch modeling already introduced to see whether this test can be judged to be measuring the same construct as that shown in the results of the Bond's Logical Operations Test (BLOT) analysis in the previous chapter.

The PRTIII-Pendulum

The Piagetian Reasoning Task (PRTIII-Pendulum) was developed in the United Kingdom (Shayer, Küchemann, & Wylam, 1976) to allow Piagetian reasoning tasks to be administered to whole class groups. Using the PRTIII, the teacher demonstrates a number of experiments in front of the class and, from time to time, the children make written responses to the questions posed on individual illustrated answer sheets. The teacher later codes each written answer from the child (a few words, sometimes a sentence or two) as 1 (correct) or 0 (incorrect) according to a set of scoring criteria derived directly from chapter 4 of Inhelder and Piaget (1955/1958; n.b., chapter 17 was the basis for BLOT). That produces the same sort of dichotomous data string for each child as that produced by the computer-scored BLOT results in the previous chapter. Any number of teacher-made tests adopt that general format of a written short-answer test given to a whole class at a time, with the teacher marking the answers right or wrong at a later time and reporting the total score as the test result. Any number of testing opportunities in the human sciences could adopt the same analytical approach profitably.

The PRTIII contains 13 items, which are scored dichotomously. The data we have for analysis in this section came from the very same 150 children who completed the BLOT in Chapter 4. We took the usual testing precaution of ensuring that half of the children completed the BLOT first, with the other half completing the PRTIII before the BLOT to neutralize any order effect.

The dispersal of the PRTIII items in terms of their difficulty locations, the error of those difficulty estimates, and the fit of those estimates to the Rasch model are illustrated using the pathway principle in Figure 5.4. The details of the item statistics for the PRTIII results from these 150 children are reported in Table 5.2. Item difficulties span a range from −3.17 logits for the easiest item

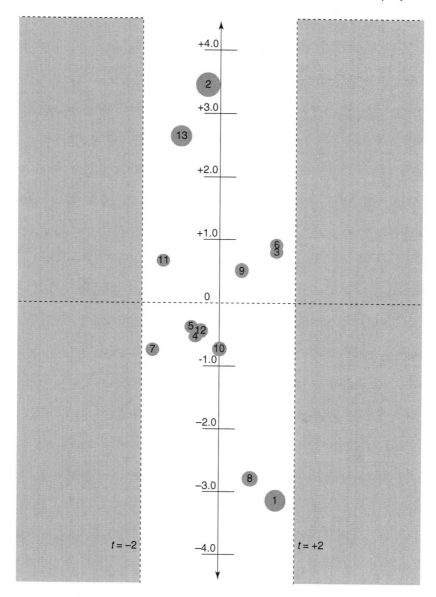

FIGURE 5.4 Variable pathway for PRTIII-Pendulum.

(item 1) to +3.40 logits for the most difficult of the PRTIII items (Item 2). All of the PRTIII items fit within the conventional limits for the infit *t* statistic, in this case, ranging from −1.4 to +1.5. At this point, we should recall that Rasch analysis routinely adopts an arbitrary 0 point for each scale: usually the mean of the test's item difficulties.

Common-Person Linking

Central to the demonstration that we need to use here is the notion that one sample of children has been the subject of two test administrations, each test of which is held to measure the same underlying construct. One very simple procedure could be adopted. We could reasonably regard all these items as attempts to measure the same underlying construct and just analyze the BLOT and PRTIII items together as one test. But this should not be regarded as sufficient for the basic purpose of establishing whether two sets of items adhere to Rasch principles sufficiently to be regarded as measuring the same construct. If the principles espoused in Chapter 4 allow us to regard the 35 BLOT items as measuring just one construct, then we could capitalize on the shared explicit theory base of the two tests to draw the same conclusion about the 48 BLOT and PRTIII items if they were Rasch-analyzed as one test. However, a possible problem with this technique is raised in Chapter 12: Fit statistics are likely to be less effective in the face of two half tests of differing origins. The procedures we demonstrate in this chapter are much more informative, based on the concept of measurement invariance that should be central to a wide range of measurement applications.

The key issue is whether the performances of one sample of students across both tests are identical enough to sustain the argument that the one dimension being assessed on each test is the same dimension for both tests. The ability estimates of the 150 UK students taking both the BLOT (Bx) and the PRTIII (By) are plotted on the corresponding x and y axes in Figure 5.5.

The key difference between the BLOT ability scale and the PRTIII ability scale is the difference in the arbitrary 0 points allotted to each scale during the

TABLE 5.2 Item Statistics for PRTIII-Pendulum

PRTIII Item No.	Difficulty Estimate	Error Estimate	Infit Mean Square	Outfit Mean Square	Infit t	Outfit t
1	−3.17	0.30	1.26	1.08	1.4	0.3
2	3.40	0.44	0.91	0.64	−0.2	0.1
3	0.8	0.22	1.17	1.09	1.5	0.4
4	−0.61	0.21	0.94	0.98	−0.6	0.0
5	−0.37	0.21	0.93	0.90	−0.7	−0.4
6	0.94	0.23	1.17	1.30	1.5	1.0
7	−0.77	0.21	0.82	0.75	−1.8	−1.3
8	−2.81	0.27	1.10	3.01	0.7	2.6
9	0.53	0.22	1.04	1.30	0.4	1.2
10	−0.81	0.21	1.00	0.86	0.0	−0.6
11	0.67	0.22	0.85	0.72	−1.4	−1.0
12	−0.41	0.21	0.97	0.83	−0.3	−0.9
13	2.60	0.33	0.79	0.67	−1.0	−0.2

Rasch analyses. First, take the mean ability score for the BLOT (*Bx*: ability estimate on test *x*) and for the PRTIII (*By*: ability estimate on test *y*) and plot that point on the graph.

The next point of interest in this comparison is the relative difficulty of the two tests being analyzed.

Recall that each of the analyses we have used for this exercise was conducted separately. The origin of the scale developed for the BLOT (0 logits) was the mean of the BLOT item difficulty estimates, and the origin of the scale developed for the PRTIII (0 logits) was the mean of the PRTIII item difficulty estimates. If the tests were of the same average difficulty for these students, the BLOT 0 and the PRTIII 0 will be identical. Usually it would be the case that the mean ability on the BLOT and the mean ability on the PRTIII also will be identical (within error). Then the intercept of the diagonal line on the *x*-axis is the adjustment that must be made to the BLOT estimates to bring them to the origin of the PRTIII estimates.

In this case, the BLOT estimates require an adjustment of −2 logits to align them with the PRTIII scale (i.e., the PRTIII is 2.28 logits more difficult for this sample than the BLOT). We already had some hint of that in the individual analyses. Whereas three students 'topped out' on the BLOT with perfect scores, only one of them did so on the PRTIII. Conversely, six students scored 0 on the PRTIII, whereas the lowest BLOT score was 5/35. All *prima facie* evidence suggests that the students found the PRTIII tougher on average than the BLOT. If the two tests were both measuring the same ability and were of the same mean

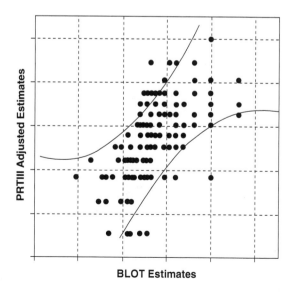

BLOT Estimates

FIGURE 5.5 Common person linking BLOT and PRTIII.

difficulty, at least 95% of the plotted points would lie within the control lines, and the diagonal line representing the modeled relations between the performances would pass through the origin point of the graph. BLOT, however, was designed to mark the transition to formal operational thinking and contains a preponderance of easier items; the PRTIII has items that extend well into the upper limits of that Piagetian stage, and the items are then, on average, more difficult.

How much variation in person estimates can be expected depends on the size of the error estimates for each of the person ability locations. The error sizes depend on the amount of good information we have about person abilities. More items in a test produce smaller measurement errors for estimates of persons taking the test. Equally, test items that are appropriately difficult for the sample produce tighter error estimates than do poorly targeted items. Moreover, in Rasch modeling, the converse is also true: More persons produce less measurement error for items, and samples that are well chosen for the test yield better item difficulty error estimates.

A quick look at the item error estimates for the BLOT (Table 4.1) will show that they are approximately the same magnitude as the item error estimates for the PRTIII (Table 5.2), mostly about 0.20 logits. This is largely because we have 150 persons to provide information about both the BLOT items and the PRTIII items; in general, the tests are well targeted by these persons. But PRTIII Item 2, however, is not as well *targeted* by this sample: The item is very difficult for these Year 9 students, and the error estimate 'blows out' to 0.44 logits as a consequence. Now, let us apply the same logic to the person error estimates in Table 5.3. This table contains a slice of the person results from the analyses of the BLOT and PRTIII. Here we have results for 23 persons. Although 150 persons provided information about the test items, we have only 35 BLOT items providing information about the persons and a mere 13 PRTIII items, one of which is arguably not targeted on most of the sample. The person error estimates yielded by the BLOT are approximately 0.50 logits (what we expect from 30–40 dichotomous items), whereas the PRTIII yields person error estimates approximating the 0.70 mark, confirming the claim that more good items provide more precise estimates of person ability than do fewer good items. The near-extreme BLOT score of 34/35 for Person 59 produces a high ability estimate (+3.93 logits) but with low precision (error = 1.03 logits).

Our investigations should not stop there. If, instead, we were to draw in a line of best fit for the data points in Figure 5.5, we could bring the temperature analogy to bear on interpreting the relationship between BLOT and PRTIII. Remember the Fahrenheit–Celsius scale relationship:

°Fahrenheit = (°Celsius × 1.8) + 32
e.g., (100°C × 1.8) + 32 = 180 + 32 = 212°F gives the boiling point of water on both scales.

For this sample of 150 persons who took both the BLOT and the PRTIII:

BLOT: person mean = 1.63 (SD = 1.37)
PRTIII: person mean = −.65 (SD = 1.89)

The relationship between PRTIII ability and BLOT ability can be calculated as follows:

$$PRTIII \text{ est} = (BLOT \text{ est} - BLOT \text{ mean}) \times PRTIII \text{ SD} / BLOT \text{ SD} - PRTIII \text{ mean}$$

$$= (BLOT \text{ est} - 1.63) \times 1.89 / 1.37 - .65$$
$$= (BLOT \text{ est} - 1.63) \times 1.38 - .65$$
$$= BLOT \text{ est} \times 1.38 - 1.63 \times 1.38 - .65$$
$$= BLOT \text{ est} \times 1.38 - 2.90$$

Uncovering the 1.38:1 relationship between PRTIII logits and BLOT logits is a timely reminder that the logit is a *probabilistic*, not *substantive*, unit and that the length of the logit needs to be monitored—just as for all other Rasch measurement properties.

> Equating of the interval scales constructed from two tests is confirmed when plots of the measures of elements common to the tests follow an identity line stochastically. When this verification fails, a necessary step is to linearly adjust the relative lengths of the logits constructed by the two tests (and intended to be based on the same underlying variable) by the ratio of the observed standard deviations of the measures common to those tests, so that both tests measure in the same substantive units.
>
> *(Linacre & Wright, 1989, p. 55)*

So what can we do with that finding? How, where could we adjust the length of the PRTIII logits to account for the 1.38:1 ratio with BLOT logits? We could replot the **common–person linking** BLOT and PRTIII in Figure 5.5. However, we first apply the ratio finding by dividing each of the PRTIII person estimates by 1.38 and then redraw the Excel graph. The SEs used to construct the 95% control lines remain the same, but those lines would now be calculated from the locations of the new PRTIII versus BLOT pairs. In effect, the vertical spread of the plots is reduced by a constant of 1.38, and the person measures show slightly improved invariance across the two tests.

As outlined before, the statistics often used in human sciences research usually do not provide individual error estimates for each person and each item. Any dispersion of scores from the perfect diagonal is regarded as unmodeled or residual variance. Consequently, test-development approaches based on the inspection of correlations are generally less than adequate. Precision in measurement derives from the amount of good information we have on which to model the measures. Measurement error must be taken into account when correlation statistics are interpreted: The more information, the smaller the error and the higher the unattentuated correlation should be. True Score Theory (TST) analysts will be more satisfied with correlations in Figure 5.6a and dissatisfied with those in Figure 5.6b. Rasch analysts would be happier with the converse: a small circle of plotted points well within the control lines of Figure 5.6 could help to justify the assertion that two tests were measuring the same variable even though the correlation coefficient was 'disastrously' low (Masters & Beswick, 1986).

Therefore, although plotting raw test scores, or counts, against each other might be more or less informative, the plotting of Rasch-modeled estimates of person ability or item difficulty can be far more useful when interpreted in the context of the precision (i.e., SE or measurement error) of these estimates. The invariance of relative person ability, whether measured by the BLOT or the PRTIII,

TABLE 5.3 Raw Scores and Ability Estimates With Errors on the PRTIII and BLOT for a Subsample of Students

Student ID No.	Score (/13)	PRTIII Ability Estimate	Error	Score (/35)	BLOT Ability Estimate	Error
58	8	0.69	0.70	29	1.83	0.48
59	9	1.20	0.74	34	3.93	1.03
60	7	0.22	0.68	28	1.62	0.45
61	3	−1.80	0.81	26	1.24	0.41
62	9	1.20	0.74	26	1.24	0.41
63	2	−2.54	0.92	29	1.83	0.48
64	9	1.20	0.74	31	2.36	0.56
65	8	0.69	0.70	31	2.36	0.56
66	7	0.22	0.68	31	2.36	0.56
67	0	Case has zero score		25	1.08	0.40
68	2	−2.54	0.92	26	1.24	0.41
70	3	−1.80	0.81	22	0.62	0.38
72	9	1.20	0.74	28	1.62	0.45
73	4	−1.21	0.74	27	1.42	0.43
74	9	1.20	0.74	31	2.36	0.56
75	2	−2.54	0.92	24	0.92	0.39
76	11	2.55	0.93	26	1.24	0.41
77	4	−1.21	0.74	30	2.07	0.51
78	7	0.22	0.68	23	0.77	0.38
79	3	−1.80	0.81	26	1.24	0.41
80	6	−0.24	0.68	26	1.24	0.41
81	8	0.69	0.70	32	2.71	0.63
82	7	0.22	0.68	33	3.17	0.75

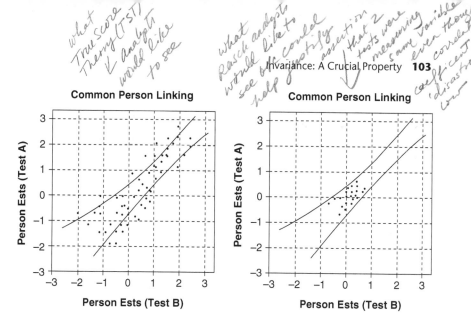

FIGURE 5.6 (a) good correlation/low invariance (b) low correlation/good invariance.

is good evidence to suggest that these test results are interchangeable. Invariance of person estimates and item estimates within the modeled expectations of measurement error over time, across measurement contexts, and so on is a key Rasch measurement property. Moreover, it is crucial to genuine scientific measurement. Disturbances to expected invariance beyond the bounds imposed by modeled error in these situations can be adduced as evidence that our measurement expectations have not been sustained in practice: that tests we had developed as useful alternatives are not that; that some test items are biased; that some test formats discriminate against some persons or group of persons; that some items are context dependent, and so on.

The principles we have described are more often used in testing situations to compare the abilities of two groups of subjects who are given the same test. Rasch modeling allows us to determine the relationships between two different groups of people who share performance on a common test. This is called common test linking. In the case of linking BLOT and PRTIII, however, the position was reversed: We had two groups of items (different tests) that had been given to the same sample (a single group of subjects). In this example, Rasch modeling was used to investigate the relations between the two tests. This benefit of Rasch modeling derives from an important principle: *the computational logic applied to persons in relation to items is exactly the same as the logic applied to items in relation to persons.* With experience in using Rasch analysis, the growing realization that these principles are exactly the same for items and for persons (e.g., estimates and errors are expressed in exactly the same units on a single scale for both; fit statistics are the same for items and for persons) allows for considerable power and flexibility in addressing a range of problems that we must address when we try to solve practical measurement questions in the human sciences. Smith (2001) summarized the basic steps for cocalibration of test instruments, while the key aspect of the conceptual basis for these procedures presented in Bond and Fox (2001) relies on earlier expositions (Masters & Beswick, 1986; Wright & Stone, 1979).

The Theory–Practice Dialogue

How could two tests be so apparently different and still measure the same underlying ability trait? The PRTIII requires a teacher demonstration of pendulum experiments while students write their answers in sentences, which the teacher later carefully assesses with the use of a detailed marking key. The BLOT is machine-marked, multiple-choice testing in its plainest form, untouched by human hands. Although the PRTIII as a whole is measurably more difficult than the BLOT, they both can be seen as two practical instantiations of the theoretical ideas expounded by Inhelder and Piaget (1955/1958); the PRTIII came from chapter 4, the BLOT from chapter 17. Both tests aim to be classroom measures of mature adolescent thinking that teachers could use to inform themselves about the relevance and suitability of particular learning experiences for their high school students.

Given that Piaget's conception of formal operational thought is regarded by many as passé or even fatally flawed, the equivalence of the PRTIII and the BLOT, despite their distinct differences, suggests that there might be more to the underlying theory than meets the critic's eye. The BLOT will provide a fine-grained analysis of the development of formal operational thinking, whereas the PRTIII will show just how developed that thinking can be. Test users who do not have the skills necessary to administer and grade the PRTIII can use the BLOT, but at the cost of the 'ceiling effect' for the most able test takers. As would be expected, both tests have strong relations with high school achievement, especially in the area of science, in which most of the research has been carried out (Adey & Shayer, 1994; Endler & Bond, 2006, 2008).

Measurement Invariance: Where It Really Matters

An *ex post facto* demonstration based on 150 students across 35 items hardly can be more than a demonstration of the invariance *principle* at work. The critics tell us that it is in large-scale empirical evaluations where our high expectations for measurement invariance are not demonstrated. Fan (1998) wrote the oft-cited report of a large-scale empirical investigation that concludes, *inter alia*, that Rasch measurement results are not worth the extra effort necessary to produce them.

In light of the previous argument and empirical evidence, Kingsbury's (2003) study of the long-term stability (i.e., invariance) of item parameter estimates in achievement testing has a number of important features. First, rather than using parameter estimates from a set of items used in a single test, it investigated the stability of item parameter estimates in two large item banks used to measure achievement in mathematics (> 2,300 items) and reading (c. 1,400 items) with students from school years 2 through 10 in seven U.S. states. (Sample sizes for the 1999–2000 school year item calibrations ranged from 300 to 10,000 students.) Second, the elapsed time since initial calibration ranged from 7 to 22 years. Finally, and most importantly (for these purposes), "the one-parameter logistic (1PL) IRT model" (Wright, 1977) was used to create and maintain the underlying measurement scales used with these banks. While *thousands* of items have been added to these item banks over the course of time, each item has been connected to the original measurement scale through the use of IRT procedures and systematic Rasch measurement practices (Ingebo, 1997).

The observed correlations between the original and new item difficulties were extremely high (.967 in mathematics, .976 in reading), more like what would be expected if items were given to two samples at the same time rather than samples separated by a time span from 7 to 20 years. Over that period, the average drift in the item difficulty parameters was .01 standard deviations of the mean item difficulty estimate. In Rasch measurement terms (i.e., focusing on impact on the measurement scales), the largest observed change in student scores moving from the original calibrations to the new calibrations was at the level of the minimal possible difference detectable by the tests, with more than 99% of expected changes being less than the minimal detectable difference (Kingsbury, 2003).

These results, of course, are not fortuitous. Ingebo (1997) reported how the Portland Public School District and the Northwest Evaluation Association deliberately implemented the Rasch model to build the original calibrated item banks stimulated by an address at an Educational Testing Service seminar in 1967. "While his measurement ideas seemed far-fetched, Dr. Wright's experimental test data [were] so promising that the Portland Public Schools initiated inspection of Rasch measurement" (Ingebo, 1997, p. 8). It seems now that some three decades later, we also have the opportunity to decide whether the promised benefits of these 'far-fetched' measurement claims would be worth the long-term effort necessary to build a Rasch-based invariant measurement system for, say, the SAT. How can it be that the Rasch model can work so well for thousands of items over many, many thousands of test administrations, yet the critics still claim it won't work for their locally developed, in-house testing?

Failures of Invariance: DIF

The principle underlying the plots of person and item invariance across testing situations is exactly that underlying the detection of Differential Item Functioning (DIF). When an item's difficulty estimate location varies across subsamples by more than the modeled error, then *prima facie* evidence of DIF exists. Indeed, Scheuneman and Subhiyah (1998) from the National Board of Medical Examiners used merely an item estimate difference greater than 0.5 logits as the criterion for detecting DIF in a 250-item medical certification test given to over 400 candidates. Given that SE estimates are inversely proportional to sample size, we could safely expect that a difference of 0.5 logit might have both statistical and substantive meaning (i.e., a genuine measured difference) on this high-stakes test. Their very basic approach, based on the violation of the Rasch model's expectation of estimate invariance, detected about 80% of the items uncovered by the more sophisticated Mantel-Haenszel procedure. Moreover, they argued, when the examiner understands the substantive construct under examination and is able thereby to posit reasonable hypotheses about the performances of subsamples of examinees, Rasch-based indications of DIF are more directly comprehensible in terms of those group differences.

When Tesio and colleagues (2002) collaborated across national boundaries (between Italy and the United States) and linked Rasch rehabilitation measures on the FIM™, they found the predicted *invariance* of item difficulty values across the two settings. They went on to reveal that variations in a few difficulty estimates (i.e., DIF) reflected differences between an incentive-driven medical system in the United States and a more family-based support system in Italy (Tesio, Granger, Perucca, Franchignoni, Battaglia, & Russell, 2002). Monitoring item calibrations is an important aspect of delivering Computer Adaptive Tests: Items showing displacement of difficulty estimates (DIF) usually are retired from the active item pool for diagnosis of the possible causes of the problem. Even with the demonstrably sound PRTIII, Shayer is always careful to recheck the item calibrations each time that task is used for a new sample: a routine and uneventful procedure that, for years, produced predictably invariant results. PRTIII item values were as good as set in stone. When a key PRTIII item concerning the application of the classic *ceteris paribus* principle became slowly but measurably easier in relation to the remaining items, the DIF was attributable to the change in the national science curriculum in the UK, which explicitly required teaching the 'hold all things equal' principle for making a 'fair test'. Theory-informed testing requires explanation when the invariance required of sound measurement is not maintained.

Most of the interest generated by examining DIF took place in the era of the sex bias of test items, especially in IQ or achievement testing. In more politically correct times, we now refer to *gender*-related DIF; and DIF is less emotive than *bias*. Two little illustrations from performances on BLOT Items 3 and 35 might be useful at this stage. This will help to show a particular depiction of DIF from a Rasch measurement perspective as well as hinting how difficult it might be to respond to the factors involved in gender-related DIF in testing.

In the previous chapter, we noted that the theoretical ICCs could be useful for understanding failures of invariance, such as DIF and understanding fit. The principles by which such actual performance versus expected performance graphs are constructed are covered in more detail in Chapter 12. Suffice it to say here that the curved ICC in each graph shows the same form as the graph for the high jumper example in Chapter 3 and for BLOT Items 6, 4, and 21 in Chapter 4. This is the graphical representation of the Rasch model's expectation of item–person performance. The line plots (continuous for males; dotted for females in Figure 5.7) show how the two groups of students actually performed. In the upper graph for BLOT Item 3, the plots of actual performances for boys and girls follow (more or less) the model's expected curve (the ICC). Certainly, there are no obvious differences in the patterns of the plots for boys and for girls.

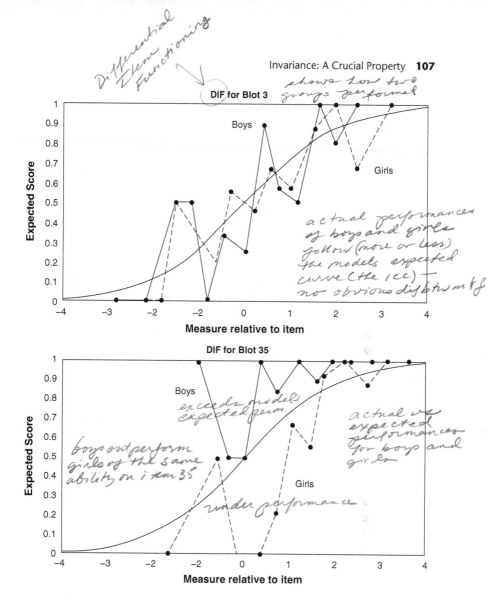

Differential Item Functioning →

DIF for Blot 3

shows how two groups performed

actual performances of boys and girls follow (more or less) the models expected curve (the ICC) — no obvious differment of

DIF for Blot 35

exceeds models expected perm

boys outperform girls of the same ability on item 35

under performance

actual vs expected performances for boys and girls

FIGURE 5.7 Comparisons of boys' and girls' performances on BLOT items: #3 (no-DIF) and #35 (gender-DIF).

That's not the case for the plots in the graph that follows, the actual versus expected performances for boys and girls on BLOT Item 35. Now, for performances of boys and girls high on the BLOT scale (to the right), the performances for boys and girls are virtually identical. But look what happens at lower levels of BLOT ability (to the left): The boys' plot (continuous) shows their actual performances really *exceed* the model's ICC of expected performance (continuous line almost exclusively above the ICC); but the girls' plot (dotted) shows that they *underperform* on Item 35 when their overall BLOT abilities levels are taken into account. Moreover, and this encapsulates the very essence of gender-related DIF, boys outperform girls *of the same ability* level on Item 35.

The examination of gender-related DIF was undertaken for the first time (*mea culpa*) for the 2007 edition of this chapter. There seemed to be a number of potential DIF candidates among the BLOT items: Some items referred specifically to male or female characters or to gender-related activities. Surely the question about matching wide tires and wheels on a motor vehicle would favor the male 'motor heads', but, no. So what about Item 35? In BLOT Item 34: "A mouse is trapped on a conveyor belt when it starts moving in direction (A) . . ." In the subsequent Item, 35, "The direction of the motion of the belt is then reversed. Which of the following would now keep the mouse near the mid-point? . . ." So why does BLOT Item 35 favor lower-ability males over females of equal ability? Is there some reference to mechanical understanding in the context of reversing the conveyor belt that gives the lower-ability boys an advantage? Do boys have a spatial geometry advantage in interpreting the item diagram? Or (tongue firmly planted in cheek) are the lower-ability girls somehow disadvantaged by the prospect of the escaping mouse? The alternative hypotheses are meant to provoke thought, not to offend; merely to suggest that the causes and potential remedies for DIF might not be obvious even when the patterns of the failed invariance are demonstrated clearly from the Rasch measurement perspective.

When we recall that the procedures for item and person estimation are mirrored, we must then also countenance the complementary situation of differential person functioning: the examinee who performs differentially on two tests of the latent trait delivered in different contexts. Part of Bunting's research not reported in Bond and Bunting (1995) involved the equating of students' results derived from the individually delivered Piagetian interview of the pendulum task (see Chapter 7) with those from the PRTIII—a demonstrated class task of the same problem (earlier in this chapter). While the common-person linking procedure *did not disconfirm* the presence of a single underlying construct, two students' results were noteworthy, especially in terms of reflecting on the underlying developmental theory. Two DIF-like results highlight the complexities of measuring and understanding the complexities of the human condition. A male student, described by his teacher as coming from a male-dominated military family, scored much better on the PRTIII-Pendulum administered in the class setting by (older, male) Bond than he did in the individual Piagetian pendulum interview administered by (younger, female) Bunting. A female student performed much better in the individual Piagetian interview with Bunting than she did in the class-group PRTIII test, where she seemed more focused on her young male peer sitting (very closely) beside her. And, what is more, *the person fit statistics in all four instances were quite unremarkable* (Bunting, 1993; Stafford, 2005). Now, try to reflect on that little theory/practice in context dialogue.

And, of course, while the many-facets Rasch model (see Chapter 8) can be used to measure the systematic severity or leniency of judges (raters), Differential Rater Functioning would alert us to the presence of rater bias—the rater who (un)wittingly changes severity according to some group characteristic. One exemplar from the 2002 Winter Olympics in Salt Lake City had Winsteps/Facets Rasch software author Mike Linacre, quoted in the Canadian press (Strauss, 2002; www.rasch.org/rmt/rmt154a.htm) under the headline: "New scoring system would have iced the gold for the Canadians." Linacre's analysis revealed how the scoring of the French judge in the figure skating final *changed in severity* in a way inconsistent with the patterns of other judges. Indeed, the French judge's scoring was inconsistent with her own earlier scoring patterns. The French judge's DRF handed the gold to the Russian pair and caused a furor. The ongoing substantive question for those in the human sciences would be, how would the theory of construct/context/rater deal with that sort of evidence?

The procedures for common-person linking of PRTIII and BLOT using Excel are given with the spreadsheet available on the book website.

Summary

Invariance is a crucial property of scientific measurement.

Person and item measures should remain invariant (within error) across all appropriate measurement conditions.

Instruments measuring one latent trait should retain their calibrations (item difficulties) in all appropriate measurement conditions (within error).

Person measures on one latent trait should remain identical (within error) regardless of which appropriate instrument is used.

In Rasch analysis, the computational logic applied to persons in relation to items is exactly the same as the logic applied to items in relation to persons.

Anchoring item values establishes measurement invariance for those items in the related analyses, but invariance must be monitored empirically to detect item 'drift' and to diagnose its likely causes.

Failures of invariance (e.g., DIF) should alert us to potential problems with the measurement instrument or to new understandings about the underlying latent trait.

Test linking is often mistakenly called **test equating**.

ACTIVITIES

Run Bond&FoxSteps and perform the analyses of the PRTIII data set.

Download the Invariance spreadsheet and instructions from the book website.

Follow the steps to implement the invariance plot (of pairs of 150 person measures) BLOT versus PRTIII.

In particular, note that the errors for *item* measures are about the same across tests, but the errors for *person* measures vary dramatically across tests. Why is that?

Work through the 'Top v Bot' spreadsheet for plotting the invariance of the pairs of 35 BLOT item measures estimated from subsamples of the top 75 persons and the bottom 75 persons. Why are the errors of the item measures relatively stable across each subsample but larger than those from the original 150-person sample?

Work through the 'BLOT odds v evens' spreadsheet for plotting the invariance of the of pairs of 150 person measures estimated from subtests of 17 even-numbered and 18 odd-numbered BLOT items. Why are the errors of the person measures relatively stable across each subtest but larger than on the whole BLOT test?

References

Adey, P., & Shayer, M. (1994). *Really raising standards: Cognitive intervention and academic achievement.* London: Routledge.

Angoff, W. H. (1960). Measurement and scaling. In C. W. Harris (Ed.), *Encyclopedia of Educational Research* (pp. 807–817). New York, NY: Macmillan.

Bond, T. G. (2004). Validity and assessment: A Rasch measurement perspective. *Metodologia de las Ciencias del Comportamiento, 5*(2), 179–194.

Bond, T. G., & Bunting, E. M. (1995). Piaget and measurement III: Reassessing the method clinique. *Archives de Psychologie, 63*(247), 231–255.

Bond, T. G., & Fox, C. M. (2001). *Applying the Rasch model: Fundamental measurement in the human sciences.* Mahwah, NJ: Lawrence Erlbaum Associates.

Bond, T. G., Rossi Ferrario, S., & Zotti, A. M. (2005, June). *Family Strain Questionnaire–Short Form for general practitioners and home-care teams.* Paper presented at PROMS, Kuala Lumpur, Malaysia.

Bunting, E. M. (1993). *A qualitative and quantitative analysis of Piaget's control of variables scheme* (Unpublished thesis, James Cook University, Townsville, Australia).

Endler, L. C. (2004). *Is student achievement really immutable? A study of cognitive development and student achievement in an Oregon school district* (Unpublished thesis, James Cook University, Townsville, Australia).

Endler, L. C., & Bond, T. G. (2001). Cognitive development in a secondary science setting. *Research in Science Education, 30*(4), 403–416.

Endler, L., & Bond, T. (2006). Tracking science achievement and cognitive development with the Rasch model: Empirical evidence of growth and heterogeneity. In X. Liu & W. J. Boone (Eds.), *Rasch measurement in science education* (pp. 74–110). Maple Grove, MN: JAM Press.

Endler, L. C., & Bond, T. G. (2008). Changing science outcomes: Cognitive acceleration in a US setting. *Research in Science Education, 38*, 149–166.

Fan, X. (1998). Item response theory and classical test theory: An empirical comparison of their item/person statistics. *Educational and Psychological Measurement, 58*(3), 357–381.

Ingebo, G. S. (1997). *Probability in the measure of achievement.* Chicago, IL: MESA Press.

Inhelder, B., & Piaget, J. (1958). *The growth of logical thinking from childhood to adolescence* (A. Parsons & S. Milgram, Trans.). London: Routledge & Kegan Paul. (Original work published 1955)

Kingsbury, G. (2003, April). *A long-term study of the stability of item parameter estimates.* Paper presented at the annual meeting of the American Educational Research Association, Chicago, IL.

Linacre, J. M. & Wright, B. D. (1989). The 'length' of a logit. *Rasch Measurement Transactions, 3*(2), 54–55.

Loevinger, J. (1947). A systematic approach to the construction and evaluation of tests of ability. *Psychological Monographs, 61*(4).

Masters, G. N., & Beswick, D. G. (1986). *The construction of tertiary entrance scores: Principles and issues.* Melbourne, Victoria, Australia: University of Melbourne, Centre for the Study of Higher Education.

Messick, S. (1995). Validity of psychological assessment. *American Psychologist, 50*(9), 74–149.

Rossi Ferrario, S., Baiardi, P., & Zotti, A. M. (2004). Update on the Family Strain Questionnaire: A tool for the general screening of caregiving-related problems. *Quality of Life Research, 13*, 1425–1434.

Scheuneman, J. D., & Subhiyah, R. G. (1998). Evidence for the validity of a Rasch model technique for identifying differential item functioning. *Journal of Outcome Measurement, 2*(1), 33–42.

Shayer, M., Küchemann, D. E., & Wylam, H. (1976). The distribution of Piagetian stages of thinking in British middle and secondary school children. *British Journal of Educational Psychology, 46*(2), 164–173.

Sherry, D. (2011). Thermoscopes, thermometers, and the foundations of measurement. *Studies in the History and Philosophy of Science, A, 42*, 509–524.

Smith, E. V., Jr. (2001). Evidence for the reliability of measures and validity of measure interpretation: A Rasch measurement perspective. *Journal of Applied Measurement, 2*(3), 281–311.

Stafford, E. (2005). What the pendulum can tell educators about children's scientific reasoning. In M. R. Matthews, C. F. Gauld, & A. Stinner (Eds.), *The pendulum: Scientific, historical & educational perspectives* (pp. 315–348). Dordrecht: Springer.

Stanbridge, B. (2001). *A radical constructivist approach to high school science teaching: Investigating its potential to extend students' meaningful learning through the optimization and possible extension of their cognitive abilities* (Unpublished doctoral dissertation, James Cook University, Townsville, Australia).

Stenner, J. (2001). The necessity of construct theory. *Rasch Measurement Transactions, 15*(1), 804–805.

Stone, M. (2001). Making Standard Measures. *Rasch Measurement Transactions, 15*(1), 792–793.

Strauss, S. (2002, February 16). New scoring system would have iced the gold for the Canadians. *Globe and Mail*, p. F6. (www.rasch.org/rmt/rmt154a.htm)

Tesio, L., Granger, C. V., Perucca, L., Franchignoni, F. P., Battaglia, M. A., & Russell, C. F. (2002). The FIMTM instrument in the United States and Italy: A comparative study. *American Journal of Physical Medicine & Rehabilitation, 81*(3), 168–176.

Thurstone, L. L. (1952). Autobiography. In G. Lindzey (Ed.), *A history of psychology in autobiography* (Vol. 6, pp. 294–321). Englewood Cliffs, NJ: Prentice Hall.

Vidotto, G., Ferrario, S. R., Bond, T. G. & Zotti, A. M. (2010). Family Strain Questionnaire—Short Form for nurses and general practitioners. *Journal of Clinical Nursing, 19*, 275–283.

Wright, B. D. (1977). Misunderstanding the Rasch model. *Journal of Educational Measurement, 14*(2), 97–116.

Wright, B. D., & Stone, M. H. (1979). *Best test design.* Chicago, IL: MESA Press.

6

MEASUREMENT USING LIKERT SCALES

The previous chapters have demonstrated how the basic features of Rasch modeling can be used to deal with simple right–wrong, or dichotomous, data. An extension of these principles allows us to extend the idea of Rasch modeling to polytomous data. One form of this approach to collecting data that has been around for a long time is the principle of the Likert scale (Likert, 1932), which usually is used to collect attitude data. Likert scales share a number of common features, regardless of which attitudes they assess, and with possible responses usually expressed in a format such as SD (strongly disagree), D (disagree), N (neutral), A (agree), and SA (strongly agree). Similarly, each Likert-scale item is provided with a stem (or statement of attitude), and the respondent is required to mark a response on the disagree–agree continuum, indicating the extent to which the statement in the stem is endorsed. An uneven number of response options might provide a 'neutral' response at the midpoint, while an even number of response options might force the respondent into choosing either a positive or negative response.[1]

Likert scales are usually regarded by psychologists as a softer form of data collection in which the researcher clearly acknowledges that the questions are requiring merely expressed opinions. Such inherent subjectivity can be attributed to many types of data collected about the human condition (Hales, 1986). However, the standard methods for analyzing Likert data immediately disregard the subjective nature of the data by making unwarranted assumptions about their meaning. These assumptions are made in order to find a quick and easy way of producing some sort of overall score in terms of, say, computer anxiety, attitudes toward a business product or service, or endorsement of particular medical practices. Thus, in this chapter, we set out to show how it is both counterintuitive and mathematically inappropriate to ignore the subjective nature of Likert data by analyzing them in the traditional way.

A standard display of Likert response options might take this form:

$$
\begin{array}{cccc}
\text{SD} & \text{D} & \text{A} & \text{SA} \\
\text{SD} & \text{D} & \text{A} & \text{SA} \\
\text{SD} & \text{D} & \text{A} & \text{SA} \\
\text{SD} & \text{D} & \text{A} & \text{SA} \\
\text{SD} & \text{D} & \text{A} & \text{SA}
\end{array}
$$

The coding for responses then could be treated in the following way:

$$
\begin{array}{cccc}
1 & 2 & 3 & 4 \\
1 & 2 & 3 & 4 \\
1 & 2 & 3 & 4 \\
1 & 2 & 3 & 4 \\
1 & 2 & 3 & 4
\end{array}
$$

where the higher number indicates a higher degree of agreement with the statement being evaluated. Thus, scoring would be conducted such that four endorsements of the SA code by a respondent results in a satisfaction score of 20, four times the amount of satisfaction indicated by the respondent who endorses the five SD categories ($5 \times 1 = 5$), or exactly twice the satisfaction of someone who endorses five SDs ($5 \times 2 = 10$).

Whenever scores are added in this manner, the ratio, or at least the interval nature of the data, is being presumed. That is, the relative value of each response category across all items is treated as being the same, and the unit increases across the rating scale are given equal value. These assumptions are conveyed when the data analysis treats SA = 4 as having a value four times greater than that of SD = 1 and does so for each and every item on the scale. On the one hand, the subjectivity of attitude data is acknowledged each time the data are collected. Yet on the other hand, the data are subsequently analyzed in a rigidly prescriptive and inappropriate statistical way (i.e., by failure to incorporate that subjectivity into the data analysis).

It is more than likely that the stem:

20. I am so afraid of computers I avoid using them. SD D A SA

indicates much higher levels of computer anxiety in educational situations than does the stem:

19. I am afraid that I will make mistakes when I use my computer. SD D A SA

Indeed, the children who respond SA on the 'mistakes' stem might routinely endorse D on the 'avoid using' stem, yet traditional analyses of the SA responses to each of the stems will contribute exactly four points to the overall computer anxiety score. A more realistic representation of the way that a sample of grade school children might actually use these two stems could be something like this:

	Less Anxious			More Anxious		
20. Avoid using			SD	D	A	SA
19. Mistakes	SD	D	A	SA		

where any move to the right indicates more anxiety overall.

From this example, we can see that endorsing SA on 'avoid using' should indicate a higher level of anxiety on the overall computer anxiety scale. This makes intuitive sense: Students who report that they 'strongly agree' with actually avoiding computers due to fear seem to show much higher levels of the underlying 'computer anxiety' construct than those who merely 'strongly agree' that they fear making mistakes.

The Rasch Model for Polytomous Data

Already, the parallels can be seen between the Rasch approach to Likert scale data and what we have detailed in the previous chapters. In particular, the Rasch model allows the item difficulty of each stem or question to be based on the way in which an appropriate group of subjects actually responded to that stem in practice. In a manner similar to that used for dichotomous data, the Rasch model establishes the relative difficulty of each item stem in recording the development of computer anxiety from the lowest to the highest levels the instrument is able to record. Therefore, each item will have a difficulty estimate. Rasch modeling also will establish the pattern in the use of the Likert scale categories to yield a single rating scale structure common to all the items on the scale. So the Rasch **rating scale model** (RSM) has just one extra feature over the model for dichotomous data: As well as reporting person estimates and a difficulty threshold estimate for each item, it provides, in addition, one set of rating scale thresholds that is common for all of the items.

In Figure 6.1, we have represented the locations of five Likert stems and five respondents drawn from a much larger number of stems and respondents on a make-believe anxiety scale. Of course, we have used the pathway analogy introduced earlier, so the principles of Rasch analysis interpretation will remain the same as before. Indeed, before reading any farther, please take a few minutes to try interpreting the key attributes of the items and the persons in Figure 6.1. The key innovation is the new item labeling: 1.1 = Item 1, Threshold 1; 1.2 = Item 1, Threshold 2; and so on.

The locations of the persons, as indications of how much anxiety they revealed in their responses, are represented by the squares as previously. The location of the square indicates the person estimate (in this case, the amount of anxiety), and the error estimates show the amount of imprecision for that location. It will be easy to recognize Tess as the most anxious person because she has the highest location on the logit scale. Ziggy is shown as the least anxious of all. Although the locations for Vicky and Wayne would be different in terms of just the person estimates alone, the size of the associated error estimates means that no meaningful difference in the anxiety levels reported by these two persons may be inferred.

— locations of scale positions show that the increase in anxiety
  implied by more from SD to A is < increase reg. to more from O to A
— shows item stems vary in level of anxiety they can actually
  detect

Measurement Using Likert Scales   **115**

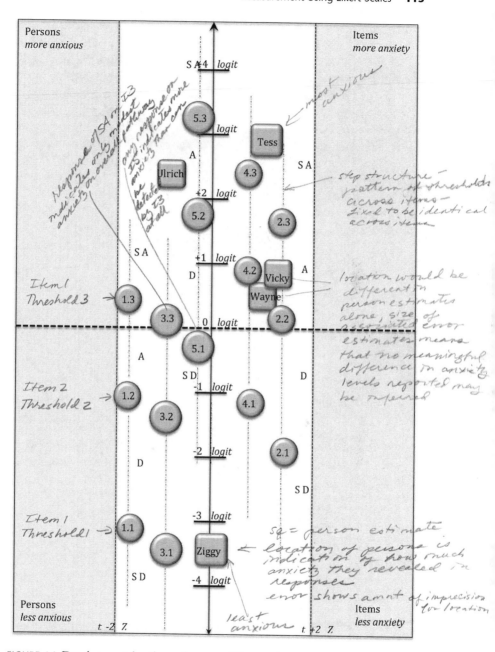

FIGURE 6.1 Developmental pathway for ersatz Likert scale.

The items, however, indicate a rather more complicated representation than we
saw with dichotomous data. For dichotomous data, each item was represented on
the developmental pathway (and in the item table) as having a single item estimate
and an associated error estimate. For rating-scale data, not only does each item have

a difficulty estimate, but the rating scale also has a series of thresholds. This is the level at which the likelihood of being observed in a given response category (below the threshold) is exceeded by the likelihood of being observed in the next higher category (above the threshold).[2] Although it might seem a little strange to talk about failure and success on Likert attitude scales, we can easily see the appropriateness of, say, failure to agree with or, even better, failure to endorse any particular response category. Similarly, success can be interpreted as agreement with or, better still, endorsement of, a particular response category. For the polytomous data we have collected with our Likert scale, we will need a number of thresholds for the anxiety scale to show the progression from each category to the next by estimating a single set of threshold values that apply to all of the item stems in the scale.

For the polytomous data we have collected with our Likert scale, we will need a number of thresholds for the anxiety scale to show the progression:

$$SD \rightarrow D \rightarrow A \rightarrow SA.$$

Therefore, what we represented in earlier chapters with dichotomous items as

✔

one item threshold estimate

✗

showed how the item difficulty estimate indicated the 50:50 probability threshold between the two possible response categories on a dichotomous item. With the rating scale model, this now is represented as

SA

Third threshold estimate

A

Second threshold estimate

D

First threshold estimate

SD

because three thresholds are needed to separate the four possible response categories on the Likert scale. But more than just that, the Rasch rating scale model does not presume the size of the **step** necessary to move across each threshold. It detects the threshold structure of the Likert scale in the data set and then estimates a single set of response category threshold values that apply to all of the item stems in the scale.

Going back to Figure 6.1, it is obvious that the thresholds for any one item (e.g., 1.1, 1.2, 1.3) are not spread equidistantly. Some steps (say, from Threshold 2 to Threshold 3) require smaller increases in anxiety than other steps (say, from Threshold 1 to Threshold 2). However, the step structure (the pattern of those thresholds across items) is fixed to be identical across every item in the Likert scale. We can see, as well, that the relative difficulty of the items also varies as it did for the dichotomous data examples. Item 1 is much easier to endorse than is Item 5, for example. We can see now that even a response of SA on Item 3 indicates only a modest amount of anxiety on the overall pathway, whereas an A response for Item 5 indicates more anxiety than can be detected by Item 3 at all.

The traditional statistical summation of Likert scale data is based on the a priori assumption that all of the items are of equal difficulty and that the thresholds between steps are of equal distance or equal value. The Rasch model makes no such assumption, and the locations of the step thresholds revealed in Figure 6.1 do not corroborate that traditional presumption. First, the locations for those scale positions, as revealed by the reality of practice, show that the increase in anxiety implied by the move from a response of SD to one of A is less than the increase required by the move from D to SA. Second, it shows that the item stems themselves also vary in the level of anxiety that they can actually detect.

Thus, the Rasch model treatment of Likert scale data is intuitively more satisfactory and mathematically more justifiable than is the traditional 'allocate 1, 2, 3, 4 and just add them up' approach. The Rasch model explicitly recognizes the SD D A SA and the subsequent coding 1 2 3 4 as ordered categories only, in which the value of each category is higher than that of the previous category, but by an unspecified amount. That is, the data are regarded as ordinal (not interval or ratio) data, and we use the Rasch model to transform the counts of the endorsements of these ordered Likert categories into interval scales based on the actual empirical evidence rather than on some unfounded assumption made beforehand.

Therefore, in the Rasch rating scale model, developed in the work of David Andrich (Andrich, 1978a, 1978b, 1978c) and Earling Andersen (Andersen, 1977), the finer detail of the item structure is shown. The analyses provide both an item estimate for each Likert stem as well as a set of estimates for the three thresholds that mark the boundaries between the four Likert response categories: SD D A SA. By analyzing the data in this manner, we can see immediately that the items do not carry the same relative value in the construct under investigation. The adding of raw scores to yield a person or item total score in Rasch measurement is justified only for those items that adhere to the model's requirements: They must pass the quality control criteria first—the evidence for that is often referred to as rating scale 'diagnostics'.

Analyzing Rating Scale Data: The Children's Empathic Attitudes Questionnaire

The following example of the Children's Empathic Attitudes Questionnaire (CEAQ) serves as a straightforward use of the Rasch rating scale model to construct a measure from Likert-type items. The CEAQ (Funk, Fox, Chang, & Curtiss, 2008), developed to measure empathy of late elementary and middle school–aged children, was piloted and revised on four separate occasions. At each administration, items were revised according to their difficulty levels and fit statistics, resulting in a 16-item version with three ordered response options for each (No, Maybe, Yes). The CEAQ findings in this chapter are based on the responses of 213 fifth, sixth, and seventh graders across two school systems (one urban and one suburban).

Figure 6.2 provides the item-map representation of responses in the format of the pathway analogy introduced earlier. The figure is a little cramped given that it represents the item difficulties, error estimates, and item fit estimates for each of the 16 CEAQ items, while for illustration purposes, it also represents the pattern of the two threshold locations for (only) a number of items. It is also worth noting that the versions of item–person maps routinely seen in Rasch analysis output from the regular analysis software programs (e.g., Winsteps) focus on the relative distributions of item difficulty and person ability estimates only. These maps do not include item fit and person fit representations on the same map as we have with our pathway map, in which the pathway between the dotted lines is meant to indicate sufficient fit.

At this point in the chapter, we have provided a map of all 16 items to show the bases of the decision to include just some of these items in a subsequent analysis. A perusal of the details in Figure 6.2 will lead to the inference that one of the items does not appear to be revealing the same underlying construct (empathy) that the others seem to be tapping. Which item is it? What is the evidence of inadequate fit? We will return to this issue as we progress through some of the basic diagnostics mentioned earlier—those that serve as quality-control indicators in determining the extent to which persons and items adhere to the model's requirements.

Item Ordering

The map for the CEAQ items also provides *prima facie* evidence for the claim made earlier in this chapter that as a general rule, Likert attitude or opinion *items* are likely to vary in terms of their difficulty, agreeability, or endorsability. Using the map and the item names in the text box, which are the easier empathy items for these grade school students to endorse? With which items is it more difficult to agree? How does the plotting of the two-item threshold values on the map provide evidence for varying item difficulty?

CEAQ ITEMS

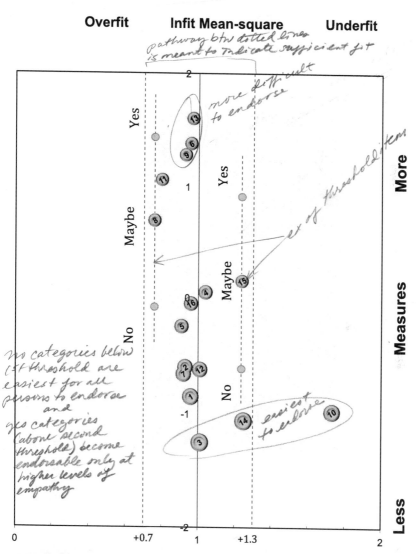

FIGURE 6.2 Developmental pathway representation of all 16 CEAQ items (some with associated threshold estimates).

TABLE 6.1 CEAQ Items

Name	Prompt
CEAQ 1	When I'm *mean* to someone, I usually feel bad about it later.
CEAQ 2	I'm happy when the *teacher* says my friend did a good job.
CEAQ 3	I would get upset if I saw someone hurt an *animal*.
CEAQ 4	I understand how *other kids* feel.
CEAQ 5	I would feel bad if my mom's friend got *sick*.
CEAQ 6	Other people's *problems* really bother me.
CEAQ 7	I feel happy when my friend gets a good *grade*.
CEAQ 8	When I see a kid who is *upset* it really bothers me.
CEAQ 9	I would feel bad if the kid sitting next to me got in *trouble*.
CEAQ 10	It's easy for me to tell when my mom or dad has a good day at *work*.
CEAQ 11	It *bothers* me when my teacher doesn't feel well.
CEAQ 12	I feel *sorry* for kids who can't find anyone to hang out with.
CEAQ 13	Seeing a kid who is *crying* makes me feel like crying.
CEAQ 14	If two kids are *fighting*, someone should stop it.
CEAQ 15	It would bother me if my friend got *grounded*.
CEAQ 16	When I see someone who is *happy*, I feel happy too.

The CEAQ pathway (Figure 6.2) shows and the values in Table 6.2 confirm that Items 13 (see another kid crying), 6 (others' problems), and 9 (another kid getting in trouble) are the more difficult-to-endorse empathy items (at the top of the maps in Figures 6.2 and 6.3). CEAQ items 3 (upset if animal hurt), 10 (mom and dad's day at work), and 14 (stopping fighting between two kids) are the easiest to endorse. We can see that the 'No' categories (i.e., below the first thresholds, 13.1, 6.1, 9.1, etc.) are of course easier for all persons to endorse, and the 'Yes' categories for the same items (i.e., above the second thresholds, 13.2, 6.2, 9.2, etc.) become endorsable only at higher levels of empathy. Only the most empathic children (see Figure 6.4) in this sample (12 children above +2.5 logits) are likely to respond 'Yes' (i.e., above the second threshold: 6.2, 9.2) for Items 6 and 9. Responding 'Yes' for item 13 (i.e., above threshold 13.2 for kid crying) is *unlikely* for any child, given the overall CEAQ measures of the children in this sample. Further, it is as easy to endorse Item 12 (feeling sorry for other kids) at the highest empathy ('Yes') level (i.e., above 12.2) as it is to respond 'Maybe' to Item 13 (seeing a kid who is crying), that is, above 13.1.

The tabular output from the Rasch analysis for Likert-type items is necessarily more complicated than the tables for dichotomous items. Although we would expect to see a single difficulty estimate and *SE* for each item, we also should expect to see estimates and errors (SEs) for each of the response thresholds. In Table 6.2, we see that each of the 16 CEAQ items has a single-item difficulty estimate and *SE*, as well as two threshold (Tau) difficulty estimates (and error estimates) recorded. However, just one set of (four) fit statistics is included for each item, just as we are used to having with dichotomous data.

TABLE 6.2 Item and Threshold Estimates (With Fit Statistics) for All 16 Children's Empathic Attitudes Questionnaire (CEAQ) Items

[handwritten: unstandardized form of fit values - mean of squared residuals] *[handwritten: weighted perf/df −2 to 2 acceptable]*

Item #	Difficulty Error (overall)	Tatus		Infit Mean Square	Outfit Mean Square	Infit Zstd	Outfit Zstd
		1 (No to Maybe)	2 (Maybe to Yes)	*[handwritten: how much misfit is revealed in data]*		*[handwritten: how likely is misfit]*	
1	−0.85	−0.74	0.74	0.96	1.08	−0.279	0.56
	0.14	0.06	0.04				
2	−0.59	−0.74	0.74	0.93	0.96	−0.61	−0.21
	0.13	0.06	0.04				
3	−1.25	−0.74	0.74	1.00	1.33	0.11	1.62
	0.15	0.06	0.04				
4	0.07	−0.74	0.74	1.03	1.11	0.45	1.08
	0.12	0.06	0.04				
5	−0.23	−0.74	0.74	0.91	0.85	−0.89	−1.18
	0.12	0.06	0.04				
6	1.38	−0.74	0.74	0.95	0.96	−0.50	−0.3
	0.11	0.06	0.04				
7	−0.65	−0.74	0.74	0.92	0.81	−0.71	−1.25
	0.13	0.06	0.04				
8	0.7	−0.74	0.74	0.75	0.73	−3.20	−3.18
	0.11	0.06	0.04				
9	1.28	−0.74	0.74	0.92	0.91	−0.88	−0.93
	0.11	0.06	0.04				
10	−0.98	−0.74	0.74	1.72	1.91	5.11	4.25
	0.14	0.06	0.04				
11	1.06	−0.74	0.74	0.79	0.76	−2.67	−2.79
	0.11	0.06	0.04				
12	−0.61	−0.74	0.74	1.00	0.96	0.12	−0.21
	0.13	0.06	0.04				
13	1.6	−0.74	0.74	0.96	0.95	−0.37	−0.42
	0.11	0.06	0.04				
14	−1.06	−0.74	0.74	1.25	1.17	1.98	1.00
	0.15	0.06	0.04				
15	0.17	−0.74	0.74	1.24	1.29	2.63	2.63
	0.11	0.06	0.04				
16	−0.03	−0.74	0.74	0.95	0.92	−0.43	−0.59
	0.12	0.06	0.04				

[handwritten: Item difficulty measurement] *[handwritten: SE Error measurement]* *[handwritten: Threshold difficulty measurements for all items]*

The detailed threshold output is very helpful to our understanding of the variable under investigation, in terms of both the structure of the Likert-scale items and the direct interpretation of any person's most probable response to each item, given that person's location.

The Rasch measurement approach to rating scale analysis as it is applied to Likert-type items uses all the foregoing information in estimating *overall* item difficulty estimates. The reduction of apparent detail in summarizing three or four

item–person map using item estimates rather than threshold estimates from the rating scale analysis

overall item difficulty

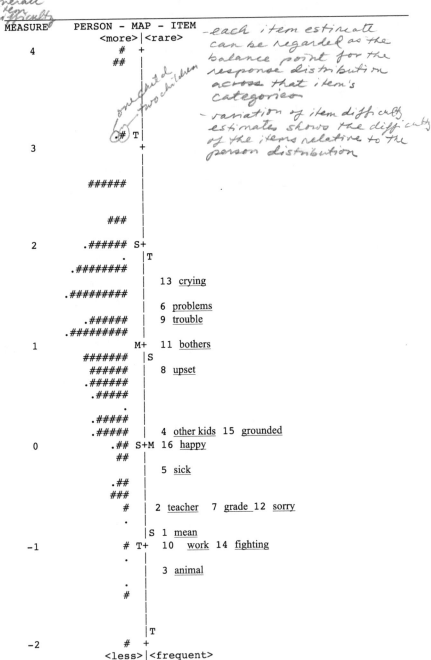

```
MEASURE      PERSON - MAP - ITEM
                  <more>|<rare>
   4               #  +
                  ## |
                     |
                     |
                     |
                     |
                   .#  T|        one out of two children
   3                 +
                     |
                     |
                ##### |
                     |
                  ### |
                     |
   2          .##### S+
                .   |T
             .####### |
                     |            13  crying
            .######## |
                     |            6  problems
              .##### |            9  trouble
            .######## |
   1                M+            11  bothers
              ###### |S
              ##### |             8  upset
              .##### |
              .#### |
                .   |
              .#### |
              .##### |            4  other kids  15  grounded
   0            .## S+M           16  happy
                ## |
                     |            5  sick
               .## |
               ### |
                #  |              2  teacher   7  grade  12  sorry
                .   |
                     |S  1  mean
  -1             #  T+           10   work  14  fighting
                .   |
                     |            3  animal
                     |
                #  |
                     |
                     |T
  -2             #  +
                  <less>|<frequent>
```

– each item estimate can be regarded as the balance point for the response distribution across that item's categories
– variation of item difficulty estimates shows the difficulty of the items relative to the person distribution

FIGURE 6.3 Item–person map for the Children's Empathic Attitudes Questionnaire (CEAQ).

or five threshold points per item in just one item difficulty estimate and one error estimate per item is not performed by discarding information, but by modeling all the relevant information according to its location along the item scale.

Figure 6.3 provides an item–person map using the item estimates rather than threshold estimates from the rating scale analysis. Each item estimate can be regarded as the balance point for the response distribution across that item's categories, and of course the variation of item difficulty estimates shows the difficulty of the items relative to each other and, in the case of the item–person map in Figure 6.3, relative to the person distribution. Rasch overall item difficulties for polytomous items are usually set according to the balance point at which the highest and lowest categories are equally probable (Wright & Masters, 1981). That is revealed in Table 6.2 where the threshold locations are −0.74 logits (i.e., below) and +0.74 logits (i.e., above) relative to each item's location.

The tables of Rasch item outputs for rating scales routinely contain two aspects that distinguish the output from that generated by the other members of the family of Rasch models: Every item has its overall estimate of item difficulty, whereas all items share a threshold structure (−0.74 and +0.74) that is common to all items. This is obvious in Table 6.2, where repeating the identical threshold structure values for every item is redundant but done to emphasize this distinctive feature of the RSM. The item difficulty estimates *vary* from item to item, but the threshold structure modeled by the Rasch analysis of the empirical data is *common* to all items. Figure 6.3 shows the overall item difficulties (the first column) from Table 6.2, whereas Figure 6.4 combines that information with the threshold estimates (the taus for two thresholds) to show the item/threshold structure of the CEAQ results. The reader can confirm that the item and threshold values displayed graphically in Figures 6.2 (pathway), 6.3 (person–item), and 6.4 (response thresholds) actually are those generated by the Rasch analysis and shown in Table 6.2. Of course, the item–person maps in Figures 6.3 and 6.4 do not display fit information.

Targeting and Reliability

We should note that moving from a dichotomous to a polytomous Rasch model should prompt us to reconsider what might constitute a suitable sample of persons for a rating scale analysis. As always, we would need a sample varied enough in the presence of the underlying psychological construct that all the response options for all of the items will be used. However, given that a typical Likert scale might have, say, four response opportunities (e.g., SD D A SA) rather than just two (✓ or ✗), we will need proportionately more persons in our sample to achieve the same density of data for each response opportunity. It should be recalled that the precision of the estimates depends on the amount of good statistical information. Whereas 40 persons might yield, say, 25 ✓ and 15 ✗ responses on a dichotomous item, those same 40 persons might yield 9 SDs, 11 Ds, 12 As, and 8 SAs on a Likert-format item.

The immediate consequence would be less measurement precision (i.e., larger error estimates) at each of the *item* thresholds as a direct result of the thinner spread of the 40 responses across the four response categories. But the *person* estimates would be more precise, as any given number of polytomous items will always provide more statistical information than the same number of dichotomous responses.

In Figure 6.3, we can discern that the targeting of this sample's empathy levels has been well, though not perfectly accomplished by the current version of the CEAQ. The higher end of the distribution of children (each '#' represents two children, and each '.' represents one child here) continues somewhat higher than the highest levels of item thresholds. In other words, a group of these students are much more empathic than we can measure with this set of items. Thus, the empathy levels of these children will not be adequately measured by the CEAQ. Thus, we need a few more items at the top end of the scale—ones that elicit higher levels of empathy—if we want more precise person estimates for those students at the top of the scale.

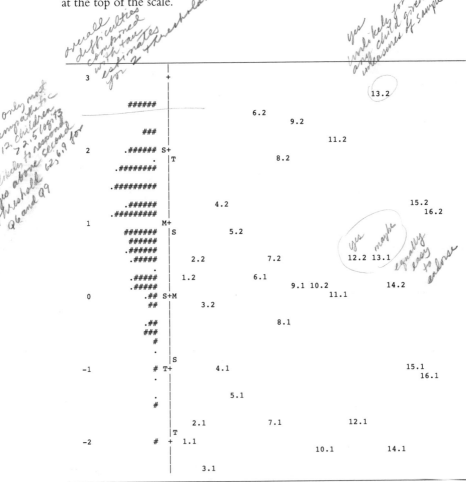

FIGURE 6.4 Children's Empathy Attitude Questionnaire response thresholds estimates for sample of 213 fifth, sixth, and seventh graders (thresholds aligned by item number).

Summary

The traditional statistical summation of Likert-type data is based on the *a priori* assumption that all items are of equal difficulty and the spaces between response options are of equal distance.

With polytomous data, not all items contribute the same amount of the latent trait.

Each item has its own Rasch estimate of item difficulty, and all items share a threshold structure that is common to all items.

Targeting and reliability are intertwined in that persons who fall above or below the set of items will have larger error estimates (SEs) as will item estimates for items where few persons are located.

Larger SEs result in lower reliability. So we need to match the difficulty of our items to the ability of our respondents to yield maximum information for constructing measurement.

Targeting can be examined both visually (Wright Maps) and statistically (mean and standard deviations for person and item distributions).

Item and person fit statistics indicate the extent to which our data do not adhere to the underlying measure. As for targeting, fit indices provide information for quality control and measure improvement.

If this is your introduction to Rasch measurement, we would advise you to complete the following activities and then to continue with Chapter 7. Return here after you have finished *all* chapters. If you already have a sound grasp of Rasch measurement principles, we invite you to go further. For additional technical information on key Rasch concepts, please refer to Appendix B.

ACTIVITIES

Open your copy of the Bond&FoxSteps software you installed from the book website.

Open the BondFoxChapter6.pdf file from the Tutorial pull-down menu.

Follow the step-by-step instructions and analyze the CEAQ data set pre-loaded into the software.

Check your results and interpretations at each stage by referring to the Tutorial file and this chapter.

Extended Understanding—Chapter 6

From the SPSS data set titled CEAQ_SPSS_FILE.sav, we have created a Winsteps file called CEAQ_WINSTEPS_FILE.txt, available online. Run this file in the Winsteps software and check that the file contains responses to the 16 CEAQ items from 213 children. You can verify this at the bottom of the initial run

File	Edit	Diagnosis	Output Tables	Output Files	Batch	Help	Specification	Plots	Excel/RSSST	Graphs	Data Setup

```
|     1      1.84      .2574     108      5*      0     -8.06    .0080|
>=================================<
|     2     -.97      .0820     108     13*      0     -6.17    .0107|
>=================================<
|     3      .78      .0361     128      7*      0     -4.66    .0069|
>=================================<
|     4      .57      .0190      18      7*      0     -3.55    .0051|
>=================================<
|     5      .42      .0116      18      7*      0     -2.62    .0037|
>=================================<
|     6      .30      .0078      18      7*      0     -1.91    .0027|
>=================================<
|     7      .22      .0054      18      7*      0     -1.39    .0019|
>=================================<
|     8      .16      .0039      18      7*      0     -1.80    .0014|
-----------------------------------------------------
Calculating Fit Statistics
>=================================<
Standardized Residuals N(0,1)  Mean: .00 S.D.: 1.02
Time for estimation: 0:0:0.171
 Processing Table 0
CEAQ_16items.sav
-----------------------------------------------------
| PERSON     213 INPUT    213 MEASURED          INFIT       OUTFIT    |
|             TOTAL     COUNT    MEASURE  REALSE  IMNSQ  ZSTD  OMNSQ  ZSTD|
| MEAN        37.7      15.9      1.06     .51    1.00   -.1   1.05   .0|
| S.D.         5.5       .6       1.11     .18     .43   1.2    .64  1.2|
| REAL RMSE    .54  TRUE SD      .96  SEPARATION  1.77  PERSON RELIABILITY .76|
|-----------------------------------------------------|
| ITEM        16 INPUT     16 MEASURED          INFIT       OUTFIT    |
|             TOTAL     COUNT    MEASURE  REALSE  IMNSQ  ZSTD  OMNSQ  ZSTD|
| MEAN       501.9     212.2      .00     .13    1.02    .0   1.05   .0|
| S.D.        67.8       .7       .91     .02     .22   1.9    .28  1.8|
| REAL RMSE    .13  TRUE SD      .90  SEPARATION  6.88   ITEM RELIABILITY .98|
-----------------------------------------------------
Output written to E:\CEAQ\ZOU056WS.TXT
CODES= 123.
easures constructed: use "Diagnosis" and "Output Tables" menus
```

FIGURE 6.5 Summary from Winsteps analysis of CEAQ_WINSTEPS_FILE.txt.

(see Figure 6.5), where it indicates that 213 Persons were MEASURED and 16 Items were MEASURED.

Once you've verified that your software runs and the results match those we have presented in this chapter, we should proceed to the basic diagnostic tables, as there is much more to be gained in understanding how this sample has responded to the CEAQ instrument.

A good starting point for gaining a quick impression of the item–person distribution is provided by the Wright Item–Person Map found in the Output Tables Menu under Table 1, Variable Maps.

Once you choose the table, that output is the basis for the threshold map shown as Figure 6.4 in this chapter. A quick comparison of the Item mean (the default is set at 0 logits by the Winsteps software) to the Person mean (located at approximately +1 logit) informs us that the sample of respondents (children) is, on average, more empathic than our measure requires. Earlier in the chapter we explored this in more detail by examining those response thresholds.

We can further investigate the measurement properties of the CEAQ by checking the output available under the Winsteps Diagnosis menu, where the first option is the Item Polarity Table (Table 26), shown in Figure 6.7.

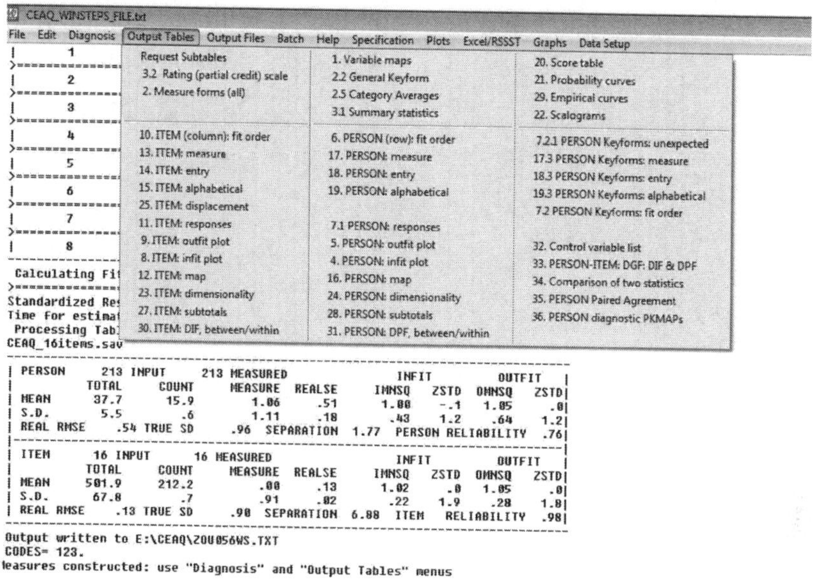

FIGURE 6.6 Output Tables menu in Winsteps.

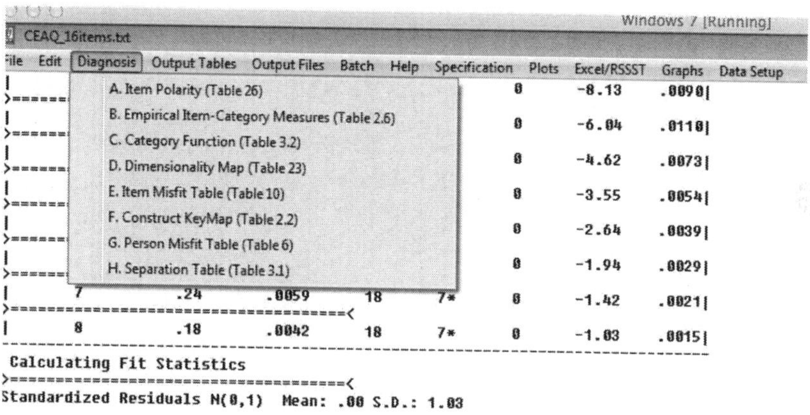

FIGURE 6.7 Output options under the Winsteps Diagnosis menu.

A. Item Polarity

Item polarity, which is a dimensionality diagnostic, is investigated by the point–measure correlation. This statistic tells us if the responses to a particular item align with the overall empathy measure. PT-MEASURE correlations that are negative or 'nearly zero' would signal problematic items not consistent with the construct.

[handwritten annotations: "tells us of the responses to an item align with the overall empathy measure" · "correlations that are negative or nearly significant" · "problematic items inconsistent w/ construct"]

TABLE 6.3 CEAQ Item Statistics in Point-Measure Correlation Order

```
ITEM STATISTICS:  CORRELATION ORDER
```

ENTRY NUMBER	TOTAL SCORE	TOTAL COUNT	MEASURE	MODEL S.E.	INFIT MNSQ	INFIT ZSTD	OUTFIT MNSQ	OUTFIT ZSTD	PT-MEASURE CORR.	PT-MEASURE EXP.	EXACT MATCH OBS%	EXACT MATCH EXP%	ITEM
10	569	212	-.98	.14	1.73	5.1	1.91	4.3	.11	.43	65.7	72.8	CEAQ10
15	496	212	.17	.11	1.24	2.6	1.30	2.6	.37	.51	56.2	57.7	CEAQ15
4	506	213	.07	.12	1.04	.5	1.12	1.1	.38	.51	54.5	58.0	CEAQ4
3	584	213	-1.25	.15	1.01	.1	1.34	1.6	.39	.41	76.8	77.4	CEAQ3
14	570	211	-1.06	.15	1.25	2.0	1.18	1.0	.43	.43	77.5	74.7	CEAQ14
1	563	212	-.85	.14	.96	-.3	1.08	.6	.48	.44	74.3	71.5	CEAQ1
6	397	213	1.38	.11	.96	-.5	.97	-.3	.49	.55	55.9	53.7	CEAQ6
2	551	213	-.59	.13	.93	-.6	.96	-.2	.51	.46	67.3	67.1	CEAQ2
16	511	212	-.03	.12	.96	-.4	.93	-.6	.51	.50	63.8	59.9	CEAQ16
5	528	213	-.23	.12	.91	-.9	.86	-1.2	.52	.49	61.6	62.3	CEAQ5
7	554	213	-.65	.13	.92	-.7	.82	-1.3	.55	.46	70.1	67.6	CEAQ7
12	549	212	-.61	.13	1.01	.1	.96	-.2	.55	.46	75.7	67.2	CEAQ12
9	402	211	1.28	.11	.93	-.9	.91	-.9	.58	.55	59.3	53.7	CEAQ9
13	377	212	1.60	.11	.97	-.4	.96	-.4	.61	.55	57.6	54.9	CEAQ13
8	453	212	.70	.11	.76	-3.2	.73	-3.2	.64	.54	65.2	53.3	CEAQ8
11	420	211	1.06	.11	.80	-2.7	.76	-2.8	.65	.54	61.2	52.9	CEAQ11
MEAN	501.9	212.2	.00	.12	1.02	.0	1.05	.0			65.2	62.8	
S.D.	67.8	.7	.91	.01	.22	1.9	.28	1.8			7.5	8.2	

For all but one of the 16 CEAQ items, our data behaved as expected, with moderate to high positive correlations (from .37 to .65). The correlation of .11 associated with Item 10, one of the easiest-to-agree-with items (see Table 6.3), appears to warrant further attention.

B. Empirical Item—Category Measures

The items in the Category Measures map are *ordered* from most agreeable (at the bottom) to least agreeable (at the top), and the logit *measures* run from left to right. We could use that display to see if the hierarchy of item measures makes sense. Instead, we will explore that a bit later by using the Construct Key Map in step F.

C. Category Function

The values of INFIT and OUTFIT mean squares of the response categories, reported in Table 6.4, are chi-square values divided by their respective degrees of freedom (Wright & Stone, 1979). The reported mean-square values (Infit MnSq for Category 2 is the lowest = 0.90; Outfit MnSq for Category 1 is the highest = 1.17) demonstrate that children's use of the categories is productive for measurement. INFIT and OUTFIT mean squares from 0.6 to 1.4 are considered to be productive for rating scale measurement (Linacre & Wright, 1994). The step difficulty in the calibration structure also advances by 1.48 logits, a little more than the generally recommended minimum of 1.4 logits (Linacre, 1999), between the *No/Maybe* Andrich threshold (−.74, highlighted in Table 6.4) and *Maybe/Yes* threshold (+.74) (.74 −(−.74) = 1.48 logits). This means that the necessary minimum of advance in step difficulties between these two categories is satisfied.

TABLE 6.4 Summary of Category Structure for the CEAQ

SUMMARY OF CATEGORY STRUCTURE. Model="R"   *chi sqvalues/df*

CATEGORY LABEL	SCORE	OBSERVD COUNT	OBSVD %	SAMPLE AVRGE	INFIT EXPECT	INFIT MNSQ	OUTFIT MNSQ	ANDRICH THRESHOLD	CATEGORY MEASURE		
1	1	521	15	-.56	-.55	1.03	1.17	NONE	(-1.98)	1	No
2	2	1113	33	.60	.59	.90	.95	-.74	.00	2	Maybe
3	3	1761	52	1.77	1.77	1.03	1.05	.74	(1.98)	3	Yes
MISSING		13	0	1.28							

demonstrate children's use of categories is productive for measurement

OBSERVED AVERAGE is mean of measures in category. It is not a parameter estimate.

step difficulty = 1.48 a little more than recommended 1.4

CATEGORY LABEL	STRUCTURE MEASURE	S.E.	SCORE-TO-MEASURE AT CAT.	----ZONE----	50% CUM. PROBABLTY	COHERENCE M->C C->M	RMSR	ESTIM DISCR		
1	NONE		(-1.98) -INF	-1.12		75% 32%	.8949		1	No
2	-.74	.06	.00 -1.12	1.12	-.91	50% 67%	.4533	1.01	2	Maybe
3	.74	.04	(1.98) 1.12	+INF	.91	77% 74%	.4974	1.00	3	Yes

means that necessary minimum of step difficulties in advance is satisfied

M->C = Does Measure imply Category?
C->M = **Does Category imply Measure?**

step difficulties btw No/Maybe Maybe/yes is satisfied

The probability curves present the Rasch modeled logistic ogives for the response category options ('1' for No, '2' for Maybe, and '3' for Yes category). They are also available as Category Characteristic Curves under the PLOTS menu. The curves summarize the sample's use of the response options in the CEAQ instrument. The vertical y-axis represents expected probability of endorsement of any given category when a child responds to a CEAQ stem. These probability levels are bounded by 0 and 1 (the floor and ceiling values). The horizontal x-axis has its origin set at 0 to represent the item's difficulty. The scale represents person ability levels *relative* to the item's difficulty. The distances are in log odds units (logits): positive locations (to the right of zero) indicate higher and higher levels of empathy. Negative locations (to the left of zero) indicate lower and lower empathy levels in respondents. In the RSM, all items/categories are modeled to have a common response structure.

Given any value of X (i.e., person estimate minus item estimate), the Rasch model expected probabilities of responses falling in the respective CEAQ categories is mapped by these ogives. As one moves along the x-axis, certain categories become more probable. The response category '2 = Maybe' has its highest probability of .5 (on the y-axis), when the child's ability is the same as the item difficulty (person–item = zero). When the person–item difference is +2, the most likely response category (probability .75) is '3 = Yes'; category '2 = Maybe' has a much lower probability (.2), and the probability of a '1 = No' response is approaching zero. The minimum threshold value for the highest probability peak for any category is expected to be .5 in order for the category to be interpreted as functioning reasonably well. In addition, one can observe that the 0 point on the x-axis also corresponds to a point on a y-axis where the ogives for No and Yes categories *cross* each other. It is the point where the probability of observing either a No or a Yes responses is *equal*. This point is called a Rasch-Andrich threshold. Ogives for categories No and Maybe cross each other at the −0.74 logit point on the

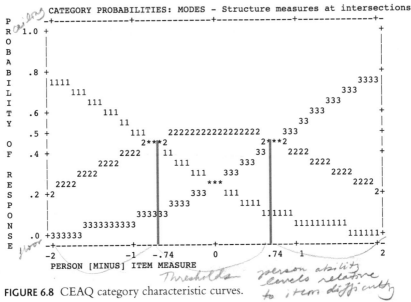

FIGURE 6.8 CEAQ category characteristic curves.

x-axis. Ogives of categories Maybe and Yes, on the other hand, cross each other at the +0.74 logit point on the *x*-axis. The expected response probabilities at these crossing of adjacent ogives is 50:50, .5, or 50% likelihood of responding to either of the adjacent response. These category ogives and thresholds as presented in Figure 6.8 demonstrate how the rating scale implemented in the CEAQ instrument functions in accord with the model expectations. The outlined diagnostic aids in Figure 6.8 for the rating scale functioning demonstrate that children made use of the categories generally as intended.

D. Dimensionality Map

The initial dimensionality indices tell us that our measure accounts for 40.9% of the person variances (rather low), roughly less than half of the individual differences among these children's responses. So something else must be influencing these responses—but is it random noise or something systematic? The factor analyses of the *residuals* indicates very little unexplained variance—in other words, there is no substantial amount of systematic/correlated information in the variance *not* accounted for by the CEAQ measure (only 1.8 eigenvalue units or 6.6% of the total variance in the whole data set, as shown in Table 6.5 and Figure 6.9).

We can examine Table 6.5 and Table 6.6 to determine which of the CEAQ items load onto that first residual factor. If we use a conventionally accepted cutoff of .40 as a meaningful factor loading, Table 6.6 reveals this first factor to consist, primarily, of responses to CEAQ questions 7, 2, and 16, which labeled as A, B, and C in the plot of residual loadings (Figure 6.9). That plot shows the

TABLE 6.5 Table of Standardized Residual Variance for CEAQ Data

```
Table of STANDARDIZED RESIDUAL variance (in Eigenvalue units)
                                            -- Empirical --    Modeled
Total raw variance in observations    =     27.1 100.0%        100.0%
  Raw variance explained by measures  =     11.1  40.9%         40.9%
    Raw variance explained by persons =      4.9  18.3%         18.3%
    Raw Variance explained by items   =      6.1  22.6%         22.6%
  Raw unexplained variance (total)    =     16.0  59.1% 100.0%  59.1%
    Unexplned variance in 1st contrast =     1.8   6.6%  11.2%
    Unexplned variance in 2nd contrast =     1.6   6.1%  10.2%
    Unexplned variance in 3rd contrast =     1.4   5.1%   8.6%
    Unexplned variance in 4th contrast =     1.3   4.7%   8.0%
    Unexplned variance in 5th contrast =     1.2   4.6%   7.8%
```

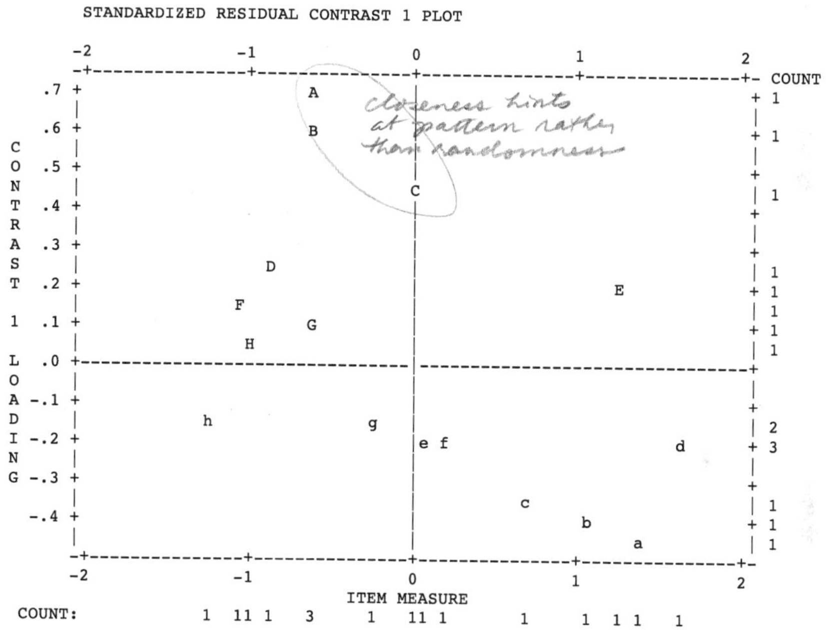

FIGURE 6.9 Plot of residual loadings for CEAQ data.

A, B, C locations to be closer to each other than they are to the other CEAQ items, hinting at a pattern—instead of random distribution—of A, B, C residuals. Is there a second dimension to the CEAQ?

Referring to the CEAQ item contents (Table 6.1), we might conclude that these items share a theme which could be called, say, 'being happy for the good fortune of others'. Whether this characteristic is theoretically a part of a general empathy construct or should be assessed independently remains for debate among researchers of empathy, but the evidence here is that these three items share some variance in common that is additional to the overall empathy measure. Granted, the percentage of variance is not large enough to create a 'measurement disturbance', but it does underline the importance of reflecting on theory to inform analysis and *vice versa*.

TABLE 6.6 Table of Standardized Residual Loadings for CEAQ Items

```
STANDARDIZED RESIDUAL LOADINGS FOR ITEM (SORTED BY LOADING)
```

CON- TRACT	LOADING	MEASURE	INFIT MNSQ	OUTFIT MNSQ	ENTRY NUMBER	ITEM		LOADING	MEASURE	INFIT MNSQ	OUTFIT MNSQ	ENTRY NUMBER	ITEM
1	.68	-.65	.92	.82	A	7 CEAQ7		-.43	1.38	.96	.97	a	6 CEAQ6
1	.60	-.59	.93	.96	B	2 CEAQ2		-.41	1.06	.80	.76	b	11 CEAQ11
1	.45	-.03	.96	.93	C	16 CEAQ16		-.36	.70	.76	.73	c	8 CEAQ8
1	.23	-.85	.96	1.08	D	1 CEAQ1		-.22	1.60	.97	.96	d	13 CEAQ13
1	.20	1.28	.93	.91	E	9 CEAQ9		-.20	.07	1.04	1.12	e	4 CEAQ4
1	.14	-1.06	1.25	1.18	F	14 CEAQ14		-.18	.17	1.24	1.30	f	15 CEAQ15
1	.11	-.61	1.01	.96	G	12 CEAQ12		-.14	-.23	.91	.86	g	5 CEAQ5
1	.03	-.98	1.73	1.91	H	10 CEAQ10		-.14	-1.25	1.01	1.34	h	3 CEAQ3

*use cutoff of
.40 as meaningful
factor loading*

E. Item Misfit Table

The items in this table (see Table 6.7) are ordered from most misfitting to least misfitting using the unweighted, unstandardized fit indicator, Outfit Mean Squares, as the ordering criterion. Item 10 emerges again as most misfitting, warranting further investigation, as *all* four fit indicators exceed the acceptable ranges. Other items have acceptable MnSq values, with only #15 exceeding Zstd = +2.0. We might ask the question about Item 8 being redundant (all fit statistics are **muted**).

TABLE 6.7 CEAQ Item Statistics in Misfit (Outfit MnSq) Order

```
TABLE 10.1 CEAQ_16items.sav                    ZOU896WS.TXT  Jun 28 15:26 2014
INPUT: 213 PERSON  16 ITEM   REPORTED: 213 PERSON  16 ITEM  3 CATS WINSTEPS 3.74.0
```

```
PERSON: REAL SEP.: 1.77  REL.: .76 ... ITEM: REAL SEP.: 6.88  REL.: .98
```

*table organized from most to
least misfitting using unweighted
unstandardized fit indicator*

```
ITEM STATISTICS:  MISFIT ORDER
```

ENTRY NUMBER	TOTAL SCORE	TOTAL COUNT	MEASURE	MODEL S.E.	INFIT MNSQ	ZSTD	OUTFIT MNSQ	ZSTD	PT-MEASURE CORR.	EXP.	EXACT MATCH OBS%	EXP%	ITEM
10	569	212	-.98	.14	1.73	5.1	1.91	4.3	A .11	.43	65.7	72.8	CEAQ10
3	584	213	-1.25	.15	1.01	.1	1.34	1.6	B .39	.41	76.8	77.4	CEAQ3
15	496	212	.17	.11	1.24	2.6	1.30	2.6	C .37	.51	56.2	57.7	CEAQ15
14	570	211	-1.06	.15	1.25	2.0	1.18	1.0	D .43	.43	77.5	74.7	CEAQ14
4	506	213	.07	.12	1.04	.5	1.12	1.1	E .38	.51	54.5	58.0	CEAQ4
1	563	212	-.85	.14	.96	-.3	1.08	.6	F .48	.44	74.3	71.5	CEAQ1
12	549	212	-.61	.13	1.01	.1	.96	-.2	G .55	.46	75.7	67.2	CEAQ12
6	397	213	1.38	.11	.96	-.5	.97	-.3	H .49	.55	55.9	53.7	CEAQ6
13	377	212	1.60	.11	.97	-.4	.96	-.4	h .61	.55	57.6	54.9	CEAQ13
2	551	213	-.59	.13	.93	-.6	.96	-.2	g .51	.46	67.3	67.1	CEAQ2
16	511	212	-.03	.12	.96	-.4	.93	-.6	f .51	.50	63.8	59.9	CEAQ16
9	402	211	1.28	.11	.93	-.9	.91	-.9	e .58	.55	59.3	53.7	CEAQ9
7	554	213	-.65	.13	.92	-.7	.86	-1.3	d .55	.46	70.1	67.6	CEAQ7
5	528	213	-.23	.12	.91	-.9	.86	-1.2	c .52	.49	61.6	62.3	CEAQ5
11	420	211	1.06	.11	.80	-2.7	.76	-2.8	b .65	.54	61.2	52.9	CEAQ11
8	453	212	.70	.11	.76	-3.2	.73	-3.2	a .64	.54	65.2	53.3	CEAQ8
MEAN	501.9	212.2	.00	.12	1.02	.0	1.05	.0			65.2	62.8	
S.D.	67.8	.7	.91	.01	.24	1.9	.28	1.8			7.5	8.2	

*most
misfitting
all four
fit
indicators
exceed
acceptable
ranges*

*redundant?
all
statistics
are "muted"*

*fit indices
< 2
all acceptable
except #15*

F. Construct KeyMap

The Winsteps Construct KeyMap is similar to the Empirical Item-Category Measures in that the items are ordered from easiest to agree with (at the bottom) to most difficult to agree with (at the top). Similarly, we can use this display to see if the vertical item hierarchy makes sense. However, the real utility of this map lies in the results displayed in the body of the map—that is, the category responses are no longer *observed empirical responses*. Rather, they represent the item–person response matrix *once the raw responses are converted to equal-interval Rasch measures* using the RSM. This transformation elevates our interpretation from describing the present (raw observed averages) to predicting the future (probabilistic responses in equal intervals) and helps guide us in making inferences about the empathy of these children from the constructed measure.

For this reanalysis, the one misfitting item (Item 10) was *omitted* due to its poor fit statistics and low PtMeas correlation, just as it was in the final version of the CEAQ published by the authors. Looking at Figure 6.10, one can see that the easiest items to endorse include those related to empathizing with others perceived as facing immediate *harm*, whereas the most difficult items to endorse are related to identifying with others' *feelings* or problems that seem beyond the responding children's usual experiences. For example, the line drawn through KeyMap (at mean person value = +1.02 logits) predicts the average child in this sample as most likely to respond '3 = yes' to perceived immediate harm, such as (easiest Item 3) being 'upset at seeing an animal hurt'. Indeed, the average child in this sample would most likely answer '3 = yes' for all easier items (i.e., 3, 14, 10, 1, 7, 12, 2, 5) up to and including Item 5, 'I would feel bad if my mom's friend got sick'. The more difficult items to empathize with (i.e., 8, 11, 9, 6, 13) would most likely receive answers of '2 = maybe' from the average child, including most difficult Item 13, 'Seeing a kid who is crying makes me feel like crying'. For the mid-levels items (i.e., 16, 4, 15), the average child is equally likely to respond 2 or 3: the Maybe/Yes threshold for those three items (indicated ':') sit right on the +1.02 logits line. Few children in this sample would be expected to respond '1 = no' to any of the questions except to the least empathic few children on the most difficult-to-endorse items. This suggests that either the least empathic (e.g., asocial) children are not represented in this sample or that situations requiring higher levels of empathy could be added to the CEAQ.

The box at the bottom of the map shows the distribution of persons, revealing the predictive validity of our measure. The left-most numbers represent the least empathic children (there are 2 in the lowest position), according to our scale, whereas those on the right agree more easily (3 are farthest to the right), or 'more empathic' *if* that is indeed what we are measuring. The average of the children's measures is signified by 'M', the mean, one standard deviation by 'S', and two standard deviations by 'T'. This can also provide a rough check of the targeting of the

EXPECTED SCORE: MEAN (Rasch-score-point threshold, ":" indicates Rasch-half-point threshold)
(ILLUSTRATED BY AN OBSERVED CATEGORY)

```
    -4    -3    -2    -1     0     1     2     3     4
    |-----+-----+-----+-----+-----+-----+-----+-----|  NUM ITEM
  1                      1    :        2       :    3  3   13  CEAQ13
  1                                                    
  1                          1    :       2        3  3   6   CEAQ6
  1                            1   :      2       :  3  3   9   CEAQ9
  1                                                    
  1                      1    :            2       3  3   11  CEAQ11
  1                                                    
  1                 1        :      2       :     3   3   8   CEAQ8
  1                                                    
  1            1   :        2       :        3       3  3   15  CEAQ15
  1                 1        :     2       :    3     3   4   CEAQ4
  1            1   :        2       :        3       3  3   16  CEAQ16
  1                                                    
  1                 1        :      2       :     3    3   5   CEAQ5
  1                                                    
  1        1    :        2       :        3          3   2   CEAQ2
  1        1    :        2       :        3          3   12  CEAQ12
  1        1    :        2       :        3          3   7   CEAQ7
  1                                                    
  1      1    :        2       :        3            3   1   CEAQ1
  1    1    :        2       :        3              3   10  CEAQ10
  1    1    :        2       :           3           3   14  CEAQ14
  1                                                    
  1    1    :           2       :        3           3   3   CEAQ3
    |-----+-----+-----+-----+-----+-----+-----+-----|  NUM ITEM
    -4    -3    -2    -1     0     1     2     3     4

                 11111 111 11 1    1
          2  2 1121 2654511232 493 9713 6 2  (3)     42  PERSON
                   T        S      M       S      T
          0        10  20 40 50 70 80 90           99  PERCENTILE
```

FIGURE 6.10 CEAQ Construct KeyMap.

CEAQ items against our sample by comparing the mean of the person distribution (the line drawn at 1.02 logits) with the mean of the items (at 0 logits). With this sample, the higher average children score is indicative of a need for empathy items that are more difficult to agree with.

G. Person Misfit Table

The misfitting persons table (Table 6.8) is interpreted in the same manner as for misfitting items—however, there are likely to be more misfitting persons than misfitting items in any given analysis. Misfitting items indicate a lack of consistency in interpreting the underlying measure, whereas misfitting persons might *also* indicate idiosyncratic responses that can stem from a multitude of nonmeasurement issues.

TABLE 6.8 Person Statistics: Misfit (Outfit MnSq) Order

PERSON STATISTICS: MISFIT ORDER

ENTRY NUMBER	TOTAL SCORE	TOTAL COUNT	MEASURE	MODEL S.E.	INFIT MNSQ	ZSTD	OUTFIT MNSQ	ZSTD	PT-MEASURE CORR.	EXP.	EXACT MATCH OBS%	EXP%	PERSON
123	45	16	2.64	.63	2.04	1.7	6.16	3.5	A -.19	.36	81.3	81.8	123.00 12 7 0.00
182	47	16	3.87	1.03	1.15	.5	3.37	1.5	B -.24	.22	93.8	93.9	182.00 13 7 1.00
21	45	16	2.64	.63	1.42	.9	2.80	1.9	C -.40	.36	75.0	81.8	21.00 12 7 1.00
101	39	16	1.12	.43	2.06	2.5	2.55	3.0	D -.17	.51	50.0	61.3	101.00 12 7 1.00
74	46	16	3.11	.75	1.00	.2	2.52	1.4	E .03	.30	87.5	88.1	74.00 11 6 1.00
152	40	16	1.31	.44	2.02	2.4	2.48	2.7	F .15	.50	56.3	65.6	152.00 99 99 1.00
205	42	16	1.74	.49	1.65	1.5	2.45	2.3	G .03	.46	62.5	70.1	205.00 11 6 1.00
187	46	16	3.11	.75	1.23	.6	2.43	1.4	H -.19	.30	87.5	88.1	187.00 12 7 1.00
112	41	16	1.51	.46	2.37	2.8	2.30	2.3	I .11	.48	50.0	68.1	112.00 12 7 1.00
40	33	16	.13	.39	2.18	3.1	2.36	3.4	J -.28	.53	50.0	50.4	40.00 12 6 0.00
149	40	16	1.31	.44	2.15	2.6	2.28	2.5	K .14	.50	56.3	65.6	149.00 13 7 0.00
20	37	16	.77	.41	2.03	2.6	2.28	2.9	L .16	.53	50.0	56.0	20.00 11 6 0.00

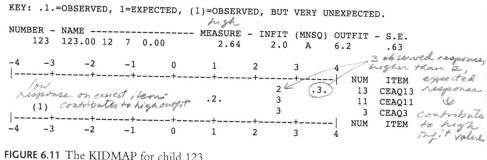

FIGURE 6.11 The KIDMAP for child 123.

Look at just a dozen of the misfitting respondents in this table excerpt. Note that the PT MEAS correlations are all negative or near zero—indicating children whose *individual* scores are contrary to those revealed in the sample's *overall* response strings. The most misfitting respondent (#123) has both high infit and outfit statistics, indicating unexpected (i.e., generally erratic) responses to items both near to and far from the child's estimated high empathy score (+2.64 logits).

Less-than-optimal targeting can also be inferred from this table—note the large standard error (1.03) for the second (*very* empathic) child, #182 (+3.87 logits). Although we can assign a high empathy score to this child, we have lower precision (less confidence) in that estimate than we would for estimates for other children. The high Outfit MnSq (3.37) suggests an unexpectedly low empathy response to an easy-to-endorse item. All other fit indicators are acceptable, revealing the potentially exaggerated impact of unweighted residuals.

The KIDMAP for child 123 (Winsteps Output Table 7.2 as displayed in Figure 6.11) reveals the response strings for this misfitting respondent (see Chapter 12). This child has a high measure on empathy (2.64 logits) yet an unexpectedly *very low* response (1) (= OBSERVED, BUT VERY UNEXPECTED) of 'No' on the easiest Item 3, 'I would get upset if I saw someone hurt an animal'; this contributes to the high *outfit*. The observed value of .3. (= OBSERVED) for Item 13, 'Seeing a kid who is crying makes me feel like crying', is unexpectedly *higher* than this child's expected response of '2 = Maybe' (= EXPECTED) to this item. This unexpected response, close to the child's measure, contributes to the high *infit* value.

H. Separation Table

Model and real reliability parameters and basic Rasch statistics for 211 nonextreme children measures (no zero or perfect scores) are presented in Table 6.9. The separation table summarizes the person and item distributions. Model parameters are calculated "assuming all misfit in the data is due to randomness predicted by the Rasch model" and real parameters defined as "assuming all misfit in the data contradicts the Rasch model" (Linacre, 2006, p. 18). The second section of the table reports reliability estimates including extreme (zero/perfect score) persons.

[handwritten margin notes: "Close which implies relative precision on model estimates"; "means these children on avg found items easy to endorse, conventionally set to 0"; "no perfect or 0 scores"; "summarizes person and item distributions"; "Rasch tends to under-estimate traditional rel. coef"]

TABLE 6.9 CEAQ Person Statistics: Reliability & Separation

SUMMARY OF 211 MEASURED (NON-EXTREME) PERSON

	TOTAL SCORE	COUNT	MEASURE	MODEL ERROR	INFIT MNSQ	ZSTD	OUTFIT MNSQ	ZSTD
MEAN	37.6	15.9	1.02	.46	1.00	-.1	1.05	.0
S.D.	5.5	.6	1.04	.11	.43	1.2	.64	1.2
MAX.	47.0	16.0	3.87	1.03	2.37	3.1	6.16	3.5
MIN.	19.0	7.0	-1.97	.39	.31	-2.7	.27	-2.4

REAL RMSE	.52 TRUE SD	.90	SEPARATION	1.75	PERSON RELIABILITY	.75
MODEL RMSE	.48 TRUE SD	.92	SEPARATION	1.93	PERSON RELIABILITY	.79
S.E. OF PERSON MEAN = .07						

MAXIMUM EXTREME SCORE: 2 PERSON

SUMMARY OF 213 MEASURED (EXTREME AND NON-EXTREME) PERSON

	TOTAL SCORE	COUNT	MEASURE	MODEL ERROR	INFIT MNSQ	ZSTD	OUTFIT MNSQ	ZSTD
MEAN	37.7	15.9	1.06	.48				
S.D.	5.5	.6	1.11	.17				
MAX.	48.0	16.0	5.12	1.84				
MIN.	19.0	7.0	-1.97	.39	.31	-2.7	.27	-2.4

REAL RMSE	.54 TRUE SD	.96	SEPARATION	1.77	PERSON RELIABILITY	.76
MODEL RMSE	.51 TRUE SD	.98	SEPARATION	1.93	PERSON RELIABILITY	.79
S.E. OF PERSON MEAN = .08						

PERSON RAW SCORE-TO-MEASURE CORRELATION = .93
CRONBACH ALPHA (KR-20) PERSON RAW SCORE "TEST" RELIABILITY = .82

[handwritten margin notes: "more conservative to use these estimates"; "fair to good in terms of yielding reliable distinctions"; "Correspond to separation G of 2.57"; "indicates (at least) two measurably and arguably qualitatively distinguishable strata of children, evidence of quantifiable empathy measure"; "estimates of sample's spread relative to precision (SE) of these measurements"; "reports reliability estimates incl. perfect & 0 scores"; "root mean square error"]

In evaluating the reliability statistics, however, it is 'more conservative' to use the nonextreme persons estimates: those actually used in the calibration of Rasch measures (Wright & Stone, 1979). There were only two children classified as extreme (perfect score, all 3s) respondents. The overall mean measure of empathy for 211 nonextreme children is +1.02 logits (SD = 1.04 logits), that is, these children, on average, found the CEAQ items easy to endorse (mean item measure is conventionally set to 0).

The model-person reliability coefficient is .79, little different from the real-person reliability coefficient of .75. This Rasch reliability coefficient might considered to be 'fair' to 'good' in terms of "yielding reliable distinctions" (Lunz & Linacre, 1998, p. 60) among children. It is important to recognize, however, that Rasch model-based reliabilities *underestimate* conventional reliability coefficients, while others, such as the interclass reliability coefficient KR-20, for example, tend to *overestimate* reliability. The estimate of reliability in Rasch models uses a procedure that acknowledges the discrete data properties rather than treating the data as continuous raw scores, which is the case in conventional reliability indicators (Linacre, 1997).

But of far greater importance are the separation indices, which are estimates of the sample's spread relative to the precision (*SE*) of those measurements (Wright & Stone, 2004). Looking at Table 6.9, we see the modeled-person separation is 1.93, which corresponds to a separation (G) of 2.57 (Wright & Masters,

TABLE 6.10 Item Statistics: Reliability & Separation   *default set at ∅*

```
          SUMMARY OF 15 MEASURED (NON-EXTREME) ITEM
-------------------------------------------------------------------------
|            TOTAL            mean item  MODEL       INFIT        OUTFIT  |
|            SCORE   COUNT     MEASURE    ERROR    MNSQ  ZSTD   MNSQ  ZSTD |
|------------------------------------------------------------------------|
| MEAN       497.4   212.2      .00        .13     1.02   .0   1.04   .1  |
| S.D.        67.7      .7       .95       .01      .14  1.5    .20  1.6  |
| MAX.       584.0   213.0     1.60        .16     1.32  3.3   1.40  3.2  |
| MIN.       377.0   211.0    -1.38        .11      .78 -2.9    .74 -3.0  |
|------------------------------------------------------------------------|
| REAL RMSE   .13  TRUE SD   .94  SEPARATION 7.17  ITEM  RELIABILITY  .98 |
|MODEL RMSE   .13  TRUE SD   .94  SEPARATION 7.40  ITEM  RELIABILITY  .98 |
| S.E. OF ITEM MEAN = .25                                                 |
-------------------------------------------------------------------------
     high                 high        high                       high
                 DELETED:    1 ITEM         all imply high model
UMEAN=.0000 USCALE=1.0000                   precision in the estimation
                                            of item measures
```

1982; Appendix B), indicates (at least) two *measurably* and arguably qualitatively *distinguishable strata* of children on the CEAQ variable, providing further evidence of a quantifiable empathy measure. This separation statistic also supports the original coding used for the rating scale. That is, the respondents were given three choices (no/maybe/yes), implying three distinct groups of children on the empathy variable. The close correspondence between G and the original number of rating scale categories serves as further support for this categorization.

This Person table also includes model and real RMSE (root mean square error) or sample dispersion values around calibrated measures (Wright, 1996). These parameters are "more realistic standard errors of measurement" (Linacre, 1998, p. 57). Model RMSE for children measures is .48, (not far from the real RMSE of .52) and implies relative precision in the model estimates of the children measures of empathy. Estimated model 'true' standard deviation for children measures is .92. A 'true' standard deviation, in Rasch models, is defined as $(SD^2_{sample} - (RMSE_{error})^{1/2}$ (Wright & Stone, 2004, p. 48). A 'true' standard deviation is to be interpreted as sample standard deviation, which has a measurement error 'RMSE' removed from it (Lunz & Linacre, 1998). Lunz and Linacre also refer to it as a "statistically unbiased standard deviation" (p. 57).

The same information for the 15 items included in the CEAQ is provided (Table 6.10). The default mean item measure in Rasch analyses is set by default at 0. The items real and model 'true' standard deviation is .94. The Rasch reliability coefficients for model and real measures are .98. These high reliability coefficients corresponded to high separation reliability values of 7.17 for model and 7.40 for real data. The real and model RMSE is .13, which implies a high model precision in the estimation of these CEAQ item measures.

Summary

In general, targeting involves matching the means and the ranges of the item and person distributions.

Diagnosis of test performance with the Rasch scale model focuses on both item and response category functioning.

Dimensionality can be examined via point-measure correlations and the primary components (factor) analysis of Rasch measurement residuals.

The Construct KeyMap results displays the category responses after the raw responses are converted to equal-interval Rasch measures using the RSM.

ACTIVITIES

Load the file CEAQ_WINSTEPS_FILE.txt (available online) into your copy of Winsteps and run the analysis as indicated earlier.

'n.b., you will need a full copy of Winsteps software to access the Diagnosis information.'

Follow the steps outlined to access the Diagnosis information for the CEAQ measure.

Insert the item format command 'IDFILE = * 10 *' to temporarily exclude misfitting Item 10 from the analysis. Which Diagnosis outputs change? Is the change for the better? Why/not?

Now access the CAIN data set from the website. Follow the analyses steps available with that file to execute the RSM analysis on the CAIN data. Follow the Diagnosis prompts. Decide on a sequence of reanalysis steps to improve the measurement properties of the CAIN. (The CAIN was the analysis undertaken for Chapter 6 in Bond & Fox 2nd ed.)

Notes

1 Our examples in Chapter 6 will not use a Neutral central response category, nor more than four response options. Countless Rasch analyses reveal those two ubiquitous practices as the sources of many measurement disturbances.

2 For clarification, these are often termed Rasch-Andrich thresholds for the RSM. An alternative conceptualization, Rasch-Thurstone thresholds, was described by Masters for the Partial Credit model (PCM; see Chapter 7) but is sometimes generalized to the RSM.

References

Andersen, E. B. (1977). Sufficient statistics and latent trait models. *Psychometrika, 42,* 69–81.

Andrich, D. (1978a). Application of a psychometric rating model to ordered categories which are scored with successive integers. *Applied Psychological Measurement, 2*(4), 581–594.

Andrich, D. (1978b). Rating formulation for ordered response categories. *Psychometrika, 43*(4), 561–573.

Andrich, D. (1978c). Scaling attitude items constructed and scored in the Likert tradition. *Educational and Psychological Measurement, 38*(3), 665–680.

Funk, J. B., Fox, C. M., Chang, M., & Curtiss, K. (2008). The development of the Children's Empathic Attitudes Questionnaire using classical and Rasch analyses. *Journal of Applied Developmental Psychology, 29*(3), 187–196.

Hales, S. (1986). Rethinking the business of psychology. *Journal for the Theory of Social Behavior, 16*(1), 57–76.

Likert, R. (1932). A technique for the measurement of attitudes. *Archives of Psychology, 22*, 5–53.

Linacre, J. M. (1997). *Judging plans and facets*. (Research Note No. 3). Chicago, IL: University of Chicago, MESA Psychometric Laboratory. Available: www.rasch.org/rn3.htm. Accessed: March 23, 2000.

Linacre, J. M. (1999). Investigating rating scale category utility. *Journal of Outcome Measurement, 3*(2), 103–122.

Linacre, J. M. (2006). *A user's guide to Winsteps*. Chicago, IL: Winsteps.com.

Linacre, J. M., & Wright, B. D. (1994). Reasonable mean-square fit values. *Rasch Measurement Transactions, 8*(3), 370.

Lunz, M. E., & Linacre, J. M. (1998). Measurement designs using multifacet Rasch modeling. In G. A. Marcoulides (Ed.), *Modern methods for business research* (pp. 44–77). Mahwah, NJ: Lawrence Erlbaum Associates.

Wright, B. D. (1996). Comparing Rasch measurement and factor analysis. *Structural Equation Modeling, 3*(1), 3–24.

Wright, B. D., & Masters, G. N. (1981). *The measurement of knowledge and attitude (Research Memorandum No. 30)*. Chicago, IL: University of Chicago, MESA Psychometric Laboratory.

Wright, B. D., & Masters, G. N. (1982). *Rating scale analysis*. Chicago, IL: MESA Press.

Wright, B. D., & Stone, M. H. (1979). *Best test design*. Chicago, IL: MESA Press.

Wright, B. D., & Stone, M. H. (2004). *Making measures*. Chicago, IL: Phaneron Press.

7

THE PARTIAL CREDIT RASCH MODEL

The extension of the Rasch model for simple dichotomous data into the rating scale model for polytomous data (Andersen, 1977; Andrich, 1978) has had an enormous impact on Rasch modeling. Although Rasch's original work had conceptualized all the subsequently developed members of the Rasch family of models, thinking up the model and developing the estimation procedures are two related but different tasks. The rating scale model is now used routinely for the analysis of Likert-type data (Chapter 6), although Andrich had originally intended the RSM for another purpose: the evaluation of written essays. It would assist the examination process by producing measures from values applied to qualitative essay rating scales by examiners. However, it also paved the way for all the Rasch procedures in common use that involve data with more than just two values (0, 1).

The rating scale model requires every item in a survey, marking rubric, or rehabilitation schedule to have the same number of response categories, as we have come to expect from **Likert scales**. The items might have 3, 4, 5, or even 6 response opportunities, but nevertheless, the number of response or scoring options must be the same for every item on the survey. That requirement often results in some unexpected problems, especially during the development or early use of such scales, including Likert scales. Just because the response form provides, for example, five response opportunities for each item, this does not ensure that all five response categories actually will be used in practice by the persons in the chosen sample. In spite of the researcher's best intention to collect data for all five categories on all items, the data set might reveal different numbers of categories than were actually used for some items (we take up this and related problems in Chapter 11). Moreover, we can easily envisage other testing situations in which it would be more useful not to be restricted to having the same number of scoring opportunities for every item or to allow rating scales with the same number of categories to have different meanings for the categories, e.g., a 5-category attitude scale and a 5-category intensity scale.

Geoff Masters from Melbourne (Wright & Masters, 1982) is usually acknowledged as the developer of the model routinely called the **partial credit Rasch model (PCM)** for polytomous data. The partial credit model specifically incorporates the possibility of having differing numbers of response levels for different items on the same test. Consider the possibility of tests in which one or more intermediate levels of success might exist between complete failure and complete success (i.e., partially correct answers). For this reason, the partial credit model is highly applicable in educational and other testing situations in which 'part marks' are awarded for 'partial success', that is, for progress between complete failure and complete success on that item. However, a very important Rasch principle must be observed in the awarding of part marks. Whereas schoolteachers might give two marks here, a half mark here, and one mark there to give a total of 3.5 (part marks) out of a possible 5 for aspects of a partially correct solution to a math problem, Rasch modeling principles and the principles of measurement more broadly require that the part marks be awarded in an *ordered* way, so that each increasing score represents an increase in the underlying ability being tested.

For example, the ordered values 0, 1, and 2 might be applied to an item as follows: 0 = totally wrong, 1 = partially correct, and 2 = completely correct; values 0, 1, 2, and 3 might be used with another item thus: 0 = totally wrong, 1 = partially correct, 2 = almost completely correct, and 3 = completely correct. So, is there a limit to the number of partial credit steps between complete failure and complete success on an item? Of course we should recur to the substantive theory we are using to guide our item writing. What does it tell us about the number of *meaningful ordered* steps between failure and success? Those who start with an explicit theoretical orientation will decide the number of steps on the basis of the guiding theory. For those with a more pragmatic bent, it will be necessary to develop an 'ordered part marks' schedule based on conceptual analysis or reflection on observations of candidates' performances. In any empirical situation such as a test, a marking key, or an observation schedule, eventually we will be limited to the number of meaningful steps that are useful in discerning the display of the varying ability levels we find in our sample. An extreme case might be the use of **visual analog scales (VAS)** in psychophysical and medical research, such as requiring subjects to indicate along a 10-cm scale just how much pain they feel in arthritic joints. Routinely, the score is read from the scale in millimeters, but there is no empirical evidence that respondents can meaningfully discriminate among the 0–100 mm = 101 response intervals on the scale. Although it is possible to use percentages as raw data, we encounter the same issues in determining how many meaningful distinctions we can make between zero and 100%.

It is the application of the partial credit Rasch model to cognitive developmental data that has paved the way for original conceptions of how fundamental measurement principles might be meaningfully applied in unexpected settings.

Indeed, this chapter is more important than it appears because it exemplifies the nature of the bridge between purely qualitative theory, methods, and ordinal data on the one hand and the construction of interval-level Rasch measures on the other. Perhaps it is timely to remind those outside the field of developmental psychology, that Piaget's epistemological theory was deliberately qualitative and notoriously nonquantitative at a time when the Anglo-American–dominated world of psychology was explicitly and strictly quantitative. A carefully arranged meeting in the United States among Piaget, Inhelder, and American psychologists titled 'Conference on Ordinal Scales of Cognitive Development' was sponsored by the California Test Bureau in 1969. The published book of the proceedings of the symposium 'Piaget and Measurement' (Green, Ford & Flamer, 1971) was reviewed by Wohlwill (1972) with the dismissive title 'And Never the Twain Did Meet'. Have hope; if we have succeeded in 'measuring Piaget' in the face of the received wisdom, then your measurement project might not be as impossible as you are sometimes told.

Let us take a well-known problem from Piaget's work. If you know anything at all about Piaget, then you know about this: 'Conservation of matter' is a flexible 'clinical interview' task often used with, for example, 3- to 7-year-olds and therefore quite unsuitable for a written task format. A child judges two balls of playdough to have the same amount. Then one of them is rolled out into a snake or sausage shape right in front of the child's eyes. The child then is asked to judge again. The question is something like, 'Does the snake have more playdough than the ball; does the ball have more playdough than the snake; or do they have the same amount of playdough?' Anyone who has watched young kids share a cupcake, pour drinks for friends, or gladly swap little coins for bigger ones will know what's coming, whereas most adults do not see what the problem could possibly be. It is only during the grade school years that children develop the understanding that the amount of playdough, amount of juice, or number of sweets will remain **invariant** no matter how the objects are rearranged.

Piaget's approach was to claim that the child who consistently conserves shows qualitatively and structurally superior thinking to the child who does not, backing his claim with detailed logical analyses of the child's inferred thinking patterns. When psychologists first tried to quantify their replications of this qualitative research, they adopted '0 = didn't conserve', '1 = did conserve' as the summary of task performance. Hindsight has shown this to be rather naïve. The extent of the reductionism and trivialization that routinely went on can be imagined: Little Johnny is interviewed for 15 minutes on three conservation tasks (amount of playdough, amount of juice, and number of sweets, each suitably rearranged) and is scored like this: 1, 1, 0 (conserves playdough and juice but misses number). Betty and the psychologist chat and play together for 20 minutes, and her efforts are scored 0, 1, 0; whereas Jane scores 1, 1, 1 after a mere 10 minutes of concentrated effort on her part. After an equally brief encounter, it seems Bill remains enchanted with the magic that makes things more or less, just by moving them around $(0, 0, 0)$. Then those with a strictly quantitative, empiricist bent would compound those errors by adding up the scores for each child: 2 for Johnny, 1 for Betty, and 3 for Jane, whereas Bill scores 0 however you look at it. Often this would be taken even one step further by claiming that 2/3 was enough to describe Johnny and Jane as 'conservers' and Betty and Bill as 'nonconservers'. Consequently, if the purpose of the research was to relate children's cognitive development to their mathematics scores, there was no meaningful result. That is hardly surprising!

Seen through the lens provided by the partial credit Rasch model, the opportunities for serious and sensitive measurement seem to multiply very productively. First, we could see that it would not be necessary to have just 0 and 1 (dichotomous) scoring. We could also have 0, 1, 2, or 0, 1, 2, 3 if we found suitable criteria to score against. Not only could we have 'items' with two or three criteria for scoring (i.e., not the dichotomous model), but we would not be constrained to the same number of steps for each item (i.e., not the rating scale model). Even more, the partial credit model allows us to mix dichotomous and **polytomous** items in the one observation schedule. Moreover, instead of providing a single overall score for each task or complete interview, we could see each task addressing a number of key aspects, each of which could be scored. Thus, the playdough task could be broken down into the following subtasks:

(a) judges initial equivalence: no = 0, yes = 1;
(b) conserves after snake transformation: no = 0, yes = 1;
(c) uses 'longer' for the snake appropriately: never = 0, inconsistently = 1, consistently = 2; and
(d) gives reasons: based on perception = 0, by rolling the snake back into a ball = 1, saying 'You didn't add or take away anything' = 2, claiming 'It's always the same no matter what you do' = 3.

Therefore, for the string of criteria or 'items' a, b, c, d, for just the first qualitative investigation (the playdough task), we could end up with Johnny's scores of 1, 1, 2, 2; Betty's 1, 1, 1, 1; Jane's perfect response string 1, 1, 2, 3; and Bill's 1, 0, 0, 0. It can be seen how we have now discriminated differences between Betty and Bill (both received 0 for playdough with dichotomous scoring) and between Jane and Johnny (both scored 1 in the dichotomous situation). Remember the ordered data matrix from Chapter 2? We can do it again (see Table 7.1).

In Table 7.1, we see the same sort of evidence for developmental sequences that we saw in the sorted dichotomous data in Table 2.2. Being on guard about making unwarranted inferences from the data, we merely observe that we have recorded ordered increases in response levels (i.e., 0 < 1 < 2 < 3, etc., or ordinal data). Further, we refrain from drawing unwarranted equivalences between the

TABLE 7.1 Ordered Data Set for Four
Children on Four Polytomous Items

Criteria	a	b	c	d
Bill	1	0	0	0
Betty	1	1	1	1
Johnny	1	1	2	2
Jane	1	1	2	3

values of 1 for Items a and b, between the scores of 2 for Items c and d, and so
forth. All we are entitled to say from these ordered data categorizations is that for
Item a, $0 < 1$, and for Item b, $0 < 1$. We may not claim that 1 (on a) = 1 (on b), or
that 2 (on c) = 2 (on d). We use Rasch modeling to estimate those relations, the
intervals between those ordered values, during the analysis process.

The data used to demonstrate the use of the partial credit Rasch model in
this chapter have been chosen for a number of important reasons. We could have
chosen a routinely used written mathematics or science achievement test, an essay
scoring guide, or a medical rehabilitation example, as long as it offered the possibility of grading responses as partly correct. Many scoring situations would suffice,
as long as the grading principle represented by the following responses is implemented: 'wrong—partly correct—right' or 'fail—some progress toward mastery—
more complete response—mastery'. However, with the current example, we can
learn something about the partial credit model while we open our eyes to the
range of possibilities for quantifying what traditionally has been seen as qualitative
data in the human sciences.

If we return to the response probability curve that we introduced in Figures 3.2 and 4.4 (for dichotomous items), then the expectations for the responses
to the question about 'judging initial equivalence' would take the same form, all
children would have a better than 50% probability of scoring 1 (= yes). We need
to modify our graph a little if we want to model the curves for a polytomous
response opportunity (e.g., 0, 1, 2 for uses the term 'longer' for the snake appropriately). Figure 7.1 shows those relationships.

Low-ability students (such as Bill) are more likely (i.e., probability exceeds
50%) to score 0 when scored on this question. High-ability students (e.g., Johnny
and Jane) have a greater than 50% likelihood of scoring the highest score for this
item (uses 'longer' consistently = 2). Betty's ability level predicts, however, that she
is more likely to score 1 (rather than 0 or 2).

To model the curves for a polytomously scored item that has four response
opportunities (e.g., gives reasons: 0, 1, 2, 3) a third threshold-based, adjacent-level
dichotomous curve must be added to the figure. Figure 7.2 shows those relationships with the most probable responses to that item reflecting the scores shown
in Table 7.1.

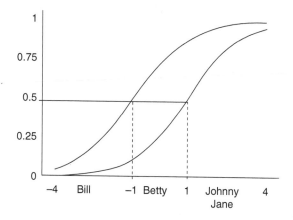

FIGURE 7.1 Response probabilities for three response-opportunity polytomous Item (c) Uses 'longer' for the snake appropriately.

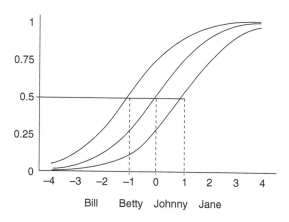

FIGURE 7.2. Response probabilities for four response-opportunity polytomous Item (d) Gives reasons.

Shayer, Küchemann, and Wylam (1976), from the University of London, had a number of reasons for developing the Piagetian Reasoning Task (PRTIII-Pendulum) for classroom use. The PRTIII-Pendulum we used in Chapter 5 was one of the demonstrated class tasks they developed to replace administration using the traditional Piagetian one-on-one clinical interview technique. The U.K. researchers wanted data collection devices that could be administered to whole classes at a time, whereas Piaget's technique was a one-on-one interview. They wanted tasks that could be used by interested school science teachers, whereas Piaget claimed that his interviewers needed one year of daily practice to become competent. They wanted tasks that could yield quantifiable data, whereas Piaget's work was notorious for its uncompromisingly qualitative approach. Well, the Rasch model cannot change the Piagetian requirements for superior interview skills or make it possible to interview 30 schoolchildren simultaneously, but it can make wonderfully quantitative what is regarded traditionally as qualitative data, while still retaining all the rich qualitative meanings. Rasch methodology can be used to construct interval-scale measures on which a whole range of the usual statistical techniques can be meaningfully employed. Indeed, the following piece of research, first reported in Bond and Bunting (1995), was inspired exactly by the existence of the partial credit Rasch model (Stafford, 2005).

Clinical Interview Analysis: A Rasch-Inspired Breakthrough

Bond and Bunting (1995) reported in much more detail than necessary here the direct replication of the pendulum task using the Genevan interview technique as reported in chapter 4 of *The Growth of Logical Thinking From Childhood to Adolescence* (Inhelder & Piaget, 1955/1958). The child is presented with a pendulum apparatus consisting of an adjustable string suspended from a fixed point and a series of weights: 40 g, 80 g, 100 g. When given a demonstration of the apparatus and provoked by an initial question such as, 'Can you show me what causes the pendulum to swing more or fewer times in some short time interval?' the child is encouraged to experiment with the apparatus to determine which of the variables (weight, length, push, angle) affects the period of oscillation. The child is asked to 'think out loud', and the interviewer asks prompting questions, seeks clarification, and challenges the child's conclusions as seems appropriate. No, this is not your usual standard test or even structured interview![1]

What was original with Bond and Bunting (1995) in this work was the detailed scoring table (Table 7.2) developed exactly from chapter 4 of Inhelder and Piaget (1955/1958). These performance criteria are far more comprehensive than any developed before, including those of Bond (1976/1995), Shayer and colleagues (1976), and others, resulting directly from a detailed rereading of the key Piagetian theoretical chapter with the possibilities opened up by partial credit Rasch modeling as the key stimulus. This probably sounds as though an excess of missionary zeal is sneaking in here, but the important claim is that when we see the old world of data through new eyes (in this case, Rasch modeling), completely new possibilities open up. We might have made a similar claim in the previous chapter for developing measures via the rating scale model, but the claim would not have been original. Many already have developed scores for Likert-type surveys, even if they have made the 'measurement' claim erroneously. Although the vast majority of standardized psychological and educational testing falls into the dichotomous tradition (of, say, IQ scores) or Likert scales (personality assessment; Michell, 1986), the PCM allows for meaningful quantification in a virtually untouched category of human sciences research, in which the data are neither dichotomous nor do they have some fixed number of response categories across items.

Therefore, when seen through the eyes of the PCM and not from the usual dichotomous/Likert viewpoint, the distinctive feature of the 15 investigative tasks

TABLE 7.2 Ordered Performance Criteria for 18 Aspects of the Pendulum Interview Task

	IIA Early Concrete	IIB Mature Concrete	IIIA Early Formal	IIIB Mature Formal
1	1.1 Able to accurately serially order lengths			
2	2.0 Unable to accurately serially order weights	2.1 Able to accurately serially order weights		
3	3.1 Able to accurately serially order push			
4	4.1 Establishes inverse relation between length and frequency of oscillation			
5	5.0 Unable to manipulate some variables	5.1 Able to vary all factors		
6	6.0 Does not make inferences. Limited to observations	6.1 Makes inferences based only on observed concrete correspondence	6.2 Makes inferences going beyond observations without needing to test all possibilities	
7		7.0 To test for length, manipulates incorrect variable and in an unsystematic manner	7.1 Manipulates incorrect variable, but makes logical deductions by inference to results on earlier experiments	7.2 Systematically manipulates lengths to test for their effects
8		8.0 Manipulates incorrect variable and is unsystematic in testing for weight	8.1 Manipulates incorrect variable, but makes logical deductions by inference to results on earlier experiments	8.2 Systematically manipulates weights to test for their effects
9		9.0 Manipulates incorrect variable and is unsystematic in test for push	9.1 Manipulates incorrect variable but makes logical deductions by inference to results on earlier experiments	9.2 Systematically manipulates impetus to test for the effect of push

(Continued)

TABLE 7.2 (Continued)

	IIA Early Concrete	IIB Mature Concrete	IIIA Early Formal	IIIB Mature Formal
10	10.0 Makes illogical deductions about the role of length (including illogical exclusion of length in favor of weight or impetus)	10.1 Excludes the effect of length (because of inaccurate observations)	10.2 Logically deduces positive relationship of affirmation or implication for the role of length	10.3 Deduces equivalence of length and frequency of oscillation
11		11.1 Makes illogical deductions about the role of weight (either illogical exclusion or positive implications)	11.2 Logically deduces a positive relationship of affirmation or implication for weight based on inaccurate observations	11.3 Excludes the role of weight
12	12.0 Preoccupied with the role of impetus as the cause of variations in the frequency of oscillation. Illogical deduction of positive implication.	12.1 Testing results in the illogical exclusion of the role of push	12.2 Logically deduces a positive relationship of affirmation or implication for push, based on inaccurate observations	12.3 Excludes the role of push
13		13.0 Does not produce combinations of length with other variables	13.1 Produces combinations of different lengths with different weights or pushes to test for effects	13.2 Produces sets of combinations of lengths with various weights and pushes to test for their effects

14

14.0 Does not produce combinations of weights with other variables

14.1 Produces combinations of different weights with different lengths to test for their effects

14.2 Produces combinations of different weights with different pushes to test for the effects

14.3 Produces combinations weights with various lengths and pushes to test for their effects

15

15.0 Does not produce combinations of push with other variables

15.1 Produces combinations of different pushes with various lengths to test for their effects

15.2 Produces combinations of different pushes with different weights to test for their effects

15.3 Produces combinations of various pushes with lengths and weights to test for their effects

16

16.0 Unsystematic method

16.1 Systematically produces all combinations, using the method of varying a single factor, while holding all else constant

17

17.0 Unable to exclude the effect of weight

17.1 Logically excludes the effect of weight

18

18.0 Unable to exclude the effect of push

18.1 Logically excludes the effect of push

in Inhelder and Piaget (1955/1958) is the careful construction of problems that are relevant and interesting to a wide sample of children. Each can engage children aged from about 5 years to 18 years. Because the focus of the work was to monitor the progress from the logical thinking of childhood to that of adolescence, children's responses to these tasks are not classified as merely right or wrong. Children's solutions are, almost invariably, partially correct, and that whole domain of partially correct answers, whether it is in mathematics problem solving, essay writing, or medical rehabilitation, is the focus of the PCM.

Scoring Interview Transcripts

Table 7.2 is a scoring guide that illustrates some important key features for those wishing to implement PCM in new testing situations. Across the top of the table, we can see the increasingly complex substages of thinking displayed: IIA (early concrete operational thought), IIB (mature concrete thought), IIIA (early formal operational thought), and, finally, IIIB (mature formal thought). The *invariant* order of stages is a critically distinctive feature of Piaget's work, just as order is the key requirement of Rasch measurement. Down the table, we have the 18 different aspects of solving the pendulum problem that Bunting found identified in the focus Piagetian chapter. It is clear that lower-level aspects of the problem (e.g., aspects 1, 3, and 4) would be scored dichotomously: 1 for meeting the performance criterion and 0 for failing to meet it. Similarly, aspects 7, 8, and 9 have three identifiable ordered levels of performance each and will yield ordered polytomous data: Criteria 7.0, 8.0, and 9.0 indicate the lowest observable levels of performance on these aspects and should be scored 0. Criteria 7.2, 8.2, and 9.2 indicate complete success on those aspects of the problem and will be scored 2. Because 7.1, 8.1, and 9.1 show partial success, each will attract the score of 1, somewhere on the ordered pathway between complete failure (0) and complete success (2).

Aspects 10 and 12 then have four ordered performance category levels and will be scored 0, 1, 2, and 3. Yet there is more: Although 16, 17, and 18 are to be scored dichotomously, successful performance on these aspects is supposed to reflect the highest level of mature thinking available to adolescents and adults. Clearly, the score of 1 here is meant to be of much greater importance than the 1 scored for successful performances on aspects 1.1, 2.1, 3.1, and 4.1. The much-lauded and much-criticized flexibility in the clinical administration of the task is not a problem for Rasch modeling. Any aspects of the problem that are not actually encountered during the interview (omitted inadvertently or deliberately) are regarded as '**missing data**', and the data file has blanks recorded at those points. (The Rasch family of models can make do with less-than-complete data sets for either items or persons. It can provide estimates of ability and difficulty based on the available data. Of course, measurement precision and the ability to detect idiosyncratic developmental patterns declines as available information decreases.)

As a procedural point, all of the interviews ($n = 58$) of the high school students were conducted by Bunting, video-recorded, and transcribed. A matrix based on Table 7.2 was used for the numerical coding of each child's performances, and the data string for each child recorded the score on each aspect of the problem (18 data points for each child), in which higher scores indicate more advanced performances. For example, the scores in column 14 (of the sample response strings that follow) indicate that Student 21 satisfied Criterion 14.1 from Table 7.2, whereas Student 65 performed to the requirements in criterion 14.3.

111111000212010000 Student 21 (least successful person)
111112212323132111 Student 65 (most successful person)

Ordered Performance Criteria for 18 Aspects of the Pendulum Interview Task

To perform a PCM analysis on the data file generated from this investigation, we need to indicate the following to the Rasch analysis software: The number of 'items' and their location in the data file. In this case there are 18 items in columns 1 to 18. What are the valid codes in the file? Codes 0, 1, 2, 3 cover all the response possibilities here. We took the care always to use 0 as the code for the lowest possible observable response category for each item. The estimation procedure should use the PCM. For some software, this is the default estimation procedure for polytomous data. In Winsteps, the default 'Groups = 0' runs the PCM: this ungroups the items, thus allowing each to have its own response structure.

Partial Credit Model Results

Figure 7.3 displays the item estimates and fit statistics from the partial credit analysis of the *méthode clinique* interview data from the pendulum problem, using the pathway principles adopted earlier in this text. Figure 7.3 combines features of the displays from the dichotomous data analyses in Chapters 4 and 5 and some features from the rating scale analysis of polytomous data in Chapter 6.

First, the result of a hypothesis test of the fit of the items ($-2 <$ infit Zstd $< +2$) is displayed using the parallel dotted lines. In this case, all the 18 items fit the Rasch model sufficiently, according to just this single criterion—not surprising since $N = 58$ is statistically small. They are all located between those lines. For each of those items that were scored dichotomously (2, 3, 4, 5, 16, 17, and 18), one item difficulty estimate per item is plotted, indicating the threshold at which the probability of scoring 0 or 1 is 50%. For those items that are scored polytomously (0, 1, 2 or 0, 1, 2, 3), either two or three difficulty thresholds are plotted. Three response categories (0, 1, 2 for Item 7) are separated by two thresholds

Pendulum Interview Criteria

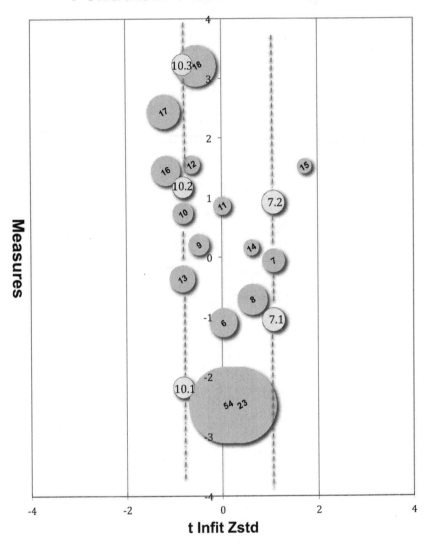

FIGURE 7.3 Pathway for Pendulum interview items.

(e.g., Estimate 7.1 separates the likelihood of scoring 0 on Aspect 7 from the likelihood of scoring 1 on Aspect 7; Estimate 7.2 separates the most probable response zones for scores of 1 and 2 on Aspect 7), whereas four response categories (0, 1, 2, 3) are separated by three threshold estimates (e.g., Aspect 10: four response categories with three estimates). Therefore, the item map in Figure 7.3 will show a number of item estimate formats:

		More likely to score 3 than below 3
		Threshold estimate 10.3
	More likely to score 2 than below 2	More likely to score 2 than below 2
	Threshold estimate 7.2	*Threshold estimate 10.2*
More likely to score 1 than zero.	More likely to score 1 than zero.	More likely to score 1 than zero.
Estimate threshold for 1	*Threshold estimate 7.1*	*Threshold estimate 10.1*
More likely to score 0	More likely to score 0	More likely to score 0
Item 2	**Item 7**	**Item 10**

The format shown depends on the number of threshold estimates needed to separate the response categories in Table 7.2. Winsteps PCM allows 254 ordered categories for each item (including 0–100, so even raw percentages can be used as data). But whether any particular testing situation can make practical and meaningful use of 10 or more response categories is an empirical question discussed in Chapter 11.

As we would expect from a task designed to elicit partially correct responses from a broad band of respondents, say, 5- to 18-year-olds, the pendulum task items cover a difficulty span of nearly 6 logits from the least difficult (6.1 at −2.58 logits) to that with the criterion most difficult to satisfy (a score of 1 on Item 18 at +3.21 logits). Given that this groundbreaking research was conducted by one undergraduate student in a very short time and that each individual interview takes a considerable time to plan, implement, transcribe, and score, a rather small sample size of 58 students was used. As a result, the error estimates for the items and thresholds remain quite large in some instances. Two influences that were mentioned before have an effect on the size of error estimates. All other things being equal (and they never are), imprecision for items will increase when items are off target for the sample and when the sample is small. But SEs for persons will be smaller when 18 polytomous items (rather than 18 dichotomous items) comprise a test. In general, more response categories provide more statistical information, which yields higher precision of the estimates for item difficulty and person ability. Precision of a threshold estimate depends most directly on the frequencies of each of the adjacent categories. Mike Linacre's rule of thumb: at least 10 observations of each category of each item for the Rasch PCM. Take a moment to look at the item error estimates in Table 7.3 and identify the more imprecise item difficulty locations (yes, they have the larger error indicators in Fig. 7.3). Then take a look at the complete item–person map in Figure 7.4 to see which of the preceding influences have contributed to the large error estimates you have identified.

TABLE 7.3 Item Estimates for Pendulum Interview Task

Item	Estimate	Error	Infit		Outfit		PtMeas Corr'n
			Zstd	MnSq	Zstd	MnSq	
1	Perfect	Score					
2	−2.48	.71	1.10	.4	1.16	.5	.05
3	−2.48	.71	1.10	.4	1.16	.5	.05
4	−2.48	.71	.96	.2	.37	−.6	.29
5	−2.48	.71	.91	.1	.30	−.7	.33
6	−1.10	.27	.99	.0	.94	−.2	.40
6.1	−2.58						
6.2	.38						
7	−.06	.22	1.19	1.1	1.14	.7	.33
7.1	−1.05						
7.2	.92						
8	−.71	.29	1.23	.6	9.90	3.4	.17
8.1	−.71						
8.2	−.71						
9	.21	.20	.91	−.5	.90	−.3	.52
9.1	−.30						
9.2	.72						
10	.74	.20	.85	−.8	.86	−.8	.60
10.1	−2.18						
10.2	1.17						
10.3	3.23						
11	.86	.17	.99	.0	1.05	.3	.50
11.1	−1.32						
11.2	1.72						
11.3	2.22						
12	1.55	.17	.88	−.6	.89	−.6	.62
12.1	−.09						
12.2	1.78						
12.3	2.97						
13	−.36	.25	.87	−.8	.84	−.9	.54
13.1	−2.22						
13.2	1.49						
14	.16	.15	1.09	.6	1.18	.5	.54
14.1	−1.73						
14.2	1.11						
14.3	1.16						
15	1.52	.14	1.31	1.7	1.50	1.6	.49
15.1	1.01						
15.2	1.23						
15.3	2.20						
16	1.45	.28	.89	−1.2	.86	−.8	.49
17	2.44	.32	.80	−1.2	.66	−1.3	.56
18	3.21	.39	.84	−.5	.60	−.9	.50

PCM Rasch-Thurstone Thresholds are shown as x.1, x.2, x.3

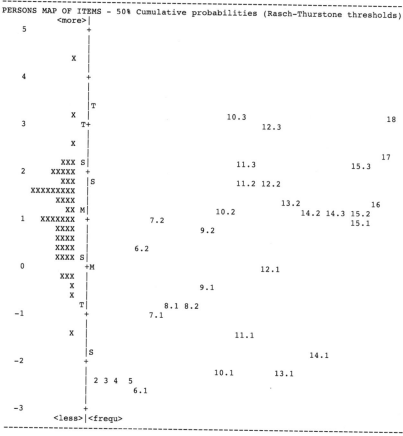

```
WINSTEPS TABLE 12.6 Bond & Fox PCM Analysis of Piagetian Interview
INPUT: 58 PERSONS 18 ITEMS  MEASURED: 58 PERSONS  17 ITEMS  49 CATS
------------------------------------------------------------------------
PERSONS MAP OF ITEMS - 50% Cumulative probabilities (Rasch-Thurstone thresholds)
           <more>|
    5           +
                |
                |
           X    |
                |
    4           +
                |
                |
                |T
           X    |                    10.3                              18
    3         T+                          12.3
                |
           X    |
                |                                                       17
         XXX  S |                    11.3                    15.3
    2    XXXXX  +
           XXX  |S                   11.2 12.2
        XXXXXXXXX|
          XXXX  |
            XX  M|                         10.2            13.2            16
    1    XXXXXXX +        7.2                       14.2 14.3 15.2
          XXXX  |              9.2                             15.1
          XXXX  |
          XXXX  |    6.2
          XXXX  S|
    0           +M                            12.1
           XXX  |
            X   |              9.1
            X   |
              T |         8.1 8.2
   -1           +         7.1
                |
            X   |                    11.1
                |S                                   14.1
   -2           +
                |                    10.1          13.1
                |  2 3 4 5
                |      6.1
   -3           +
           <less>|<frequ>
------------------------------------------------------------------------
```

FIGURE 7.4 Item–person map for Pendulum interview.

Interpretation

What guidelines do these considerations provide for sample selection for further research using the pendulum task in this Piagetian clinical interview format? First, we need to give the task to a larger sample, but what sort of larger sample? We can look at the distribution of the persons in the Wright map in Figure 7.4: most clustered between 0 and +2 logits and very few outside that. When we see, as well, that the items at the extremes of the difficulty range are dichotomous items but that they have error estimates about the same size as those for polytomous Items 10, 11, 12, and 13, we should conclude that the next sample should include both more-able persons on the pendulum task to make estimates for 16, 17, and 18 more precise, as well as less-able persons to enhance the precision of Items

1, 2, 3, 4, and 5. This is in keeping with what we already know: Inhelder and Piaget (1955/1958) designed this task for use with a broad age range (say, 5–18 years), whereas the breadth of the sample for this study was restricted deliberately to 12- to 15-year-olds for two important reasons. First, it was the transition from concrete to formal thought that Bunting was investigating, not early concrete or mature formal thinking. Second, the investigation sought to avoid compounding the measurement of cognitive development with other age-related variables such as amount of education or exposure to formal science instruction. An increase in sample size would implicate both of these variables, as well as the possibility, indeed likelihood, that the team of interviewers/scorers necessary to administer the task to a larger sample would not do their work with the consistency that the investigator aimed to achieve with $n = 58$. The many-facets Rasch model that we introduce in Chapter 8 addresses the issues of rater behavior and has the promise of modeling the effects of such influences.

But this raises an important issue for those wanting to Rasch-calibrate their research instruments. Drawing a sample at convenience or randomly from a target population will likely produce a distribution of person abilities that, as we see in Bunting's case, looks roughly normal. To get measures for each of the items that are equally precise (small enough SEs), we need to search out those with much more and much less of the underlying ability targeted by our instrument. In essence, our desired distribution will look more rectangular (i.e., uniform) than normal. We should ensure that the person distribution should extend beyond the range of the items and that persons should be equally dispersed across that range. This would result in imprecise measurement of persons at the extremes—but not to the point of being misleading. We would still have no doubt that the high performers are high performers and the low performers are low performers, but we are focusing on the calibration of the instrument here. Conversely, when we seek more precise measures of our persons, the items should extend beyond the range of person abilities and be equally dispersed along that range. But remember that each polytomous item has a much wider operational range than does a dichotomous item; often a rating scale for even one item has an operational range wider than the whole person sample. And there is always the *caveat* that more well-targeted items produce more precise person measures and that more well-targeted persons will improve the precision of item measures.

The Theory–Practice Dialogue

First, we also must acknowledge that empirical results such as these, derived from small and restricted samples, hardly can do more than point the way to the undoubted promise of larger-scale investigations, although there are some hints in these results that show the possibility for theory–practice dialogue. We are reminded that Piaget was notorious for using what were regarded as small samples. For well-conducted research with small samples, we expect larger samples merely to tweak our findings. In this case, the data from the pendulum task, at its first iteration, demonstrate sufficient adherence to the Rasch measurement specifications to be regarded as producing measures of cognitive development. These results are not bad for an explicitly qualitative approach that has faded from favor, in part, for not yielding suitably quantifiable results using traditional statistical approaches. Those who are interested can refer to the research report (Bond & Bunting, 1995) to see the correspondences, and lack of them, between interpretations derived from Piaget's theory and the empirical results. Unless these findings are refuted by further research, only some fine-tuning of the underlying Piagetian theory or its interpretation is required. Although that report recommended that future replications of the task include the provision of a suitable timing device for accurately assessing the pendulum's swing, this conclusion was derived from the opportunity that the interviewer had to pursue children's responses actively in the interview situation, not as a result of the Rasch analysis. We are not suggesting that Rasch modeling is the universal panacea for measurement in the human sciences. Nothing replaces thoughtful theory-driven research, and Rasch measurement is a highly effective tool that belongs in every social scientist's toolbox.

Unidimensionality

The use of Rasch modeling in the Bond and Bunting (1995) research showed the value that the concept of order has within a framework of unidimensionality. Interpretations of item and item step order as well as person order are clearly central in developmental and educational research, with clear implications for measuring physical skill acquisition and medical rehabilitation as well. Hand in hand with a clear concept of the variable under examination is the Rasch concept of **unidimensionality**, that is, do all the items relate to the same latent variable, and do they all point in the same direction along it? Although often taken for granted in the quantitative analysis of human sciences data, the point is an important one in the construction, meaning and the application of Rasch measurement, especially in novel settings where the exact nature of the latent variable is still being discovered.

In an address to the Rasch Special Interest Group (SIG) at the American Educational Research Association (AERA), Keeves (1997) reminded the audience of the primary role of unidimensionality in the longitudinal testing of educational achievement such as the international studies regularly being conducted by the International Association for the Evaluation of Educational Achievement (IEA). For the sort of scaling and equating required for these efforts, he indicated:

> Fulfillment of the requirement of unidimensionality is a matter of degree not just a matter of kind as Bejar (1983, p. 31) has pointed out:
>
>> Unidimensionality does not imply that performance on items is due to a single psychological process. In fact, a variety of psychological processes are involved in responding to a set of test items. However, as long as they function in unison—that is, performance on each item is

affected by the same process and in the same form—unidimensionality will hold.

Thus a science test can involve physics, chemistry, or biology content and test different skills, knowledge, understanding, application and analysis (to use the terms of the Bloom taxonomy, in the tradition of the University of Chicago) provided the processes involved operate in concord, the requirement for unidimensionality will be satisfied. This demands empirical testing as well as logical analysis.

(Keeves, 1997, p. 4)

In Keeves's example, the unidimensional latent variable is 'science'. However, for many subject teachers, there will be three distinct unidimensional latent variables: 'physics', 'chemistry', and 'biology'. Whenever we look closely at any latent variable, we discover that it contains subordinate latent variables. We must choose the level of aggregation that corresponds to our purposes and ask, 'Is there a coherent unidimensional latent variable at that level?'

This provides an interesting context for the interpretation of Rasch modeling results in terms of the theory–practice dialogue. If our aim is to put into systematic practice a particular conception of one psychological, educational, or health-related quality of life construct at a time, our success at that is represented empirically by the development of a unidimensional test. The unsuccessful aspects of that attempt, especially in terms of inadequate item fit or item disorder (i.e., lack of construct validity), require us to revisit our theory-driven intentions. Perhaps it is not the theory that fails the test but our efforts to operationalize the theory into practice via a test, an observation schedule. Perhaps it is the marking scheme that falls short. Items should be included in tests because very good reasons exist for having them there. Test developers should be committed to the items they develop: Item misfit then signals to the investigator, 'Think again!'—not the usual—'Throw it out!' We will be no further advanced in our attempts at measurement if we include items in our trial on some semblance of face validity and then just dispose of them on a whim when they misfit our measurement model.

When both our theoretical considerations and our empirical evidence suggest to us that our efforts to develop a test of some underlying latent trait have been successful, then evidence of misordered items or persons suggests that refinement of our ideas is necessary. As a principle that can be applied more generally in test development and use, however, we have indicators of both unidimensionality and order that beg for interpretation in the context of the theory that generated the test and the practical situation that produced the results.

Summary

The Partial Credit Model allows for the number and calibrations of response thresholds to vary across items (*cf.* RSM).

PCM response categories must be ordered. Higher scores indicate partial successes that are closer to total success on an item. (*n.b.* They are partial marks, not part marks.)

Application of the PCM offers potential for bridging the qualitative/quantitative divide that permeates much human science research.

Substantive (content) theory and Rasch (measurement) theory work hand in hand for the construction of response category descriptions, ordering, interpretation, and test refinement.

If this is your introduction to Rasch measurement, we would advise you to complete the activities that follow and then continue with Chapter 8 and to return here after you have finished all chapters. If you already have a sound grasp of Rasch measurement principles, we invite you to go further.

Bond&FoxSteps

The complete data file, control lines, and tutorial for this analysis are preloaded into the Bond&FoxSteps software that is available on the book website.

ACTIVITIES

1. Go to your copy of the Bond&FoxSteps Rasch software and select the tutorial for Chapter 7. Run the analysis on the preloaded data file and interpret the output according to the instructions in the tutorial pdf.
2. Restart Bond&FoxSteps. Copy and paste the data only from the Bond-FoxChapter7.txt file into the interactive window and use the buttons to reconstruct the analysis that was run automatically by the preinstalled file.
3. Go to the source document (Bond & Bunting, 1995) and read directly the theory–practice dialogue for using Rasch analysis for this investigation.

Extended Understanding—Chapter 7

Category Functioning

We have a rather simple way of checking whether the categories used in this Partial Credit Model analysis actually function in the way that we expected. In Extended Understanding in Chapter 6, we introduced the Category Characteristic Curves (CCCs) to examine the functioning of the response options for the CEAQ. In Figure 7.5, the CCCs for two well-functioning aspects of the Interview are shown. Note that only one set of category curves is required for the RSM but that each PCM item will have its own unique category structure.

The criteria for scoring Item 7 focus on the child's ability to test for the effects of length while experimenting with the pendulum apparatus. The criteria for the

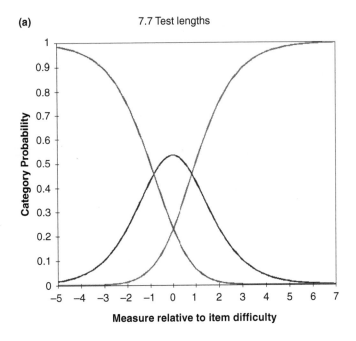

(a)

7.7 Test lengths

Category Probability

Measure relative to item difficulty

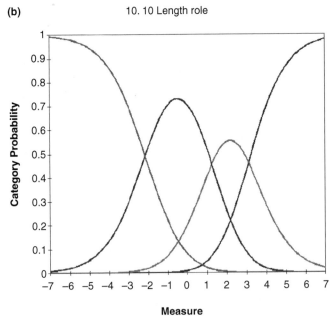

(b)

10. 10 Length role

Category Probability

Measure

FIGURE 7.5 Category Characteristic Curves for well-functioning (3-category) Item 7 and (4-category) Item 10.

ordered performance categories for Item 7 from the scoring rubric in Table 7.2 progress from 7.0, 'for length, manipulates incorrect variable . . .' through 7.1, 'makes logical deductions about length by inference . . .' to 7.2. 'Systematically manipulates lengths to test for their effects'. Figure 7.5a reveals that each of those *three* categories is actually observed in the collected data and that each, in turn, becomes the most likely observed category as the person measure increases along the underlying latent trait (from L to R). Figure 7.5b shows that the *four* ordered categories for Item 10, in which the children investigate and draw conclusions about the length of the string and the period of the pendulum, function just as well.

The points at which the curves intersect will correspond to the Rasch-Thurstone thresholds shown for 7.1 and 7.2 and for 10.1, 10.2, and 10.3, in Table 7.3. The item and threshold estimates for Item 8, however, suggest that neither the three categories nor the CCCs are functioning as theorized for that item. (Winsteps Table 14.3 counts 4 children's performances classified at level 8.0 and the remaining 54 at level 8.2; for this sample of children, none were identified as inferring the correct conclusions about the role of weight in spite of manipulating the wrong variable.) The Item 8 criteria performed dichotomously, in spite of the theory-based expectation that all three could be observed.

Rasch measurement theory can be quite readily applied to the concept of ordered categories as was shown with the RSM (Chapter 6). The principle can be stated quite simply: For ordered categories, the higher category should have the higher average measure of persons responding in that category. The statistic (AVERAGE MEASURE in the extract from Winsteps Table 14.3) is the average Rasch measure of the persons responding in each category. So the ordering of the categories from lowest to highest should be matched by the ordering of the average of the person measures for those categories, for example, categories: 7.0, 7.1, 7.2, and average measures: 0.18, 1.09, and 1.38. This tells us directly and immediately that the theory-based category ordering for Item 6 from the Inhelder and Piaget text works empirically with a sample of children more than half a century and half a world away. Item 10 categories work just as well. Although average person measures for Item 8 work well, only two, not three categories were actually observed. For Item 15, some misordering was observed: The average measure (2.11) for the five children's performances rated in category 1 is the highest for all four categories. Checking back to Table 7.2, we find that the performance criteria for Items 14 and 15 are different from the rest: each has *two* alternative—not ordered—criteria at the IIIA-Early Formal stage. Clearly, the data for scores of 2 and 3 should be collapsed for Items 14 and 15. But one alarm bell is ringing—many categories have low (or even zero) counts. It would be more convincing if we could draw our conclusions from a larger sample—a minimum count of, say, 10 per category, would be better for resolving the potential theory/practice dissonances.

Part of the quest for unidimensionality involves the empirical evidence revealed in the Rasch analysis of the test data. Remember Keeves: 'This demands empirical testing as well as logical analysis'. So what empirical evidence might we consider? Four aspects of evidence are worthy of consideration.

ENTRY NUMBER	DATA CODE	SCORE VALUE		DATA COUNT	%		AVERAGE MEASURE
7	0	0		5	9		.18
	1	1		21	36		1.09
	2	2		32	55		1.38
8	0	0		4	7		.57
	2	2		54	93		1.22
10	0	0		2	3		.21
	1	1		27	47		.75
	2	2		23	40		1.36
	3	3		6	10		2.64
15	0	0		26	45		.57
	1	1		5	9		2.11
	2	2		15	26		1.51
	3	3		12	21		1.67

Point–Measure Correlations

The column 'PtMeas Corr'n' in Table 7.3 shows most of the Pendulum Interview items as having values between $c.$ +0.3 and $c.$ +0.6. First: all correlations should be positive, and, second: they should not be near zero. The r_{pm} is computed in the same way as the traditional point biserial correlation from statistics, except that Rasch *measures* replace total scores. The near-zero (but positive) values for Items 2, 3, and 8 might be cause for some concern. However, since the point–measure correlations for extreme items are expected to be near zero, the observed values of the correlations must be compared with their expected values before thinking of rejecting the items. In practice, problems with point–measure correlations will also appear in the category average measures.

Fit Statistics

The Rasch model is a mathematically expressed, theoretical ideal, just like Pythagoras's Theorem, so no real data will ever fit the Rasch model. Fit statistics are part of the quality control mechanisms used to judge whether the misfit of the data to the model undermines the suitability of the data collection device (in this case, an interview and performance criteria) as a measure of the underlying latent trait. If you check the Zstd and MnSq statistics in both the Infit and Outfit columns of Table 7.3, very little is worth noting except for the extreme Outfit statistics for Item 8 (again).

Dimensionality: Primary Components Factor Analysis of the Rasch Residuals

The item and person Rasch measures and the category structures from this PCM analysis explain a very substantial 85.9% of the total variance in the data set. If the data fitted the model perfectly, 91.2% would have been explained. The unexplained variance in the data is 14.1%. This includes the Rasch-predicted randomness in the data, as well as any departures in the data from the Rasch measurement criteria. Those departures are the evidence for multidimensionality. Remember that prior to the calculation of the contrasts, the Rasch dimension has been extracted from the data. Residuals are those parts of the observations not explained by the Rasch dimension. According to Rasch specifications, these should be random and show no structure. The variance explained is dominated by the variance of the persons and the items. The important aspect is how much variance (the eigenvalue) is in the first contrast. Here it is 3.7 of 17 (item) units. This indicates a secondary subdimension/strand/component/artifact among the items with the strength of about four items. Then, we would need to look at the items loading at opposite ends of this contrast (the top and bottom of the plot in Winsteps Table 23.1) to infer the *substantive definition* of the contrast. We would then look at the disattenuated correlations between the person measures loading on the different item clusters (Winsteps Table 23.0) to see if the contrast is a reflection of statistically different person estimates produced by those subsets of items.

TABLE 7.4 Standardized Residual Variance for Pendulum Interview Task

Table of STANDARDIZED RESIDUAL variance (in Eigenvalue units)		Empirical			Modeled
Total variance in observations	=	121.0	100.0%		100.0%
Variance explained by measures	=	104.0	85.9%		91.2%
Unexplained variance (total)	=	17.0	14.1%	100.0%	8.8%
Unexplned variance in 1st contrast	=	3.7	3.0%	21.5%	
Unexplned variance in 2nd contrast	=	2.2	1.8%	13.0%	
Unexplned variance in 3rd contrast	=	1.7	1.4%	9.8%	
Unexplned variance in 4th contrast	=	1.5	1.2%	8.8%	
Unexplned variance in 5th contrast	=	1.3	1.1%	7.9%	

Summary

Category Characteristic Curves provide a rather simple way of checking whether the categories used in any Partial Credit Model analysis actually function as expected.

A simple Rasch measurement principle for ordered categories requires that the higher category should have the higher average measure of persons responding in that category.

Then, the ordering of response categories from lowest to highest should be matched by the ordering of the average of the person measures for those categories.

Safer conclusions can be drawn from larger samples; adopting a minimum count of, say, 10 per category would be better for resolving response category issues.

The evidence from point–measure correlations, fit statistics, and the PCA of Rasch residuals should be considered together to illuminate the theory–practice nexus.

ACTIVITIES (Extended Understanding)

Run the Chapter 7 data again in Bond&FoxSteps. This time, rescore the responses in categories for Items 14 and 15 from 0123 to 0112, so that the scores of 1 and 2 are combined.

Use:
```
NEWSCORE=0112; collapses 2nd and 3rd categories
RESCORE=000000000000011000; rescore Items 14 and 15
```

Consult Bond&FoxSteps Table 23 to look at the Standardized Residual Variance for Pendulum Interview Task. Check the contrasts for competing dimensions. The last table of that output (23.99) suggests possible local item dependencies (which correspond quite well with item contents). What is the balance of evidence for unidimensionality over multidimensionality?

Use Winsteps or Ministeps and select the preloaded data file for Chapter 7. Run the analysis and examine the output in terms of the Extended Understanding discussion from earlier.

1. Look at the CCCs in terms of the category functioning. Which polytomous items are/not functioning as intended? Why? How could that be remedied?
2. Access Table 14.3 to inspect the statistics that summarize the category functioning. What evidence do you find for well-performing and poorly performing categories? Be sure to note the category counts, especially where categories do not function as intended.

Note

1   The standard view of the Piagetian method can be summarized adequately by Wallace (1965): "Results obtained by such a flexible procedure as the méthode clinique do not lend themselves to statistical treatment" (p. 58). Indeed, even Piaget himself subscribed to that view. As a consequence, standardized individual interview procedures were developed, class tasks such as Shayer's (Shayer, Küchemann, & Wylam, 1976) were substituted, or pencil-and-paper tests such as Bond's (1976) were written to provide the sort of data amenable to statistical analyses.

References

Andersen, E.B. (1977). The logistic model for m answer categories. In W. E. Kempf & B. H. Repp (Eds.), *Mathematical models for social psychology* (pp. 59–80). Vienna, Austria: Hans Huber.

Andrich, D. (1978). Rating formulation for ordered response categories. *Psychometrika, 4*, 561–573.

Bejar, I. I. (1983). *Achievement testing: Recent advances.* Beverly Hills, CA: Sage.

Bond, T. G. (1995). *BLOT—Bond's logical operations test.* Townsville, Queensland, Australia: James Cook University. (Original work published 1976)

Bond, T. G., & Bunting, E. M. (1995). Piaget and measurement III: Reassessing the *méthode clinique. Archives de Psychologie, 63*(247), 231–255.

Green, D. R., Ford, M. P., & Flamer, G. B. (Eds.). (1971). *Piaget and measurement.* New York, NY: McGraw Hill.

Inhelder, B., & Piaget, J. (1958). *The growth of logical thinking from childhood to adolescence* (A. Parsons & S. Milgram, Trans.). London: Routledge & Kegan Paul. (Original work published 1955)

Keeves, J. P. (1997, March). *International practice in Rasch measurement, with particular reference to longitudinal research studies.* Invited paper presented at the annual meeting of the Rasch Measurement Special Interest Group, American Educational Research Association, Chicago, IL.

Michell, J. (1986). Measurement scales and statistics: A clash of paradigms. *Psychological Bulletin, 100*(3), 398–407.

Shayer, M., Küchemann, D.E., & Wylam, H. (1976). The distribution of Piagetian stages of thinking in British middle and secondary school children. *British Journal of Educational Psychology, 46*(2), 164–173.

Stafford, E. (2005). What the pendulum can tell educators about children's scientific reasoning. In M. R Matthews, C. F. Gauld, & A. Stinner (Eds.), *The pendulum: Scientific, historical & educational perspectives* (pp. 315–318). Dordrecht: Springer.

Wallace, J. G. (1965). *Concept growth and the education of the child.* Slough, UK: National Foundation for Educational Research.

Wohlwill, J. F. (1972). An never the twain did meet. *Contemporary Psychology, 6*, 334–335.

Wright, B. D., & Masters, G. N. (1982). *Rating scale analysis.* Chicago, IL: MESA Press.

8

MEASURING FACETS BEYOND ABILITY AND DIFFICULTY

Many of those who use other statistical methods for analysis in the social sciences tend to criticize the Rasch measurement approach for being simplistic. How could any human abilities seriously be regarded as unidimensional? Surely, even in the simplest forms of testing (e.g., color-in-the-bubble multiple-choice testing) shouldn't we make some allowance for guessing, lack of concentration, and the like?

The response is that the Rasch approach is simple, not *simplistic*. The aim is to develop fundamental measures that can be used across similar appropriate measurement situations, not merely to describe the data produced by administering Test *a* to Sample *b* on Day *c*. Rasch modeling addresses itself to estimating properties of persons and tests that go beyond the particular observations made during any testing situation. Wright (1998) summarized it succinctly: "I don't want to know which questions you answered. I want to know how much . . . you know. I need to leap from what I know (observed raw score) and don't want—to what I want (ability estimate) but can't know. That's called **inference**."

So far, we have focused on just two aspects of the measurement situation, on just two **facets** of the single underlying dimension being measured: One facet is the level of ability or attitude expressed by the person, whereas the second facet is the level of difficulty or **endorsability** of the item, stem, or prompt. The testing situation, therefore, can be viewed as an opportunity to collect data, some observable evidence of the interaction between the person and the test that provides empirical evidence about the existence of a latent trait revealed in the test items and any person's performance on them.

Of course, it does simplify matters quite remarkably to regard the person simply in terms of which items were 'bubbled' on a computer scan sheet and to regard the discipline of, say, mathematics in terms of 150 multiple-choice stems with four response options each. Surely, reading ability plays a part, along with the person's motivation, propensity to guess, and the like. Surely, some items are more clearly written; some have better diagrams; some are based on everyday experiences, whereas some are a little esoteric. Undoubtedly this is the case, but Rasch modeling works from the principle that the key predominant underlying attribute of the measurement situation is the latent trait expressed in the items, elicited from the candidates, and recorded in the performances when each test candidate and each test item interact. To the extent that the test performances are driven *primarily* by the person's ability and the item's difficulty, the Rasch model principles hold. Any **aberrant** performance, either by items or by persons, would be flagged by the fit statistics for closer monitoring.

However, we easily can imagine measurement situations in which other aspects of the testing situation routinely interpose themselves between the ability of the candidates and the difficulty of the test (e.g., when judges are used to evaluate test performances in terms of performance criteria). The most notorious of these usually occurs at Olympic Games time, for example, in the platform diving or gymnastics sections of the summer games, or the figure skating competition of the winter games. Even the least-informed of us sit stunned in front of our television screens at what appears to be, shall we say, inconsistent behavior among and between judges. The TV scorecards usually show the country of origin for each judge, and many of us shake our heads in disbelief at what appear to be obvious, repeated, and often systematic discrepancies between judges' scorecards. Two general properties of judges' behavior seem worthy of note. The first is that some judges seem to be more lenient or more severe than other judges, right across the board. The second, the one that gets us the most riled, is what we would call bias, judgment that seems to be more lenient or more severe depending on the competitor, the competitor's country, that country's political alliances, and so on.

Why then, in important evaluation situations, do we continue to act as though the judge, **rater**, or examiner has merely a benign role? On a personal level, we might try to avoid the tough marker, complain that some judges are biased against us, or avoid the examiner's specialist topic, but we might as well face it; in high-stakes testing, we often have the suspicion that the marker, not the candidate or the test, might mean the difference between pass and fail, that the scorer rather than the performance determines silver, not gold.

Does this then not show the inadequacy of the fundamental Rasch principle of unidimensional measurement? Do we not need to consider more than just the test and the candidate? Well, no and yes, in that order! Clearly, we have suggested here that judge or rater **severity**, at least, needs to be taken into the equation. This chapter argues that many other facets of the testing situation profitably can be considered as key aspects of the measurement process if we believe they systematically influence the overall score. Moreover, we show how the many-facets Rasch model, developed in the work of Mike Linacre of Chicago (Linacre, 1994), successfully models these more complex situations, and does that successfully, all within the Rasch model's requirement for measurement along one single dimension at a time. In the conceptualization of the **many-facets Rasch model (MFRM)**, the raters are regarded as independent experts who apply their understanding to rate person performances. They are not seen as human clones who are merely implementing the scoring rubric and are expected to behave in machine-like manner.

A Basic Introduction to the Many-Facets Rasch Model

Let us reconsider our earlier proposition that person ability and item difficulty are the key contributors to the performances that we wish to measure. If we had a little logit scale of item difficulty, it might look like this:

```
. . . . . . . .  1 . . . . . . .  2 . . . . . . .  3 . . . . . . .  4 . . . . . . .  5 . . . . . . .  6 . . . . . . .
easier                                                              harder
```

so that a person who is successful on harder and harder items has ability located farther toward the 'harder' end of the scale:

```
. . . . . . . .  1 . . . . . . .  2 . . . . . . .  3 . . . . . . .  4 . . . . . . .  5 . . . . . . .  6 . . . . . . .
easier                                  B          W                harder
```

Here Bill has 1 logit less ability than Wendy. Now consider that their performances, say short written answers to questions, are rated by two different judges, one who generally is tough and another who generally is more lenient:

```
. . . . . . . .  1 . . . . . . .  2 . . . . . . .  3 . . . . . . .  4 . . . . . . .  5 . . . . . . .  6 . . . . . . .
easier                                  BW                          harder
```

Now the ability estimates for Bill and Wendy are so close that they cannot be meaningfully separated by this testing situation. We can guess that Bill had the easy judge, whereas Wendy had the tough one. If the judge situation were reversed, we could have expected a result such as the following:

```
. . . . . . . .  1 . . . . . . .  2 . . . . . . .  3 . . . . . . .  4 . . . . . . .  5 . . . . . . .  6 . . . . . . .
easier                  B                                W          harder
```

It seems reasonable to presume that the examiners are not behaving in a random or precipitous way. They do know their area of expertise; they can discriminate better from lesser displays of ability; they both understand and use the marking guide sensitively and diligently; and both would be able to argue the 'correctness' of the scores they give. As examiners, one is routinely tougher, and one is routinely easier.

Let us imagine giving a small set of short-answer examination papers for candidates Charles, Jenny, Bill, Wendy, and Harry to examiner Easy and then to examiner Tough for rating. Look at the likely outcome:

Judge Easy:

```
........   1 .......  2 .......  3 .......  4 .......  5 .......  6 .......
Less ability          C        J        B        W    H    More ability
```

Judge Tough:

```
........   1 .......  2 .......  3 .......  4 .......  5 .......  6 .......
Less ability    C         J        B        W    H            More ability
```

We will put the pass mark at 3 on this scale. Greater than 3 is a passing grade. Charles has no chance. Judge T will fail both Bill and Jenny, but Judge E will give both of them a passing grade. Sure, you might be happy if Judge T (rather than Judge E) were accrediting your future brain surgeon, but what if the testing result was that your kid (B or J) just missed the entrance cutoff for college? Or if receiving physiotherapist home visits depended on the cut score? Whatever the assessment situation, if we were serious about measurement of ability in a judged situation, we would want to be sure that passing or failing depended more on candidate ability than on luck of the draw with examiners. We could fire one of the examiners, but which one? Better than that, we could give one or both of them some retraining in use of the marking guide. But judges are notoriously impervious to retraining. Even better still, we could model the difference in the severity of the judges, check the probability that the differences are systematically applied by each, and use all the available information we have to decide the cutoff point for the test.

Why Not Use Interrater Reliability?

We can imagine that the **interrater correlation** shown in the preceding example will be just about perfect (i.e., +1), although the effects on passing or failing at the level of 3 would be quite different depending on which judge the candidate had. Try it. Use your spreadsheet or calculator to work out the correlation between the sets of scores in Table 8.1.

The correlation is +1.0 (perfect), but Judge T fails Candidates f, g, h, and i, whereas Judge E fails only Candidates h and i. And shouldn't we remember Stevens's (1946) warning that neither **Pearson's r** nor **Spearman's rho** should be applied to ordinal data such as these?

A candidate in any of the preceding situations has to be considerably more able to get the same rating from the severe Judge T than a less able candidate would receive from the lenient Judge E. Because we have a complete set of data for

TABLE 8.1 Ratings for Eight Candidates by Judge Easy and Judge Tough

Candidate	Judge Easy	Judge Tough
a	7	6
b	6	5
c	5.5	4.5
d	5	4
e	4.5	3.5
f	4	3
g	3.5	2.5
h	3	2
i	2	1

raters, we can conclude that Judge T is just one 1 logit harder on candidates than Judge E: Adjusting Judge E's ratings by one logit to the left or Judge T's ratings by one logit to the right reveals the general consistency in the judging behavior. Therefore, the problem with intercorrelations between judge ratings is that they can demonstrate only consistency among the rank orders of candidates. They do not tell us anything about the severity or leniency differences between judges (i.e., judge discrepancies in difficulty levels). They can't answer the measurement question, 'By how much?' In standard settings, it has been effectively demonstrated (e.g., Plake, 1998; Stone, 2001) that judges simply seem obliged to disagree. Short of attempting to force normative interrater agreement by iteration, it seems a rather hopeless situation merely to calculate rater agreements. Would it not be better to model the measurement relationship between raters and to monitor the Rasch quality-control mechanisms to ensure raters, like items and persons, are performing consistently?

When we understand that raters involved in the evaluation process might influence the location of person ability estimates, we can imagine how various other facets of human performance measurement might intervene in that process in a scientifically lawful (i.e., measurable and therefore accountable) way. We might want to determine whether the short form and the standard form of a test treated candidates equally, and, if not, by how much they differed. While we are looking at the test facet, we could consider whether parallel tests actually produced equivalent measures of candidates. If we routinely change our accreditation or entrance tests to keep them secure, we would want to monitor whether we could rely equally on all forms of such tests. Likewise, if we reasonably harbor a suspicion that some attributes of the candidates are consistently important aspects of their performances, we could examine one or more facets related to candidates, such as gender, first language, cultural grouping, and the like. Moreover, the standard treatments of rater reliability do not enable us to 'correct' or adjust for differences in rater severity/leniency or other impacting facets of the judged assessment situation. But the MFRM does, because from this particular Rasch analysis we can obtain a fair average measure of the candidate performance, that is, an interval-scale person measure corrected for severity/leniency, version of the assessment procedure, and so forth.

Relations Among the Rasch Family of Models

We can now enlarge our understanding of Rasch's original (i.e., two-facets) model that the probability of any correct response is a function of the ability of the person and the difficulty of the item (i.e., probability = function of (ability − difficulty)), to include other additional facets of the examination process. The probability of any correct response is a function of the ability of the person and the difficulty of the item, with appropriate allowance made for the severity of the rater and for which particular form of the test was taken (i.e., probability = function of (ability − difficulty − rater − test)).

Linacre's (1992) conception of the many-facets Rasch model shares an interesting property with the rating-scale and partial credit models: When the extra facets (e.g., rater, test, or candidate) are not required to model the added complexities of the measurement situation, then the equation conflates to the basic two-facets Rasch model: probability = function of (ability − difficulty).

Data Specifications of the Many-Facets Rasch Model

Interestingly, evaluations and examinations that do not adopt the many-facets Rasch model to deal with the 'rater severity' problem deal with the role of the examiner in two remarkably contrasting manners. The first, of course, is just to ignore the problem: All grades or scores are taken at face value, and no attempt is made even to check whether the scores assigned by raters differ at all. The second approach goes to the other extreme: It requires that all examiners grade the same set of papers or assess the same set of video-recorded performances in an attempt to ensure that all raters assign the same grade to any one candidate. A less demanding practice of examiner pairing is widely used to provide some check on rater behavior. Of course, as we have seen, correlation indices are not indicators of this exact agreement intention, and **interrater agreements** of 90% mean little if agreement, say within one grade level, is counted as perfect.

Although it might not be necessary for all examiners to score all tests, the subset of double-, triple-, or quintuple-marked performances must be large and must be graded by all (two, three, or five) judges. Any performances not assessed by all those judges cannot be used to check rater behavior.

Now, with the Rasch model, we can take advantage of a property of the model that we have come across before. *The Rasch model is quite robust in the face of* missing *data: It does not require a perfectly complete matrix of values as the starting point for calculations.* True score-based statistics require a complete data set, so perfectly good data often are discarded because the set is incomplete or some inauthentic datum (e.g., an average or typical score) is interpolated into the gap. On the other hand, the Rasch model requires only sufficient density of data to permit the calculations. Where the data matrix is empty, no information is interpolated. Therefore, a data set to detect rater severity effects does not require the very costly procedure of having all five judges rate all 500 candidates. Provided the judges' rotation roster is carefully thought out to provide sufficient links through the data set, it should not be necessary for any paper/performance/candidate to be assessed by more than two judges. The many-facets Rasch model's approach to monitoring the rater severity effect provides for the most parsimonious allocation of double marking that is consonant with the calculation of rater effect estimations. Indeed, single marking is all that is required if examinees each provide more than one performance to be assessed. The important element is that some suitable link(s) be provided across the sets of examinees, performances, and raters. Linacre provides quite detailed requirements for minimal marking schedules in a number of places (Linacre, 1997; Lunz & Linacre, 1998).

Of course, given what we already know about the density of the data submitted for Rasch analysis, that more targeted data will produce more precise estimates (smaller SEs) than will fewer data, we can be sure that the scoring roster requiring all raters to grade all questions for all candidates will produce the most precise estimates of ability, difficulty, and **rater severity**. The point is that a complete scoring roster can be too demanding, too expensive, or too time consuming, or it often can be just plain impractical in a practical performance situation. The robust nature of the Rasch model in the face of missing data means that sufficiently accurate estimates of these three facets can be calculated with much less demanding (i.e., substantially incomplete) marking rosters. Linacre (1997) displayed three judging rosters for ratings from the Advanced Placement Program of the College Board. The complete judging plan of 1,152 ratings illustrates the ideal plan for both conventional and Rasch analysis. This complete judging plan meets the connection requirement among all facets because every element (essays, examinees, and judges) can be compared directly and unambiguously with every other element.

A much less judge-intensive plan of only 180 ratings also is displayed, in which less precise Rasch estimates for all facets can be obtained because the facet-linking overlap is maintained. The Rasch measures would be less precise than with complete data because 83% fewer observations are made. Linacre's final table reveals the minimal judging plan, in which each of the 32 examinees' three essays is rated by only one judge. Each of the 12 judges rates eight essays, including two or three of each essay type, so that the examinee–judge–essay overlap of these 96 ratings still enables all parameters to be estimated unambiguously in one frame of reference. Of course, the saving in judges' costs needs to be balanced against the cost of low measurement precision, but this plan requires only 96 ratings, 8% of the observations required for the complete judging plan. Lunz and Linacre

(1998) reported the successful implementation of such a minimal judging plan (Linacre, 1997).

Rating Creativity of Junior Scientists

An incidental part of a study commissioned by the U.S. Navy provided Guilford (1954) with a set of ratings data via which he introduced some innovative approaches to the examination of and adjustment to ratings of examinees by a panel of experts (Linacre, 1992, chap. 10). The data, summarized in Table 8.2 revealed how three senior scientists (named *A*vogadro, *B*rahe, and *C*avendish for our purposes) rated seven junior scientists (1–7) on five traits of scientific creativity (a–e).

Ratings were awarded on each of five traits using an ordinal rating scale that ranged from 1 to 9, with 9 meaning most creative. Following the principle established in Tables 4.1 and 5.2 of this volume, the data from Guilford's table have been ordered to show examinees in descending order of performance and items in descending order of difficulty, left to right. Examiners also appear in order of leniency: in general, Scientist A gives higher ratings than does Scientist B, who is more lenient than Scientist C.

Most examples of many-facets Rasch analysis contain so many examinees, raters, or both that it is often difficult to conceptualize how the data matrix might actually appear on paper (i.e., in two dimensions). Guilford's published exemplar provides the essentials for a many-facets conceptualization of his data. It is small enough that it can be easily transformed into a format that the reader can analyze and interpret. (Bond&FoxFacets is available on the book website. It is a tailored version of the Minifac and FACETS software available at www.winsteps.com.)

TABLE 8.2 Ratings of Seven Junior Scientists on Five Creativity Traits by Three Senior Scientists (after Guilford, 1954, p. 282)

		Hard			Creativity Traits									Easy		
		Trait e			Trait c			Trait b			Trait a			Trait d		
Examinee	Judge:	A	C	B	A	C	B	A	C	B	A	C	B	A	C	B
High 2		5	5	2^g	5	5	5	7	7	7	9	7	8	8	7	7
5		5	7	3	7	7	3	7	7	4	9	9	2^f	8	7	2^f
7		5	7	4	5	7	5	7	7	3	7	7	3	5	5	5
1		3	3	3	3	5	4	5	5	5	5	5	6	5	7	6
3		1	5	6^f	3	5	3	3	5	5	3	3	4	7^g	5	6
4		3	1	5^f	1	3	4	3	3	6	7	5	5	3	3	5
Low 6		1	3	2	3	3	6^f	5	3	4	3	3	4	5	5	4

^{g}*most* unexplained ratings according to Guilford's descriptive model
^{f}*most* unexpected ratings according to many-facets Rasch analysis (using FACETS software)

Helpfully, Guilford provided his own interpretation of rater behavior based on the light shed on the problem by analyses conducted under true score theory.

Guilford (1954, pp. 282–288) developed a descriptive model based on treating the senior scientists' ratings of junior colleagues as linear measures of performance. For later comparison, it is useful to record what conclusions Guilford came to from the results of his analyses: First of all, he detected evidence of judge–examinee interaction, in which he concluded that Judge A tended to overvalue Examinee 5, Judge B tended to overvalue Examinee 4 but undervalued Examinees 5 and 7, and Judge C tended to overvalue Examinee 5 and undervalue Examinee 4. Thus Judge B disagreed with Judges A and C about Examinees 4 and 5. Were judge–item interaction significant, then Judge A would tend to see examinees higher on Item a and lower on Items c and e than the other judges. In the raw data, Judge B's ratings correlated negatively with those of both Judges A and C, but, after removing explained effects, Guilford found that all judges' ratings then correlated positively. Unfortunately, the existence of the highly significant judge–examinee interactions indicates that there is no way of inferring how each of the senior scientists will use the creativity rating scale traits to judge the next junior scientist to join the group. That means that although Guilford's descriptive analyses, like all of those derived from true score theory, might help to clarify the relations, the findings cannot generalize beyond the current data set. Harking back to Wright's statement—these analyses provide what we don't want—descriptions of raw data—instead of what we want and don't have—estimates of judge leniency and severity. Such estimates are what science is made of—inference and prediction beyond our present sample.

Given that the data array must represent more than just the two facets of analysis conducted using the dichotomous, PCM, and RSM Rasch models (items and persons), the structure of the data file must, in this case, represent three facets of data from a 3D array in a 2D flat text file format. The complete data file that follows contains all of the data needed for the analysis, ordered according to the display in the original Guilford (1954) chapter. Each data line (e.g., line three: 1,3,1–5,3,3,3,7,1) contains, first, identifiers for the facets (e.g., 1, 3, 1–5 indicates 1 = first Judge A, 3 = third Junior Scientist c, and 1–5 indicates values for Items 1–5 will follow) and then introduces the ratings (must be between 1 and 9) for five items or indicators: 3, 3, 3, 7, 1; that is, the ratings given by 1 (first Judge A) to 3 (third Junior Scientist c) on 1–5 (the five traits of creativity, numbered 1 to 5) are 3, 3, 3, 7, 1, and so forth.

```
Data =
1,1,1-5,5,5,3,5,3
1,2,1-5,9,7,5,8,5
1,3,1-5,3,3,3,7,1
1,4,1-5,7,3,1,3,3
1,5,1-5,9,7,7,8,5
```

```
1,6,1-5,3,5,3,5,1
1,7,1-5,7,7,5,5,5
2,1,1-5,6,5,4,6,3
2,2,1-5,8,7,5,7,2
2,3,1-5,4,5,3,6,6
2,4,1-5,5,6,4,5,5
2,5,1-5,2,4,3,2,3
2,6,1-5,4,4,6,4,2
2,7,1-5,3,3,5,5,4
3,1,1-5,5,5,5,7,3
3,2,1-5,7,7,5,7,5
3,3,1-5,3,5,5,5,5
3,4,1-5,5,3,3,3,1
3,5,1-5,9,7,7,7,7
3,6,1-5,3,3,3,5,3
3,7,1-5,7,7,7,5,7
```

The many-facets Rasch model to be estimated considers the ability of the candidate, the difficulty of the item, and the difficulty of each rating category over the previous category (i.e., an **RSM** for items) and the severity of the judge. Guilford's analysis consisted of a sequence of analytical steps in which relevant information from earlier analyses was incorporated where appropriate into later analyses. In the many-facets Rasch model procedure, the facets are estimated *concurrently* so that they might be considered *separately*. The Bond&FoxFacets software and control and data files are available on the book website. The control lines given on the book's website will allow the interested reader to replicate this analysis with FACETS (or the free Minifac) Rasch software package. Alternatively, the pathway in Figure 8.1 shows estimates, errors, and fit indicators for the main facets: raters, examinees, and traits.

Although not included here, the FACETS tables for this analysis show unremarkable fit statistics. That is, the ratings (Scale 1–9), items (Traits a–e), judges (Senior Sci, A, B, C) and junior scientists (A–F) all perform sufficiently predictably to be considered in a single Rasch measurement frame of reference. Because of that, the Wright map of the Scientific Creativity variable is instructive (Fig. 8.2). When the many facets are estimated simultaneously, the information about any one facet can be read off the map, all other facets taken into consideration. All other facets considered (i.e., item and category difficulty as well as judge severity), Betty is the most creative junior scientist (+0.66 logits, err. = 0.18), while Fred (est. −0.29; err. 0.19) is the least creative. While the criteria for indicators 'daring' (est. −0.29; err. 0.15) and 'attack' (est. −0.27; err. 0.15) are the easiest to satisfy, it takes a higher level of Scientific Creativity to be judged as having Enthusiasm. Senior Scientist B (est. +0.24; err. 0.12) can be seen as just measurably more

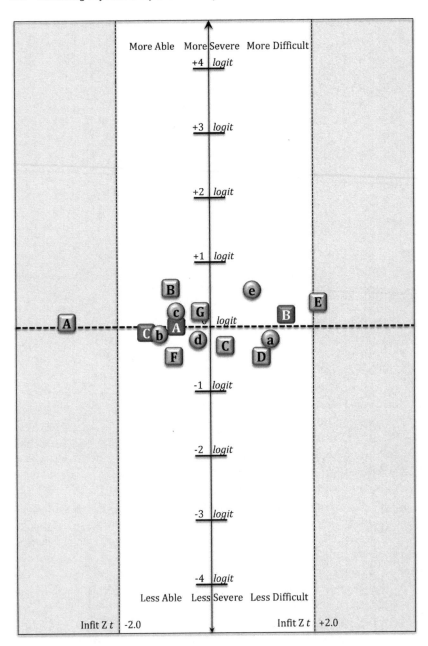

FIGURE 8.1 Pathway of the many-facets Rasch analysis of scientists' ratings.

demanding than Scientist C (est. −0.09; err. 0.1), but not Scientist A (est. +0.04; err. 0.1). The latter two senior scientists (A and C) are equally demanding of junior scientists when they rate them on the 9-category, 5-indicator Scientific Creativity scale.

```
All Facet Vertical "Rulers".
-------------------------------------------------------------------------
|Measr|+Junior|-Traits              |+Junior|-Senior sci|+Junior |Scale|
-------------------------------------------------------------------------
+   1 +       +                      +       +           +       +(9)  +
|     |       |                      |       |           |       | 7   |
|     |       |                      |       |           |       |     |
|     | 2     |                      | *     |           | Betty | --- |
|     |       | Enthusiasm           |       |           |       |     |
|     | 5     |                      | *     |           | Edward| 6   |
|     | 7     |                      | *     |           | George|     |
|     |       | Clarity              |       | Brahe     |       | --- |
|     |       |                      |       |           |       |     |
+   0 *       +                      *       * Avogadro  *       * 5   *
|     | 1     | Basis                | *     | Cavendish | Anne  |     |
|     | 3     |                      | *     |           | Chris | --- |
|     |       | Attack       Daring  |       |           |       |     |
|     |       |                      |       |           |       | 4   |
|     | 4     |                      | *     |           | David |     |
|     | 6     |                      | *     |           | Fred  |     |
|     |       |                      |       |           |       | --- |
|     |       |                      |       |           |       |     |
|     |       |                      |       |           |       | 3   |
+  -1 +       +                      +       +           +       +(1)  +
-------------------------------------------------------------------------
|Measr|+Junior|-Traits              | * = 1 |-Senior sci|+Junior |Scale|
```

FIGURE 8.2 Wright map for the many-facets Rasch analysis of scientists' ratings (from FACETS; Linacre, 2006).

Many-Facets Analysis of Eighth-Grade Writing

McNamara's (1996) book *Measuring Second Language Performance* clearly championed the application of Rasch measurement to second-language testing. Since then, very few in second-language and applied linguistic studies could have ignored McNamara's claims concerning the particular benefits of Rasch measurement in language testing. What is often fundamental to language testing is the assessment of candidates' performances by panels of judges. Examinees' language ability is often collected as a permanent record, say, a written paragraph or essay, or observed in a transient situation, such as an oral presentation, simulated telephone call, or discussion, and human judges are responsible for assigning quantitative grades to those performances based on a set of marking criteria. Inevitably, judges disagree, in spite of their shared expertise and judges' training, and fairness to candidates demands some sort of moderation. The various forms of qualitative moderation operate by obliging one expert to defer to the judgment of another. Typical practices of quantitative moderation involve some sort of averaging, often after outlying scores have been consigned to the waste bin (after Bond, 2015). It is clear from McNamara's argument (see McNamara & Knoch, 2012), that the many-facets Rasch model (MFRM; Linacre, 1989) is the measurement model of choice for judged language testing: "In fact, FACETS had revealed a problem that was common to all performance tests, the vulnerability of the score to rater effects, a point that as Linacre had pointed out in his PhD thesis had been recognized for over 100 years, but conveniently forgotten" (McNamara & Knoch, 2012, p. 12).

The many-facets Rasch model exemplar included here is taken from the work of Engelhard (1992, 1994), in which he examined rater severity and other aspects of the writing ability assessment in the high-stakes Eighth Grade Writing Test administered annually to all eighth-grade students in the state of Georgia. Each student was asked to write an essay of no more than two pages on a writing task randomly assigned from a set of eight topics (labeled a–h). The 1,000 marked scripts were selected randomly from the spring 1990 cohort of examinees, with 82 raters (or essay markers) having graded the essays. Each of the student essays was graded "by two raters, on each of the following five domains: content/organization, style, sentence formation, usage and mechanics", using "a four-category rating scale (ranging from inadequate [1] to minimal [2] to good [3] to very good [4]) . . . The final rating pattern used to estimate student writing ability consists of 10 ratings (2 raters × 5 domains = 10 domains)" (Engelhard, 1992, p. 177).

Of course, reliance on rater allocation of grades on five criteria across assigned topics in a high-stakes, statewide educational assessment requires that the raters grade with the same severity, that the essay topics be equally demanding, and that the grades across domains reflect similar levels of essay writing ability. Indeed, raters for the Georgia writing tests must meet rigid training and testing requirements. The estimated interrater reliability for this set was .82, which is comparable with the usual requirements of state education authorities. The essay topics had been constructed with the explicit intention of producing tasks of equal difficulty. So which variables might impact any student's final score? Clearly, the aim is to give a fair score to every student according to each student's ability. What should not impact that score but might include the severity/leniency of the rater pair; the difficulty of the writing topic randomly assigned; the relative difficulty of the writing domains; as well as the rating scale used for grading the essays. It is worth remembering that the assessment practices used for this essay grading were meticulously designed and implemented to *ensure* that the scores given to the student essay would reflect student ability alone, with all other potential influences controlled.

Engelhard's (1992) many-facets Rasch analysis of the writing assessments used the following facets: essay writing ability of the student (B), the difficulty of the randomly assigned writing task (T), the severity of the rater (R), the difficulty of the writing domain (D), and the difficulty of the rating scale step (F). Engelhard's conception of his measurement problem would take the following form:

$$\text{Probability} = \text{function of } (B - D - T - R - F).$$

As expected, the writing ability estimates of the 1,000 students used for this investigation varied considerably: Raw essay scores from 10/40 to 39/40 yielded estimates that varied from a low of −6.84 logits to a high of +7.07 logits. Figure 8.3 (after Engelhard, 1992, p. 179) reports the estimates for raters (R), tasks (I), and domains (D).

The map of the task difficulty (T) facet shows that the intention to produce eight essay writing prompts of equal difficulty has almost been realized: The most difficult writing task (c, 'all-expense-paid trip'; estimate = +0.12; error = 0.06) is measurably more difficult than the easiest task (b, 'experience that turned out better'; estimate = −0.16; error = 0.06). Therefore, although these writing prompts/tasks show small, statistically significant differences in difficulty, for all practical assessment purposes, the prompt writers have succeeded in producing eight essay-writing topics of approximately equal difficulty. The evidence demonstrates the empirical equivalence of task difficulty; students' final grades do not need to be adjusted to account for differential difficulty of writing tasks.

The calibrations for the five writing domains (D) show greater variation in difficulty. Whereas the three domains of content/organization, usage, and mechanics, and sentence formation could be regarded as equally difficult, allowing for the error of the estimates, the style domain was the most difficult at +0.50 logits (error = 0.05). The sentence formation domain, with a difficulty estimate of −0.28 (error = 0.05), was significantly easier to score well on.

The plots of rater severity in Figure 8.3 tell a much more varied tale, however. A group of approximately 20 raters (located around the 0 origin of the scale) could be regarded has having graded the essays with the same middling severity (allowing for measurement error). However, the remaining 60 raters are spread across more than a 3.5-logit severity range, with the most severe rater (11) estimated at +1.78 logits (error = 0.66) and the most lenient rater (19) estimated at −1.74 logits (error = 0.48).

Engelhard (1992, p. 177) pointed out that these raters were highly trained. They had to undergo rigorous training and then qualify by achieving at least 62% perfect agreement and 38% adjacent category agreements to become operational raters. During the actual essay grading period, unidentifiable 'validity' papers were included in each packet of 24 essays for grading so that rater agreement was continuously monitored. Then, to ensure fairness, every essay was graded by two raters, with papers showing large between-rater discrepancies being rescored by a third rater. The high interrater reliability mentioned earlier (.82) reveals how successful rater training and monitoring was when monitored through the eyes of conventional statistics. This is an exemplary implementation of the best that conventional judged assessments has to offer.

Despite these remarkable efforts, the measurement of rater severity, using the many-facets Rasch model, reveals that variation in rater severity still could have a remarkable and unaccounted-for impact on student writing assessment scores. Table 8.3 has been derived from Engelhard's (1992) Table 5 (pp. 185–186) to show the impact of the variations in rater severity on the observed and expected ratings of essay writing for four selected students. Students 43 and 522 from this sample received identical total raw scores of 27/40 when their completely identical ratings across five writing domains by two raters were added together. They even shared a common rater (106), who is shown in Figure 8.3 as a moderately severe

	Raters	Writing Tasks	Domains
	Severe	*Hard*	*Hard*
+2.0			
.	11		
.			
.			
+1.5			
.			
.	101 82		
.			
.	106 77 66		
+1.0			
.	35 18		
.	110 3 61 96 60 63		
.	31 65 79		
.	120		
+0.5	41 23 48 53		S
.	32 20 72 100		
.	103 14		
.	80 105 69 45 74 16		
.	7 75 52 70 40 34	d c	
0.0	85 102 93 71 58	g h f a e	M
.	114 113 21		C/O U
.	94 64	b	
.	12 119 73 118 37		SF
.	4 95 112 90 104 49		
-0.5	116 51 57 97		
.	24 76 111 86 26		
.	59		
.	27 44 115 55		
.			
-1.0	109 117		
.			
.	6		
.			
.	89 87		
-1.5			
.	25		
.	19		
.			
.			
-2.0			
	Lenient	*Easy*	*Easy*

FIGURE 8.3 Calibrations of rater severity, writing task, and writing domain difficulties (from Engelhard, 1992).

rater (estimate = +1.13), well above the mean. The essay of Student 43 received its other ratings from a lenient rater (26, estimate = −0.65 on Figure 8.4); the second rater for Student 522 was another severe rater (82, estimate = +1.29). The Rasch ability estimates—the fair measures of writing ability—in the right column are based directly on the identical raw scores (27/40 for Students 43 and 522) but incorporate allowances for the unequal severity of the rater pairs derived from the modeled estimates of rater severity plotted in Figure 8.3. Relying on raw scores alone would underestimate the writing ability of Student 522 by a considerable amount (1.99 − 1.16 = 0.83 logits).

Similarly, Students 621 and 305 received completely identical ratings yielding equal raw score totals of 22/40 each. The essay of Student 621 was graded by two severe raters (82, estimate = +1.29, and 66, estimate = +1.06), whereas the scores of 22/40 for student 305 came from a severe rater (61, estimate = +0.81) and a lenient rater (55, estimate = −0.85). How unfortunate for Student 621: relying on raw scores alone and ignoring rater severity underestimated that student's writing ability by more than 1 logit this time (0.08 − [−1.18] = 1.26 logits).

It should be kept in mind that the pairs of raters for each preceding essay were in perfect accord with their allocation of grades for each essay (i.e., interrater reliability would be perfectly high for these essays). They exceeded the stringent agreement demands of the assessment system. However, the many-facets Rasch modeling of the essay-grading data, made possible because raters could be linked together across common essays, showed very considerable differences in rater severity. The range of rater severity in this tightly monitored grading system is more than 3.5 logits and clearly overwhelms the much smaller difficulty differences in the allocated writing topics and the variations across the writing domains. More importantly, differences in rater severity have the potential to impact severely the essay-writing ability estimates of these eighth-grade students. The fit statistics of these raters and ability estimates suggest that these effects are not the result of erratic judge behavior. The judges performed very consistently, well within the Rasch model's stringent expectations. However, the judges are consistently more or less lenient than each other, so much so that it would be

TABLE 8.3 Observed and Expected Ratings for Selected Students

Student	Domain					Domain					Raw Score	Infit Mean Square	Outfit Mean Square	Rasch Ability
	C/O	S	SF	U	M	C/O	S	SF	U	M				
	Rater 26					Rater 106								
43	2	3	3	3	3	3	3	3	2	2	27	0.9	0.9	1.16
	Rater 82					Rater 106								
522	2	3	3	3	3	3	3	3	2	2	27	0.9	0.9	1.99
	Rater 66					Rater 82								
621	2	2	3	2	3	2	2	2	2	2	22	0.6	0.6	0.08
	Rater 55					Rater 61								
305	2	2	3	2	3	2	2	2	2	2	22	0.5	0.4	−1.18

Note: C/O = Content Organization; S = Style; SF = Sentence Formation; U = Usage; M = Mechanics.

unfair not to adjust students' final grades according to the allocation of examiner pairs. The exemplary but conventional treatment of interrater reliability did not prevent the differences in rater severity/leniency from impacting student essay scores. But from the MFRM analysis, we can obtain a **fair average** measure of each student's essay writing ability: an interval-level-scale person measure corrected, in this assessment, for severity/leniency differences of this highly-trained raters.

Engelhard (1992) further pointed out that misfitting raters could be identified. Their apparently erratic grade allocations could be identified by student essay number. Therefore, the essay could be reexamined, and those occasional inconsistencies of the examiners could be monitored more effectively. When the grade allocations of overfitting raters were examined, they typically showed little variation of grade allocation within essays, although most raters gave varying domain grades within most essays most of the time. Instead, overfitting raters gave 44444, 33333, or 22222 across the five writing domains, indicating a holistic rather than an analytic approach to essay evaluation. In a later paper based on a section of similar eighth-grade essay-grading data (15 raters across 264 compositions), Engelhard (1994) showed how the many-facets Rasch model could be used to reveal typical rater errors other than severity, such as halo effect, central tendency, and restriction of score range.

Summary

The basic Rasch measurement model is both strict and simple. It prescribes the two attributes that matter when the interaction between a person and an item is modeled: the ability (agreeability) of the person and the difficulty (endorsability) of the item. We have illustrated, however, several instances in which it might be more reasonable to determine whether test responses are affected by other sources of systematic variance in the data collection situation such as the time of the test, the particular task, the cultural or language group of the candidates, or the severity of the judge. We could regard these additional facets as decompositions of the original single Rasch difficulty facet, for example, in which a number of aspects of the assessment process contribute to the difficulty the candidates face in revealing their abilities. In these demonstrably more complex circumstances, we then can estimate the extent of those influences on the quality and fairness of our measures. The values for these separate facets, created on the same logit scale as person ability and item difficulty (i.e., in the same manner as thresholds are represented), are estimated, while the parameter separation so fundamental to the construction of sound and reproducible measures is maintained. The many-facets Rasch model provides for the simultaneous estimation of facet parameters so that they may be examined separately. Whether the many-facets model is the most suitable for any particular analysis requires consideration. For example, do the judges actually interact in the examining process (as in an oral assessment) or merely observers of the performances? Or do the senior nurses certifying the new graduates dis-cuss and share in the patients' treatments or just stand back, observe, and tick the checklisted behaviors? In the end, one must ask whether the model used provides a sufficient measurement summary of the assessment occasion. In the face of these developments, further reliance on **interrater correlations** between judges as the criterion for high-quality ratings is, at best, ill informed. Interjudge correlations tell us only about the consistency between judges in their rank ordering of can-didates, and consistency is a necessary but not sufficient condition for producing valid ratings. We need to know whether the judges' ratings (or different tasks or examination timings, for example) result in the same decisions for candidates of the same ability. But how can we know this without estimating the relative sever-ity of the different judges or other potentially confounding assessment facets? We cannot, yet we need exactly this type of information to make valid, equitable comparisons among respondents to give fair ability measures. Without estimating such relevant individual facets separately, these sources of systematic variance go unmonitored, confounding our efforts to construct useful measures and hence biasing important decisions.

If this is your introduction to Rasch measurement, we would advise you to complete the activities that follow and then continue with Chapter 9 and to return here after you have finished all chapters. If you already have a sound grasp of Rasch measurement principles, we invite you to go further.

Extended Understanding—Chapter 8

Invariance of Rated Creativity Scores

So, having completed the MFRM analysis of the judgments of junior scientists' creativity ratings, is everything 'hunky-dory', as they say in the classics? Well, no. If we return to take the principle of measurement **invariance** (from Chapter 5) seriously, we would require that the creativity estimates of junior scientists should remain *invariant* across judges (especially after we have already taken into account the differences in judge severity). In Figure 8.4, taken directly from the FACETS output, we have plotted the creativity of each junior scientist as judged by senior scientists A and C (less severe) on the horizontal axis against that candidate's esti-mate as judged by senior scientist B (more severe), alone. The modeled identity (or invariance) line is dotted in that FACETS figure.

Estimated measures of junior scientist creativity are not invariant across senior scientist ratings. Clearly, while Judge B is marginally more severe than the others, it is more important to note that Judge B's ratings vary too much from those of Judges A and C to be considered part of the same measurement system. We saw a hint of that in Table 8.2: While Guilford (1954) concluded that judges A and B each produced one of the most unexplained ratings in his analyses (indicated by the superscript g in Table 8.2), the MFRM analysis attributed all five of the most unexpected ratings to Judge B (indicated by the superscript f). As a judge,

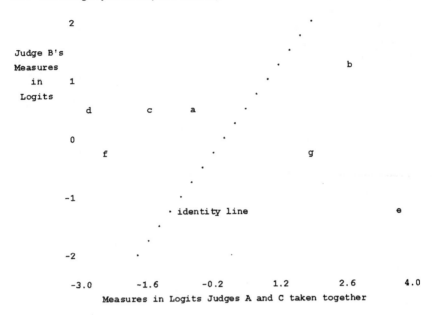

FIGURE 8.4 Judge B's candidate measures plotted against those of Judges A and C together. An approximate expectation line is drawn in. Points are identified by junior scientist code (a–f).

B's performance is too idiosyncratic. Its seems that the Navy examinations board should have seriously considered retiring Senior Scientist B from the scientific creativity judging panel. The control file for this many-facets Rasch analysis is given at the end of Chapter 8. More detailed consideration of this analysis is given in chapter 10 of Linacre's (1992) expository text on the many-facets Rasch model.

Rasch Measurement of Facets Beyond Rater Effects

The uses of the many-facets Rasch model to provide fair person measures in assessments based on judged performances do not need to stop here. We could use the MFRM to investigate whether some other facets of some judged performance assessment could be modeled profitably. The many-facets model allows all the relevant facets of a measurement situation to be modeled concurrently in order that they can be examined independently. The lack of invariance termed 'differential item functioning' (DIF) in the less complex models of the Rasch family can be generalized to the concept of 'differential facet functioning' (DFF) in the MFRM to detect whether the invariance expected under the model's requirements actually are instantiated empirically or whether some sort of bias exists.

Summary

Performance assessments require judges to rate candidates according to a set of criteria.

The underlying problem is that judges, even when highly trained, do not make equal assessments of equal performances.

Complete marking of performances where all judges rate all performances of all candidates are often prohibitive. The same is true for double and triple marking.

The MFRM scales the leniency/severity of judges on the same interval measure (logits) units as for items and persons.

The fair average measure of the candidate performance is an interval-scaled person measure, corrected for the additional facet, for example, the severity/leniency or the particular version of the assessment procedure and so forth.

Empirical investigations of judged performances reveal the influence of the judge can often be more crucial to pass/fail decisions than is candidate ability.

The usual Rasch quality control statistics/diagnostics monitor adherence of all facets (item/person/judge) to the model's requirements.

Suggested Reading

Engelhard, G. (1992). The measurement of writing ability with a many-faceted Rasch model. *Applied Measurement in Education, 5*(3), 171–191.

ACTIVITIES

1. Download the Bond&FoxFacets software from the website. Double-click on the icon to install it on your computer. The free copy of Bond&FoxFacets is already fully loaded with a specially prepared tutorial using the Guilford data file. BondFoxChapter8.pdf is the Bond&FoxFacets tutorial for the Guilford data. That data file is already loaded into the Bond&FoxFacets software. Run the Facets analysis of the Guilford data file using the BondFoxChapter8.pdf as your tutorial guide.

2. Download the data file essayschap8.txt from the website. It contains data and control files for a Facets analysis of judged performance data for 50 young ESL students on their three written essays, as judged by their four (ESL) teachers. Follow the principles from the tutorial guide for Chapter 8 to run your own independent analyses of the new file.

References

Bond, T. (2015). Enhancing the capacity of English language teachers to develop English language testing: Lessons from the Orient. In V. Aryadoust & J. Fox (Eds.), *Trends in language assessment research and practice: The view from the Middle East and the Pacific Rim.* Newcastle: Cambridge Scholars.

Engelhard, G. (1992). The measurement of writing ability with a many-faceted Rasch model. *Applied Measurement in Education, 5*(3), 171–191.

Engelhard, G. (1994). Examining rater errors in the assessment of written composition with a many-faceted Rasch model. *Journal of Educational Measurement, 31*(2), 93–112.

Guilford, J.P. (1954). *Psychometric methods* (2nd ed.). New York, NY: McGraw-Hill.

Linacre, J.M. (1989). *Many-facet Rasch measurement.* Chicago, IL: MESA Press.

Linacre, J.M. (1992). *Many-facet Rasch measurement.* Chicago, IL: MESA Press.

Linacre, J.M. (1994). Constructing measurement with a many-facet Rasch model. In M. Wilson (Ed.), *Objective measurement: Theory into practice* (Vol. 2, pp. 129–144). Norwood, NJ: Ablex.

Linacre, J.M. (1997). *Judging plans and facets (Research Note No. 3).* Chicago, IL: University of Chicago, MESA Psychometric Laboratory.

Linacre, J.M. (2006). *Facets Rasch measurement computer program.* Chicago, IL: Winsteps.com.

Lunz, M.E., & Linacre, J.M. (1998). Measurement designs using multifacet Rasch modeling. In G.A. Marcoulides (Ed.), *Modern methods for business research* (pp. 44–77). Mahwah, NJ: Lawrence Erlbaum Associates.

McNamara, T.F. (1996). *Measuring second language performance.* New York, NY: Longman.

McNamara, T.F., & Knoch, U. (2012). The Rasch wars: The emergence of Rasch measurement in language testing. *Language Testing, 29*(4), 555–576.

Plake, B.S. (1998). Setting performance standards for professional licensure and certification. *Applied Measurement in Education, 11*(1), 65–80.

Stevens, S.S. (1946). On the theory of scales of measurement. *Science, 103*, 677–680.

Stone, G.E. (2001). Understanding Rasch measurement: Objective standard setting (or truth in advertising). *Journal of Applied Measurement, 2*(2), 187–201.

Wright, B.D. (1998). *Introduction to the Rasch model* [Videotape]. Chicago: MESA Press.

9

MAKING MEASURES, SETTING STANDARDS, AND RASCH REGRESSION

This chapter introduces three important applications of Rasch measurement principles and techniques to solve the sorts of problems that many of us encounter in our human sciences research. To address these issues, we have invited three of our colleagues to share their expertise directly with you. The first author, Yan Zi, from the Hong Kong Institute of Education, created a Rasch interval-level measurement scale from a large data bank of fitness indicators routinely used in Hong Kong primary schools. Yan's contribution to this chapter demonstrates the use of Rasch diagnostics to decide which indicators/items to include or exclude in constructing the Rasch Measurement Physical Fitness Scale (RMPFS). The second author, Gregory Stone from the University of Toledo, explains the rationale and demonstrates practices for objective standard setting for test data and for judged performances using raters. Stone explains how to use Rasch measurement to set cut points for setting standards for high-stakes decision making. The third author, Svetlana Beltyukova from the University of Toledo, uses Rasch measurement to extract a set of airline attributes to predict overall passenger satisfaction with airline performance. For this task, she introduces the Rasch regression model that Ben Wright pioneered in 2000.

Creating a Measure from Existing Data: The RMPFS (Yan Zi, HKIEd)

The main purpose of this study (reported in detail in Yan & Bond, 2011) was to develop, to the extent that it was both useful and possible, a Rasch Measurement Physical Fitness Scale (RMPFS) combining all, or at least some, of the indicators routinely used in Hong Kong primary schools. A successful scale would then calibrate person ability (students' overall physical fitness levels) and item difficulty (difficulty levels of each of the physical fitness indicators) in a single, stable fitness measurement framework.

Although physical fitness is regarded as a multifaceted concept, whether a uni-dimensional fitness index can be constructed is the subject of this evidence-based empirical investigation. The study aimed to generate a unidimensional index of physical fitness for children, for tracking changes in fitness levels over time as well as estimating fitness differences between groups of children.

Method

Data

Fitness data used in this study were retrieved from the existing physical fitness assessment records database of a large Hong Kong primary school. The data set covers this school's students' physical fitness records at each year level from primary 1 (6 years old) to primary 6 (12 years old) for the academic years from 2002–03 to 2006–07. There are two rounds of students' records for each academic year except 2002–03, for which the records for the second semester were not entered into the school's database. A total of 9,439 student records were kept in the data pool for scale development. The details of the sample used in this study are presented in Table 9.1.

Physical Fitness Indicators

There are nine fitness indicators administered in the school, including BMI, the 6-minute run, the 9-minute run, 1-minute sit-ups, standard push-ups, modified push-ups, right handgrip, left handgrip, and sit-and-reach. The 6-minute-run test is administered to students in Grades 1 to 3 only, and the 9-minute-run test is administered to students in Grades 4 to 6 only. It is worth noting that while meters indicate equal amounts of difference on the length or distance scales, that indication has only ordinal meaning when it is used as the score units

TABLE 9.1 Sample Distribution

Academic year	2002–03		2003–04		2004–05		2005–06		2006–07		Total
Semester	1st	2nd	1st	2nd	1st	2nd	1st	2nd	1st	2nd	
Male	510	–	556	551	572	574	592	590	606	598	5149
Female	458	–	472	468	492	489	488	487	468	468	4290
Total	968	–	1028	1019	1064	1063	1080	1077	1074	1066	9439

Age	6	7	8	9	10	11	12	13	Total
Male	837	900	877	845	813	779	94	4	5149
Female	666	701	727	742	717	672	61	0	4290
Total	1503	1601	1604	1587	1530	1451	155	4	9439

representing fitness in the 6- or 9-minute-run test. The standard push-ups test is administered only to male students in Grades 3 to 6, and the modified push-ups test is administered to all students in Grades 1 and 2, as well as to female students in Grades 3 to 6.

Data Analysis

The Rasch analyses adopted the partial credit model (PCM) given that the definition of the rating scale is unique for each of the physical fitness indicators. Although Winsteps can accommodate up to 255 category levels per item, using more than the necessary category levels is likely to confuse the meaningful interpretation of the results (see Chapter 11). It is unlikely that primary students' performances on physical fitness indicators have more than about 10 qualitatively different levels; a 10-m difference in a 6-minute run test or 1 cm in a sit-and-reach test will mean little in overall physical fitness levels, even if such a small difference could move a child's fitness estimate from a lower to a higher response category for that one indicator. Linacre (2000) recommended a Poisson logarithmic transformation to yield more reasonable numbers of ordered categories to help the interpretation of the results and the detection of departures from fit to the model more clearly. The transformation can be expressed as

$$\text{Scored category} = 1 + 8 \times \frac{\log\left(\text{observation} + 1\right) - \log\left(L + 1\right)}{\log\left(H + 1\right) - \log\left(L + 1\right)} \tag{1}$$

where L is the lowest value of the observations, and H is the highest value of the observations. The number 8 was chosen after some preliminary investigative analyses to yield 9 categories.

Seven Criteria to Investigate the Quality of Physical Fitness Indicators

This study explicitly adopted the Rasch 'data-fit-the-model' approach (Bond & Fox, 2007) in developing the physical fitness scale: The measurement properties of the intended RMPFS were held to be more important than the existence of the data. The following criteria were utilized in the scale development to investigate the quality of indicators for retention or exclusion:

- *Investigations from a practical perspective.* Practical considerations might uncover some important factors detrimental to scale development.
- *Fit statistics for indicators.* Relatively more stable mean square (MNSQ) statistics (Smith, Rush, Fallowfield, Velikova, & Sharpe, 2008) were used as fit criteria for indicator quality assurance.

- *Point–measure correlations for indicators.* The point–measure correlation coefficient (Linacre, 2006) higher than +.4 indicates consistency of indicator polarity in the scale.
- *Rasch reliability.* Rasch person reliability and item reliability indices were used to indicate replicability of person and item placements along the trait continuum.
- *Variance explained by measures.* A higher proportion of variance explained by Rasch measures means that the scale has better capacity for predicting performances of both items and persons.
- *Category function.* Well-functioning response category structures indicate the successful implementation of polytomous Rasch measurement.
- *Influence of underfitting persons.* The impact of extremely misfitting persons on the fitness scale quality was investigated.

Results and Discussion

After the iterative developmental procedure, only four out of nine physical fitness indicators satisfied the criteria adopted for the Rasch measurement investigations and were retained to form the final version of RMPFS. Scales 1 to 5 displayed in Table 9.2 are intermediate scales before Scale 6—the final version of RMPFS—was finally established.

TABLE 9.2 Scale Properties at Each Stage of RMPFS Development

	MNSQ		*Point–Measure Correlation*	*Rasch Reliability Person Item*	*Variance Explained by Measures*
	Infit	*Outfit*			
Scale 1: 8-indicator 9-category					
6-minute Run	1.03	1.03	0.58	0.52 1.00	62.1%
9-minute Run	1.09	1.09	0.65		
1-minute Sit-ups	0.93	0.91	0.63		
Right Handgrip	0.76	0.75	0.73		
Left Handgrip	0.74	0.72	0.73		
Sit-and-Reach	1.21*	1.27*	0.42		
Standard Push-ups	1.01	1.01	0.70		
Modified Push-ups	1.49*	1.48*	0.47		
Scale 2: 7-indicator 9-category					
6-minute Run	1.10	1.10	0.61	0.66 1.00	60.6%
9-minute Run	1.15	1.15	0.68		
1-minute Sit-ups	1.07	1.05	0.64		
Right Handgrip	0.78	0.78	0.76		
Left Handgrip	0.75	0.75	0.76		
Standard Push-ups	1.01	1.02	0.74		
Modified Push-ups	1.57*	1.58*	0.51		

	MNSQ		Point–Measure Correlation	Rasch Reliability Person Item	Variance Explained by Measures
	Infit	*Outfit*			
Scale 3: 6-indicator 9-category					
6-minute Run	0.93	0.92	0.70	0.60 1.00	62.6%
9-minute Run	0.95	0.95	0.75		
1-minute Sit-ups	0.90	0.90	0.69		
Dominant Handgrip	1.11	1.10	0.65		
Standard Push-ups	0.88	0.88	0.78		
Modified Push-ups	1.26*	1.27*	0.6		
Scale 4: 4-indicator 9-category					
6-minute Run	0.92	0.91	0.73	0.63 1.00	66.9%
9-minute Run	0.90	0.90	0.79		
1-minute Sit-ups	0.97	0.98	0.70		
Dominant Handgrip	1.09	1.08	0.70		
Scale 5: 4-indicator 7-category					
6-minute Run	0.92	0.95	0.72	0.62 1.00	68.7%
9-minute Run	0.90	0.91	0.79		
1-minute Sit-ups	0.95	0.99	0.73		
Dominant Handgrip	1.10	1.10	0.71		
Scale 6 (RMPFS): 4-indicator 7-category without Underfitting Persons					
6-minute Run	0.93	0.96	0.78	0.77 1.00	81.5%
9-minute Run	0.85	0.88	0.86		
1-minute Sit-ups	0.95	1.00	0.79		
Dominant Handgrip	1.11	1.13	0.79		

Note: *Misfitting item.

Consideration of BMI

BMI was excluded due to conceptual and practical reasons. BMI is a rough index appropriate for reporting adiposity at the population level but not for individuals due to prediction error (Heyward, 2002, p. 183; Stratton & Williams, 2007). BMI is a trait with an inverted U-shaped (∩) distribution so that neither a higher BMI nor a lower BMI score necessarily stand for a better level of physical fitness. This distinctive feature of BMI contradicts a key requirement of the Rasch model: that all items should function in the same (linear) direction along the latent trait under measure.

Consideration of Sit-and-Reach

Sit-and-reach, used to assess flexibility, is distinct from the other indicators in that students' performances for other indicators, but not sit-and-reach, increase monotonically with students' age. So the correlation matrix shows flexibility to have relatively low correlations with the other physical fitness indicators (see Marsh & Redmayne, 1994). Moreover, the results in Table 9.2 show that when the sit-and-reach was excluded from the RMPFS, the Rasch person reliability increased appreciably from .52 to .66, even though the raw score range of the scale was reduced.

Consideration of Handgrip

Rasch principal components analysis (PCA) of residuals shows that right handgrip score and left handgrip score have quite high loadings on the first contrast factor, and the correlation between their residuals is .52; that is, they share about 27% of their variance in common, suggesting a separate fitness subdimension comprising right handgrip and left handgrip, with local dependency between the two. From the Rasch perspective, one promising solution is to use dominant handgrip instead of right and/or left handgrip, so the higher of right and left handgrip score was chosen as the dominant handgrip result for each student. Note that local dependence would be likely between the 6- and 9-minute run or between standard and modified push-ups, but no single case in the data set has scores on both the 6- and 9-minute run or standard and modified push-ups.

Consideration of Push-Ups

The properties of Scale 3 (see Table 9.2) show that the standard push-ups and modified push-ups have poor fit to the Rasch model. Two reasons are likely to explain noise introduced to these two indicators. The partner school of this study used these two indicators as supplementary tests for a small portion of students (14.4% for standard push-ups and 20.2% for modified push-ups) only before academic year 2005 to 2006. Second, the push-ups tests have no time limit but have an assumption about students' willingness to try their best until exhaustion. But this does not always seem to be the case in practice, especially for supplementary tests, to which students often attach less importance. Considering the misfit shown by these two indicators and the possibility of measurement noise introduced by them, it is reasonable to exclude them from further RMPFS development. The properties of a 4-indicator scale in Table 9.2 (Scale 4) are much better than those of previous versions: Person reliability increased from .60 to .63, and variance explained by measures increased considerably from 62.6% to 66.9%.

Optimizing Response Category

The results of Rasch analyses adopting 9-category items showed that the response category structure was not optimal because of the uneven distribution of respondents among categories, reversed average measures and threshold calibrations, and the submersion of some category probability curves. Therefore, principled collapsing of some adjacent and potentially redundant categories was undertaken in order to obtain a meaningful and interpretable category structure for each indicator. The first principle ensured a reasonable number of respondents in each category, and the second ensured that average measures for categories and threshold difficulties increase monotonically with reasonable increments. Finally, a 7-category structure was developed and examined in detail according to Linacre's (2002) guidelines: Point–measure correlation coefficients of all four indicators range from .71 to .79; the number of observations of all categories for each indicator ranges between 14 and 3,496 with a mean of 879; observations across categories for all indicators display unimodal distributions, peaking in a central category and showing smooth decreases to categories 1 and 7, respectively; and average measures of categories for all indicators advance monotonically. The outfit and infit MNSQs for all categories range between .79 and 1.44, with most of them are very close to 1.0. Threshold calibrations of categories for all indicators advance monotonically. The distances between adjacent threshold calibrations are all larger than 1.0 logit and less than 5.0 logits with only two exceptions. Therefore, Scale 5 based on the 7-category data replaced Scale 4, which had been constructed from 9-category data (see Table 9.2).

Influence of Underfitting Persons on the RMPFS

Two methods might be used to improve Rasch measurement scales: One is to eliminate 'bad' items; the second is to exclude temporarily the data from misfitting persons (Verhelst & Glas, 1995). Since only four 'acceptably good' indicators are retained in Scale 5 (see Table 9.2), the alternative was undertaken in order to improve the quality of the scale. Given that underfitting persons (MNSQ >> 1.0) are more detrimental to measures than are overfitting persons (MNSQ << 1.0), and Linacre (2002) claimed MNSQs higher than 2.0 indicate more noise than information, persons with either outfit MNSQ or infit MNSQ > 2.0 on Scale 5 were temporarily excluded from the next phase of the scale construction. The final version of the RMPFS was based on 8,469 retained cases (after 1,185 cases were excluded), which had at least 1 score for any of the 4 remaining indicators. That scale (see Table 9.2) shows marked improvement in Rasch person reliability (.62 to .77) as well as in variance explained by measures (68.7% to 81.5%).

Properties of the RMPFS With Subsamples

Because the RMPFS came from a longitudinal data set, most students have several records over time in the data set, meaning that some records might be considered dependent: performances of the same student at different times. All available data were included so that the construction the RMPFS included as many good-quality data as were available. However, Rasch modeling requires independent records in order that the Rasch model features such as sample-distribution-free measurement and local independence of measures might not be compromised. To investigate the source of such concerns, separate Rasch analyses were undertaken so that each person has only one record in each analysis.

Table 9.3 reveals that the properties of the RMPFS across each of the six consequent independent subsamples are quite good (infit and outfit MNSQs: .74 to 1.19; point–measure correlations: .69 to .87). The Rasch item reliabilities

TABLE 9.3 Scale Properties of the RMPFS for Subsamples

Sample		Measure (SE)	MNSQ		Point–Measure Correlation	Rasch Reliability Person Item
			Infit	Outfit		
Overall	R9	1.25 (0.03)	0.85	0.88	0.86	0.77 1.00
	DH	0.96 (0.02)	1.11	1.13	0.79	
	R6	−0.61 (0.03)	0.93	0.96	0.78	
	SU	−1.59 (0.02)	0.95	1.00	0.79	
2003/1	R9	2.63 (0.08)	0.79	0.81	0.85	0.78 1.00
	R6	−0.06 (0.08)	0.90	0.99	0.75	
	DH*	−1.13 (0.06)	1.12	1.12	0.78	
	SU	−1.44 (0.06)	0.93	0.97	0.77	
2004/1	R9	2.33 (0.09)	0.80	0.84	0.86	0.80 1.00
	DH	−0.18 (0.06)	0.99	1.00	0.82	
	R6	−0.31 (0.08)	1.01	1.04	0.72	
	SU	−1.84 (0.06)	0.98	1.05	0.76	
2005/1	R9	2.15 (0.09)	0.87	0.89	0.82	0.76 1.00
	DH	0.45 (0.06)	1.00	1.01	0.81	
	R6	−0.45 (0.08)	0.96	1.00	0.74	
	SU	−2.14 (0.06)	1.01	1.00	0.76	
2005/2	R9	3.37 (0.08)	0.74	0.75	0.87	0.80 1.00
	DH	−0.45 (0.07)	1.16	1.19	0.77	
	R6	−0.88 (0.07)	0.85	0.85	0.79	
	SU	−2.03 (0.06)	0.99	1.01	0.78	
2006/1	R9	1.56 (0.09)	0.82	0.83	0.86	0.76 1.00
	DH	0.93 (0.06)	1.11	1.15	0.74	
	R6	−0.46 (0.08)	0.99	1.04	0.69	
	SU	−2.03 (0.06)	0.92	1.01	0.74	
2006/2	R9	2.04 (0.09)	0.88	0.89	0.83	0.77 1.00
	DH	0.11 (0.07)	1.10	1.12	0.79	
	R6	−0.74 (0.08)	0.88	0.92	0.78	
	SU	−1.42 (0.07)	0.97	1.00	0.78	

Note: *Indicator out of order.

remain at 1.00, and person reliabilities approximate .80. Standard errors of item estimates are slightly larger than those derived from the total data set due to the decrease of the sample sizes. The ordering of the item difficulty is consistent with that for the overall sample with only one exception (2003–1)—dominant hand-grip easier than 6-minute run. But, given that item ordering remained invariant in every other instance, the person dependence in the results for the whole data set can be considered a nonissue.

Age Dependent or Age Related?

While it could be easy to conclude that the RMPFS merely reflects changes that are determined by children's age, Figure 9.1 based on RMPFS Rasch interval-level measures shows a more comprehensive analysis. Although there are systematic differences in fitness levels, on average, between boys and girls at each age, the overlap across sexes and age groups remains quite substantial. The conclusion easily drawn from those graphs is that increases in children's fitness are merely related to but not dependent on children's age. A boy with an RMPFS measure of 3.17 logits (See Figure 9.2a) might be the fittest boy in the first year of primary school, aged 6 years, or an 11-year-old of above-average fitness for his age group. Similarly, almost any 9-year-old girl (except for the very fittest) could have a fitness level that appears in any age group of 6- to 11-year-old girls (See Figure 9.2b).

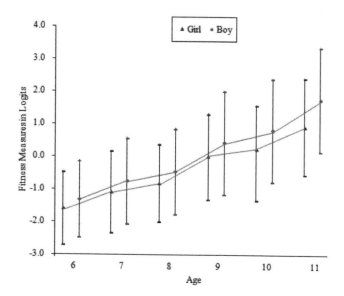

FIGURE 9.1 Fitness development by age and sex ($M \pm 1$ SD).

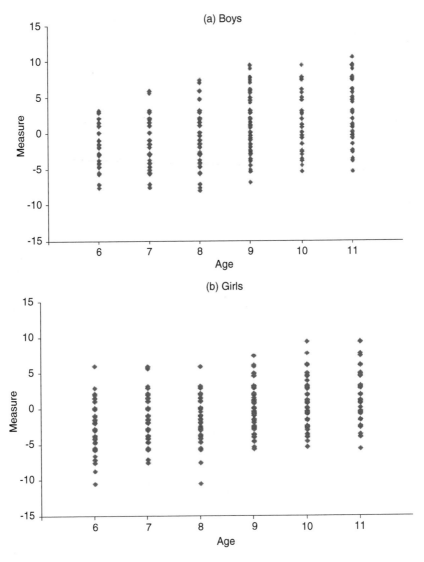

FIGURE 9.2 Distribution of fitness levels for (a) boys and (b) girls.

The Final Version of RMPFS

Through a theory-driven, iterative developmental procedure guided by Rasch model measurement perspectives as well as practical considerations, eventually four physical fitness indicators, including the 6-minute run (R6), 9-minute run (R9), 1-minute sit-ups (SU), and dominant (not left or right) handgrip (DH) were successfully calibrated to form the RMPFS, thereby integrating three key components of physical fitness—cardio-respiratory fitness, muscular endurance, and muscular strength. The other six routinely used fitness indicators—BMI, sit-and-reach, right handgrip, left handgrip, standard push-ups, and modified push-ups—were excluded from the RMPFS primarily because of violation of the Rasch model's requirements or sometimes for other, more practical considerations. The RMPFS now provides a single overall person measure of health-related physical fitness suitable for use with primary school children in Hong Kong.

Table 9.4 presents the indicator properties of the RMPFS. The item measures for the four indicators range from −1.59 logits to +1.25 logits, with small SEs of .02 or .03 logits: Quite precise difficulty estimations are due primarily to the large calibration sample. Infit and outfit MNSQs (.85 − 1.13) indicate sufficient fit to the Rasch model for practical measurement purposes, in this case, low-stakes monitoring of school children's overall fitness levels. The point–measure correlations approximate .80, evidence that all the indicators function in the same direction as instances of the underlying physical fitness latent trait. Rasch person reliability is acceptable, at .77—a consequence of retaining only four RMPFS indicators.

The Wright item–person map of the four-indicator RMPFS is shown in Figure 9.3. The students' fitness levels ($M = -.21$, $SD = 2.78$) are well targeted by difficulty levels of the RMPFS physical fitness indicators ($M = .00$, $SD = 1.16$). The indicators' difficulty range (−1.59 to 1.25 logits) is much smaller than the range of students' ability (−12.86 to 11.17 logits). The response threshold levels for each indicator on the right-hand side of the map (from R6_1 at −11.31 logits to DH_7 at +10.94 logits) reveals that, overall, the RMPFS fitness indicators provide good targeting for this sample of Hong Kong primary school students.

The ICCs (item characteristic curves) and CCCs (category probability curves) further support the valid functioning of the scale: Empirical ICCs match the theoretical ICCs reasonably well (Figure 9.4a), especially for students with median fitness levels (located around the middle of the curves), and CCCs satisfy the requirements of Linacre (2002).

TABLE 9.4 Scale Properties of the Final Version of RMPFS

	Measure (SE)	MNSQ		Point–Measure Correlation
		Infit	Outfit	
6-minute Run	−0.61 (0.03)	0.93	0.96	0.78
9-minute Run	1.25 (0.03)	0.85	0.88	0.86
1-minute Sit-ups	−1.59 (0.02)	0.95	1.00	0.79
Dominant Handgrip	0.96 (0.02)	1.11	1.13	0.79

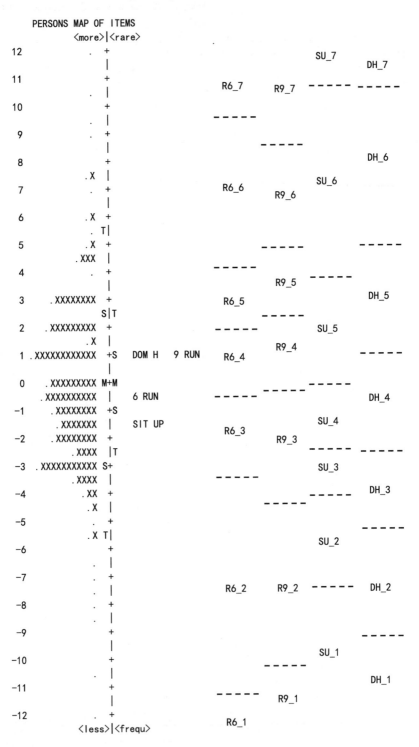

FIGURE 9.3 Wright map of the RMPFS.

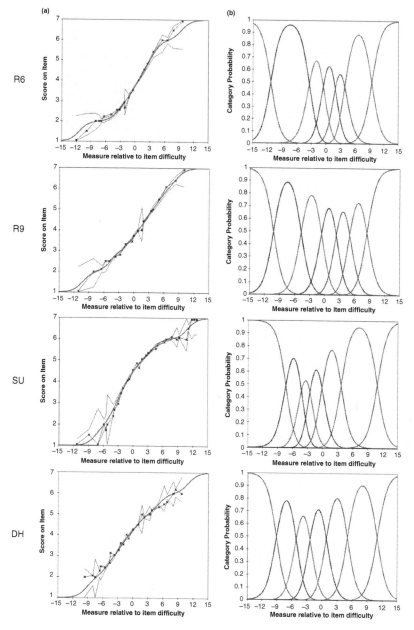

FIGURE 9.4 (a) Empirical and expected ICCs and (b) category probability curves for RMPFS indicators.

Each performance category for each of the four indicators (Figure 9.4b) has a distinct peak in the graph, meaning that each category for each indicator was the most probable performance level for groups of persons with a specified physical fitness level. The absence of category threshold disordering and that the threshold calibrations advance monotonically with category indicate that higher RMPFS performance categories correspond to higher measures of overall physical fitness.

This overall RMPFS measure combines core fitness components cardio-respiratory fitness, muscular endurance, and muscular strength—but is not the simple average of the performances on different components. On the basis of overall fitness measures derived from using the RMPFS, it would now be possible to construct a norm-based scoring system for specific age groups of Hong Kong students.

Objective Standard Setting: The OSS Model (Gregory Stone, U Toledo)

There are many methods and variations used for the establishment of criterion-referenced performance standards, and each is supported by a host of proponents offering a legion of validity evidence to demonstrate their usefulness (Cizek & Bunch, 2007; Hambleton & Slater, 1997; Kane & Case, 2004; Stone, 2001, 2009; Stone, Koskey, & Sondergeld, 2011). Unfortunately, for most methods, the most fundamental of requirements is frequently ignored: A criterion-referenced standard must represent the *body of content* knowledge, skills, and/or abilities necessary for a passing test taker to have *mastered* in order to be considered as meeting minimal requirements. Although the definitional process involves measurement, measurement is not the exclusive consideration. Establishment of the standard is also an *evaluative* exercise during which subject-matter experts (SMEs) must participate in defining both minimal competency and other parameters. Both the measurement and evaluative exercises must reflect the goal of establishing the reasoned criterion standard in order for the outcome, the pass point, to be truly meaningful. In this chapter, the Rasch-based objective standard-setting models (OSS and OSSJME) for the establishment of criterion-referenced performance standards on dichotomous (multiple-choice) and polytomous (judge-mediated) examinations will be introduced to show how measurement and evaluative exercises are combined to ensure the validity of decisions about the cut score.

The Tradition of Standard Setting

The many models associated with criterion-referenced standard setting can be divided into two major categories: those that base the criterion on SME *predictions* of test taker performance on selected items and those that base the criterion on SME definition of *essential content*. The former include the **Angoff method** (Angoff, 1971) and those of Nedelsky and Ebel (Ebel, 1979; Nedelsky, 1954). The latter include Rasch-based models, including **OSS** (Draney & Wilson, 2011; Stone, Beltyukova, & Fox, 2008; Stone, Koskey, & Sondergeld, 2011) and the **bookmark method** (Karantonis & Sireci, 2006).

Arguably, the Angoff model is the most popular current method for the establishment of passing standards. Generally, the model requires SMEs to review a selection of items, used as they are seen in the examination, and to *predict* the number of hypothetical, minimally competent test takers who *will* answer each item correctly. The summation of the proportion predictions becomes the raw standard, prior to an iterative process of review. That **iterative process** usually takes place after the initial standard is set and might consist of many forms of discussion. SMEs are then provided with some form of real exam data—actual item difficulties, for example—and a discussion often takes place concerning whether the SMEs wish to alter their predictions based on the actual data presented. Impact data, that is, the number of test takers who might have passed on earlier examinations had the new standard been implemented, might also be presented. There could be several iterative rounds during this process until the exercise reached a successful conclusion: The standard produces a passing rate that is acceptable to the group.

Through such normative processes of iteration along with the addition of a stable measurement protocol (e.g., Rasch measurement), traditional standard-setting models can achieve stable standards over time. However, the *meaningfulness* of the standard is as much dependent on process as it is on the stability of the standard, and it is in the *process* that the traditional models reveal fatal flaws. Criterion-referenced standards must reflect *content*. Specifically, as stated, they must reflect the essential content necessary for the test taker to have mastered in order to be certified as passing. Yet the decisions required of SMEs in the traditional models are not of actual *content* specification but rather of *performance*—relative to content. Furthermore, these 'hypothetical test taker' predictions are known to be poor (Plake et al., 1991) and require an entire post-hoc iterative exercise to overcome that shortcoming. The leap from predictions of success to content specification is broad and unachievable. No outcome originating from a false premise can be reasonable, with or without iteration, or the other innumerable post-hoc 'modifications' that have become so associated with the Angoff model. There simply can be no meaningful content definition that originates from predictions of test taker success.

The Objective Standard-Setting Model

Most readers of this text will be willing to consider our assertion that the Rasch model provides the ideal framework within which we might situate an empirically driven approach to the establishment of criterion-referenced passing standards. OSS begins from the Rasch principle that there exists an underlying variable (a construct; a latent trait), typically operationalized by a content-balanced examination. It will be our goal to establish the portion of that content that is essential for a test taker to have mastered in order for that person to be considered a passing candidate. Thus the job of the standard setter is to define that portion of essential content. Decisions made by the SMEs engaged in the process must therefore be directed specifically toward the *definition* of content.

More than traditional models do, OSS views standard setting as a balanced process. OSS requires SMEs to make qualitative judgments about content; SMEs are, after all, experts in their content areas. They tend not to be psychometricians or fortunetellers, and thus asking them to make hypothetical predictions requires they move beyond their expertise. In contrast, OSS deploys SMEs in roles in which they possess the exact competencies to succeed. OSS uses the Rasch measurement model to perform the measurement function, that is, to translate SME qualitative decisions onto a quantitative scale. The outstanding Rasch feature, to convert SME judgments about a qualitative, meaningful construct into a quantitative, interval-level measurement scale, allows for this seamless translation. The simplicity of translation offers two relatively straightforward mechanisms within the OSS model family that can be used for both traditional, dichotomously scored exams (i.e., MCQ tests; Chapter 4) and judge-mediated examinations (involving raters; Chapter 8). These models will now be demonstrated on both components of a high-stakes health care certification test.

Objective Standard Setting for Dichotomous Examinations

A 12-member health care certification panel annually administers a two-component, high-stakes examination to professionals applying for certification. The written examination and its oral counterpart are designed to evaluate the level of test taker proficiency relative to the knowledge, skills, and abilities associated with common tasks performed by physicians in hospitals and offices on a routine basis. The certification is considered a major step toward the practice of medicine in the United States. Hospital privileges are frequently granted on the basis of earning this certification, and insurance reimbursement is often tied to certification status. The 200-item, multiple-choice test is used to establish a single pass point such that test takers must achieve that level in order to proceed toward certification. Items are content balanced across the selected discipline. To evaluate the performance of the examination and to score test takers, the board adopted the Rasch model.

To begin the evaluation process, the 12 SMEs engage in a discussion to describe carefully the characteristics, knowledge, skills, and abilities associated with the minimally competent (i.e., passing) candidate. Essentially, the SMEs create a consensus description of passing candidates that is used later to guide their decision making. During the group discussion, it was important that SMEs described the passing candidate as thoroughly as possible according to the *content* specification of the examination content blueprint. The content blueprint reflects academic curricula, professional task analyses, and other sources of validity evidence, making

TABLE 9.5 Steps in Objective Standard Setting for Dichotomous Examinations

	Subject Matter Expert Engagement	*Measurement Translation*
Step 1 Definition	SMEs individually review items, answering the following question: *"Is the content as it is presented in the item essential for the minimally competent (passing) test taker to have mastered?"*	Rasch item difficulties associated with the selected essential items are averaged for each SME. The grand average across SMEs becomes the raw standard.
Step 2 Refinement	SMEs individually review a short, content-balanced presentation of items in item difficulty order, centered ±1 SEM around the raw standard. SMEs place a mark at the point where the items move from essential to nonessential.	The average of points becomes the refined standard.
Step 3 Error	SMEs discuss and determine how measurement error will be used in the standard.	A balanced approach to error may be used, or error may be used to protect the 'innocent test taker' or the 'public'.

that blueprint the most complete reflection of the multifaceted professional and the most appropriate basic description of the successful test taker. The importance of this discussion cannot be overemphasized. Once the description of the minimally competent professional is established, the 12 SMEs are then ready to engage in the three-step OSS process (see Table 9.5).

Step one represents the fundamental definitional process, wherein the SMEs define which portion of the content presented on the examination is essential for passing candidates to have mastered. SMEs were provided with a recently administered copy of the examination. The items on the examination had been Rasch calibrated, but those item difficulties are not shared with the SMEs during step one. Instead, the examination is presented to the group just as it was presented to the test takers but with the correct answers keyed. SMEs are asked to read each item in its entirety, carefully, and then, when finished, each was asked to answer the following question: "Is the content as it is presented in the item *essential* for the minimally competent (passing) test taker to have mastered?" The exercise is conducted with each SME individually. At the conclusion, 12 sets of 'essential item pools' exist, representing those items selected by each of the 12 SMEs as essential for minimally competent (passing) candidates to have mastered. The essential item pool represents a qualitatively meaningful selection of the total test content, a definition as it were, that specifies what each of the SMEs believes is essential for test takers to have mastered vis-à-vis the examination. It is a qualitative decision using SME content expertise that will then be quantified as a measurement device.

OSS requires a set of item calibrations before the pass criterion can be quantified. While some might find this a limitation, from our perspective, it is clearly a natural requirement for *measurement*. The pass criterion might be described qualitatively at any time during step one, but it cannot be quantified until the item calibrations are used in the calculation of the passing standard.

Quantifying the SMEs' essential item pools is quite straightforward. Each item in the essential item pool has an associated Rasch item difficulty calibration. Because the mean is statistically one of the better representations of any normally distributed set, the mean of the Rasch calibrations of those essential items provides a reasonable representation of each SME's item pool. Table 9.6 presents results derived from the essential item pools from the 12 panel members. Item means were calculated independently for each SME's pool, then the grand mean across all SMEs was calculated. This final grand mean is considered the *raw standard*.

TABLE 9.6 OSS Step One: Calculating the Raw Standard

SME #	Number of Essential Items Selected	Mean Item Difficulty of Essential Items (logits)
1	69	1.34
2	87	1.45
3	95	1.29
4	78	1.48
5	83	1.41
6	87	1.38
7	81	1.45
8	73	1.39
10	85	1.46
11	92	1.42
12	94	1.47

Grand mean across SMEs 1.41

Although the raw standard is the fundamental representation of the essential item pools, the grand mean calculation does risk washing out some degree of specificity in the selection of items. This is an inevitable risk in any standard-setting process. OSS step two reintroduces content specification after the raw standard quantification in order to refine the meaning of the standard. Step two involves the use of a modified, limited bookmark approach to help clarify the passing point by presenting an array of items to SMEs and asking them to clarify the passing point: a content-balanced set of 20 items, whose item difficulties are centered around the raw standard and fall between ±1 *SE* of it. Table 9.7 presents the set of items offered to the SMEs during the OSS bookmarking in step two.

TABLE 9.7 Step Two Refinement of the Raw Standard via Modified Bookmark Exercise

Item (Content Category)	Logit Difficulty		Essential v. Non-Essential Mark
J (4)	1.63		
I (5)	1.60		
H (2)	1.56		
G (3)	1.54		
F (1)	1.53		
E (3)	1.51		
D (5)	1.50		
		→	SME 12 = 1.485
C (2)	1.47		
		→	SME 3, 8, 11 = 1.455
B (4)	1.44		
		→	SME 1, 2, 5, 7, 10 = 1.435
A (1)	1.43		
		→	SME 4, 6, 9 = 1.420
A (2)	1.41		
B (3)	1.40		
C (1)	1.39		
D (5)	1.37		
E (4)	1.35		
F (4)	1.33		
G (1)	1.29		
H (5)	1.25		
I (3)	1.22		
J (2)	1.20		

Mean refined standard = 1.44

The item difficulties of the upper 10 items are at or *above* the raw standard and spread relatively evenly across the standard error range. The item difficulties of the lower 10 items are at or *below* the raw standard and spread evenly across the standard error range. SMEs were presented with the ordered set of 20 items and were instructed to review each item carefully. The item difficulty information is not provided, but SMEs are informed that the items are arranged in difficulty order. After the review, each SME is asked independently to draw a mark at the point in the list where the content of the items shifted from essential to nonessential. Table 9.7 presents the results from the marking exercise, revealing that SME judgments are clustered around four items. The refined standard for each individual is calculated as in the following example: SME 12 marked the shift from essential to nonessential between Item C (1.47 logits) and Item D (1.50 logits), so SME 12's refined standard is his/her mean 1.485 logits. The grand mean of all 12 SME refined standards becomes the final refined passing standard. The final standard refined via step two bookmarking was 1.44, or .03 logits higher than the original raw standard.

A feature unique to OSS is the acknowledgement and use of measurement error in standard setting. All measurement, and all human evaluations, include some degree of error or imprecision. Standard setting is no exception. The ways in which error may be used largely mirror the ways in which error can be problematic in any measurement process. OSS step three requires that error be addressed in formulating the standard in one of the following three ways: (a) Error might lead to the incorrect failure of a test taker, and the test taker might be harmed not because of lack of mastery but because of measurement imprecision or some other flaw in the examination process. We could then use error to err on the side of caution and *protect the innocent test taker* from our inability to conduct a perfect assessment. (b) Conversely, the test takers might also guess or find items easy to answer if poorly written. That limits our ability to evaluate their true mastery, and we might wish to have more confidence in our 'pass' decision. Moreover, the examination might be of such high stakes and the possible consequences to public health (in this case) so severe that we want to be quite sure of our 'pass' decision. Then we choose to err on the other side of caution to *protect the public*. (c) The third, in a balanced approach, used likely most often, we acknowledge the error but favor neither test taker nor public.

In all instances, we can use the SE associated with the person measures to adjust the refined standard. Standard errors are used as confidence intervals, such that to establish a 95% confidence level in the passing standard, the SE would be multiplied by the Z-score of 1.95. Table 9.8 demonstrates how standard error confidence intervals can be used to construct the final standard: for example, protecting the public with 95% confidence sets the pass standard at 1.85 logits,

TABLE 9.8 OSS Step Three—Using Error to Calculate the Final Standard

Decision	RS + Confidence (SE) = Final Standard	Passing Rate %
Protect the Public with 95% Confidence	1.44 + 1.96 (.21) = 1.85 logits	59%
Protect the Public with 68% Confidence	1.44 + 1.00 (.21) = 1.65 logits	67%
Balanced Approach to Error	1.44 + 0.00 (.21) = 1.44 logits	78%
Protect the Test Taker with 68% Confidence	1.44 − 1.00 (.21) = 1.23 logits	85%
Protect the Test Taker with 95% Confidence	1.44 − 1.96 (.21) = 1.03 logits	91%

Refined standard (RS) = 1.44 (SE = .21) and Confidence expressed as a Z-score allowing only 59% of candidates to pass; protecting the candidate with the same 95% confidence interval, would allow 91% pass the lower standard set at 1.03 logits.

When decisions with high confidence are made (i.e., with 95%), passing and failing rates are more likely to be unacceptably high or low, particularly from a political or motivational point of view, so the standard-setting exercise must also be weighed in these terms. So use of error is an evaluative exercise; although the calculation of the passing standard is a measurement operation, as with all OSS decisions, the theoretical imperative behind the decision is both philosophical and practical.

OSS maintains its clear connection to the meaning of criterion-referenced standard setting throughout the three-step process. In the first two steps, SMEs engage in content-based decisions and specify what content was essential to the mastery learning process and what content might be handy to know but not essential. Quantification occurs through the OSS Rasch measurement process rather than through SMEs' speculation. In the final step, error is explicitly acknowledged and used to inform decision making through an evaluative discussion. Rasch measurement construct definition makes this possible; dialogue and engagement of SMEs makes standard setting meaningful.

Objective Standard Setting for Judge-Mediated Examinations

Tests that are rated by human judges pose special difficulties for standard setting. While test takers might respond to many, if not all, of the same items, each performance is in some sense unique: Each is graded not by a single correct or incorrect key but rather by judges, against a rubric, along a continuum of correctness. Graded essays, orally administered *vivae voce*, practical and performance assessments, and any evaluation in which a human judge uses an evaluative rubric are all considered here judge-mediated examinations.

Typical standard-setting exercises for such examinations require SME panels to be gathered and engaged in sample performance ratings. SMEs will frequently rate several dozen previously rated examinations during the standard-setting exercises—a process that might take several days to complete. The advent of OSS using the many-facets Rasch model offers a better and more parsimonious solution to the setting of pass standards on performance-based examinations. Rather than requiring a separate standard-setting exercise (alluded to earlier), objective standard setting for judge-mediated examinations (OSSJME) is incorporated into the actual judge examination rating process *during* the examination and yields data for the many-facets Rasch model analysis, reducing time and expense and improving the transparency of the information gathered. The basic many-facets Rasch model (Chapter 8) for performances being graded on a typical rating scale is shown as:

$$\log\left(P_{nijk} / P_{nij(k-1)}\right) = B_n - D_i - C_j$$

where

P_{nijk} = the probability of test taker n being graded k by judge j on item i,
$P_{nij(k-1)}$ = the probability of test taker n being graded $k - 1$ by judge j on item i,
B_n = the ability estimate of test taker n,
D_i = the difficulty of item i, and
C_j = the severity of judge j.

OSSJME adds an additional (S_p) facet, such that:

$$\log\left(P_{nijk} / P_{nij(k-1)}\right) = B_n - D_i - C_j - S_p$$

where the additional facet S_p = the likelihood of selecting pass-fail category p relative to pass-fail category $p - 1$.

Examiners evaluate test takers as usual, using whatever rating form or rubric is usually employed. At the bottom of that form, a single standard-setting holistic evaluation question is added. The question that forms the basis for the standard setting asks the rater to consider the performance holistically and to evaluate that performance using a rating such as the following:

Clear Failure — Borderline Failure — Borderline Pass — Clear Pass

The exemplar elaborating the OSSJME process uses data from the oral presentation component of the same high-stakes health care certification group used in the OSS procedure. In that example, the certification group requires test takers to engage in an orally delivered examination in addition to the 200-item multiple-choice test. The oral presentation is designed to evaluate critical-thinking skills not easily assessable via traditional M-C testing. Test takers are presented with case studies (considered *items* in the multifaceted model), and each test taker is required to interact with examiners orally by providing answers to questions posed by examiners. The case studies are much like 'simulated patients', presenting a case history and other basic information to the physician, who is then required to evaluate patient status and outline appropriate treatment. The quality, depth, and completeness of test taker responses are scored on a rating form with a 4-point Likert-type rating scale. At the end of each case presentation and scoring, examiners ($N = x$) evaluate the performance of the test taker holistically across the entire case presentation and rate the performance using the Clear Failure/Borderline Failure/Borderline Pass/Clear Pass grade options.

TABLE 9.9 OSSJME Many-Facets Standard

Raw Average (Original Scale)	Rasch Measure (SE) Logits	Pass Decision	Passing Rate
1.76	3.26 (.07)	1 = Clear Pass	
2.40	1.47 (.05)	2 = Borderline Pass	89%
—	0.47	Calculated Midpoint	82%
2.91	−0.53 (.03)	3 = Borderline Fail	71%
3.68	−4.20 (.09)	4 = Clear Fail	

Data are analyzed using Linacre's FACETS computer program for the many-facets model.

Table 9.9 presents the FACETS analysis for just the modeled 'standard-setting' facet: each rating (Clear Failure, Borderline Failure, Borderline Pass, Clear Pass) is associated with a logit ability measure, each representing a particular level of mastery. These logit estimates are then used to establish the pass standard. For this certification process, the passing standard for the examination is positioned midway between ability measures for Borderline Pass and Borderline Failure. Routinely, this midpoint is taken as the pass standard; however, this decision, like that for the M-C examination, is based on the professional judgments of the certification SME group. By adopting the Borderline Failure value as the standard, the benefit of the doubt for measurement imprecision (SE) is used in favor of the test taker. By adopting the Borderline Pass value as the standard, the certification group makes the decision to hold test takers to a higher level of confidence in the passing decision and, thereby, to 'protect the public'. Use of the midpoint represents the balanced approach. Table 9.9 presents the impact on passing rates of each standard on the sample of test takers in our example.

Fair Standards

Standard setting is inherently both evaluative and measurement oriented. OSS and OSSJME promote the specifically qualitative decisions made by content experts and using the Rasch measurement model to quantify those SME decisions effectively. OSS requires SMEs to make clear and direct decisions regarding the essential content presented in written examinations. OSSJME requires evaluators to review content-directed performances of test takers and to compare those performances to a set of content-defined criteria. Both are firmly rooted in qualitative, content-based criteria and not in predictions of success or normative manipulations inherent in other models. Criterion standards must demonstrate this content-directed connection to be fair and reasonable. The establishment of the validity of standards must begin with this important consideration.

Rasch Regression (Svetlana Beltyukova, U Toledo)

More than a decade ago, Ben Wright introduced a method for creating a predictive yardstick for a dichotomous outcome of gout diagnosis using probabilistic Rasch analysis (Wright, 2000a; Wright, Perkins, & Dorsey, 2000). He named that method Rasch regression and wrote his 'recipe' for it (Wright, 2000b). In his method, he extended Rasch regression to the ordinal outcome of probable, possible, and uncertain diagnosis of Alzheimer's disease (see Hughes, Perkins, Wright, & Westrick, 2003).

Unlike the routinely used least-squares regression, Rasch regression goes beyond merely maximizing the explained variance in the **dependent variable** (DV) by identifying the set of predictors that, together, represent a meaningful linear variable. Essentially, it builds upon routine Rasch analysis procedures to define the variable that *maximizes person separation* into levels that are *predefined* by the dependent variable. The usual Rasch diagnostics (fit statistics, scale functioning, item and person dimensionality, etc.) are used to assess the utility of regressing the dependent variable(s) on the **independent variables** (IV). The most useful diagnostic, however, is the Rasch principal components analysis of the residuals (Rasch PCA) to identify which IVs contribute the most useful information in predicting the DV.

Airline Passenger Satisfaction Data

The following description of Rasch regression uses data from Airs@t survey developed by the International Air Transport Association (IATA) and M1nd-Set (an expert in travel market research) to assess passenger satisfaction. The Airs@t survey is used by airlines worldwide to track passenger satisfaction and to compare it with that of other airlines. Survey items refer to passenger experiences with the airline preflight, in flight, and postflight as well as ask for an overall rating of the airline performance.[1] Beltyukova and Fox (2013) were invited to analyze these data with the Rasch model to determine which of the surveyed airline attributes predicted *overall rating of airline performance* (OVERALL).

The data used were collected from 40,400 business-class passengers on long-haul (i.e., 5 hours or longer) flights operated by 22 major airlines flying 11 different aircraft. Almost 78% of the sample were males, and 92% were in the age range of 26 to 64. The sample sufficiently differed on the DV—*overall rating of airline performance*: 3,077 (8%) rated it as poor or fair, 9,750 (24%) as good, 17,763 (44%) as very good, and 9,810 (24%) as excellent. The important condition for Rasch regression of "collect[ing] a sample of persons who differ substantially in your dependent variable" (Wright, 2000b) was clearly satisfied.

Sixty-five items representing different aspects of flight experience were selected to explore their utility in predicting the *overall rating of airline performance*.

Item selection was based on existing research by Perroud and colleagues (2006). According to that model, airlines should consider and differentiate among BASIC items (e.g., on-time departure), PERFORMANCE (KEY) items (e.g., cabin- and crew-related features), and BONUS items (e.g., in-flight entertainment). Further, these three classifications of attributes impact passenger satisfaction and dissatisfaction in different ways, so each should be prioritized by airlines based on this satisfaction/dissatisfaction combination. However, because our goal was to extract a linear measure to predict satisfaction (i.e., setting aside dissatisfaction for the moment), we hypothesized that BASIC items would be the *easiest* to endorse as being satisfied, followed by PERFORMANCE (KEY) items, and finally, BONUS items would be most difficult for passengers to endorse as satisfying. This hypothesis was based on Perroud's observations that BONUS items reveal their full potential to drive satisfaction once both *basic* and *performance* attributes have been satisfied. Thus, it would make sense that BONUS items would be found at the most difficult end of the satisfaction measure. PERFORMANCE (KEY) items, however, are claimed to impact greatly on both satisfaction and dissatisfaction—*but only when satisfaction with BASIC attributes has been achieved.* Again, this implies the expected placement of Airs@t items on a linear continuum, with BASIC at the bottom (easiest) followed by PERFORMANCE (KEY). Finally, a fourth type of item (SECONDARY), which includes features such as 'seat control operation', consistently had been observed as having a weak impact on both satisfaction and dissatisfaction. Thus, we did not hypothesize these items as large contributors to our proposed satisfaction variable. Using this framework, the 65 Airs@t survey items were classified according to the type of attribute they represented: 9 'basic', 18 'performance/key', 13 'bonus', and 25 'secondary' items for the regression analyses. Originally, the Airs@t data set contained five response options, but in what follows, the data are analyzed as four response options, with the *poor* and *fair* response categories collapsed.

Rasch Regression Using the Anchored Formulation

The Rasch regression analysis presented here is referred to by Wright (2000a) as the 'anchored' approach. This approach anchors the persons at their DV values to achieve maximum separation of persons on their outcome classification. The best set of predictors (based on Rasch diagnostics) is then chosen to define the linear measure that is predictive of the DV.

Step 1. The first step required that the 40,400 passengers be anchored at their dependent variable values. For this, the data file was sorted by passengers' responses to Airs@t item 1, *overall rating of airline performance* (OVERALL), so that the new data file for subsequent analysis had passengers ordered, in four groups, from least to most satisfied according to their response on (*only*) item 1 (e.g., the first 3,077 passengers responded either Poor or Fair to item 1). The following person anchor file (PAFILE) command, then, anchors the Person measure for each successive group of respondents at 1, 2, 3, or 4 logits, respectively). Person anchor information is written as the following command in the Winsteps program:

```
PAFILE=*
1–3077          1; poor and fair overall performance
3078–12827      2; good overall performance
12828–30590     3; very good overall performance
30591–40400     4; excellent overall performance
*
```

This step incorporated the dependent variable (as anchored person measures), and a Rasch rating scale model (RSM) analysis was conducted using only the 65 survey items (as the independent variables).

Given that Winsteps identifies items according to their order, the data file was now set up so that the dependent variable (DV—OVERALL) was located in the first column, followed by the 65 (IV) survey items. The dependent variable would now be identified as item 1, the first survey item as item 2, the second as item 3, and so forth. By setting up the data file in this manner, it is easy to exclude the dependent variable from the RSM analyses with the simple command:

```
IDFILE = *
1
*
```

This eliminates the dependent variable from the analyses; however, the *information* from the dependent variable is incorporated through the PAFILE, where each person is anchored at the appropriate dependent variable value, as shown.

After running the RSM on this data file, the results of the Rasch PCA were examined to determine which of the 65 observed independent variables (items) clustered together and contributed to the discrimination among the four DV groups. Rasch PCA of residuals identified 56 items with loadings on the measure of > .30 (see Table 9.10). These included all basic (9 items), all performance/key (18 items), all bonus (13 items), and 16 out of 25 secondary items; that is, all the items that had loadings of ≤ .30 were secondary attributes. This was consistent with the model espoused by Perroud and colleagues (2006) in which secondary items had less impact on overall passenger satisfaction with airline performance.

Step 2. A set of Rasch diagnostic statistics (item and person reliability and separation indices, item fit indices, and percentage of variance explained) were compared for a series of stepwise Rasch analyses performed on the 56-item

TABLE 9.10 'Anchored' Approach to Rasch Regression: Results of the Rasch PC A With 65 Input Items

CONTRAST	LOADING	MEASURE	INFIT MNSQ	OUTFIT MNSQ	ENTRY NUMBER	ITEM
1	.65	2.60	.75	.78	18	K_18
1	.62	2.48	.90	.94	14	K_18_3
1	.62	2.11	.99	1.00	63	S_19_6
1	.61	2.69	.97	.99	15	K_18_4
1	.60	2.47	1.05	1.06	20	K_19_3
1	.60	2.58	.96	.98	21	K_19
1	.59	2.33	.97	.98	13	K_18_2
1	.59	2.57	1.01	1.03	16	K_18_5
1	.58	1.91	.86	.85	9	B_20
1	.58	2.14	.95	.97	7	B_20_6
1	.57	1.69	.92	.90	2	B_20_1
1	.56	3.22	.91	.94	41	BO_21
1	.56	2.39	.88	.91	25	K_22_3
1	.56	2.52	1.12	1.15	62	S_19_5
1	.55	2.62	1.12	1.14	19	K_19_1
1	.55	2.65	1.03	1.06	17	K_18_7
1	.55	2.51	.84	.86	27	K_22
1	.54	2.24	1.11	1.14	60	S_18_1
1	.54	1.95	1.02	1.01	5	B_20_4
1	.54	2.18	.93	.95	10	B_22_4
1	.54	2.02	1.17	1.18	61	S_19_4
1	.54	1.90	1.00	.99	3	B_20_2
1	.53	1.78	1.04	1.05	6	B_20_5
1	.52	2.78	1.10	1.15	31	BO_18_6
1	.52	2.45	.94	.96	26	K_22_2
1	.52	3.19	1.20	1.25	37	BO_21_4
1	.51	1.75	1.02	.99	4	B_20_3
1	.51	3.09	1.14	1.19	38	BO_21_5
1	.51	3.11	1.23	1.27	40	BO_21_9
1	.50	2.96	1.18	1.22	39	BO_21_6
1	.50	2.98	1.15	1.19	36	BO_21_7
1	.49	2.16	1.01	1.04	56	S_17_1
1	.49	2.86	1.36	1.38	30	BO_19_2
1	.49	2.38	.96	.99	12	K_17
1	.48	2.48	1.10	1.14	59	S_17_4
1	.48	2.05	.98	1.01	65	S_23_2
1	.47	2.62	1.04	1.06	23	K_22_1
1	.47	2.17	1.12	1.16	57	S_17_2
1	.45	2.26	.92	.95	28	K_23
1	.44	3.00	1.16	1.20	34	BO_21_8
1	.43	3.16	1.37	1.42	33	BO_21_2
1	.43	2.99	1.20	1.23	35	BO_21_3
1	.41	3.39	1.25	1.31	32	BO_21_1
1	.40	1.77	1.26	1.29	55	S_12
1	.39	1.73	1.37	1.42	49	S_12_2
1	.37	2.36	.90	.93	22	K_22_5
1	.37	3.00	1.30	1.36	29	BO_14
1	.37	1.96	1.24	1.26	64	K_23_1
1	.36	2.08	1.01	1.01	8	B_20_7
1	.36	2.85	1.41	1.48	43	S_14_1
1	.34	1.47	1.26	1.33	51	S_12_4
1	.34	2.50	.99	1.00	24	K_22_6
1	.34	1.61	1.34	1.38	50	S_12_3
1	.32	3.21	1.55	1.63	44	S_14_2
1	.32	2.38	1.57	1.64	58	S_17_3
1	.31	2.43	1.38	1.42	66	S_23_3
1	.30	2.71	1.59	1.67	45	S_14_3
1	.29	1.70	1.65	1.72	48	S_12_1
1	.24	2.96	1.43	1.51	47	S_14_6
1	.24	2.55	1.40	1.47	46	S_14_5
1	.22	2.30	1.08	1.10	67	S_23_4
1	.18	1.81	1.39	1.45	53	S_12_6
1	.12	1.92	1.33	1.38	54	S_12_7
1	.08	2.08	1.52	1.59	52	S_12_5
1	.06	3.70	1.44	1.37	42	S_21_10

data file until no items showed misfit; that is, misfitting items were deleted at each step until no more items misfit the model (see Table 9.11). The resulting definition of the prediction yardstick consisted of 36 items representing all basic attributes (9 items), almost all performance/key attributes (15 out of 18) and bonus attributes (8 out of 9), but very few secondary items (only 4 out of 25). This solution was largely consistent with the hypothesized linear satisfaction variable and yielded the highest percentage of variance explained by the measure (57%).

Step 3. The resulting logit scale was then recalibrated into a more user-friendly 0 to 100 scale. Rescaling logits to an operational range of 0 to 100 was chosen to improve interpretability of the results as "the increments of 10 units up or down [this] scale change the outcome odds by a factor of 3" (Hughes, Perkins, Wright, & Westrick, 2003, p. 369).

Step 4. We now, from Step 3, have all values on a 0 to 100 scale. The analysis was rerun to provide anchor files for item measures, person measures, and rating scale thresholds from the final 36-item solution. This was accomplished by using the Output Tables menu in Winsteps and saving all three types of anchor files (calibrated 0–100): IAFILE (Item Anchor FILE), PAFILE (Person Anchor FILE), and SAFILE (Step Anchor FILE), with descriptive file names for later use.

The following command lines were added to the Winsteps control file for the subsequent, Step 5, analysis:

```
PAFILE=PAFILE_36_items.txt
IAFILE=IAFILE_36_items.txt
SAFILE=SAFILE_36_items.txt
```

Step 5. With the person, item, and threshold anchor commands in the control file, the dependent variable data column (#1) was reintroduced to the analysis by 'commenting out' the earlier command to ignore column 1. The addition of semicolons instructs Winsteps to ignore the command.

```
;IDFILE = *
;1
;*
```

In effect, this anchors all of the independent variables at their previously calibrated measures and reintroduces the dependent variable (OVERALL) into the analysis, *unanchored*. Figure 9.5 shows the 36-Item Construct Key Map (Winsteps Table 28.2), which is now our 'prediction yardstick', with the dependent variable 'OVERALL' (*overall rating of airline performance*) moved to the bottom of the yardstick for ease of interpretation. Wright and colleagues called this map "The Complete Story on One Page" (2000, p. 39) because it shows the definition of the passenger satisfaction variable based on the Rasch-selected 36 items that formed the best linear variable for predicting passenger satisfaction from the

TABLE 9.11 'Anchored' Approach to Rasch Regression: Results of the Stepwise Rasch Analyses

Items in Analysis	Person Separation	Person Reliability	Item Separation	Item Reliability	Infit MNSQ	Outfit MNSQ	# Items Misfit	Variance Explained	Item Types			
									Basic	Key	Bonus	Secondary
45 items	4.50	.95	66.35	1.00	0.59–1.49	0.63–1.86	2	52.1%	9	18	9	9
43 items	4.48	.95	65.83	1.00	0.60–1.25	0.63–1.34	1	52.9%	9	17	9	8
42 items	4.47	.95	66.39	1.00	0.60–1.27	0.63–1.35	1	53.3%	9	17	9	7
41 items	4.45	.95	67.41	1.00	0.60–1.19	0.63–1.32	1	53.7%	9	17	9	6
40 items	4.42	.95	68.29	1.00	0.60–1.22	0.64–1.44	1	54.1%	9	16	9	6
39 items	4.38	.95	68.90	1.00	0.60–1.17	0.64–1.32	1	54.5%	9	16	9	5
38 items	4.35	.95	69.68	1.00	0.60–1.17	0.64–1.32	1	54.8%	9	15	9	5
37 items	4.32	.95	69.86	1.00	0.60–1.17	0.64–1.32	1	55.2%	9	15	9	4
36 items	4.28	.95	70.42	1.00	0.62–1.25	0.65–1.22	0	57.2%	9	15	8	4

available data. Distributions of the four subgroups of passengers (i.e., those who rated the overall airline performance as *poor and fair, good, very good*, and *excellent*) were obtained by running each of the four groups separately using the PSELECT command and added to the bottom of the construct key map to enhance interpretation of the results and evaluation of the utility of regressing the dependent variable on the resulting 36 items. Table 9.12 provides summary descriptive statistics for each subgroup of passengers.

The regression yardstick produced by the anchored Rasch aligned with our original hypothesis (based on Perroud's work), with all the basic attributes at the lower end of the measure (easiest to endorse), followed by performance/key attributes and by bonus attributes at the top (most difficult to endorse; see Figure 9.5). Point–measure correlations for the 36 items (ranging from .67 to .79) indicated a strong relationship among these items (see Table 9.13). The point–measure correlation for the dependent variable with the anchored linear yardstick was .72, and fit statistics were .81 (infit) and 1.14 (outfit), thus indicating a satisfactory solution for predicting *overall rating of airline performance* from the 36 items (see Table 9.13). Finally, the ordering of the subgroup means was meaningful, that is, mean measures increased with the increase in the overall satisfaction rating and the four group means were statistically distinct (see Table 9.13), suggesting that stable patterns in responses to the 36 items separating the four groups could be identified. Drawing a line through the mean of each subgroup (see Figure 9.5) showed the following:

Business-class passengers who rated overall airline performance as:

- *poor and fair* (DV code of 1) would be expected to rate all the basic and half of the performance/key attributes as good and the more difficult performance/key attributes and all bonus attributes as poor or fair;
- *good* (DV code of 2) would be expected to rate all the basic attributes as very good and all the performance and bonus attributes as good;
- *very good* (DV code of 3) would be expected to rate all the basic and performance/key attributes as very good and the most difficult bonus attributes as good; and
- *excellent* (DV code of 4) would be expected to rate all the basic and performance/key attributes as excellent and all the bonus attributes as very good.

TABLE 9.12 'Anchored' Approach to Rasch Regression: Subgroup Separation Analysis

Subgroup based on DV value	Mean	Std. Error	n
Poor and Fair	36.39	0.07	3,077
Good	44.71	0.18	9,750
Very good	54.45	0.06	17,763
Excellent	69.10	0.13	9,810

Note. All pairwise group comparisons were significant at $p < .0001$.

TABLE 9.13 Item Statistics in Measure Order

ENTRY NUMBER	TOTAL SCORE	TOTAL COUNT	MEASURE	MODEL S.E.	INFIT MNSQ	INFIT ZSTD	OUTFIT MNSQ	OUTFIT ZSTD	PT-MEASURE CORR.	PT-MEASURE EXP.	EXACT MATCH OBS%	EXACT MATCH EXP%	ITEM
41	87745	38445	57.65A	.06	.82	-9.9	.80	-9.9	.76	.73	61.2	56.2	BO_21
37	86841	37750	57.35A	.06	1.19	9.9	1.16	9.9	.70	.73	52.8	56.0	BO_21_4
40	89777	38111	56.38A	.06	1.24	9.9	1.23	9.9	.68	.73	52.2	55.8	BO_21_9
38	87931	37142	56.18A	.06	1.16	9.9	1.16	9.9	.69	.73	54.7	55.7	BO_21_5
34	68122	28091	55.34A	.07	1.22	9.9	1.23	9.9	.68	.73	54.4	56.1	BO_21_8
35	61506	25268	55.23A	.07	1.25	9.9	1.22	9.9	.68	.73	53.6	56.1	BO_21_3
36	91793	37717	55.02A	.06	1.20	9.9	1.20	9.9	.67	.73	53.7	55.6	BO_21_7
39	91471	37350	54.77A	.06	1.21	9.9	1.19	9.9	.68	.73	54.3	55.6	BO_21_6
15	105227	40149	51.80A	.06	.88	-9.9	.86	-9.9	.74	.72	60.7	56.1	K_18_4
17	105995	40158	51.47A	.06	1.06	8.3	1.11	9.9	.70	.71	57.1	56.2	K_18_7
19	107483	40395	51.09A	.06	1.09	9.9	1.06	5.7	.71	.71	56.2	56.4	K_19_1
23	105907	39776	51.08A	.06	1.16	9.9	1.16	9.9	.68	.71	55.3	56.4	K_22_1
18	107841	40326	50.85A	.06	.62	-9.9	.65	-9.9	.79	.71	70.9	56.4	K_18
21	108573	40394	50.61A	.06	.86	-9.9	.83	-9.9	.75	.71	62.4	56.5	K_19
16	108636	40377	50.57A	.06	.94	-9.6	.91	-8.2	.74	.71	60.1	56.5	K_18_5
62	109779	40361	50.05A	.06	1.09	9.9	1.10	9.0	.69	.71	57.7	56.7	S_19_5
27	109459	40100	49.89A	.06	.84	-9.9	.82	-9.9	.74	.71	63.4	56.8	K_22
24	41485	15063	49.73A	.09	1.00	.3	.97	-1.4	.71	.71	59.7	57.0	K_22_6
14	110648	40304	49.61A	.06	.82	-9.9	.84	-9.9	.73	.70	64.7	56.9	K_18_3
20	111157	40393	49.48A	.06	.93	-9.9	.90	-9.6	.74	.70	61.4	56.9	K_19_3
26	109967	39755	49.25A	.06	.98	-2.7	.99	-.5	.70	.70	60.6	57.0	K_22_2
25	111803	39935	48.65A	.06	.90	-9.9	.93	-6.2	.70	.70	62.9	57.3	K_22_3
22	42749	15062	48.21A	.09	.87	-9.9	.88	-6.5	.71	.70	64.6	57.6	K_22_5
13	114593	40390	47.95A	.06	.90	-9.9	.87	-9.9	.73	.70	62.8	57.6	K_18_2
1	115106	40400	47.73	.06	.81	-9.9	1.14	9.9	.72	.69	64.9	57.7	OVERALL
60	116645	40338	46.96A	.06	1.15	9.9	1.20	9.9	.65	.69	59.4	58.1	S_18_1
10	116785	39962	46.41A	.06	.95	-6.8	.96	-3.1	.68	.69	62.4	58.4	B_22_4
7	117485	39831	45.93A	.06	.96	-6.3	.99	-.8	.68	.68	61.9	58.7	B_20_6
63	119751	40383	45.59A	.06	.86	-9.9	.85	-9.9	.72	.68	66.5	58.8	S_19_6
8	45578	15195	45.19A	.10	1.01	.5	.98	-.9	.69	.68	62.4	59.2	B_20_7
61	121761	40390	44.65A	.06	1.15	9.9	1.12	8.0	.66	.67	60.9	59.4	S_19_4
5	121901	39947	43.98A	.06	1.02	2.9	.99	-.7	.68	.67	62.7	59.8	B_20_4
9	124164	40377	43.48A	.06	.80	-9.9	.75	-9.9	.72	.67	68.3	60.1	B_20
3	122435	39758	43.46A	.06	1.00	1.4	.97	-2.2	.68	.67	63.8	60.2	B_20_2
6	119090	37852	42.24A	.06	1.05	6.0	1.14	8.1	.64	.66	64.1	61.1	B_20_5
4	127405	40350	41.83A	.06	1.04	5.2	.99	-.9	.67	.65	64.7	61.2	B_20_3
2	128548	40338	41.22A	.06	.87	-9.9	.83	-9.9	.69	.65	68.3	61.7	B_20_1
MEAN	101977	36971	49.38	.06	1.00	-.6	1.00	.0			60.8	57.6	
S.D.	22911.4	7197.7	4.47	.01	.15	8.8	.15	8.3			4.6	1.7	

Note that the mean for subgroup 4 (*excellent*—measured at rescaled value of 69) just exceeds the value of 62 (the Rasch-Andrich threshold between categories 3 and 4) on Item 1 Overall (D1 47.73 + F3 14.45; item 1 difficulty plus the threshold value), where the probability of rating an airline as excellent (4) rather than as good (3) exceeds 50%. Similarly, the mean for subgroup 3 (*very good*— measured at 54) just exceeds the value of 47 (the Rasch-Andrich threshold between categories 2 and 3 [D1 47.73 + F2 −1.14] obtained by adding the 2/3 threshold value to 47.73 item difficulty value), where the probability of rating an airline as *very good* begins to fail and the odds in favor of rating the airline as good increase.

Last but not least, given that the odds change by a factor of 3 for any 10-unit change on the measure, odds can be calculated for any measure position. Thus, for example, knowing that the odds of rating an airline as either *excellent* or *very good* are even at person measure 62, these odds become 3:1 at person measure 72, 1:3 at person measure 52, 1:9 at person measure 42, and so on. Combining this information with the knowledge of group means, it would be expected that the passengers who rated the airline as *very good* (group mean is 54) would have about 30% probability of rating the airline as *excellent*, while passengers who rated the airline as *good*

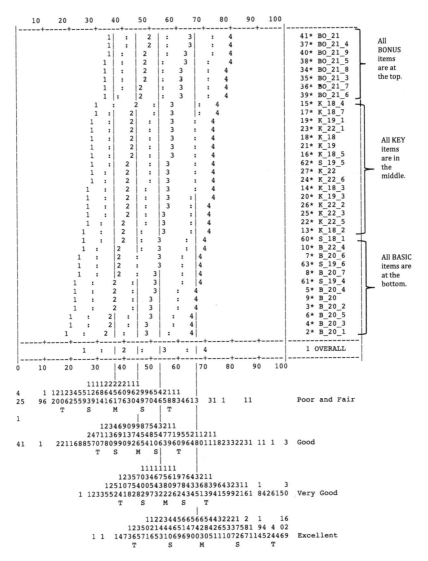

FIGURE 9.5 Predictive yardstick of passenger overall rating of airline performance.

(group mean is 45) would have about 12% likelihood of rating it as *excellent*. Similar calculations and comparisons can be made for any measure position.

In summary, all of the findings obtained with the 'anchored' approach were consistent with the hypothesized linear variable based on the satisfaction trends reported by Perroud and colleagues (2006), who indicated that passengers needed to be satisfied with the basic and performance/key attributes first *before* bonus attributes became important.

Rasch Regression: Alternative Approaches

Wright (2000a) introduced two *other* approaches to Rasch regression, with each being a slight variation of the 'anchored' approach demonstrated already. His 'open mind' approach *requires* no information/restrictions about the classification of persons on the DV (dependent variable). The goal is to achieve maximum separation of persons *independent* of their outcome classification (dependent variable score). This eliminates Step 1 of the anchored approach and, instead, relies on a series of Rasch analyses to extract the best possible latent independent variable, which is later used to evaluate the extent to which it can predict the dependent variable. This approach "optimizes the inferential stability" (p. 43) of the dependent variable predictions because the linear measure formed by the independent variables has been constructed "independently of any DV distribution and also of any sample dependent covariance among the IV" (p. 43).

Wright's 'shortcut' approach falls in between the other two approaches in that all independent and dependent variables are analyzed together, without any anchoring. Following is a summary the steps for conducting the Rasch regression using each approach.

Steps	Regression—Anchored	Open mind	Shortcut
1	Anchor the persons at DV value.	X	X
2	Run the IVs.	unanchored	unanchored w/DV
3	Rescale logits to 0–100, etc.	✓	✓
4	Retain IVs with highest loadings from PCA.	✓	✓

Regardless of the approach, the key step in each analysis is to identify a set of items that function well together as a unidimensional Rasch measure, in this case, of airline satisfaction. This is achieved by an iterative procedure of analysis, consideration of fit and dimensionality statistics, and the successive deletions of misfitting items.

With the 'open mind' approach (i.e., not anchoring the independent variables on their dependent variable values), a series of stepwise Rasch analyses (see Table 9.14) was performed on this data set until no items showed misfit. The resulting definition of the prediction yardstick consisted of the *same* 36 items obtained with the anchored approach, suggesting comparable inferential stability of the two approaches.

For the 'shortcut' formulation, the results were somewhat similar to the other two approaches (Table 9.15). Three additional items retained using this approach (1 performance/key, 1 bonus, and 1 secondary) were those removed during the final iterations of the stepwise Rasch analyses in the other two approaches. In this analysis, these items (#28, #31, and #65) had borderline outfit mean square statistics of 1.32, 1.31, and 1.37. The rank ordering of the 36 items common across

TABLE 9.14 'Open Mind' Approach to Rasch Regression: Results of the Stepwise Rasch Analyses

Items in Analysis	Person Separation	Person Reliability	Item Separation	Item Reliability	Infit MNSQ	Oufit MNSQ	# Items Misfit	Variance Explained	Item Types Basic	Key	Bonus	Secondary
65 items	4.70	.96	45.26	1.00	0.56–1.66	0.60–1.90	16	48.4%	9	18	13	25
49 items	4.65	.96	67.90	1.00	0.58–1.57	0.61–1.75	5	52.0%	9	17	12	11
44 items	4.49	.95	62.25	1.00	0.60–1.26	0.63–1.35	2	52.8%	9	17	9	9
42 items	4.47	.95	66.39	1.00	0.60–1.27	0.63–1.35	1	53.3%	9	17	9	7
41 items	4.45	.95	67.41	1.00	0.60–1.19	0.63–1.32	2	53.7%	9	17	9	6
39 items	4.38	.95	68.90	1.00	0.60–1.17	0.64–1.32	1	54.5%	9	16	9	5
38 items	4.35	.95	69.68	1.00	0.60–1.19	0.64–1.37	1	54.8%	9	15	9	5
37 items	4.32	.95	69.86	1.00	0.60–1.19	0.64–1.31	1	55.2%	9	15	9	4
36 items	4.28	.95	70.39	1.00	0.62–1.22	0.67–1.26	0	57.2%	9	15	8	4

TABLE 9.15 'Shortcut' Approach to Rasch Regression: Results of the Stepwise Rasch Analyses

Items in Analysis (including DV)	Person Separation	Person Reliability	Item Separation	Item Reliability	Infit MNSQ	Outfit MNSQ	# Items Misfit	Variance Explained	Item Types			
									Basic	Key	Bonus	Secondary
66 items	4.76	.96	45.19	1.00	0.56–1.66	0.60–1.90	16	48.6%	9	18	13	25
50 items	4.71	.96	67.55	1.00	0.58–1.57	0.61–1.75	5	52.1%	9	17	12	11
45 items	4.56	.95	62.29	1.00	0.60–1.26	0.63–1.34	2	53.0%	9	17	9	9
43 items	4.54	.95	65.96	1.00	0.60–1.27	0.63–1.35	1	53.4%	9	17	9	7
42 items	4.52	.95	66.95	1.00	0.60–1.19	0.64–1.32	2	53.9%	9	17	9	6
40 items	4.46	.95	68.41	1.00	0.60–1.17	0.63–1.28	0	56.1%	9	16	9	5

the three approaches remained exactly the same, and the amount of variance explained was also very similar.

Discussion

Three different approaches to conducting Rasch regression analyses have been illustrated. The so-called anchored approach provided direct information to the analysis with regard to the classification of the persons into four satisfaction groups on the dependent variable (OVERALL). The 'open mind' approach emphasized the potential of the Rasch model to extract a stable and meaningful latent variable and examine its ability to discriminate groups of persons on the conceptually relevant dependent variable. Finally, Wright's 'shortcut' approach represented a pooled run in which the dependent variable was examined together with the independent variables that were conceptualized as contributing useful information to the measurement of the construct and beyond the information provided by the dependent variable. All three Rasch regression approaches yielded almost identical results, and they were consistent with the model of passenger satisfaction with airline performance, which is consistent with the claim for measurement objectivity obtained with the Rasch model. In addition, the applied appeal of the Rasch regressions is that "the resulting positional relationships are complete, easy to see and easy to interpret" (Wright, 2000a, p. 43). But is the more intensive anchored regression approach worth the extra work? It seems that what you get out of the one-page construct map plus the added distributions and lines for means for each DV group is worth the extra effort taken for the complete Rasch regression approach using DV group anchors. While the simpler variations identify the same DV items, more or less, you don't get the mapped 'Complete Story on One Page'.

Summary

While we advocate the use of the Rasch model before data collection takes place, Rasch principles can be used to construct a Rasch measure from existing data sets.

While some response options might have almost unlimited ordered categories (e.g., number of meters complete during a 12-minute run), it is an empirical issues as to how many useful measurement distinctions can be made between the extremes.

Although meters and seconds indicate interval-level differences on the length or time scales, those indications have only ordinal-level meaning on fitness, VAS, and other scales.

Rasch measurement diagnostic indicators underlie seven criteria that can be used to justify the inclusion or exclusion of items for creating measures.

Establishment of OSS standards is an *evaluative* exercise, supported by Rasch measurement, in which subject-matter experts (SMEs) define minimal competency.

The Rasch-based objective standard-setting model (OSS) is used for the establishment of criterion-referenced performance standards on multiple-choice tests.

The OSSJME extends these principles to ensure the validity of cut-score decisions in judge-mediated examinations.

Rasch regression goes beyond maximizing explained variance in the DV to identify the set of predictors that represent a meaningful linear variable.

Rasch regression procedures focus on how to choose a set of predictors that best separates persons on a dependent variable of interest.

The more intensive anchored Rasch regression approach provides the added benefit of the mapped 'Complete Story on One Page'.

ACTIVITIES

Please read

Yan, Z., & Bond, T. (2011). Developing a Rasch measurement physical fitness scale for Hong Kong primary school–aged students. *Measurement in Physical Education and Exercise Science, 15*(3), 182–203.

Stone, G. E., Koskey, K.L.K., & Sondergeld, T.A. (2011). Comparing construct definition in Angoff and objective standard setting models: Playing in a house of cards without a deck. *Educational and Psychological Measurement, 71*(6), 942–962.

Wright, B.D. (2000b). Rasch regression: My recipe. *Rasch Measurement Transactions, 14*(3), 758–759.

Wright, B.D., Perkins, K., & Dorsey, J.K. (2000). Rasch measurement instead of regression. *Multiple Linear Regression Viewpoints, 26*(2), 36–41.

Note

1 Airs@t survey and research can be found on the IATA website (www.iata.org/services/ statistics/intelligence/Pages/passenger-satisfaction-survey.aspx) and in Perroud, Ray, and Friedrichsen (2006).

References

Angoff, W. (1971). Scales, norms and equivalent scores. In R. L. Thorndike (Ed.), *Educational measurement* (pp. 506–600). Washington, DC: American Council on Education.

Beltyukova, S., & Fox, C. (2013, October). *Diagnostic mapping of key drivers for predicting airline satisfaction of business class passengers.* International Air Transport Association (IATA) Forum, Miami, FL.

Bond, T. G., & Fox, C. M. (2007). *Applying the Rasch model: Fundamental measurement in the human sciences* (2nd ed.). Mahwah, NJ: Erlbaum.

Cizek, G. J., & Bunch, M. B. (2007). *Standard setting: A guide to establishing and evaluating performance standards on tests.* Thousand Oaks, CA: Sage.

Draney, K., & Wilson, M. (2011). Understanding Rasch measurement: Selecting cut scores with a composite of item types: The Construct Mapping procedure. *Journal of Applied Measurement, 12*(3), 298–309.

Ebel, R. L. (1979). *Essentials of educational measurement.* Englewood Cliffs, NJ: Prentice-Hall.

Hambleton, R., & Slater, S. (1997). Reliability of credentialing examinations and the impact of scoring models and standard-setting policies. *Applied Measurement in Education, 10*(1), 19–38.

Heyward, V. H. (2002). *Advanced fitness assessment and exercise prescription* (4th ed.). Champaign, IL: Human Kinetics.

Hughes, L. F., Perkins, K., Wright, B. D., & Westrick, H. (2003). Using a Rasch scale to characterize the clinical features of patients with a clinical diagnosis of uncertain, probable or possible Alzheimer disease at intake. *Journal of Alzheimer's Disease, 5*(5), 367–373.

IATA. (2014). *Airs@t—Satisfaction survey.* Retrieved from www.iata.org/services/statistics/intelligence/Pages/passenger-satisfaction-survey.aspx

Kane, M., & Case, S. (2004). The reliability and validity of weighted composite scores. *Applied Measurement in Education, 17*(3), 221–240.

Karantonis, A., & Sireci, S. G. (2006). The bookmark standard-setting method: A literature review. *Educational Measurement: Issues and Practice, 25*(1), 4–12.

Linacre, J. M. (2000). New approaches to determining reliability and validity. *Research Quarterly for Exercise and Sport, 71*(2), 129–136.

Linacre, J. M. (2002). Optimizing rating scale category effectiveness. *Journal of Applied Measurement, 3*, 85–106.

Linacre, J. M. (2006). Data variance explained by Rasch measures. *Rasch Measurement Transactions, 20*(1), 1045–1054.

Marsh, H. W., & Redmayne, R. S. (1994). A multidimensional physical self-concept and its relations to multiple components of physical fitness. *Journal of Sport & Exercise Psychology, 16*(1), 43–55.

Nedelsky, L. (1954). Absolute grading standards for objective tests. *Educational and Psychological Measurement, 14*(1), 3–19. doi:10.1177/001316445401400101

Perroud, D., Ray, D., & Friedrichsen, C. (2006). Improving the travel experience. Greater profits through effective satisfaction measures. *Leisure,* pp. 1–11.

Plake, B. S., Melican, G. J., & Mills, C. N. (1991). Factors influencing intrajudge consistency during standard setting. *Educational Measurement: Issues and Practice, 10*(2), 15–16.

Smith, A. B., Rush, R., Fallowfield, L. J., Velikova, G., & Sharpe, M. (2008). Rasch fit statistics and sample size considerations for polytomous data. *BMC Medical Research Methodology, 8.* Retrieved from www.biomedcentral.com/1471–2288/8/33

Stone, G. E. (2001). Objective standard setting (or truth in advertising). *Journal of Applied Measurement, 2*(2), 187–201.

Stone, G. E. (2009). Introduction to the Rasch family of standard setting methods. In E. V. J. Smith & G. E. Stone (Eds.), *Criterion referenced testing: Practice analysis to score reporting using Rasch measurement models* (pp. 138–147). Maple Grove, MN: JAM Press.

Stone, G. E., Beltyukova, S., & Fox, C. (2008). Objective standard setting for judge-mediated examinations. *International Journal of Testing, 8*(2), 180–196.

Stone, G. E., Koskey, K.L.K., & Sondergeld, T. A. (2011). Comparing construct definition in Angoff and objective standard setting models: Playing in a house of cards without a deck. *Educational and Psychological Measurement, 71*(6), 942–962. doi:10.1177/0013164410394338

Stratton, G., & Williams, C. A. (2007). Children and fitness testing. In E. M. Winter, A. M. Jones, R.C.R. Davison, P. D. Bromley, & T. H. Mercer (Eds.), *Sport and exercise physiology testing guidelines* (pp. 211–223). New York, NY: Routledge.

Verhelst, N. D., & Glas, C. A. (1995). The one parameter logistic model. In G. H. Fischer & I. W. Molenaar (Eds.), *Rasch models: Foundations, recent developments, and applications* (pp. 215–237). New York, NY: Springer.

Wright, B. D. (2000a). Multiple regression with WINSTEPS: A Rasch solution to regression confusion. *Multiple Linear Regression Viewpoints, 26*(2), 42–45.

Wright, B. D. (2000b). Rasch regression: My recipe. *Rasch Measurement Transactions, 14*(3), 758–759.

Wright, B. D., Perkins, K., & Dorsey, J. K. (2000). Rasch measurement instead of regression. *Multiple Linear Regression Viewpoints, 26*(2), 36–41.

Yan, Z., & Bond, T. (2011). Developing a Rasch measurement physical fitness scale for Hong Kong primary school–aged students. *Measurement in Physical Education and Exercise Science, 15*(3), 182–203.

10

THE RASCH MODEL APPLIED
ACROSS THE HUMAN SCIENCES

We have already lamented that the large majority of empirical studies in the human sciences do not include the deliberate construction of a variable before the statistical analyses are undertaken. Raw scores, or counts, are treated as *measures*, and analyses often are conducted at the item level rather than the variable level. This becomes even more problematic when advanced statistical models with a multitude of indicators, as is done with hierarchical linear modeling (HLM) and structural equation modeling (SEM) (Bond, 2015). Here, problems we encounter in one poorly designed statistical analysis are compounded across several constructs (variables) and their interrelationships. However, over the past decade, there has been a noteworthy increase in the number of studies published using the Rasch model, and those appear across a remarkable breadth of human sciences disciplines. Scrolling through the studies that have cited our first two editions of this book would reveal the following constructs as some of those that would appear: engagement in videogame playing; clinical staging and disease progression in dementia; learning progression of energy concepts; posttraumatic stress disorder; knowledge of mathematical equivalence; difficulty of healthy eating; occupational performance; and morphological awareness, to name but a few. In this chapter, we summarize a few, more recent studies to illustrate of the variety of applications in which Rasch measurement has been used to advance theory and practice. In each example, the researchers have interpreted their empirical results from the Rasch analysis in in light of the underlying theory to advance the use of the measure for diagnosis and prediction.

Rasch Measurement in Health Sciences

Diagnosis of Gout Using Laboratory Indicators

Perkins, Wright, and Dorsey (2000) illustrated the use of Rasch measurement to produce a clear, simple picture of the relation between laboratory abnormalities in the diagnosis of gout. Ninety-six sets of medical record observations were submitted for analysis—half for patients diagnosed with gout and half for patients not diagnosed with gout. Each observation had values recorded for indicators routinely considered in the diagnosis of gout: uric acid, gender, age, diabetes, hypertension, weight, height, body surface area, nephrolithiasis, diuretics, cholesterol, triglyceride, blood urea nitrogen, and creatinine. Rasch measurement techniques were used in an attempt to establish a single dimension for diagnosing gout. Because blood chemistries in mg/dl, height, and weight are recorded as continuous variables, each of the physical science data points (X) was rescored linearly to its nearest integer code, using the conversion

$$Y = (X - Min.Value) / ((Max.Value - Min.Value) / 9).$$

The resultant coding, which simplified the physical science measurements to 10 equal-size steps, has a monotonic relation with the original physical science variables.

Usual Rasch analysis procedures (estimates and fit indices) were followed by the deletion of items that did not contribute useful information. In this case, Perkins and colleagues (2000) then used the Winsteps principal components analysis of the Rasch residuals to identify significant relations among the diagnostic items. The plot of the factor loadings of residuals against the Rasch item measures in Figure 10.1 shows a clear separation of the male corpulence cluster from the blood chemistry cluster. Note that the gout diagnosis is located in the center of the blood chemistry cluster at the bottom. The triglyceride variable was also removed from the measurement model because person separation was improved by setting aside triglyceride information. Finally, a medical variable defined by the three blood chemistries (uric acid, blood urea nitrogen, and creatinine) was established as the best linear variable for predicting gout that could be supported by the laboratory data. This allows for the probabilities for gout diagnosis to be read off for any particular blood chemistry results, as well as for the identification of patients with and without gout who do not fit the gout variable.

Producing a Shortened Version of an Existing Instrument: The FSQ

Individuals caring for chronically ill patients at home often carry stressful psychological loads, which remain undetected by medical professionals. Caregivers are often the 'hidden patients' and, as a consequence, their problems are routinely underestimated and undertreated (Hill, 2003). Their own problems can increase both health and social costs and often cause upheavals in ongoing caregiver–patient relationships. Therefore, clinical nurses, general practitioners, and other members of home care teams have to recognize the psychological problems of caregivers. To do so, they need to be able to assess the problem's severity quickly and to monitor it over the course of the at-home treatment, without having recourse to specialist training in psychological diagnosis.

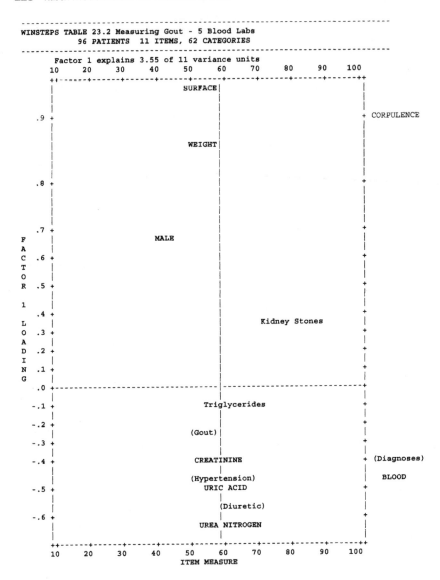

```
WINSTEPS TABLE 23.2 Measuring Gout - 5 Blood Labs
          96 PATIENTS  11 ITEMS, 62 CATEGORIES

     Factor 1 explains 3.55 of 11 variance units
     10     20     30     40     50     60     70     80     90     100
```

FIGURE 10.1 Winsteps map of Rasch residual principal components.

The research reported by Vidotto, Ferrario, Bond, and Zotti (2010) aimed to fulfill these requirements by developing a psychometrically sound short form of a previously validated questionnaire, the Family Strain Questionnaire, which could be implemented and interpreted without requiring the usual sophisticated psychological training. The Italian Family Strain Questionnaire (FSQ—Rossi Ferrario, Baiardi, & Zotti, 2004) in its original form is a semistructured interview plus 44 dichotomous items, based on a stress-appraisal coping model (Lazarus &

Folkman, 1984), usually administered by registered psychologists in about 20 minutes. It aims at investigating the caregivers' subjective perceptions of emotional burden, problems of social participation, the need for more information about the patient's disease, satisfaction with family relationships, and thoughts about the patient's impending death. The interpretation of the FSQ takes further skill to obtain the factorial scores and requires a clinical psychologist or a trained health professional to administer the interview and/or to interpret the time-consuming factor scoring of those results.

An existing data set consisting of the responses to the 44 items by the principal home caregivers (n = 811) was analyzed using the Rasch model to inform the item-reduction process (Linacre, 1995; Vidotto, Ferrario, Bond, & Zotti, 2007). Thirty-five items were selected and administered to a new convenience sample of 40 caregivers of patients from a major rehabilitation clinic in Italy. Reverse-scored items (1, 3, 11, and 34) were recoded so that a caregiver's response of '1' always indicated a higher level of stress than a '0' response. Examination of the results led to the removal of items 3, 4, 11, 15, and 34 before reanalysis. For each item, the series of misfit indicators (p. 278) revealed whether the information provided by the item reflected aspects other than caregiver stress. Items were removed for a variety of substantive reasons (p. 277), but note that items 3, 11, and 34 were three of the five reverse-scored items. The remaining 30 items that appeared to be the best candidates for an FSQ short form were then reanalyzed.

The reduced FSQ 30 set of 30 items showed very good fit statistics and maintained the diagnostic qualities of the original form. The elimination of the five items noted improved the summary item-fit statistics, while person and item reliabilities remained identical to those of the FSQ 35. An invariance comparison revealed a generally tight dispersion of the plots between estimates for caregiver stress based on the analysis of all FSQ 35 items and the FSQ 30 reduced-item version. These considerations confirmed that eliminating the misfitting FSQ 35 questions (3, 4, 11, 15, and 34) had little impact on the estimated stress of caregivers, while it improved the measurement qualities of the FSQ scale.

FSQ-SF

The resulting 30 items form the Family Strain Questionnaire—Short Form (FSQ-SF) that caregivers can complete in about 5 minutes. This brief measure can indicate the severity of stress and allows categorization of caregivers by level of psychological risk, which is also represented on the reverse of the questionnaire form by a graphic tool. The resulting (FSQ-SF) was administered to a new convenience sample of 40 caregivers of patients from a major rehabilitation clinic in Italy who cared at home for patients affected by cancer, dementia, or respiratory failure. To simplify interpretation, all 30 FSQ-SF items were expressed in the same direction, so that a 'Yes' response always indicated more stress than a 'No' answer. Second, the FSQ-SF items were listed in order of severity of stress—corresponding to the results of the Rasch item reanalysis—so that the scale ranges from the lowest to the highest stress indicators. The items were grouped into areas of increasing psychological risk, and each group was named based on the level of need for psychological consultation (see Figure 10.2 for a free translation of the Italian scoring instructions and interpretations). The generic labels for each stress level are indicative of the type of follow-up required:

OK; R (Recommended); SR (Strongly Recommended); U (Urgent).

The Rasch person statistics table (Vidotto et al., 2010, p. 280) for the FSQ-SF (N = 40 caregivers) reported ordered caregiver stress estimates, error, and fit statistics as well as the clinically judged OK, R, SR, and U interpretation cutoffs. The strong Rasch measurement properties of the FSQ-SF and innovative scale representation mean that nurses and general practitioners can use it to routinely scan for increased strain in the caregivers of their long-term patients. Given that the daily use of the FSQ-SF does not benefit from the quality-control aspects of Rasch analysis, a modification to the scoring procedure (Rule 5 of directions for use; see Figure 10.2) provides an additional safeguard against the potential underestimation of caregiver strain. While a Guttman-like response sequence was the basis of the interpretations of the total score, allowances had to be made for misfitting response strings in the absence of fit statistics.

Ongoing monitoring and refinement of the FSQ-SF should investigate the extent of the measurement invariance (see Chapter 5) of the short form against

```
30  29  28  27  26  25  24  23  22  21  20  19  18  17  16  15  14  13  12  11  10  9  8  7  6  5  4  3  2  1  0
-------------------------------------------------+...................-.......................+------------------+....................
            U                          SR                    R          OK
```

....

FSQ-SF Instructions for health professionals:

Purpose
The Family Strain Questionnaire-Short Form **FSQ-SF** is designed to allow the general practitioner or other health professional to screen caregiver related problems rapidly.

The correct use of this schedule provides the following indications:
Area U: the **urgent** need to refer the caregiver to a psychologist and/or psychiatrist (= Urgent);
Area SR: the need to **strongly recommend** the caregiver to seek psychological evaluation and support (SR= Strongly Recommended);
Area R: the need to advise the caregiver to seek counselling if the level of perceived stress increases (R= **Recommended**), *or*,
Area OK: an indication that the caregiver is apparently **coping** at present.

Generally, the higher the total score, the more serious the level of strain perceived by the caregiver and the more at risk is that person's condition.

Please note: this schedule does not provide a psychological diagnosis or specify any form of intervention. Such evaluation remains the proper responsibility of the specialist to whom you should recommend the caregiver, where indicated.

Directions for use
1) Ask the caregiver to complete the schedule (*e.g.* while waiting for his/her appointment or during the home-visit). Advise the caregiver to read the instructions carefully, to complete the patient's information first and then complete the questionnaire. This should take about ten minutes.
2) Please check that the caregiver provides responses to all thirty questions.
3) Fold the form along the dotted line (*i.e.* covering the NO responses) and count the total number of YES responses.
4) Circle the number which corresponds to the total of YES responses. The total score corresponds to one of the following areas: OK, R, SR, U (along a scale of increasing perception of strain).
5) If caregiver's score is <20 and the caregiver has answered YES to any of the questions numbered 24 to 30, then *increase* the total score by 1 for each of these.
6) Circle the code for the area which corresponds to the final total.

FIGURE 10.2 FSQ-SF Severity Scale with instructions for medical and nurse personnel.

the original FSQ. The original data set (N = 811) would allow for comparison of the Rasch measures and interpretations of the FSQ against those based on the factorial scoring methods used with the original, keeping in mind Vickers's considerations (Vickers, 2004) concerning interpreting total scores from multifactorial instruments.

Uncovering HRQoL Measurement Disturbances With DIF Analysis

In examining the extent to which a commonly used set of self-reported health status indicators could be combined to form a Rasch interval-scale overall health measure, measurement disturbances revealed as DIF provoked deeper understandings of health status related to anxiety/depression.

The EQ-5D descriptive system and the EQ Visual Analogue Scale (EQ-VAS) were developed by the EuroQol Group (1990) for deriving the preference-weighted single indices used for health-system economics studies involving trade-offs. The EQ-5D-3L has five items (Gudex, 2005) classifying health in terms of mobility (MO), self-care (SC), usual activities (UA), pain/discomfort (PD), and anxiety/ depression (AD). It offers three response categories so that higher levels indicate greater health deficits such as 1 = no problem, 2 = some problem, and 3 = extreme problem, a coding scheme that gives lower *scores* for healthier respondents. The original 20-cm visual analog scale of the EQ-VAS ranges from 0 to 100, with 0 representing the worst imaginable health and 100 indicate the best imaginable health. EQ-VAS directly elicits respondents' self-assessment on their current general health status (Williams, 2005).

Given the brevity of the EQ-5D, its insensitivity in measuring health preferences in various health conditions has led to various 'bolt-on' experiments by adding different disease-specific items to the existing EQ-5D system. This study investigated the extent to which the five EQ-5D items and the EQ-VAS together could form a valid measure of health-related quality of life (HRQoL) in a U.S. representative sample diagnosed with the most prevalent chronic health conditions.

Data extracted from the 2-year panel (2002–2003) from the Medical Expenditure Panel Survey (MEPS) were from respondents who (1) were ≥18 years of age; (2) had complete EQ-5Ds, and (3) reported a primary ICD-9-CM code for one of the top 10 most prevalent chronic health conditions (Table 10.1). The 101 ordered VAS categories were collapsed to form a 9-category item to ensure sufficient frequency of endorsement for each EQ-VAS category, and the EQ-VAS coding was reversed to be consistent with the EQ-5D (Gu, Bond, & Craig, 2009, 2010).

The Rasch rating scale model (RSM) was used to calibrate the responses on the five items and the Rasch partial credit model (PCM) for the 9-category VAS scores. Fit of the six items to the Rasch model was assessed by using the INFIT mean square (INFIT MNSQ < 1.4).

TABLE 10.1 EQ-VAS Respondents ($N = 2,057$)

Mean age (SD)			52.05 (16.53)		
	n	%		n	%
RACE			DISEASE		
White	1610	78.27	Hypertension	336	23.53
Black	337	16.38	Diabetes	215	15.06
Asian	57	2.77	Arthropathy	170	11.90
Other	53	2.58	Depression	168	11.76
VAS			Back Disorder	159	11.13
0–20	49	2.38	Joint Disorder	80	5.60
21–30	50	2.43	Chronic Sinusitis	79	5.53
31–40	75	3.65	Anxiety	74	5.18
41–50	169	8.22	Asthma	74	5.18
51–60	137	6.66	Cholesterol	73	5.11
61–70	244	11.86			
71–80	470	22.85	GENDER		
81–90	515	25.04	Female	1196	58.14
91–100	348	16.92	Male	861	41.86

The mental health item anxiety/depression (AD) consistently showed misfit in the original EQ-5D five-item scale. The overall fit of data to the Rasch model was enhanced with the inclusion of categorized VAS item.

Misfit was shown by the anxiety/ depression mental health item, especially with 2002 data, and improved fit in 2003, especially *with* the inclusion of VAS. In order to investigate further the unpredicted measurement disturbance for the AD item, two invariance checks across sample where made on the basis of the medical literature on anxiety and depression. The first DIF comparison calibrated item difficulties for males versus females; the second looked at invariance of item difficulties across the 10 groups of chronic health conditions. Remember, DIF analysis checks for item difficulty invariance across selected sample subgroups while keeping the overall person measures equivalent.

Results showed significant gender-related DIF ($p < 0.01$) on the EQ-5D anxiety/depression mental health item (see Figure 10.3a for the 2002 data subset), meaning that males reported significantly less anxiety/depression than did females with the same overall measure of HRQoL on the EQ-5D VAS. Of course, this might mean that males suffer less from anxiety/depression than do females with the same health status or that the males underestimate or underreport their actual anxiety/depression levels.

The data were then examined for item measurement invariance across the 10 identified disease groups. Figure 10.3b reveals that the 2003 item measures for *four* of the EQ-5D items and the VAS remained invariant, but there was significant *disease-related DIF* ($p < 0.01$) on the anxiety/depression item for two disease groups: those for respondents diagnosed with depression or anxiety. That

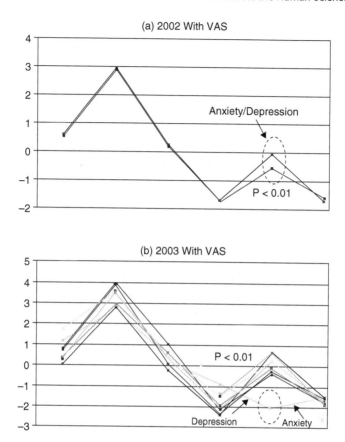

FIGURE 10.3 (a) Gender-related DIF with VAS–2002; (b) Disease-related DIF with VAS–2003.

DIF remained whether or not the VAS was included and occurred in both years. Responses from the VAS consistently fit the Rasch model (INFIT MNSQ < 1.4) over the two time points and across all 10 disease groups.

Reanalyses using a gender split on the anxiety/depression item improved fit to the model among males (in 8 out of 10 first-year and 9 out of 10 second-year disease groups). When enhanced by the inclusion of the VAS, the EQ-5D descriptive system exhibited satisfactory Rasch measurement qualities, and further enhancement was achieved by purging the gender and disease effects. Results compared across both years revealed the crucial measurement property of invariance for the EQ-5D. The findings suggest that (1) the EQ-5D descriptive system and the EQ-VAS can be combined to provide an overall measure of HRQoL and (2) together, they might serve as a suitable measurement framework for deriving population preference weights and (3) important gender-specific reporting differences create measurement disturbances for the anxiety/depression item and for the anxiety and depression disease groups (Gu, Bond, & Craig, 2009, 2010).

Applications to Physical Therapy

Throughout this book, we have emphasized the advantages of the Rasch measurement model over **classical test theory** in many ways. Because one of our greatest emphases has been on using the model to establish the construct validity of an instrument, it seems appropriate to include in this chapter an outstanding example of such an application. We briefly summarize a study by Campbell, Kolobe, Osten, Lenke, and Girolami (1995), in which they examined the construct validity of the Test of Infant Motor Performance (TIMP). Their article was proclaimed the best published in the journal *Physical Therapy* for that year (Linacre, 1996).

The TIMP is intended for use by physical therapists to detect deviations from an infant's normal path of development. These detections must be made as early as possible in order that effective interventions can be quickly implemented. Detection of deviations involves close contact between the therapist and baby, during which the therapist observes "both spontaneous and provoked actions of babies ranging in age from premature to 4 months old" (Linacre, 1996, p. 489). The therapist then rates these actions according to a strict protocol learned during training.

Using therapist ratings of videotaped babies of a variety of ages, impairment levels, and racial origins, Campbell and colleagues (1995) constructed measures with a many-facets Rasch model. They plotted measures of development separately for normal and high-risk children. The comparison of the two sets of measures revealed that although high-risk babies start lower on the scale and grow more slowly, the difference was slight, indicating the critical importance of precise measurement at this stage (Campbell et al., 1995). Moreover, their research provided empirical validation of a key theory of fetal development: The plots revealed that 7.5 months after conception is a pivotal point in motor development.

Measuring Behavioral Change

The measurement of a person's *willingness and ability to change* has been a subject of research since the beginning of the 1980s. The research rationale centers on the argument that if mental health treatment providers are able to identify a client's willingness to change a problematic behavior (e.g., eating disorder, substance abuse, gambling, domestic violence, etc.) during the client intake process, they could match their interventions with appropriate techniques to improve the effectiveness of treatment. A widely accepted theory of change characterizes the change process across five stages, in which a person progresses through precontemplation, contemplation, preparation, action, and maintenance (Prochaska, 1979; Prochaska & DiClemente, 1982). To build on this theory, a change measure, known as the University of Rhode Island Change Assessment (URICA), was developed to identify the client's stage of change (McConnaughy, Prochaska, & Velicer, 1983).

The URICA consists of 32 items (representing four stages of change) with five Likert-style response options. The preparation stage was omitted because the researchers struggled to identify the items that would measure uniquely just that stage. More importantly, scores on the precontemplation-stage items correlated negatively with those from all other items (McConnaughy et al., 1983; McConnaughy, DiClemente, Prochaska, & Velicer, 1989). The researchers decided to represent a person's stage of change by *subtracting* the precontemplation scores from the summation of the contemplation, action, and maintenance stage scores (Project MATCH Research Group, 1997, 1998). Rather predictably, subsequent studies adopting this approach yielded a series of problems and confusion in understanding stages of change. For example, researchers using this approach struggled to interpret why some people scored highly on several stages of change simultaneously (e.g., above average on precontemplation, below average on contemplation and maintenance, and close to average on maintenance). A common 'solution' was to cluster clients by their scoring patterns, producing two to nine different change profiles that did not fit the theorized progression and were inconsistent across different research projects. As with many strong theories in the human sciences, these researchers were well intentioned in measuring a construct crucial to their field but lacked access to the proper tools to do so. Addition, subtraction, and correlations among ordinal-level data lead only to a Tower of Babel situation—that is, construct confusion abounds in spite of the intention to speak a common language and to make stable inferences to improve clinical practice.

Therefore, Zaporozhets, Fox, Beltyukova, Laux, Piazza, and Salyers (2014) conducted a recent study to construct a measure of linear progression that would provide clinically meaningful information about clients' readiness to change. The study consisted of two sets of Rasch analyses. During the initial analysis ($N = 255$) cases, researchers identified the subset of 11 URICA items that then were piloted on a new sample of 318 cases drawn from three different clinical programs. The second set of Rasch analyses was conducted on the combined sample ($N = 573$). Rasch analysis confirmed that the identified subset of items demonstrated a linear progression across the four stages of change in a meaningful way. The new 11-item instrument, the Toledo Measure of Change (TMC-11) satisfies Rasch measurement requirements, including the specification that the interval-level measures remain invariant (within error) across identified subgroups and over time.

At this point, it would be beneficial to return to an important concept learned. In Chapter 3, we noted that using 'Rasch fit indicators should be an iterative learning experience: uncovering more about the variable, how it is revealed in person and item performances, discovering how our data collection can be better controlled, and so forth'. With the URICA, the researchers used a theory-driven approach to interactively delete subsets of persons and items while comparing the Rasch diagnostics for each output. By having a strong *theory* as a guide and four experts on the team with extensive experience with treating behavioral change in *clinical practice*, the Rasch analyses provided the appropriate *analytical tools* to guide the researchers in deciding what sort of items should be retained.

The iterative approach taken in this research included examination of Rasch person and item reliability estimates to determine the extent to which participant responses and item progression remained stable across different samples.[1] Further, the rating scale functioning was analyzed to identify categories that respondents used meaningfully. The middle category *undecided* was removed or combined in different analyses in order to improve fit, reliability, and variable meaning—without having to administer several versions of the scale to the same participants. This analysis was repeated until 7 items were identified as sharing a common theme representing Stage 1, Stage 2, and Stage 4. Then, an additional 4 items were identified to represent Stage 1, Stage 2, and Stage 3 better. For example, 'Trying to change is pretty much a waste of time for me because the problem doesn't have to do with me' (Stage 1), 'I think I might be ready for some self-improvement' (Stage 2), 'At times my problem is difficult, but I am working on it' (Stage 3), 'It worries me that I might slip back on a problem I have already changed, so I am here to seek help' (Stage 4).

The TMC-11, replicated on yet another sample, confirmed a linear order of the four stages of change. Stage 1, precontemplation, required the least degree of change from a person to endorse, followed by Stage 2, contemplation, and Stage 3, action. Stage 4, maintenance, required the highest degree of change to endorse. (Figure 10.4 shows the Wright map of this item progression, with the largest gap between contemplation and action items.) Seven of the 11 items differed from each other by at least two item standard errors, indicating stability of the measure. Further, 55.9% of the raw variance in the data was explained by the Rasch linear model, and person reliability was .85.

The resulting TMC-11 is very easy to use in clinical settings because it is short and does not require any scoring. Researchers organized all items by their degree of difficulty (degree of readiness to change) from the easiest to the most difficult item to endorse (see also the FSQ-SF). Hence, the mental health treatment provider can identify person's stage of change just by checking the pattern of the responses and noting where the person stopped endorsing change statements. In addition, the mental health treatment provider can easily identify items about which a client was not certain and follow up on them in clinical dialogue. For example, if a person endorsed the item 'I think I might be ready for some self-improvement' but was undecided about the item 'Maybe this place will be able to help me' (both Stage 2 items), the clinician can enquire further about that person's doubts. This approach helps to keep the person's evaluation individually sensitive, allows accurate application of appropriate clinical techniques, and saves

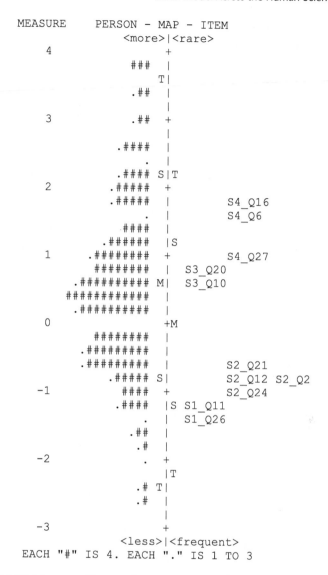

```
MEASURE      PERSON - MAP - ITEM
                 <more>|<rare>
   4                   +
               ###     |
                      T|
               .##     |
                       |
   3           .##     +
                       |
              .####    |
                .      |
              .#### S|T
   2         .#####    +
             .#####    |              S4_Q16
                .      |              S4_Q6
               ####    |
             .#####   |S
   1       .#######    +              S4_Q27
           #######     |     S3_Q20
         .######### M|     S3_Q10
       ###########    |
       .#########    |
   0                  +M
          #######     |
        .########     |
        .########     |              S2_Q21
          .#### S|              S2_Q12 S2_Q2
  -1        ####      +              S2_Q24
          .####      |S S1_Q11
              .       |     S1_Q26
            .##       |
            .#        |
  -2         .        +
                     |T
          .# T|
          .#        |
                     |
  -3                 +
              <less>|<frequent>
     EACH "#" IS 4. EACH "." IS 1 TO 3
```

FIGURE 10.4 Wright map of item and stage progression for the URICA variable.

clinicians from making the erroneous assumptions that would arise if we merely computed the mean of the two items' ordinal scores.

Rasch Measures as Grist for the Analytical Mill

Many of the sophisticated data analysis techniques routinely used in human sciences research explicitly required interval-level data as input. Stevens's quote from 1946 might be considered a truism, but it is no less true for that:

As a matter of fact, most of the scales used widely and effectively by psychologists are ordinal scales. In the strictest propriety the ordinary statistics involving means and standard deviations ought not to be used with these scales, for these statistics imply a knowledge of something more than the relative rank-order of data.

(p. 679)

The vast majority of these statistical techniques (and, of course, the software packages that implement those analyses) *require* interval data; the scores derived from our data collections are merely ordinal-level data at best. We have also known this for close to a century, and, for the same period of time, we have conveniently forgotten or failed to acknowledge that. The following investigations report using Rasch interval-level measures in ANOVA, HLM, and SEM analyses. Our contention is that Rasch measurement is, at present, uniquely positioned to fulfil the requirement of converting ordinal data into interval measures for analysis purposes.

Demographic Variables in Student Satisfaction

In Australia, the Course Experience Questionnaire (CEQ) is a survey instrument of 25 items that is administered annually to the cohort of students who have graduated from all of the nation's universities. It surveys graduates about the quality of the courses they have recently completed. Important in this context, CEQ results are used to compare courses and institutions. Factor analysis identified five factors (clear goals, good teaching, appropriate assessment, generic skills, appropriate workload) among responses to 24 Likert-type items with five ordered response options from strongly disagree to strongly agree. The methods of analysis and reporting of comparative CEQ data code each item response option, then provide means and standard deviations both for items and for subsets of items. Methods similar to this are typical in Likert-style survey analyses (see Chapter 6). The reanalyses of 1996 CEQ data (Curtis & Keeves, 2000) were premised on the authors' concern that traditional analyses treat the data as "interval and that a particular response option indicates the same level on the underlying trait for all items. Our concern is that graduates' responses are ordinal and therefore should be analysed differently" (Curtis & Keeves, 2000, p. 74). Moreover, "if policy decisions are to be based on the results of the survey or if the survey instrument is to be modified over time while still permitting comparisons, we contend that the alternative and superior analytical techniques that are available should be used" (p. 74). The results of the Rasch analyses are reported in greater detail in Curtis (1999) and are similar to those of Waugh (1998): eight of the 25 items misfit the measurement model, but the 17 remaining items do form a coherent measure. This, in spite of evidence from both exploratory and confirmatory factor analyses confirming a single underlying factor and five separate factors (as identified in the CEQ structure), nested within that overall CEQ factor. In particular, Rasch analysis suggests that the overall perception of course quality by recent graduates of Australian universities is most strongly influenced by (only) three of the five CEQ factors: good teaching, generic skills, and clear goals (after Curtis & Keeves, 2000).

Analysis of the CEQ data can be taken further because the graduates responding to the CEQ survey provide considerable demographic data (age, sex, mode of study, English-speaking background, employment status, etc.). In order to ascertain whether there are differences among course types, Curtis undertook a two-way analysis of variance using individual GSI scores as the criterion measure and both course type and institution as categorical variables. The Graduate Satisfaction Index (GSI) is merely a linear transformation of the Rasch logit scale, centered on a mean of 500 with each logit rescaled to 100 units (see chapter 10, 2nd ed). The ANOVA revealed differences among broad fields of study: Nationally, students of the humanities and social sciences (GSI mean = 527.06; SD = 104.02) were much more satisfied that those studying engineering (GSI mean= 476.14; SD = 73.21) or architecture (GSI mean = 480.90; SD = 82.34). In other words, the GSI for any institution could be regarded as a function of its student × course mix: "taking the mean GSI for all graduates of an institution would bias the institutional score in favor of those universities with high proportions of humanities graduates and against those with high proportions of engineering graduates" (Curtis & Keeves, 2000, p. 76).

Correcting for the course mix of each institution allowed for GSI comparisons to be based on actual versus expected GSIs rather than on means across institutions. This revealed a higher proportion of Australian universities to be performing close to course-weighted GSI expectations than would be obvious from the results of traditional analyses. Using Rasch-based GSI interval-level person satisfaction measures along with indicators of student demographics for 2- and 3-level hierarchical level modeling (HLM) revealed characteristics at the individual student levels as being implicated. Moreover, controlling for both institutional-level and student-level characteristics provides for findings that are unexpected in the light of earlier, traditional statistical analyses, showing the benefit of using genuine interval-level measures as the input for further appropriate statistical analyses:

> Multilevel analysis has permitted influences of variables that were previously confounded to be disaggregated. For example, in earlier studies, it was reported that employment status at the time of completing the CEQ did not influence graduates' perceptions of their courses. By separating effects at individual and course levels, we have been able to show that employment status is significant. In the past, its influence has been masked by course type because of different rates of graduate employment from different courses.
>
> *(Curtis & Keeves, 2000, p. 81)*

Using Rasch Measures for Structural Equation Modeling

For many in the human sciences, structural equation modeling (SEM) has become the instrument of choice. In some circles, it seems like the default option for almost all analyses. For those who are more thoughtfully wedded to SEM, our advice would be spread over two steps: First, that Rasch analysis should be adopted to guide the construction and quality control of measurement scales for *each* of the variables that feature in the research. Second, that the interval-level person Rasch measures and their standard errors (*SEs*) that derive from each of those instruments should be *imputed* into the SEM software for the calculation of the relationships between those variable measures.

An SEM project conducted by Boon, Millar, Lake, Cottrell, and King (2012) reported on an important government-funded project that investigated social community resilience subsequent to one of four persistent and pervasive meteorological hazards in Australia: flood, drought, bushfire, and cyclone. (If the crocs, snakes, and sharks don't get you, then the weather just might!) The variables were organized according to Bronfenbrenner's bioecological systems theory (1992), which arranges the constructs (factors) that impact individual resilience according to their theorized proximity to and, hence, influence upon any individual. Instruments to collect data on constructs such as resilience, sense of place, connectedness, preparedness, and the like were developed from the literature and refined using Rasch analysis of data collected during instrument trialing (Boon et al., 2012, p. 60).[2]

The data collected with those refined instruments for the major project across four disaster-impacted communities were, in the first instance, modeled for SEM analysis using AMOS 19 software. The chief investigator found the results of that analysis resulted in poor fit indices for the proposed models due to colinearity problems between the many items comprising the factors: Items informing one SEM factor, say individual resilience, also had significant loadings upon other factors, for example sense of place. This meant that the proposed SEM models were neither statistically nor theoretically robust: These problems were solved when the Rasch computed person measures for each construct were used to model the theoretically proposed relationships in SEM. So for the second SEM analysis, person measures and standard errors for each latent variable, derived from previously Rasch-analyzed data on each part of the data collection instrument, were imputed into AMOS. The poor fit indices of the SEM models from the first analyses converted to relationships with excellent fit indices, which were in keeping with the theoretical precepts of the investigation.

The overall model of resilience ($N = 1,008$) showed the common links between the various variables across the four impacted communities: It explained 39% of the variance in resilience and 22% of the variance for leaving the community after the disaster. Moreover, it accounted for 36% of the variance in preparedness

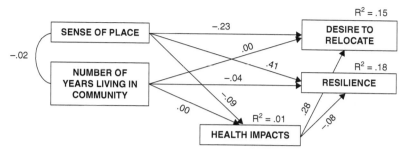

FIGURE 10.5 SEM model of links among sense of place, number of years, health impacts, desire to relocate, and resilience (based on imputed Rasch person measures for each variable).

and 20% of the variance in adaptability for the total sample (p. 241). SEM models developed from imputed Rasch measures for each of the impacted communities revealed both common links and individual differences across sites (Boon et al., 2012). Subsequent research reports analyzing relationships identified in the project and using the Rasch person measures for the identified latent constructs have been published (Boon, 2014).

The SEM diagram in Figure 10.5 illustrates how the construct 'sense of place' (connectedness with others in the community and actual locality) predicts their disaster resilience (standardized regression weight, β = .41) and precludes a desire to leave (β = $-.23$) after the disaster experience. Health impacts of a disaster are not related to the number of years living in a community, an expected finding, but the SEM highlights that health problems sustained as a result of a disaster can induce a desire to leave the community (β = .28) to relocate.

Conclusion

Even the roughest estimates in the growth of Rasch measurement research (Figures 10.6 and 10.7) reveal remarkable growth since the commencement of the current millennium. Citations of the previous two editions of this text (Figure 10.6) are now running at well over 300 per annum, three times the number of citations of a decade ago. Research mentioning the Rasch model (Figure 10.7) has increased about fourfold, having doubled (2001–2007) and then doubled again (2007–2013).

A more thorough investigation across areas of research interest will show that the growth in research report numbers is accompanied by an increase in the diversity of research topics over the same period

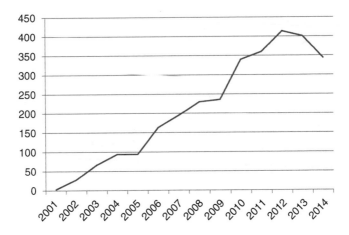

FIGURE 10.6 Citations of *Applying the Rasch Model* (2001–2014).

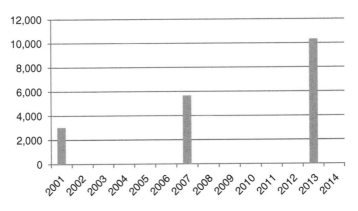

FIGURE 10.7 Citations including 'Rasch Model' (2001–2007–2013).

Summary

The purpose of this chapter is to introduce readers to innovative measurement practices and the wide range of applications of the Rasch model across the human sciences.

A simple search of Google Scholar using appropriate key words usually provides research-area-specific Rasch model exemplars.

Searching within the citations of this text, using key words (e.g., HRQoL) will also yield research exemplars.

Rasch Measurement Transactions (accessed at www.Rasch.org) provides a host of summaries of research papers suitable for entry-level and experienced researchers.

ACTIVITIES

Access Google Scholar or your usual research citation index and search for reports that include 'Rasch model' or similar.

Within those search results, search for results by year (or years) of your own choosing.

Then, within the earlier 'Rasch model' search results, search for references including key words from your own area(s) of research interest.

Access *Rasch Measurement Transactions* (www.Rasch.org) and search that site for references including key words from your own area(s) of research interest.

Notes

1 Procedures and criteria are explained in the original publication.
2 Disclaimer: Bond was the Rasch measurement consultant to the project team.

References

Bond, T. (2015). Enhancing the capacity of English language teachers to develop English language testing: Lessons from the Orient. In V. Aryadoust & J. Fox (Eds.), *Trends in language assessment research and practice: The view from the Middle East and the Pacific Rim*. Newcastle: Cambridge Scholars.

Boon, H. J. (2014). Disaster resilience in a flood-impacted rural Australian town. *Natural Hazards, 71*(1), 683–701.

Boon, H. J., Millar, J., Lake, D., Cottrell, A., & King, D. (2012). *Recovery from disaster: Resilience, adaptability and perceptions of climate change*. Gold Coast, Australia: National Climate Change Adaptation Research Facility.

Bronfenbrenner, U. (1992). *Ecological systems theory*. Philadelphia, PA: Jessica Kingsley.

Campbell, S. K., Kolobe, T. H., Osten, E. T., Lenke, M., & Girolami, G. L. (1995). Construct validity of the Test of Infant Motor Performance. *Physical Therapy, 75*(7), 585–596.

Curtis, D. D. (1999). *The 1996 course experience questionnaire: A re-analysis* (Unpublished doctoral dissertation, Flinders University of South Australia, Adelaide).

Curtis, D. D., & Keeves, J. P. (2000). The Course Experience Questionnaire as an institutional performance indicator. *International Education Journal, 1*(2), 73–84.

The EuroQol Group. (1990). EuroQol—a new facility for the measurement of health related quality of life. *Health Policy, 16*, 199–208.

Gu, N.Y., Bond, T. G., & Craig, B. M. (2009, September). (EQ-5D +VAS) × Rasch = HRQoL measure. Poster presentation at the EuroQol Group's 26th Plenary Meeting, Paris.

Gu, N. Y., Bond, T. G., & Craig, B. M. (2010). (EQ-5D + VAS) × Rasch = HRQoL measure. *Rasch Measurement Transactions, 2*(3), 1215–1216.

Gudex, C. (2005). The descriptive system of the EuroQol instrument. In P. Kind, R. Brooks, & R. Rabin (Eds.), *EQ-5D concepts and methods: A developmental history* (pp. 19–27). Netherlands: Springer.

Hill, J. (2003). The hidden patient. *Lancet, 362,* 1682.

Lazarus, R. S., & Folkman, S. (1984). *Stress, appraisal and coping.* New York: Springer.

Linacre, J. M. (1995). Prioritizing misfit indicators. *Rasch Measurement Transactions, 9*(2), 422.

Linacre, J. M. (1996). Year's best paper in physical therapy. *Rasch Measurement Transactions, 10*(2), 489–490.

McConnaughy, E. A., DiClemente, C. C., Prochaska, J. O., & Velicer, W. F. (1989). Stages of change in psychotherapy: A follow-up report. *Psychotherapy: Theory, Research, Practice, Training, 26,* 494–503. doi:10.1037/h0058468

McConnaughy, E. A., Prochaska, J. O., & Velicer, W. F. (1983). Stages of change in psychotherapy: Measurement and sample profiles. *Psychotherapy: Theory, Research, Practice, 20,* 368–375. doi:10.1037/h0090198

Perkins, K., Wright, B. D., & Dorsey, J. K. (2000). Using Rasch measurement with medical data. In Bezruczko, N. (Ed.), *Rasch measurement in health sciences* (pp. 221–234). Chicago, IL: MESA Press.

Prochaska, J. O. (1979). *Systems of psychotherapy: A transtheoretical analysis.* Homewood, IL: Dorsey Press.

Prochaska, J. O., & DiClemente, C. (1982). Transtheoretical therapy: Toward a more integrative model of change. *Psychotherapy, Research and Practice, 19,* 276–288. doi:10.1037/h0088437

Project MATCH Research Group. (1997). Matching alcoholism treatments to client heterogeneity: Project MATCH posttreatment drinking outcomes. *Journal of Studies on Alcohol, 58,* 7–29.

Project MATCH Research Group. (1998). Matching alcoholism treatments to client heterogeneity: Project MATCH three-year drinking outcomes. *Alcoholism: Clinical & Experimental Research, 22,* 1300–1311. doi:10.1097/00000374-199809000-00016

Rossi Ferrario, S., Baiardi, P., & Zotti, A. M. (2004). Update on the Family Strain Questionnaire: A tool for the general screening of caregiving-related problems. *Quality of Life Research, 13,* 1425–1434.

Stevens, S. S. (1946). On the theory of scales of measurement. *Science, 103,* 677–680.

Vickers, A. J. (2004). Statistical consideration for use of composite health-related quality of life scores in randomized trials. *Quality of Life Research, 13,* 717–723.

Vidotto, G., Carone, M., Jones, P. W., Salini, S., Bertolotti, G., & Quess Group. (2007). Maugeri Respiratory Failure questionnaire reduced form: A method for reducing questionnaire using the Rasch model. *Disability and Rehabilitation, 29,* 991–998.

Vidotto, G., Ferrario, S. R., Bond, T. G., & Zotti, A. M. (2010). Family Strain Questionnaire—Short Form for nurses and general practitioners. *Journal of Clinical Nursing, 19,* 275–283.

Waugh, R. F. (1998). The Course Experience Questionnaire: A Rasch measurement model analysis. *Higher Education Research and Development, 17*(1), 45–64.

Williams, A. (2005). The EuroQol instrument. In P. Kind, R. Brooks, & R. Rabin (Eds.), *EQ-5D concepts and methods: A developmental history* (pp. 1–18). Netherlands: Springer.

Zaporozhets, O., Fox, C., Beltyukova, S., Laux, J., Piazza, N., & Salyers, K. (2014). Measurement and evaluation in counseling and development. *Association for Assessment and Research in Counseling,* 1–16. Retrieved from www.sagepublications.com

11

RASCH MODELING APPLIED

Rating Scale Design

Anyone who has taught survey construction or attempted to construct such a scale has encountered the numerous options available for developing response options. These options are accompanied by a bewildering range of opinions about what the best options are. Often a simple 'yes/no' suffices for responses, sometimes a frequency scale ('never/sometimes/often/always') is called for, and, almost certainly, a Likert-type scale ('strongly disagree' to 'strongly agree') is considered, if not automatically chosen as the default. What many fail to consider is the critical role of the response options—both the number of categories and their definitions—on the quality of the data collected. Any ambiguity in the questions and scales attenuates reliability, which in turn affects validity. We must keep validity forefront in our minds at every stage of any test-construction process, but one key place where this is often overlooked is in rating scale construction. Validity arguments should be addressed throughout the entire process and begin with the logic and theory behind the construction of the survey items. And remember that validity, unlike reliability, is *not* established by reference to some simple statistic. Validity is an argument that entails judgment about *meaning*. Meaning stems from theory: from the type of questions we ask, the way that we ask them, of whom we ask them, and how we summarize and interpret the data. Thus, how rating scales are constructed—right from the very beginning—matters greatly. Rating scale construction then should be viewed as the researcher's one-shot chance at communication with the respondents as they attempt to use the response restrictions we imposed to record their attitudes, behaviors, or achievements on the construct of interest.

Even after great care has been taken to develop an unambiguous rating scale, the assumptions about both the quality of the measures and the utility of the rating scale in facilitating interpretable measures should be tested *empirically*. Not many seem to be aware that such empirical tests exist. Instead, those working in the Stevens tradition make *assumptions* that, say, 'a 7-point scale yields the most variability' or 'a 4-point scale with no middle category forces the respondent to choose', or 'the semantic differential is what is used in my discipline'. These conventions are not scientifically justified and hence are not sufficient as the basis for either choosing a rating scale or failing to test its utility and validity after it is administered. Instead, survey developers resort to some formulaic approach to rating scale construction—one that stifles thought, creativity, and, hence, meaning, in the process. So many opinions exist with so little empirical evidence to support them. But whether one collects data using such a conventional, formulaic approach or a more reflective, tailored approach, the functioning of that rating scale must be tested empirically. A beauty of the Rasch rating scale model (RSM) is its capacity to show us empirically exactly how the respondents used our rating scale and its provision for iterative procedures that allow us to extract the most meaning from the data. That is, it enables us to explore which categorizations of responses yield higher-quality measures than do other categorizations (Linacre, 1999; Wright & Linacre, 1992). From this basis, Chapter 11 expands on the analysis of rating scale data presented in Chapter 6 by discussing Rasch guidelines and procedures for investigating empirically the utility of rating scales in the development of high-quality valid measures.

These investigations give explicit consideration to the influence of both the number and the labeling of response-option categories in this process. We address these issues to demonstrate specifically how the design of rating scales has a large impact on the quality of the responses elicited and to show how the Rasch model provides an appropriate framework for carrying out such empirical investigations.

Let's suppose that a group of employees is asked to rate the extent to which they agree with the statement, 'My boss is supportive of my work'. Both the type of elicited responses and the inferences made about perceived supervisor support will depend on how many and what kind of response options are provided. We can examine the following set of possible response options:

Option A		Disagree		Agree	
Option B		Disagree	Neutral	Agree	
Option C	Strongly disagree	Disagree	Neutral	Agree	Strongly agree
Option D	Strongly disagree	Disagree		Agree	Strongly agree

Option A is designed as a yes-or-no (dichotomous) type: My boss is either supportive or not. Option B allows for a middle-of-the-road response to be included so respondents are not forced into choosing either of the extremes. Option C allows for more definition to the variable of interest (i.e., it depicts perceived support with five marked points along a continuum). Option D follows that principle but obliges employees to report their bosses as somehow supportive or not; no soft option there. When presented with one of these rating scales, the employees are required to express their perceptions within the restrictions *imposed* by the response options, and to the extent that the respondents can communicate effectively their perceptions within those restrictions, the quality of the measures will be enhanced. We have all been given surveys with not enough response options, too many options, ambiguous options, or questions we don't even understand. Little wonder that some respondents leave the survey incomplete; others will select just any response, even ones that don't make sense, just to get through the task. Imagine the futility of trying to make meaning out of data produced by such endeavors.

At this point, we go beyond recommending the careful design of the rating scale and begin to question how well our scale actually worked. Did the respondents need more categories (as provided in Option C) to express themselves? Did they actually use more categories when we offered more response alternatives? Do the number and type of categories preferred by respondents also work best for the measurement analysis? These questions focus on the important empirical issue: What is the practical number of response categories for the optimal measurement of this variable, and how should they be labeled? The solution should be tailored to every construct and sample and cannot be determined by a one-size-fits-all formulaic approach. However, all other things being equal, it might be better to err a little on the side of too many rather than too few categories. The analyst can collapse existing rating scale categories but cannot create new ones during the analysis to maximize meaning after the data are collected. The downside is that the question of how the sample might have responded given the collapsed scale remains open. The best advice is to ensure the appropriateness of the rating scale options and labeling for the construct and sample *before* the major data collection process is underway.

Here is a commonly used 7-point scale as an example:

Option E	Strongly disagree	2	3	4	5	6	Strongly agree

Would this rating scale communicate more effectively than Options A through D? Is it actually useful to add more response categories, with or without labeling, or do the distinctions between, say, five and six categories now become blurred, thereby introducing confusion for the respondents and ultimately lowering the quality and meaning of the scores (Fox, Gedeon, & Dinero, 1994)? There is research suggesting that although the addition of response categories might increase reliability, it does so only if these additional categories are not arbitrary (Linacre, 1995; Wright & Linacre, 1992). Chang (1994) explained that an increase in the number of response alternatives might introduce error by allowing respondents to draw more freely on divergent frames of reference. In such a situation, it is difficult for a "common language" (Lopez, 1996) to be shared between the respondent and the investigator via the rating scale. In short, two people might perceive the same level of supervisor support, yet one may check 5 and the other 6, simply because the introduction of too many response options muddles the definition of the variable in question. With Options A and B, the category definition and meaning is much more constrained than in Options C and D.

The empirical evidence is there is no definitive optimal number of response categories that applies to all rating scales. Whereas five response categories might work for measuring one construct, a simple yes-or-no type of response might be better for another. It is therefore the job of the survey developer to determine empirically the optimal number of response categories and their labeling every time a new rating scale is developed or when an existing rating scale is used with a new population. Thus, the researcher must discover empirically rather than merely assert the optimal number of rating scale categories for measuring a given construct (Lopez, 1996).

The strategy for determining the optimal number of response categories requires examination of Rasch measurement diagnostics. Statistics guide us in assessing how the categories are functioning to create an interpretable measure. Here we fall back on the principles espoused throughout this volume: Do we have reliable data for persons and items? Do the categories fit the model sufficiently well? Do the thresholds indicate a hierarchical pattern for the rating scale? Are there enough data in each category to provide stable estimates?

If sufficient problems are diagnosed in the existing rating scale, a general remedy is to reduce the number of response options by collapsing problematic categories with adjacent, better-functioning categories and then to reanalyze the data. Diagnostics from the new analysis then are compared with those from the original analysis, and a determination is made as to whether the collapsing helped to improve variable definition. At no point would we *ever* 'go so far as to blindly recommend collapsing categories'. Thoughtful *post hoc* investigation of rating scale category functioning is commended to those who wish to clarify the meaning of their already-collected data, especially in the cases where investigators intend to improve data collection procedures in subsequent iterations of the research enterprise. Always, the goal is to produce the rating scale that yields the highest-quality measures for the construct of interest. It is preferable to do that before the event but acceptable to do it after the data are collected. Winsteps software provides a wide variety of output formats that can be indispensable for investigating rating scale quality and performance.

Category Frequencies and Average Measures

The simplest way to assess category functioning is to examine category use statistics (i.e., category frequencies and average measures) for each response option (Andrich, 1978, 1996; Linacre, 1995, 1999). Category frequencies indicate how many respondents actually chose any particular response category, summed for *each* category across *all* items. These category frequencies summarize the distribution of all responses across all categories, allowing a very quick and basic examination of rating scale use.

Two features are important in the category frequencies: shape of the distribution and number of responses per category. Regular distributions such as uniform, normal, bimodal, slightly skewed distributions are preferable to those that are irregular. Irregular distributions include those that are highly skewed (e.g., distributions having long tails of categories with low responses; Linacre, 1999). However, skewed distributions are common in the real world of clinical data, often with the most interesting patients located somewhere in that long tail.

Categories with low frequencies also are problematic because they do not provide enough observations for an estimation of stable category threshold values. Hence, these are the categories that should be considered for collapsing into adjacent categories. Exactly how these collapsing decisions should be made is detailed later in the chapter. A recommended minimum number of responses per category is 10 (Linacre, 1999).

Average measures are useful for 'eyeballing' initial problems with rating scale categories. Average measures are defined as the average of the ability estimates for all persons in the sample who chose that particular response category, with the average calculated across all observations in that category (Linacre, 1995). For example, if the average measure is −1.03 logits for Category 1, that is the average of the ability estimates for *all* persons who chose Category 1 on *any* item in the survey. Average measures should increase as the variable increases. If average measures increase *monotonically* across response categories, that indicates that, on average, those with higher ability/stronger attitudes endorse progressively higher categories, whereas those with lower abilities/weaker attitudes endorse progressively lower categories. When this pattern is violated, as indicated by a lack of monotonicity in the average measures, collapsing categories might be considered.

Table 11.1 shows sample output for a well-functioning 4-category (three-threshold) rating scale. The category frequencies (i.e., the observed count) have at least 10 responses in each category but show a negatively *skewed* distribution. Average measures appear in the next column. The average measure for

TABLE 11.1 Category Frequencies and Average Measures for Well-Functioning Four-Category Rating Scale

Category Label	Observed Count	Average Measure
1	63	−1.03
2	341	+0.34
3	884	+1.37
4	1,179	+3.12

Category 1 is −1.03 (i.e., the average agreeability estimate for all persons endorsing response option 1 across any item is −1.03 logits). For all persons who answered 2 on any item, the average estimate is +0.34 (i.e., these persons are more agreeable on average than the persons who answered 1). These average measures function as expected (i.e., they increase monotonically, −1.03 < +0.34 < +1.37 < +3.12, across the rating scale response categories 1, 2, 3, 4).

Thresholds and Category Fit

In addition to adequate category frequency and the monotonicity of average measures, other pertinent rating scale characteristics include threshold (or step) calibrations and category fit statistics (Lopez, 1996; Wright & Masters, 1982). From Chapter 6, threshold calibrations are the 50:50 point difficulties estimated for choosing one response category over the adjacent category (e.g., how difficult it is to endorse 'strongly agree' over 'agree'). As for average measures, step calibrations should increase monotonically. Thresholds that do not increase monotonically across the rating scale are considered *disordered*.

The magnitudes of the distances *between* adjacent threshold estimates also are important. Between-threshold distances should indicate that each step defines a distinct position on the underlying variable. That is, the threshold estimates should be neither too close together nor too far apart on the logit scale. Guidelines recommend that thresholds should increase by *at least* 1.4 logits to show empirical distinction between categories but *not more than* 5 logits so as to avoid large gaps in the variable (Linacre, 1999). Threshold estimates presented in Table 11.2 illustrate that our rating scale meets these criteria (a: −2.05 < −0.01 < +2.06 and b: −2.05 to −0.01 = 2.04 logits; −0.01 to +2.06 = 2.07 logits).

One method of visually inspecting the distinctions between thresholds is to examine the probability curves, which show the probability of endorsing any given rating scale category for every agreeability–endorsability $(B - D)$ difference estimate. Each response category should have a distinct peak in the probability curve graph, illustrating that each is indeed the most probable response category for some portion of the measured variable. Categories observed to be 'flat' on the graph might be useful as long as they span a large portion of the variable. If, however, these flat categories are overshadowed and made redundant by

TABLE 11.2 Thresholds for a Well-Functioning Four-Category Rating Scale

Category Label	Threshold
1	None
2	−2.05
3	−0.01
4	+2.06

other categories, they might not aid in defining a distinct point on the variable. Problematic thresholds—those that are disordered or too close—will show up on the graph, often as flattened probability curves spanning small sections of the measured variable.

The graph in Figure 11.1 illustrates the probability of responding to any particular category, given the difference in estimates between any person ability and any item difficulty. For example, if a person's ability were 1 logit lower than the difficulty of the item ($B - D = -1$ on the x-axis), that person's probability of endorsing a 4 is close to zero, of endorsing either a 1 or a 3 is close to 0.2, and of endorsing a 2 is close to 0.55 on that item. This person therefore is most likely to endorse Category 2 on this item. For persons with ability estimates higher than the given item difficulty (e.g., $B - D = +3$ on the x-axis), the most probable response (c. 0.7) is a 4. This graph shows that each of the response categories 1, 2, 3, and 4 in turn is the most probable across some section of the measured underlying variable.

The threshold estimates in Table 11.2 correspond to the *intersections* of the rating scale category curves in Figure 11.1, the point at which there is an equal probability (50:50 likelihood) of choosing either of two adjacent response category options. For example, the first threshold in Table 11.2 is −2.05. A vertical line drawn from the intersection of the 1 and 2 probability curves in Figure 11.1 intersects with the x-axis at −2.05. Please take a few minutes to find the corresponding points in Figure 11.1 for each of the other two thresholds seen in Table 11.2. Each threshold estimate represents a distinct and separate point on

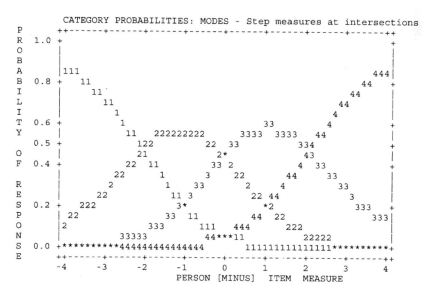

FIGURE 11.1 Response category probability curves for a well-functioning 4-category rating scale.

TABLE 11.3 Category Fit for a Well-Functioning Four-Category Rating Scale

Category Label	Outfit Mean Square
1	1.10
2	1.11
3	0.81
4	1.02

the measured variable, and each response category is the most probable response category for some part of the continuum.

Fit statistics provide another criterion for assessing the quality of rating scales. Outfit mean squares greater than 2 indicate more misinformation than information (Linacre, 1999), meaning that the particular category is introducing more noise than meaning into the measurement process. Such categories warrant further empirical investigation and thus might be considered as candidates for collapsing with adjacent categories. Table 11.3 shows the fit of each rating scale category to the unidimensional Rasch model, well under the criterion of mean square statistic less than 2.0 (Linacre, 1999).

The rating scale diagnostics discussed so far include category frequencies, average measures, threshold estimates, probability curves, and category fit. These diagnostics should be used in combination. Typically, they tell the same story in different ways. For example, if one category has a very low frequency, the thresholds are likely to be disordered, and the probability curves will not have distinct peaks for each of the rating scale categories. Similarly, the average measures might be disordered, and the fit statistics will be larger than expected. This will not be the case in every situation, but these diagnostics, when used in combination, are very useful in pointing out where we might begin to revise the rating scale to increase the meaning we derive from the measure.

Revising a Rating Scale

When rating scale diagnostics indicate that some categories were used infrequently or inconsistently by respondents, adjacent categories can be combined and the data reanalyzed. The aim here is to eliminate noise and improve variable clarity (Fox et al., 1994; Linacre, 1999; Wright & Linacre, 1992). Look again at the example in Option E at the beginning of the chapter. Do respondents understand the intended difference between a 5 and a 6 on this rating scale? Is it possible that given two respondents with the same attitude, one might circle 5 and the other might circle 6? If respondents cannot make a distinction between the meaning of Categories 5 and 6 and hence use them in an inconsistent manner, unreliability is introduced into the measure, and category diagnostics will show where we might have erred in the development of the rating scale. On the basis of this information, collapsing of categories together can, in many cases, improve the representation and interpretation of the measure.

Revision of the rating scale should come at the *pilot* phase in the development of the measure, because the measures and diagnostics subsequent to collapsing might not correspond to those based on the original response categories. Just as item format and content are pilot tested in the first phase of measure development, so should the number, type, and labeling of rating scale categories be. The collapsing of categories from pilot data can be used in an exploratory manner to investigate the best match between diagnostics and respondent use, with the optimal categorization being used in the final phase of the instrument development. Of course, there is never any guarantee that the newly collected data will substantiate the final category choice.

An Example

In this example, 221 elementary science teachers were asked to rate the frequency with which they used different pedagogic strategies for teaching science (e.g., writing reflections in journals, developing portfolios, working to solve real-world problems, engaging in hands-on activities). The rating scale categories were labeled as follows:

1	2	3	4	5
Never	Rarely	Sometimes	Often	Always

The rating scale diagnostics output is shown in Table 11.4 and Figure 11.2. The first obvious problem we see in Table 11.4 is that Category 4 has only

TABLE 11.4 Diagnostics for Problematic Rating Scale

Category Label	Observed Count	Average Measure	Infit Mean Square	Outfit Mean Square	Threshold Calibration
1	190	−2.08	0.77	0.83	None
2	207	−0.86	0.93	1.01	−1.51
3	179	0.15	1.13	1.88	−0.36
4	7	1.71	0.33	0.90	3.57
5	113	1.18	1.45	1.47	−1.70

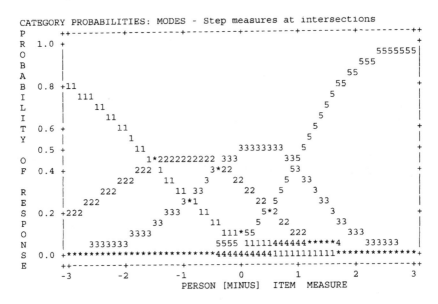

FIGURE 11.2 Response category probability curves for a problematic rating scale.

seven observations in all, across all prompts. Even without recurrence to the 'frequency > 10' criterion, the very low count in comparison to all others must be a cause for caution. This problem is reflected in the average measure values, the step calibrations, and the probability curves. The average measures for Categories 4 and 5 are disordered. Respondents who endorse 'always' (Category 5) have lower overall measures on average (1.18 logits) on this variable than do respondents who endorse 'often' (average measure = 1.71 logits). This is counterintuitive. More evidence of the problem is revealed in the threshold calibrations, in which thresholds 3 (+3.57) and 4 (−1.70) are disordered, and in Figure 11.2, in which the probability curve for Category 4 is flat (i.e., it is *never* the most probable category at *any* value along the *x*-axis).

These rating scale problems impede our interpretation of the construct frequency of pedagogic strategies. When it is easier on average to endorse 'always' than to endorse 'often', we have direct empirical evidence that our respondents are not using our rating scale in the way we intended. One potential solution is to try collapsing the rating scale categories to see if that improves variable interpretation.

Guidelines for Collapsing Categories

The first guideline for collapsing rating scale categories is that what we collapse must make sense (Wright, 1996; Wright & Linacre, 1992). That is, category collapsing should never be thoughtless or arbitrary. The question is, will the new pivot point between, say, agree/disagree and rarely/often responses be based on substantive considerations? In the example described, our infrequently used category was 'often'. Does it make sense to collapse the 'often' category with 'sometimes'? Does it make more sense to collapse 'often' with 'always'? In this particular example, there does not seem to be a compelling substantive reason to do either, so which should be preferred: collapse the 'often' category up with 'always' or down to 'sometimes'?

A second guideline for collapsing category data indicates that we should attempt to create a more (rather than less) uniform frequency distribution (Linacre, 1995, 1999). Collapsing Category 4 'often' into Category 5 'always' improves the frequency distribution slightly. The Winsteps codes for collapsing Category 4 upward into Category 5 are '12344', indicating that we want to analyze four categories instead of five, with the codes for the last two categories (4 and 5) being treated as the same response (4 and 4). The complete software commands can be found online at the book website.

Table 11.5 and Figure 11.3 present the results from this categorization of the variable (i.e., with 'often' and 'always' treated as the same response). With four categories instead of five, we now have enough observations in each of the response categories. The average measures and step calibrations are now monotonic, and the probability curves show that each category represents a distinct portion of the underlying variable. Thus, collapsing Categories 4 and 5 has improved our rating scale diagnostics.

In addition to those guidelines derived from the literature, we would also suggest collapsing the original Category 4 downward into Category 3 for comparison purposes (12334). This is because the guidelines for collapsing are just that—guidelines. This is a common precept for Rasch modeling: Analysis is undertaken to develop and measure the meaning of a concept in practice. There can be no fixed rules to which we must adhere whereby the meaning or significance of a result becomes completely void when some arbitrary value is passed. It is therefore important to maintain a scientific approach to our investigations and explore the empirical consequences of all likely recategorizations before settling on the preferred one. To facilitate this, Table 11.6 and Figure 11.4 are included to show the results from collapsing Category 4 downward into Category 3 (12334).

TABLE 11.5 Diagnostics for 12344 Collapsing

Category Label	Observed Count	Average Measure	Infit Mean Square	Outfit Mean Square	Threshold Calibration
1	190	−2.3	0.72	0.79	None
2	207	−0.83	0.97	0.92	−1.74
3	179	+0.79	0.88	1.33	−0.12
4	120	+1.96	1.39	1.31	+1.86

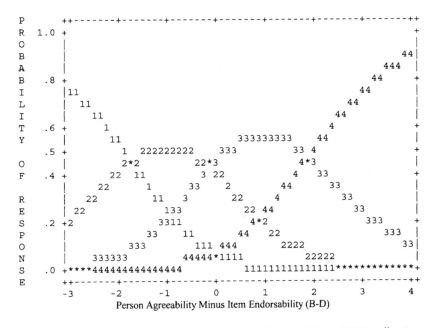

FIGURE 11.3 Response category probability curves after 12345 >> 12344 collapsing.

It is clear that the collapsing improved category definition in both cases. Collapsing 'often' up, then down (12344 then 12334) resulted in monotonic step ordering and distinct category definitions. But what is the evidence for deciding which is the better of the two?

When comparing several categorizations of the same rating scale, we also can look at indicators other than category diagnostics. For example, we can assess the quality of the various reliability and validity indices for the whole variable and compare these across each recategorization (Lopez, 1996; Wright & Masters, 1982). Chapter 3 argues that person and item separation should be at least

TABLE 11.6 Diagnostics for 12334 Collapsing

Category Label	Observed Count	Average Measure	Infit Mean Square	Outfit Mean Square	Threshold Calibration
1	190	−2.49	0.72	0.79	None
2	207	−0.84	0.94	0.90	−1.74
3	186	+0.83	0.87	1.27	−0.15
4	113	+1.91	1.43	1.34	+1.88

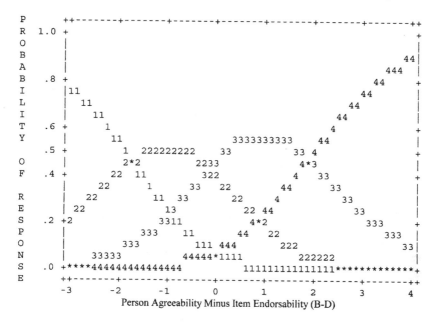

FIGURE 11.4 Response category probability curves after 12345 >> 12334 collapsing.

2, indicating that the measure separates persons, items, or both into at least two distinct groups. Table 11.7 shows that categorization 12344 yielded the higher reliability (and, consequently) for both persons and items.

With respect to validity, we will look at both the item ordering and fit. That is, does one categorization of the variable result in a better ordering of items along the underlying variable, one that is more consistent with the theory that generated the items in the first place? Do items misfit under one categorization but not another? These reliability and validity issues are addressed in previous chapters, but the same principles continue to apply here as well. Here they help us gain a fuller picture of how we can best refine the rating scale. Whereas the rating scale diagnostics help us in determining the best categorization, knowledge of Rasch reliability and validity indices tells us how the measure is functioning as a whole.

TABLE 11.7 Comparison of Three Categorizations

Categorization	Average Measures	Fit	Step Calibrations	Person Separation	Item Separation
12345	Disordered	< 2.0	Disordered	1.36	6.91
12344	Ordered	< 2.0	Ordered	2.06	8.23
12334	Ordered	< 2.0	Ordered	1.90	8.16

Problems With Negatively Worded Items

At the heart of this chapter is our contention is that any practice undertaken for scale development must be tested empirically to demonstrate that the measure functions as intended. A common recommendation and practice in survey construction is to include some negatively worded items as a check against response bias, social conformity, response set, or dishonesty. If we wanted to 'catch out' such responders with the CEAQ (from Chapter 6), we would be advised to write some stems with *negative* content and then to *reverse* the scoring for those items.

So, CEAQ 3 becomes:

I would *not* get upset if I saw someone hurt an *animal*.   No   Maybe   Yes

and CEAQ 15 becomes:

It *wouldn't* bother me if my friend got grounded.   No   Maybe   Yes

Remember that the scoring for the (all positive) CEAQ items was No = 0, Maybe = 1, Yes = 2, so that higher item and total scores means *more* empathy. For analysis purposes, then, we would *reverse* the coding/scoring for these two items: i.e., No = 2, Maybe = 1, Yes = 0. This practice is intended to make the direction of the variable uniform so that a higher score (2) will always represent 'more' of the variable—in this case, more empathy.

Let's suppose then a child responds 'No' (now coded as 2) to 'It *wouldn't* bother me if my friend got grounded'. This reverse coding, and hence item interpretation, is thought to be equivalent to responding 'Yes' to 'It *would* bother me if my friend got grounded'. But do these two versions mean the same thing? Conventional wisdom claims that they do, and survey practice routinely implements that wisdom unquestioningly. But such practice conveniently ignores two principles: First, Piaget (and other psychologists) warns us that negations are more difficult than assertions; double negations are even more difficult again. Secondly, item writing and interpretation are acts of communication: requiring reversed responses to negatively worded items is just a likely to destroy communication as it is to trap disingenuous responses. But the important issue that persists is whether the reverse-coded negative item can be interpreted the same way as a positive item is a question that should be tested empirically using the Rasch model—and quite often we find that the substantive meaning does change when we attempt to interpret reverse-coded negative items within the same measurement framework.

The potential problems have been documented across a wide range of studies. In the Rasch world, Wright and Masters (1982) first demonstrated the problems by plotting the estimates for the positively worded items against those for the negatively worded items ('for' and 'against' items) on a series of questions about attitudes toward drugs (using the procedures for the *invariance* plots in Chapter 5 and following). Person measures should remain invariant (within error) across subsets of items from the same test. Wright and Masters demonstrated the inconsistencies that can arise from posing negatively worded questions, reverse scoring, and scaling them along with positive ones. They concluded that analyzing 'for' and reverse-scored 'against' simultaneously often does not yield the best quality measures. Only when the two subsets of items yield invariant measures for the sample of persons does the conventional practice maintain the substantive meaning of the variable. In spite of the empirical evidence of the Wright and Masters demonstration, the practice of using negatively worded items is still very prevalent.

In addition to plotting the pairs of estimates for the two types of items, potential problems are likely to be flagged by other Rasch diagnostics, in particular, point–measure correlations and/or Rasch PCA of residuals. Low or negative point–measure correlations and/or residual factors associated with the negatively worded items indicate potential issues. Developing the Family Strain Questionnaire—Short Form (FSQ-SF; Chapter 10) encountered these issues with reverse-scored items. The final 30 items of the FSQ-SF were expressed in the same direction, so that a 'Yes' response always indicated more stress than a 'No' answer.

The analysis by Conrad, Wright, McKnight, McFall, Fontana, and Rosenheck (2004) of the Mississippi Scale for Combat-Related Posttraumatic Stress Disorder (M-PTSD; Keane et al., 1988; Litz et al., 1992; Keane et al., 1997), found a second, competing measurement factor formed by *reverse-coded* items. They concluded that the use of reversed items with such patients (i.e., the intended subjects for the M-PTSD) caused confusion and subsequent measurement disturbances:

> A good final example of this in the M-PTSD was the item, 'I do not feel guilt over things that I did in the military' where the response, 'not at all true', indicated high PTSD. To answer this correctly, we would expect the most disturbed patients to reverse the most common pattern of their responses, i.e., from 5 to 1, to indicate high PTSD. At the same time, we expect them to use a double negative to indicate a negative quality. In other words, to say, 'It is not at all true that I do not feel guilty' indicates that I feel guilt which is a negative feeling. Even healthy people who are feeling well psychologically would have to stop and think about that one.
>
> *(Conrad et al., 2004, pp. 14–15)*

Conventional wisdom in the Rasch world is, 'Two negatives don't necessarily make a positive'. If you think they do, then demonstrate that empirically.

The Invariance of the Measures Across Groups

A final step in investigating the quality of the new measure is to compare the estimates across two or more distinct groups of interest (e.g., male/female, Christian/

Jewish, employed/unemployed, married/divorced/never married) to examine whether the items have significantly different meanings for the different groups. This is called differential item functioning (DIF). We take the same example as before, the reported frequency of pedagogic strategies among elementary science teachers. Suppose we want to compare the frequency of use of those different pedagogic strategies with that of a sample of elementary mathematics teachers. We can use the data from both groups in the Excel spreadsheet for common item linking (see Chapter 5), plotting item estimates (difficulties and errors) for science teachers against those for mathematics teachers to examine whether the frequency of usage is measurably different for science and mathematics teachers. Any difference in the frequency of pedagogic strategies between the groups can be examined more closely to see why any particular strategy was not rated the same for both groups (Figure 11.5).

Examination of DIF follows the same procedures as those outlined in Chapter 5 on invariance. Comparing persons across two tests to determine the invariance of the ability estimates, however, DIF (based on common item-linking principles) models the invariance of item difficulty estimates by comparing item estimates across two or more samples. The procedure requires that item difficulties be estimated for each sample separately and that the item calibrations be plotted against each other (as in Figure 5.1).

The model for invariance of item estimates is represented by a straight line with a slope of 1 (i.e., 45°) through the mean item difficulty estimates from each sample (i.e., 0 logits for each). Control lines show which items do not display invariance within the boundaries of measurement error, across the two person samples (see Wright & Masters, 1982, pp. 114–117). Given that the model requires that relative item estimates remain invariant across appropriate samples of persons (see Chapter 5), items revealing DIF should be investigated closely to determine what might be inferred about the underlying construct and what that implies about the samples of persons in which DIF is detected. In achievement testing, for example, DIF is regarded as *prima facie* evidence of item bias. However, it takes detailed knowledge about the construct and the samples of relevant persons to determine just what can be learned from DIF, how it can be avoided, and whether it should be.

We can see from the plot that all but one of the items fall within the 95% control lines, meaning that the item calibrations remain invariant (within error) if we conduct separate estimates of the items for each of these groups of teachers. Investigation of this one item that fails the invariance requirement reveals that for math teachers, it was much more difficult for them to agree with the statement, 'I know a variety of pedagogical strategies to help my students become engaged in the material' than it was for science teachers. At face value, this result might be puzzling, but as always, we must confer with the substantive experts to help shed light on these empirical results. In this case, the explanation was simple—due to difficulties in scheduling professional-development workshops, the math teachers had not yet been exposed to the unit on engagement

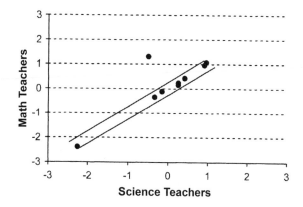

FIGURE 11.5 Differential item functioning (DIF): math versus science teachers.

strategies and thus did not express as much confidence (agreement) with that survey statement as did the science teachers, who were fresh out of that exact training with new ideas. Just as for misfitting data, we don't just throw out items because they don't behave as expected. Instead, we need to investigate the reasoning and make adjustments as necessary to our study design, interpretations, and/or analyses. The evidence of DIF might just be the very information that is central to your investigation.

Summary

In this chapter we discussed how the number and labeling of rating scale categories can have a substantial influence on the quality of the inferences made from the data: Empirical evidence shows that some categorizations yield higher-quality data than others. Given that there is no definitive optimal number of response categories that applies to all rating scales, the utility of any rating scale should be tested empirically using the Rasch diagnostic statistics. Our examples are based on the diagnostics provided in Winsteps.

Several aspects of the diagnostic information are indicative of response patterns that run counter to expectation. These, typically, warrant consideration of collapsing adjacent categories. The recommended steps are to:

- Examine category frequencies and average measures to identify categories with low frequencies and lack of monotonicity across average measures.
- Check to see that category thresholds tell the same story as the category frequencies and average measures.
- Category thresholds should increase monotonically as well as progress at intervals by at least 1.4 logits and no more than 5.0 logits.
- Look for category fit statistics with outfit mean squares greater than 2.

When rating scale categories were used infrequently or inconsistently by respondents, adjacent categories can be combined and the data reanalyzed. The aim here is to eliminate noise and improve variable clarity.

Guidelines for collapsing include:

- Deciding which categories to collapse is not arbitrary; it must make sense. This would include but not be limited to avoiding collapsing categories with qualitatively different meanings (e.g., disagree and agree).
- The resultant frequency distribution should be closer to uniform.
- Different possible, meaningful categorizations should be considered and each compared in terms of reliability, fit, other diagnostics, and variable meaning.

These practices aid the researcher in constructing measurement-based meaning from data that are often fraught with ambiguity and inconsistency. The ultimate goal in category diagnosis and subsequent collapsing is to extract the most reliable and meaningful measures possible.

Suggested Readings

Linacre, J.M. (1999). Investigating rating scale category utility. *Journal of Outcome Measurement, 3*(2), 103–122.

Linacre, J.M. (2002). Optimizing rating scale category effectiveness. *Journal of Applied Measurement, 3*(1), 85–106.

Wright, B.D., & Linacre, J.H. (1992). Combining (collapsing) and splitting categories. *Rasch Measurement Transactions, 6*(3), 233–235.

Applied

Zhu, W., Timm, G., & Ainsworth, B. (2001). Rasch calibration and optimal categorization of an instrument measuring women's exercise perseverance and barriers. *Research Quarterly for Exercise and Sport, 72*(2), 104–116.

ACTIVITIES

Read: Wright, B. D., & Linacre, J. H. (1992). Combining (collapsing) and splitting categories. *Rasch Measurement Transactions, 6*(3), 233–235.

Access the CAIN control and data file from the book website.
Check the number and labeling of the CAIN response options.
Import the file for analysis.
Check the CCCs and diagnostic information.

Implement a variety of collapsing strategies and decide on the most appropriate collapsing option.

Check whether the R (reverse-scored items) cause measurement disturbances. Look at the Rasch diagnostics. You might try a negative items-versus-positive items invariance plot.

(Remember, consider eliminating items that continue to misfit the model).

Exemplar software commands for collapsing response categories are provided online at the book website.

References

Andrich, D. (1978). Scaling attitude items constructed and scored in the Likert tradition. *Educational and Psychological Measurement, 38*(3), 665–680.

Andrich, D. (1996). Measurement criteria for choosing among models with graded responses. In A. von Eye & C.C. Clogg (Eds.), *Categorical variables in developmental research: Methods of analysis* (pp. 3–35). San Diego, CA: Academic Press.

Chang, L. (1994). A psychometric evaluation of 4-point and 6-point Likert-type scales in relation to reliability and validity. *Applied Psychological Measurement, 18*(3), 205–215.

Conrad, K.J, Wright, B.D., McKnight, P., McFall, M., Fontana, A., & Rosenheck, R. (2004). Comparing traditional and Rasch analyses of the Mississippi PTSD Scale: Revealing limitations of reverse-scored items. *Journal of Applied Measurement, 5*(1), 1–16.

Fox, C., Gedeon, J., & Dinero, T. (October, 1994). *The use of Rasch analysis to establish the reliability and validity of a paper-and-pencil simulation.* Paper presented at the annual meeting of the Midwestern Educational Research Association, Chicago, IL.

Keane, T.M., Caddell, J.M., & Taylor, K.L. (1988). Mississippi Scale for Combat-Related Posttraumatic Stress Disorder: Three studies in reliability and validity. *Journal of Consulting and Clinical Psychology, 56*, 85–90.

Keane T.M., Newman, E., & Orsillo, S.M. (1997). Assessment of war-zone–related PTSD. In J.P. Wilson & T.M. Keane (Eds.), *Assessing psychological trauma and PTSD: A handbook for practitioners* (pp. 267–290). New York, NY: Guilford Press.

Linacre, J.M. (1995). Categorical misfit statistics. *Rasch Measurement Transactions, 9*(3), 450–451.

Linacre, J.M. (1999). Investigating rating scale category utility. *Journal of Outcome Measurement, 3*(2), 103–122.

Linacre, J.M. (2002). Optimizing rating scale category effectiveness. *Journal of Applied Measurement, 3*(1), 85–106.

Litz, B.T., Penk, W.E., Gerardi, R., & Keane, T.M. (1992). Behavioral assessment of posttraumatic stress disorder. In P. Saigh (Ed.), *Post-traumatic stress disorder: A behavioral approach to assessment and treatment* (pp. 50–83). Boston, MA: Allyn and Bacon.

Lopez, W.A. (1996). The resolution of ambiguity: An example from reading instruction. Doctoral dissertation, University of Chicago. *Dissertation Abstracts International, 57*(07), 2986A.

Wright, B.D. (1996). Comparing Rasch measurement and factor analysis. *Structural Equation Modeling, 3*(1), 3–24.

Wright, B.D., & Linacre, J.H. (1992). Combining (collapsing) and splitting categories. *Rasch Measurement Transactions, 6*(3), 233–235.

Wright, B.D., & Masters, G.N. (1982). *Rating scale analysis*. Chicago, IL: MESA Press.

Zhu, W., Timm, G., & Ainsworth, B. (2001). Rasch calibration and optimal categorization of an instrument measuring women's exercise perseverance and barriers. *Research Quarterly for Exercise and Sport, 72*(2), 104–116.

12

RASCH MODEL REQUIREMENTS

Model Fit and Unidimensionality

It is in vain to do with more what can be done with fewer.

—William of Occam

It would be difficult to deny the claim that the most contentious issue in Rasch measurement is that of fit. Outside Rasch measurement circles, we continue to perplex the rest of the psychometric world by insisting that our task is to produce empirical data that fit the Rasch model's specification. Others in IRT talk of fit in what many consider to be conventional terms (i.e., how well does the model fit the data). Of course, the concept of fit must be considered hand in hand with the requirements for unidimensionality, equal discrimination, and local independence of items. The concept of unidimensionality reflects the Rasch model's focus on the process of fundamental measurement. It is a prerequisite that our data fit the model sufficiently in order to achieve invariant interval-level measurement. Indeed, the benefits and attractive properties of Rasch measurement exist *only* to the extent that the data fit the model's demanding requirements. This is consistent with the position emphasized throughout this text: Even in the most complex measurement situations, individual attributes should be measured one at a time.

The Rasch model is a theoretical mathematical description of how fundamental measurement should operate with social/psychological variables. Its task is not to account for the data at hand but rather to specify what kinds of data conform to the strict prescriptions of scientific measurement. There is no doubt, however, that mathematical models do not hold exactly in the real world. Instead, they describe an unattainable idealization, just as they do in all sciences. Check for the existence of genuine Pythagorean right-angled triangles. We all learned Pythagoras's theorem in school: The square on the hypotenuse of a right angled triangle is equal to the sum of the squares on the other two sides. Or, mathematically: $c^2 = a^2 + b^2$.

Apparently, this rule for constructing square corners was known for centuries before Pythagoras formalized the mathematical proof. And it was used for the construction of buildings that persisted since antiquity. What our teachers forgot to tell us, and the ancients did not learn from Pythagoras, is that Pythagorean triangles exist only in the minds of theoretical geometers, not in actual building practice nor in our geometry exercise pads. But close enough is good enough! If your empirical triangles fit closely enough to Pythagoras's theoretical ideal, the corners of your buildings will still look square two millennia later. Empirical data describe what the imperfect real world is like. If your right-angled triangle turns out wrong-angled, then your measuring instrument or how you are using it needs examination. Let's be quite up front about this: no real, empirical data will ever fit Rasch's theoretical ideal. The question is, 'Do our data fit the model close enough to support the measurement decisions we want to make?'

The Data, the Model, and the Residuals

In Rasch measurement, we use fit statistics to help us detect the discrepancies between the Rasch model prescriptions and the data we have collected in practice. In a number of places so far, we have used an item–person matrix to show the interactions between person ability and item difficulty. Each cell in the complete matrix has an entry, x_{ni}, representing the *actual* observed score (x = either 0 or 1 for dichotomous data) that resulted when Person n took Item i. Table 12.1 shows a portion of the ordered matrix of actual observed scores from Table 2.3, where schoolchildren A through N answered math questions a through l. When we order that matrix according to the difficulty of the items and the ability of the persons, we have the opportunity to compare the Rasch model prescriptions with what we actually find in the data set. The estimation procedure in Rasch analysis has two distinct phases: first, calibration of the difficulties and abilities and second, estimation of fit.

In the dichotomous model, the Rasch parameters, item difficulty and person ability, are estimated from the pass-versus-fail proportions for each item and each person. (The pass/fail proportion = number correct/number incorrect: $n / [N - n]$.) For item difficulty, the estimate is calculated from the proportion of the persons that succeeded on each item. Person ability is calculated from the proportion of items on which each person succeeded. The result of that iterative process is a set of all the item calibrations (i.e., one for each item) and a set of all possible person measures (i.e., one for every possible total score).

If we then take a second, same-size but empty matrix, we can substitute the estimated Rasch measures. We put person logit measures in place of the $n / [N - n]$ proportion for each person and item logit measures in place of the n / N proportion

TABLE 12.1 Some Actual or Observed Scores (x_{ni}) From Table 2.3 (Ordered)

Persons	Items					Person Total
	i	*a*	*b*	. . .	*g*	
J	1	1	1		1	9
C	1	1	1		0	8
E	1	0	1		0	7
. . .						. . .
H	0	1	0		0	2
Item Total	11	10	7	. . .	1	

for each item (see the ability and difficulty Rasch estimates in Table 12.2). Given that there is a direct monotonic curvilinear transformation of $n / [N - n]$ proportions into logit values (remember Figure 2.1?), the items and persons maintain their exact *orders* (but now we have estimated the *intervals* between them). Next, we take the corresponding pair of parameter values for, say, Person N and Item *i* and substitute those values into the Rasch model (Formula 3 in Appendix B) to obtain an expected response value, E_{ni}, for that particular item–person pair (i.e., the expected response value E when Person N encounters Item *i*). By repeating that calculation for every item–person pair and entering the resultant value in the appropriate cell, we use the Rasch model to generate a complete matrix of the theoretically *expected* response values based on those person and item calibrations. Table 12.2 shows the Rasch-modeled correct response probabilities (E_{ni}) for Persons J, C, E, . . ., H encountering Items *i, a, b, . . ., g* (E_{ni} is the expected response value for Person N on Item *i*).

TABLE 12.2 Rasch Expected Response Probabilities (E_{ni}) Based on Item and Person Estimates

Persons	Items					Ability Estimate
	i	*a*	*b*	. . .	*g*	
J	0.26	0.50	0.77		0.95	+1.52
C	0.20	0.40	0.70		0.94	+1.19
E	0.12	0.27	0.56		0.89	+0.58
. . .						. . .
H	0.02	0.04	0.14		0.50	−1.52
Difficulty Estimate	+2.59	+1.59	+0.32	. . .	−1.52	

Residuals

The difference between the actual observed score in any cell (x_{ni}; Table 12.1) and the expected response value for that cell (E_{ni}; Table 12.2) is the response **residual** (y_{ni}; Table 12.3). If the expected response value for a cell is high, say, estimated at 0.95 (i.e., $E_{Jg} = 0.95$), then we can calculate the (unstandardized) residual in which the actual score is 1 (x_{Jg}; we observed that Person J actually scored 1 on Item g). So capable Person J performed as expected on rather easy Item g and scored 1 (i.e., $x_{Jg} = 1$). Then $y_{Jg} = x_{Jg} - E_{Jg} = 1 - 0.95 = +0.05$ (a small residual), whereas if that capable Person J had unexpectedly scored 0 for easy Item g (i.e., $x_{Jg} = 0$), then $y_{Jg} = x_{Jg} - E_{Jg} = 0 - 0.95 = -0.95$ (a large residual). For the first case, the residual is low, indicating that the actual response was close to the Rasch model's expectation. The alternative possibility, with the much larger residual, indicates that such an actual performance would be quite different from the Rasch-modeled expectation.

It then is easy to imagine a third similarly sized matrix that for each item–person pair contains the score residual for that cell (y_{ni}) when the expected response value (E_{ni}) is subtracted from the actual score (x_{ni}). Table 12.3 is a matrix of response residuals (y_{ni}) derived from Table 12.1 actual scores (x_{ni}) and Table 12.2 expected response values (E_{ni}). When the person's ability is the same as the item's difficulty, the residual value will be +0.50 if the answer given is correct ($1 - 0.50 = +0.50$) or −0.50 if the person gives the wrong response ($0 - 0.50 = -0.50$). Residual values range from almost −1 to almost +1; negative values are always derived from incorrect (0) responses and positive residual values from correct (1) responses.

There is an obvious problem (one frequently encountered in statistics) in trying to aggregate a total residual score for any item or person. Because any actual score (x_{ni}) will be either 0 or 1, and every expected response value (E_{ni}) will be a decimal fraction ($0 < E_{ni} < 1$), the residual will always be a negative fraction for all actual scores of 0 and a positive fraction for all actual scores of 1. Just adding those residual values for any item or person string results in totals of 0.0 for every person and every item: The negative residuals cancel the positives.

TABLE 12.3 Matrix of Response Residuals ($y_{ni} = x_{ni} - E_{ni}$)

Persons	Items					Residual Total (Person)
	i	a	b	$...$	g	
J	0.74	0.30	0.23		0.05	low
C	0.80	0.60	0.30		−0.93	high
E	0.88	−0.27	0.44		−0.89	high
...						...
H	−0.02	0.96	−0.14		−0.50	modest
Residual Total (Item)	high	modest	low		high	

However, squaring each of those residual values will result in all positive values (e.g., $+0.052^2 = +0.0025$ and $-0.952^2 = +0.9025$). These *squared* residual values can then be aggregated by summing down any relevant item residual column or along any person residual row. Although the expected residual is an impossible-to-achieve 0, residual values outside of ±0.75 are seen as *unexpected*. In practice, each raw residual (y_{ni}) is standardized by using the variance of that residual, and it is the standardized residual (z_{ni}) that is used to calculate fit statistics.

Fit Statistics

Rasch suggested the use of chi-square fit statistics to determine how well any set of empirical data met the requirements of his model. Rasch analysis programs usually report fit statistics as two chi-square ratios: infit and outfit mean square statistics (Wright, 1984; Wright & Masters, 1981).

Outfit is based on the conventional sum of squared standardized residuals, so for Person n, each standardized residual cell is *squared* and the string of those squared residuals, one for each and every item encountered by Person n, is summed and its *average* (mean) found by dividing by the number of items to which Person n responded, hence '**mean squares**'.

Infit is an information-weighted sum. The statistical information in a Rasch observation is its model variance, that is, the square of the model standard deviation of the observation about its Rasch expected value. This variance is larger for *well-targeted* observations and smaller for *extreme* observations. To calculate infit, each squared standardized residual value in the response string, say, the residual z_{ni} for each of the items encountered by Person n, is weighted by its variance and then summed. Dividing that total by the sum of the variances leaves the differential effects of those weightings in place.

Therefore, infit and outfit statistics are reported as mean squares in the form of chi-square statistics divided by their degrees of freedom, so that they have a ratio scale form with an expected value of $+1$ and a range from 0 to positive infinity. Infit and outfit mean square values are always positive (i.e., > 0). In this form, the mean square fit statistics are used to monitor the compatibility of the data with the model. Infit and outfit mean square statistics address the question: How *much* misfit exists in the data?

An infit or outfit mean square value of $1 + x$ indicates $100x\%$ more variation between the observed and the model-predicted response patterns than would be expected if the data and the model were perfectly compatible. Thus, an infit mean square value of more than 1, say, 1.30 (i.e., $1 + 0.30$) indicates 30% (100×0.30) more variation in the *observed* data than the Rasch model *predicted*. An outfit mean square value of less than 1, say, 0.78 ($1 - 0.22 = 0.78$) indicates 22% (100×0.22) less variation in the observed response pattern than was predicted by the model.

The idea of the response string showing more variation than expected is a concept with which most are comfortable. This happens when a person's responses are more *haphazard* than expected: A capable person gets easier items *unexpectedly* wrong (e.g., 0010011110, where items are ordered easiest to most difficult), or a less able person gets harder items *unexpectedly* correct (e.g., 1101000110).

Expectations of Variation

Now, the Rasch model is a **stochastic** or **probabilistic** model, and from that viewpoint, a perfect **Guttman** response pattern, 1111100000, is unrealistically and unexpectedly perfect. It shows too little variation (i.e., much less variation than the Rasch model predicts). A Guttman response string would have a mean square value considerably less than 1. According to the probabilistic principles incorporated in the heart of the Rasch model, a more realistic and expected response pattern would look more like this: 1110101000, and the mean square fit value would be much closer to + 1. (*N.B.* All of these exemplar response strings have a score of 5 correct answers out of 10.)

Infit and outfit statistics also are reported in various standardized forms (e.g., as a *t* or *Z* distribution) in which the expected value is 0. For example, both of these mean square fit statistics can be transformed into an approximately normalized *t* distribution with $df = \infty$ by applying the Wilson-Hilferty transformation. We should note that *t* is a Student's *t*-statistic which needs its accompanying *df*. So the *Z* statistic used for fit statistics is actually *t* with infinite degrees of freedom. Some Rasch software packages show "*t*" even when they are reporting *Z*. Technically, $Z = t_\infty$. These normalized versions of the statistics are referred to as the ZSTD INFIT and the ZSTD OUTFIT in Winsteps (Linacre, 2006, p. 200). ZSTD INFIT is the Standardized Weighted Mean Square and ZSTD OUTFIT is the Standardized Unweighted Mean Square (Wright & Masters, 1982, p. 100). When the observed data conform to the model, the *Z* or *t* values have a mean near 0 and a standard deviation near 1. Using the commonly accepted interpretation of *Z* and *t* values, infit and outfit *Z* values greater than +2 or less than −2 generally are interpreted as having less compatibility with the model than expected ($p < .05$). Normalized or **standardized infit** and outfit statistics could have either positive or negative values. *Negative* values indicate *less* variation than modeled: The response string is closer to the Guttman-style response string (all easy items correct then all difficult items incorrect). *Positive* values indicate *more* variation than modeled: The response string is more haphazard than expected (Table 12.4).

TABLE 12.4 Fit Statistics and Their General Interpretation

Mean Squares	t Z	Response Pattern	Variation	Interpretation	Misfit Type
> 1.3	> 2.0	Too haphazard	Too much	Unpredictable	Underfit
< 0.75	< −2.0	Too determined	Too little	Guttman	Overfit

We must emphasize here that underfit to the model (i.e., unpredictable, erratic responses or noise) and overfit to the model (i.e., determinacy or Guttman-style response pattern) have different implications for measurement. Underfit degrades the quality of the ensuing measures. Underfitting performances are those that should prompt us to reflect on what went wrong. Overfitting performances might mislead us into concluding that the quality of our measures is better than it really is. In many practical measurement situations in the human sciences, it is quite likely that overfit will have no practical implications at all. The technical implications are smaller standard errors and inflated separation/reliability, so take some care there. Lack of local independence of items could be likely. It might be useful to note when overfit occurs—for example, when an 'item answers an item' because the solving algorithm can be copied from one item to another (resulting in violations of the local independence requirement). Or in case of item redundancy, when items of a questionnaire are just 'synonyms' or replications of other items. With a strong developmental theory such as Piaget's, we might expect rather muted fit indicators (overfit to the Rasch model): Preoperational thought strictly precedes concrete operational thought, which is the logically necessary precursor of formal operational thought, and so forth. In physical rehabilitation, we would not be surprised if indicators for standing, stepping, walking, and climbing stairs exhibited overfit. Development of these skills is expected to be heavily interrelated. One of the regular candidates for overfitting is the last typical item on a consumer satisfaction survey, 'In summary, how would you rate . . .?' Statistically and substantively, it adds little to our knowledge, but it doesn't do any harm to our findings.

The last of the mandatory SFT (Student Feedback about Teaching) items (see Bond, 2005a; Bond & Fox, 2007), 'Overall, the quality of this staff member's teaching was . . .' produced the predicted overfitting indicators: Infit MnSq: 0.54; Outfit MnSq: 0.54. On the other hand, including a question such as 'This teacher's punctuality was . . .' results in underfit: Infit MnSq: 1.53; Outfit MnSq: 1.57. While the question about punctuality was included in the SFT at the time of its development for important reasons, it is clear that 'punctuality' taps some off-trait aspects of university life other than just those tapped by the remaining SFT items (i.e., Item 13 'Punctuality' is not related to the good teaching construct as are other SFT questions). Adding responses to questions such as SFT 13 to give an overall satisfaction score would spoil the measure. In fact, SFT reporting procedures eschew the calculation of a total satisfaction score. Further, it is the case that eliminating the underfitting items is likely to shift the fit frame of reference and often leads to the overfitting items falling into line.

Even the terms 'overfit' and 'underfit' cause problems for some readers in this field. Underfit refers to **noisy** or erratic item or person performances, those that are not sufficiently predictable to make useful Rasch measures. Underfit is detected when the fit statistics are too high to meet the Rasch model's requirements (i.e., over the fit cutoffs). Overfit reflects item or person performances that

TABLE 12.5 General Descriptors for Levels of Misfit

Misfit statistic too low	Predicted fit statistic	Misfit statistic too high
e.g., $Z < -2.0$	e.g., $-2.0 < Z < +2.0$	e.g., $Z > +2.0$
e.g., MnSq < 0.7	e.g., $0.7 <$ MnSq < 1.3	e.g., MnSq $> +1.3$
1111100000	1110101000	0100100010
Less than modeled	Modeled	Larger than modeled
Overfit	Good fit	Underfit
Deterministic	Stochastic	Erratic
Muted	Productive for measurement	Noisy
Too good to be true—likely due to item dependence	Expected	Unexpected—likely due to poor item/special knowledge/guessing
Guttman	Rasch	Unpredictable

are almost too good to be true; they yield Guttmann-like response patterns. Over-fit is detected when the fit statistics are too low to meet the Rasch model's expectations (i.e., under the fit cutoffs). In essence, for items, this generally indicates a lack of local independence, that is, the items are not working independently of each other, as in the summary survey item. So a number of questions based on the same information (a paragraph of prose, a diagram, or one of Piaget's tasks) might overfit (exhibit too-good fit statistics) because they lack local independence. (In an important sense, rather than talking about *fit* statistics, perhaps we should always keep in mind that we are talking about the estimation of *misfit*. For any cells in which the empirical data do not match the Rasch model prescription, the difference between the data and prescription, the residual, contributes toward misfit. But, conventionally, we use the term 'fit statistics', so we are obliged to stay with that.) (See Table 12.5.)

Our conception of misfit must include the idea that every response string is actually possible in practice, although some response strings are more probable than others. Although the Guttman pattern remains the most probable, all other patterns are probable, although some are highly improbable. The Rasch model, as a probabilistic or stochastic model, regards the perfect Guttman pattern (1111100000) as too rigid. The Rasch expectation is that there is a zone of uncertainty or unpredictability around the person's level of ability. Linacre and Wright (1994) described the following response strings and provided infit and outfit mean square values for each (Table 12.6).

The interpretation of fit statistics, more than any other aspect of Rasch modeling, requires experience related to the particular measurement context. Then,

> [w]hen is a mean-square too large or too small? There are no hard-and-fast rules. Particular features of a testing situation, for example, mixing item

types or off-target testing, can produce different mean-square distributions. Nevertheless, here, as a rule of thumb, are some reasonable ranges for item mean-square fit statistics.

(Wright, Linacre, Gustafsson, & Martin-Loff, 1994; Table 12.7)

Unfortunately, many readers will scour this text merely to cite the page to support that the fit values they have reported are within some acceptable bounds. Our guidelines are much more equivocal: Fit statistics should be used to assist in the detection of problem item and person performances, not just to decide which

TABLE 12.6 Diagnosing Misfit

Response Strings				Infit Mean Square	Outfit Mean Square	Fit Type
Easy	... Items	... Hard	Diagnosis			
111	... 0110110100	... 000	Modeled	1.1	1.0	Good Fit

This would be regarded as an ideal Rasch model response string.

111	... 1111100000	... 000	Deterministic	0.5	0.3	Overfit

Is an example of a Guttman or deterministic pattern. Note that the outfit and infit mean square statistics are too low to be believed.

011	... 1111110000	... 000	Carelessness	1.0	3.8	Underfit

This suggests carelessness with an easy item.

000	... 0000011111	... 111	Miscode	4.3	12.6	Underfit

This response string is too bad to be believed and suggests that the responses might be miscoded.

111	... 1111000000	... 001	Lucky Guessing	1.0	3.8	Mixed

On the other hand, unexpected success on the most difficult item suggests lucky guessing.

111	... 1000011110	... 000	Special Knowledge	1.3	0.9	Mixed

This highly improbable pattern suggests the presence of special knowledge, either the knowledge that is missing in the string of failures or special knowledge that allowed the unexpected string of successes.

TABLE 12.7 Some Reasonable Item Mean Square Ranges for Infit and Outfit

Type of Test	Range
Multiple-choice test (high stakes)	0.8–1.2
Multiple-choice test (run of the mill)	0.7–1.3
Rating scale (Likert/survey)	0.6–1.4
Clinical observation	0.5–1.7
Judged (where agreement is encouraged)	0.4–1.2

items should be omitted from a test. Indeed, merely omitting the overfitting items (e.g., $Z < -2.0$ or MnSq < 0.70) could rob the test of its best item—the other items are not as good as these.

For fit mean squares, we expect values close to 1 when the data fit the model. But how close is good enough? Now, our interpretations of mean-squares indicators do not take sample size into account, although it is easy to demonstrate that mean squares fit statistics will get closer and closer to 1.0 just by increasing sample size. But, of course, the standardized (transformed) versions of fit statistics (Z or t) are designed to take sample size into account (using the mean and variance of the mean-squares statistic). So, problem solved; except as we have already argued, no set of data can have perfect fit to the Rasch model. The consequence is that even the smallest amount of misfit must become significant (i.e., > 2.0) when the sample size becomes large enough. Margaret Wu (personal communication, 2004; Wu & Adams, 2007, p. 23) expressed that these characteristics of Rasch residual based fit statistics place us in a dilemma.

> If we use mean-square fit values to set criteria for accepting or rejecting items on the basis of fit, we are likely to declare that all items fit well when the sample size is large enough. On the other hand, if we set limits to fit z values as a criterion for detecting misfit, we are likely to reject most items when the sample is large enough. So, with a large enough sample, every item should fit according to mean squares, but every item should mis-fit according to z.

So while a set of general guidelines like those listed will be helpful for researchers embarking on Rasch modeling, a considerable bibliography of relevant material exists. Articles published by Smith (e.g., 1991, 1994, 2000; Smith, Schumacker, & Bush, 1998) provide good starting points for a more thoroughly informed view of issues concerning fit statistic interpretation. What remains disturbing are the journal articles that cite these Bond & Fox pages as justifying their fit cutoffs, along with the reviewers who demand and accept those citations uncritically.

Fit, Misfit, and Interpretation

In Chapter 4, we alerted you to the use we would make of ICCs from the BLOT to help us reflect on the idea of misfit. Figure 12.1 contains an interesting representation of fit for actual person performances (the jagged empirical ICC) against the Rasch-modeled expectations (the smooth model ICC) for Item 4, the BLOT item at the midpoint on the BLOT item–person logit scale (0.0). The BLOT item output in Table 4.1 gives the following summary for Item 4:

Item	Estimate	Error	Infit MnSq	Outfit MnSq	Infit t	Outfit t
4	0.00	0.22	1.00	0.88	0.0	−0.4

Both infit and outfit mean square values are reported as close to the expected 1.0 and the standardized versions of those fit statistics, and infit and **outfit** *t* are close to the expected 0 values. So,

Q1: How *much* misfit to the model for Item 4?
A1: Very little; Infit MnSq 1.00 and Outfit MnSq 0.88 are very close to 1. And,
Q2: How *likely* is it that Item 4 misfits the model?
A2: Very unlikely; infit *t* 0.0 and outfit t −0.4 are very close to 0.

The smooth curve in Figure 12.1 is the single ICC for Item 4 from Figure 4.4 and models the expected performance of the interaction between persons and that item when the performances fit perfectly to the Rasch model (an impossible expectation). The plotted points on the jagged curve represent the actual performances of 150 students from Chapter 4 and were selected from the output

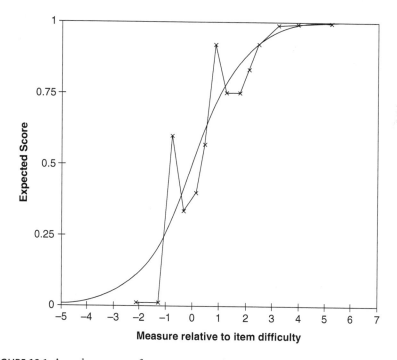

FIGURE 12.1 Actual person performance versus theoretical ICC for an item with good fit: BLOT 4 (again).

options in Winsteps. To understand fully the potential meaning of this graph, it is worth thinking through the steps involved in producing the plot of actuals.

First of all, the $B - D$ calculation for each person is made: BLOT Ability $B -$ Item 4 difficulty (D). In this case, D_4 (conveniently) $= 0.0$. Persons with similar $B - D$ values are grouped together (in this case, at intervals of 0.4 logits), and the actual scores for every person in each group (i.e., 0, 1, 1, 0, 0, . . .) are totaled and the mean value (total / n) calculated. Each plotted point then represents the mean score $(0 \leq x \leq 1)$ on the vertical axis for the group of students with ability estimates within ± 0.2 logits of the location on the horizontal axis. Indeed, Winsteps actually plots the mean score (on y) against the mean of the measures within the interval (on x).

Now the plotted points of mean *actual* responses from each of 14 groups of students, grouped at intervals of 0.4 logits along the BLOT ability–difficulty logit scale, show quite remarkable proximity to the Rasch-modeled *expectation* of performances (the ICC). Yes, there is a slight deviation away from the modeled curve, at around -1.0 and $+1.0$ logits relative to the item difficulty, but this is the sort of *actual* versus *model* match that yields those very acceptable fit statistics. In other words, this is extremely close to the degree of variation of *actual* around *expected* that the Rasch model predicts.

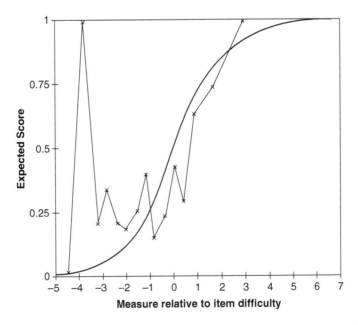

FIGURE 12.2 Actual person performance versus theoretical ICC for an item with poor fit: BLOT 21 (again).

Now the actual versus theoretical comparison in Figure 12.2 paints a much less favorable picture for BLOT Item 21, the most difficult of the BLOT set.

The segment of output for Item 21 from Table 4.1 shows its fit characteristics to be poor from any perspective: Every one of the four fit indicators is noticeably higher than expected by the Rasch model, although an Infit MnSq value of 1.27 would not usually raise eyebrows. Performances on this item are more erratic than expected, although the Rasch model *does* predict correctly about 100 out of 150 responses. Poor fit means that the performance of about 50 students on BLOT Item 21 cannot be predicted comfortably by what is known about those persons' performance on the BLOT test overall (BLOT ability estimate).

Item	Estimate	Error	Infit MnSq	Outfit MnSq	Infit t	Outfit t
21	2.33	0.2	1.27	1.75	2.6	3.4

So how is that revealed in Figure 12.2? The smooth curve is the single-model ICC for Item 21 from Figure 4.4, and the plotted points represent the actual performances of the sample of 150 students from Chapter 4. Again, the figure comes from the output options in Winsteps. Note that this time, the value on the horizontal axis is the calculated B (BLOT ability) − D (Item 21 difficulty) as Item 21's difficulty estimate is +2.33 logits (i.e., not 0 as for Item 4). If we covered the eight plotted points on the left side of the graph, we could conclude, rather generously, that the able groups of students to the right perform close to the Rasch model's expectation: not wonderfully so, but 'good enough for government work'. Now cover that right side of the graph and look on the left at the summaries of groups of person performances on BLOT Item 21 for the less-able portion of the BLOT sample. These students perform above expectations almost right across the board, so the probabilistic expectations of success that we have derived from the Rasch model for persons and items don't hold up here—especially where the less able two thirds of the students meet with the most demanding item. In Chapter 4, 'Going Further', we diagnose the misfit problem step by step to conclude that guessing by less-able students is the likely problem. We can look for some empirical evidence for that conjecture by running Winsteps again, this time implementing the 'CUTLO' option, which cuts off responses from persons with a low probability of success on an item. Linacre (2006) suggests,

> Use this if guessing or response sets are evident . . . Example: Disregard responses where examinees are faced with too great a challenge, and so might guess wildly, i.e., where examinee measure is 2 or more logits lower than item measure: CUTLO = 2.

(p. 83)

Here are the item statistics for Item 21 after CUTLO = 2 was executed:

```
|ENTRY   TOTAL                    MODEL|  INFIT   |   OUTFIT  | PTMEA|
|NUMBER  SCORE  COUNT  MEASURE  S.E.  | MNSQ   ZSTD| MNSQ  ZSTD|  CORR.|
|   21    48    121   2.59    .21| 1.18   1.8| 1.26  2.0|   .34|
```

So the 29 ($N = 150 - 121$ Counts) lowest-performing BLOT candidates were set aside for this analysis ($D - B > 2$ logits). With the Item 21 performances of those potential guessers put aside, MnSq statistics are 1.18 and 1.26: ZStds are 1.8 and 2.0. QED?

Guessing is an off-trait behavior that can be detected by careful Rasch-modeled examination and the problems associated with it minimized. Ingebo (1997) reported on the strategies employed to minimize the potential effects of guessing on the thousands of item-difficulty parameters in the NWEA multiple-choice item bank that Kingsbury (2003; Chapter 5) later reported as having remarkably invariant estimates over decades of testing use: The lowest 15% of the student distribution was routinely put aside for the item-calibration processes. Further, Andrich, Marais, and Humphry (2012) adopted Waller's guessing principles and used Andersen's theorem to examine the potential impacts of random guessing on item estimates in a simulated data set and another using Advanced Raven's Progressive Matrices.

When the difficulty–ability difference ($\beta - \delta$) is 1 logit (rather than the conservative 2 logit difference used for BLOT), the probability of obtaining a correct response is 0.27. So, in a second Rasch model analysis, all responses of persons to items where the probability of a correct response was less than 0.30 from the standard first analysis were converted to missing data. In that case, the item estimates for the most difficult items *increased* when potential guessers were *removed*. The follow-up study of Andrich and Marais (2014) used the same ARPM data set to estimate the effect of potential guessing on person *ability* estimates. They revealed that when the Waller-based procedure was applied, more-able persons (i.e., those least likely to guess) have greater increases in ability estimates than do less-able persons, (i.e., those most likely to guess). Indeed, Andrich and Marais concluded that in order to avoid disadvantaging the more proficient persons, Waller's procedure should be used when the Rasch model is used to analyze multiple-choice items.

We can change the focus for examining fit from looking at the performance of individual items to looking at the performance of individual persons. We should expect to be able to diagnose persons in a manner that corresponds with our diagnoses of items. The kidmap for Student 1 (Figure 12.3) summarizes that student's performance according to the Rasch model's expectations. In the kidmap option in the QUEST software, the item difficulties are displayed in the usual Rasch fashion, with the easiest items at the bottom of the map and the most difficult items at the top. The items located on the left side of the map are those on which this particular child was successful, and the items on the right side of the map

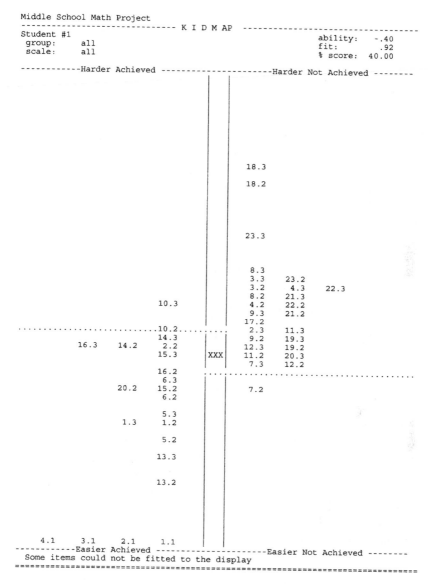

Middle School Math Project
------------------------------- K I D M AP --------------------------------------
Student #1   ability: -.40
    group: all   fit: .92
    scale: all   % score: 40.00

-----------Harder Achieved --------------------Harder Not Achieved --------

FIGURE 12.3 Kidmap for Student 1 showing good fit to the model (Infit mean square = .92).

are those that the child did not complete successfully. The child's ability estimate of −.40 logits is plotted in the center column, with the dotted line on the left indicating the upper bound of the ability estimate (ability estimate plus one standard error: $b_n + s_n$) and the dotted line on the right indicating its lower bound (ability estimate minus one standard error: $b_n − s_n$. The fit index, an infit mean square value of 0.92, indicates a pattern of performance that closely approximates the predicted Rasch model response pattern based on the child's ability estimate: The expected fit value is +1.0. Item 10.3 is correct despite a less than 50% probability of success, whereas Item 7.2 is incorrect, a little against the Rasch expectation of a slightly more than 50% probability of a correct response. The 0.92 infit mean square value indicates a performance close to that predicted by the Rasch model, and the kidmap corroborates that visually.

The infit mean square value of +1.78 for Student 16 indicates that the pattern of responses shown in the Figure 12.4 kidmap is more haphazard than the Rasch model would expect for an estimated ability of +.45 logits. Following the principles outlined in the previous interpretation, we can detect the unexpected responses made by Student 16: Item 3.3 is the only item that the student gets unexpectedly correct, but the difficulty estimate of this item step is so close to the upper bound of the estimated ability for Student 16 that it could be just disregarded in terms of affecting misfit. The items that are unexpectedly incorrect, however, paint a different picture: These are the source of the misfit, estimated at 78% (1.78 − 1.0 × 100%) more variation than the Rasch-modeled expectation. Given that the items unexpectedly incorrect for Student 16 are relatively on target for the student's ability, the impact of this performance shows up more clearly in the weighted (infit) statistics than in the unweighted (outfit) statistics (Table 12.8).

But how can this be of value diagnostically to the investigator? A comparison between the two kidmaps is a good place to start. Student 16 (est. = +0.45) was completely unsuccessful at a group of items that were well within that student's ability (revealed by this testing). Student 1 (est. = −0.41) has considerably less ability overall, as revealed by this investigation, but this student was able to successfully complete all the items in groups 14, 15, 16, and 19. In terms of Table 12.6, the response pattern of Student 16 is consonant with that shown as 'special knowledge missing'. To the child's teacher, however, this indicates the possibility of a developmental gap in this child's understanding of fundamental mathematical concepts. Of course, the teacher first would ensure that the child actually was present at school on the occasions when this material was covered in school lessons before going on to investigate further the reasons behind this apparent deficiency. New remedial teaching should first account for this lack of understanding in order to be more effective than teaching that just provided general remediation.

There is an interesting sidelight to these kidmaps and the issue of fit that could help us further understand the qualitative–quantitative nexus in the investigation of human behavior. The original researcher who had undertaken the qualitative interview of each student in this middle school mathematics investigation asked the data analyst to explain the meaning of the Rasch output. During that process, Kidmaps 1 and 16 were generated solely on the basis of the fit statistics shown in the group output. Kidmap 1 was chosen as the first student in the output with unremarkable fit values, whereas Kidmap 16 was chosen as the first in the sample where misfit seemed apparent. The segments of output for those two students

```
Middle School Math Project
----------------------------- K  I  D  M  A  P-------------------------------
  Candidate: 16                                        ability:    .45
  group:     all                                       fit:       1.78
  scale:     all                                       % score:  62.22

-----------Harder Achieved --------------------Harder Not Achieved --------

                                        |  |
                                        |  |
                                        |  |
                                        |  |
                                        |  |
                                        |  |
                                   18.3 |  |
                                        |  |
                                   18.2 |  |
                                        |  |
                                        |  |
                                        |  |
                                   23.3 |  |
                                        |  |
                                        |  |
                              3.3    8.3 |  |
............22.3.....4.3.....3.2 23.2....
                                        |  |   8.2    21.3
     22.2    10.3     4.2            |  |
                      9.3        |XXX|   21.2
                                 |  |    17.2
     11.3    10.2     2.3 ...............................................
                      9.2            14.3    19.3
             12.3     2.2            14.2    16.3    19.2
             20.3    11.2            15.3
             12.2     7.3
                                    16.2
                      6.3
             20.2     7.2            15.2
                      6.2

                      5.3
              1.3     1.2

                      5.2

                     13.3

                     13.2


     4.1     3.1     2.1     1.1 |  |
------------Easier Achieved ---------------------Easier Not Achieved -------
  Some items could not be fitted to the display
================================================================================
```

FIGURE 12.4 Kidmap for Student 16 showing inadequate fit to the model (Infit mean square = 1.78).

TABLE 12.8 Case Statistics for Students 1 and 16

Case ID No.	Actual Score	Possible Score	Ability (Logits)	Error	Infit Mean Square	Outfit Mean Square	Infit t	Outfit t
01	18	23	−0.41	0.30	0.93	0.68	−0.19	−0.17
16	28	23	+0.45	0.30	1.78	1.50	2.41	0.82

are shown in Table 12.8. When shown what the high misfit values for Student 16 revealed in terms of unexpected errors in the response pattern, the interviewer took out the handwritten case notes for that student. The top of the page was annotated with an expression of the interviewer's surprise that an apparently capable student had performed so poorly on a whole group of obviously easier questions. The investigator was both surprised and delighted that the misfit values had alerted the data analyst to a case on quantitative grounds that the investigator had noted while conducting the qualitative interview.

Fit: Issues for Resolution

Notwithstanding the important distinction raised earlier about the relation between the data and the Rasch model, Rasch analysis procedures share a number of general features with other data-modeling techniques. After the initial estimation of approximate item difficulties and person abilities, these initial values are used to estimate improved difficulty and ability estimates. This iterative process is repeated for the purpose of reducing the marginal totals of item and person residuals to as close as possible to zero. Generally speaking, Winsteps estimation iterations continue until the largest marginal residual is less than the default level of 0.5 score points (while the largest change in any person or item estimate is less than 0.01 logits). Iterations cease when marginal residuals are acceptably small or when the biggest change in any estimate is too small to matter. However, although marginal residuals are very small, individual response residuals can remain large. It is these that form the basis of fit analysis.

This leads to a rather counterintuitive paradox: A test made up of two equal-size but unrelated sets of items can produce more acceptable fit estimates than a test attempting to measure one attribute that includes a small number of poorly constructed items. Think of it this way. In the example of the 'two different halves' test, there is no single underlying attribute on which person performance is being measured. The estimation iterations simply will be repeated until the default change in residual values is recorded, and perhaps all items will 'fit'. For a well-constructed test, in which two or three items are not working as well as the others, the underlying latent attribute is defined, psychometrically, by the performances of the persons on the large number of items. The interactions between the persons and the large number of good items will dominate the estimation process. When the residuals are reduced as far as possible for the bulk of the data set, the two or three less adequate items will show evidence of misfit. This is the caution behind using the process of common-person linking between BLOT and PRTIII in Chapter 5. One alternative is to pool the data and conduct one analysis of all the data. In the original investigation, both techniques were used.

This leads us back, conveniently, to the value of theory-driven research. Misfit indicators are likely to be less reliable when data collection devices have been assembled haphazardly. How can data analysis be expected to discriminate between equally poor items? It is not unreasonable to suggest, however, that misfit indicators could be very useful in helping the investigator understand where the theory-driven measurement intentions went astray in empirical practice: A small number of less satisfactory items might be detected against a backdrop of a larger number of successful items.

Misfit: A Fundamental Issue

"Refereeing papers for European journals, in particular, reveals to me that our Rasch colleagues in Europe usually require a broader range of fit indicators than we have in the US and Australia, and are often more stringent in the application of misfit cutoffs" (Bond, 2005b, p. 336). For those who wish to conduct other, perhaps more rigorous tests of fit, the most appropriate reference is that of Fischer and Molenaar (1995). In part of the next chapter, we review the relation between the Rasch measurement model and the requirements for fundamental measurement in the social sciences following the prescriptions for axiomatic conjoint measurement (Cliff, 1992; Luce, 1995; Luce, Krantz, Suppes, & Tversky, 1990; Michell, 1999).

In the Interim

One interesting sidelight to come from the never-ending search for ways to detect important deviations from the important unidimensionality requirement of Rasch modeling has been the application of factor analysis techniques to the residual matrices (Wright, 1996). If the Rasch-modeled person–item interaction information extracted from the data matrix leaves a random dispersion of residuals, then the claim is that the solution accounts for just one dimension. The presence of factor loadings in the analysis of residuals would suggest the presence of more than one underlying test dimension. Winsteps facilitates this analysis and interpretation in its Tables 23.3 and 24.3, Principal Components Analysis of Residuals, which decomposes the matrix of item or person correlations based on residuals to identify other possible factors (dimensions) that might be affecting response patterns

(Linacre, 1998; Smith, 2000). Alternatively, ConQuest software (Wu, Adams, & Wilson, 1998) provides methods for assessing whether a single Rasch dimension or two or more closely related Rasch dimensions provide the most parsimonious summary of data–model fit.

Detecting Multiple Dimensions

One of the distinctive features of the Rasch approach to scientific measurement has been revealed by the insistence that our attempts at making measures should proceed by one clearly theorized construct at a time. That is, the Rasch model requires that measures must be unidimensional. But, of course, that underlies our problem. How do we know when we have established a unidimensional measure suitable to our measurement purposes? All attempts at summarizing data are compromises; many would claim that the only strictly unidimensional test is the single-item test, and even that one item might be revealed as tapping more than one underlying trait (e.g., reading the prompt, calculating the answer, writing the response, etc.). Generally, practitioners of Rasch measurement rely on the indicators of misfit to reveal the extent to which any item or person performance suggests more than one underlying latent trait is at work.

Given our current knowledge of the possible inadequacies of fit indexes for this purpose and our deeper understanding of the nature of scientific measurement structures (Chapters 1 and 13), it would be remiss of us not to reflect on the possible consequences of treating two or more dimensions as one or to suggest how recent developments in the field can help us deal with this potential problem. We adopt a two-pronged approach: The first looks at how we can use factor analytical approaches to help us detect extraneous dimensions in our data; the second outlines how a more sophisticated Rasch-based model makes comparisons between multidimensional and unidimensional measurement structures.

So the identification of possible multiple dimensions within a data set must remain one of the main focuses of measurement construction in the human sciences. Given that factor analysis still remains the single most common statistical tool for diagnosing dimensionality, it is no wonder that our understanding of underlying measurement constructs remains so limited. In practice, factor analyses, due to their sample dependency and use of ordinal-level data, provide dimensionality information that is only partially replicable across other samples of interest and further perpetuates the notion that scientific measures can be developed and diagnosed using correlational methods.

Factor Analysis—Problems and Promise

Factor analyses are based on correlations of sample-dependent ordinal-level data, typically requiring complete data matrices for analysis. Not only are complete data sets unrealistic for most investigations (Wright, 1996), but the solutions to missing-data problems result in data loss (using casewise deletions) or distortions of the data matrix (using pairwise deletions or missing data imputation).

The major problem is that factor analysis does not require the construction of linear, interval-level measures or factor scores from the outset, and hence the factor sizes and factor loadings rarely are reproduced when new sets of relevant data are reanalyzed with the same procedure (Wright, 1996). Furthermore, even though the confirmation of a factor structure is based on its reproducibility with another data set, the confirmation procedure includes neither fit statistics nor standard errors for loadings (Wright, 1996).

This dependence on sample-dependent correlations, without analysis of fit or standard errors, severely limits the utility of factor analysis results. It continues to appear as if factor analysis is an obligatory step in establishing the validity of a measure, yet few seem to be able to explain how the results help in understanding or improving the measure. Factor analysis is far removed from the idea of constructing a linear measure and often serves as a compulsory yet misleading exercise in the construct validation process. Thus, two major concerns with factor analysis are: It does not provide information on which items and which persons work toward defining a useful yardstick (i.e., it does not serve to construct linear measures) nor on the extent to which they do so (e.g., using fit indices, standard errors). Rather, it identifies correlations with the underlying variable but not locations on it (Schumacker & Linacre, 1996). It does not provide a defensible framework (i.e., it is based on sample-dependent correlations) for understanding the magnitude of and relations among possible subscales. This leads to a variety of possible yet arbitrary interpretations of the resulting factors.

Rasch Factor Analysis

'Rasch factor analysis' (first introduced by Wright in 1996) can be a somewhat misleading term, but, simply put, it involves, first, a regular Rasch analysis procedure (using the ordinal-level descriptive data to construct a linear measure), followed by a factor analysis of the (ordinal-level) residuals that remain after the linear Rasch measure has been extracted from the data set (Linacre, 1998). A factor analysis of these residuals is used to identify any common variance among those aspects of the data that remained unexplained or unmodeled by the primary Rasch measure. This use of factor analysis procedures, (i.e., after a linear variable has been constructed), can be quite informative because it provides information supplemental to understanding what common variance in the data is not accounted for by the linear Rasch measure under investigation.

Linacre (1998) suggested three stages to the investigation of data dimensionality. First, any negative-point biserial correlations (from traditional statistics) should be examined to identify potentially problematic items. Second, misfitting persons and items should be diagnosed using Rasch fit indicators. Third, these procedures should be followed by the examination of dimensionality using Rasch Factor

Analysis. If any substantial and interesting dimension is identified from the Rasch Factor Analysis, the researcher should consider creating a separate measure for this dimension (Linacre, 1998).

The identification of common variance in the residuals is not always meaningful. Both the size of the factor (that is, the amount of variance for which it accounts) and the nature of the factor (reflection of response styles or item content, e.g., Linacre, 1998) need to be considered in assigning importance to additional dimensions that might emerge. The nature of any additional dimension must be assessed by the researcher. Hopefully, that reflection will be theoretically driven, but, realistically, it is often based on pragmatic reasoning. For example, one easily can conceptualize a mathematics test functioning as a single dimension even though it contains items on both subtraction and addition. Others might find it useful to construct two different measures—one of subtraction ability and one of addition ability. Wright and Stone (2004, p. 20), using characteristics of stones (rocks, etc.), illustrate some of the decisions that one might make.

Principal components analysis of stone residuals might identify a subset of stones that has something in common. When we examine these stones, we might find that smooth stones are harder to lift than rough stones of similar weight, which would produce a telltale set of similar residuals. This would identify a secondary and probably unwanted variable of smoothness operating in our stones data and give us the opportunity to decide whether we want to measure stones on two variables (i.e., weight and smoothness) or control the intrusion of smoothness by ensuring that all of the stones that we use to build our strength/weight measure are equally smooth. When constructing a strength/weight yardstick, we would then take care to use stones of similar smoothness in order to clarify our definition of strength/weight. Principal components analysis of person residuals might also show a second variable—this time the effect of wet hands on lifting. The natural resolution of this disturbance to the construction of a strength/weight yardstick is to control for hand wetness.

Analysis of a Psychotherapy Measure—An Example

The Symptom Checklist 90 Revised (SCL-90-R; Derogatis, 1975, 1994) is one of the most commonly used psychological assessment instruments today. The instrument consists of a checklist of symptoms on a 5-point Likert scale, ranging from (0) not at all distressed to (4) extremely distressed, for symptoms the patient might have experienced over the past week. The SCL-90-R is composed of nine symptom subscales and three global indices. The subscales include Somatization, Obsessive-Compulsive, Interpersonal Sensitivity, Depression, Anxiety, Hostility, Phobic Anxiety, Paranoid Ideation, and Psychoticism. The three global indices of distress/psychopathology are the Positive Symptom Total Index (number of symptoms), Positive Symptom Distress Index (intensity of distress), and the Global Severity Index (calculation of both number of symptoms and intensity of distress).

As with many psychological inventories, clinicians interpret the scores based on responses to individual items as well as scale scores (Derogatis & Savitz, 1999).

As with the factor analysis of other psychological instruments, investigations into the dimensionality of this inventory have resulted in mixed support for the hypothesized subscale structure of the SCL-90-R (Derogatis & Savitz, 1999). What has been consistent, however, is the finding of relatively high intercorrelations among the subscales (ranging from .59 to .67; see Clark & Friedman, 1983; Dinning & Evans, 1977, Holcomb, Adams, & Ponder, 1983). This evidence pointed toward the potential utility of the factor analysis of the Rasch model residuals to investigate the dimensionality of the checklist. If the 'subscales' are so highly intercorrelated, might they work together to form a single meaningful yardstick that measures global distress? If so, we could develop an equal-interval measure that would remain invariant (within standard error estimates) for diagnosing distress levels and then measuring change in those levels over time. The Rasch Factor Analysis could be used to detect any substantial and meaningful variance that was not captured by that primary global distress yardstick.

> Therefore, we performed a Rasch factor analysis, that is, an analysis of response residuals among items in order to see if we could find any evidence for the presence of unsuspected secondary variables, after removing variance due to the primary "Distress Yardstick".
>
> *(Wright & Stone, 2004)*

The team of researchers (Elliott, Fox, Beltyukova, Stone, Gunderson, & Zhang, 2006), in the beginning stages of instrument investigation, used data from two different psychotherapy outcome studies on process-experiential therapy (Elliott, Watson, Goldman, & Greenberg, 2004; Greenberg, Rice, & Elliott, 1993), both conducted at the University of Toledo. The first group of clients was recruited through a depression study, and all were diagnosed with major depressive disorder or related affective disorders. The second group was a naturalistic sample, in therapy for a variety of Axis I and Axis II disorders (SCID-1 & SCID-II; First, Spitzer, Gibbon, & Williams, 1995).

Principal Components Analysis of Rasch Residuals

Figure 12.5 shows the factor plot of the standardized residuals after the primary Rasch dimension has been extracted. This map plots the item measure (Rasch estimate in logits) against the magnitude of the PCA factor loading of its residual, based on the standardized residual of each item from the Rasch dimension. Thus, items that have substantial variance that remains unexplained by the primary Rasch measure have higher factor loadings (seen at the top of the map). The vertical spread of these items helps diagnose whether these items are clustered in particular levels of the measure (e.g., clustered as more or less difficult). Items that are

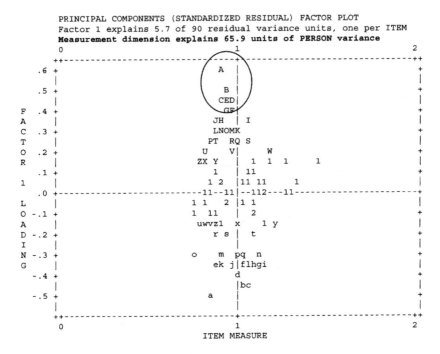

PRINCIPAL COMPONENTS (STANDARDIZED RESIDUAL) FACTOR PLOT
Factor 1 explains 5.7 of 90 residual variance units, one per ITEM
Measurement dimension explains 65.9 units of PERSON variance

FIGURE 12.5 Winsteps dimensionality map for SCL-90-R residuals.

clustered together with loadings substantially greater than zero are those requiring further investigation for measurement disturbances (Wright & Stone, 2004).

When describing secondary dimensions in the data, Wright and Stone (2004) used the analogy of identifying a branch of items that are distinguishable from the main stem or yardstick (p. 30). The substantiality of any such additional factor(s) is then evaluated by comparing the ratio of variance of the residual factor to that of the yardstick (Rasch measure) as a whole (Wright & Stone, 2004).

The heading in Figure 12.5 indicates that the first factor extracted from the residuals accounts for 5.7 units (items) out of 90 residual variance units (items).

Further, the yardstick (Rasch measure) dimension explains 65.9 units of the person variance. These indices are then used to calculate a factor sensitivity ratio (Wright & Stone, 2004) by taking the common residual units divided by the yardstick (analogous to systematic or explained variance) units. Here, dividing 5.7 (residual variance units) by 65.9 (Rasch measure variance units) yields .086; that is, 8% to 9% of the yardstick stability is affected by this factor representing unexplained relations between the item residuals after the Rasch measure was extracted.

Table 12.9 (a truncated table from Winsteps; Linacre 2006) lists the factor loadings, indicating seven items (69, 61, 79, 21, 88, 76, and 37) with substantial positive loadings on the factor discovered in the item residuals (i.e., with off-dimension loading of .4 or greater).

TABLE 12.9 Winsteps Output for Loadings on First Dimension of Residuals

FACTOR	LOADING	MEASURE	INFIT MNSQ	OUTFIT MNSQ	ENTRY NUMBER		I
1	.59	.90	.82	.77	A	69	69
1	.49	.93	.93	.87	B	61	61
1	.44	.90	.86	.81	C	79	79
1	.44	.97	1.05	1.18	D	21	21
1	.43	.93	1.23	1.15	E	88	88
1	.42	.94	1.08	1.00	F	76	76
1	.40	.95	.88	.83	G	37	37
1	.37	.88	.98	.93	H	83	83
1	.36	1.05	.98	.95	I	70	70
1	.33	.89	.75	.72	J	41	41
1	.32	.97	.94	.88	K	90	90
1	.31	.87	.77	.74	L	36	36
1	.30	.98	.91	.81	M	80	80
1	.30	.92	.95	.91	N	18	18
1	29	.90	.92	.87	O	77	77
1	.27	.84	.77	.73	P	54	54
1	.27	.98	.95	.90	Q	43	43
1	.26	.97	1.15	1.04	R	22	22
1	.25	1.06	.97	.84	S	50	50
1	.23	.88	1.02	1.08	T	89	89
1	.21	.83	.82	.79	U	26	26
1	.21	.96	1.02	.98	V	68	68
1	.19	1.18	1.20	1.23	W	73	73
1	.17	.79	.81	.80	X	29	29
1	.16	.87	.85	.80	Y	32	32
1	.14	.79	.85	.87	Z	28	28
1	.14	1.08	1.56	1.62		84	84
1	.14	1.19	1.18	1.90		63	63
1	.14	1.44	1.23	.70		16	16
1	.13	1.26	1.15	1.01		7	07
1	.11	1.06	1.20	1.48		85	85
1	−.52	.86	1.31	1.50	a	1	01
1	−.47	1.04	1.11	1.16	b	39	39
1	−.43	1.04	1.17	1.13	c	49	49
1	−.40	.99	1.08	1.27	d	40	40

Note: Factor 1 is the principal components analysis of standardized residual correlations for items (sorted by loading). Factor 1 explains 5.7 of 90 residual variance units, one per ITEM Measurement dimension explains 65.9 units of person variance.

The seven positive items appear to have a common meaning of social anxiety. These items are:

69. Feeling very self-conscious with others
61. Feeling uneasy when people are watching or talking about you
79. Feeling of worthlessness

21. Feeling uneasy with the opposite sex
88. Never feeling close to another person
76. Others not giving you proper credit for your achievements
37. Feeling that people are unfriendly or dislike you

The four items (1, 39, 49, and 40) that are substantially negatively correlated with the factor have a common meaning that could be labeled, 'physical anxiety'.

These items are:
  1. Headaches
39. Heart pounding/racing
49. Hot/Cold Spells
40. Nausea/Upset Stomach

This secondary variable identified by the Rasch factor analysis provides evidence of a small influence of another dimension that might be labeled 'social distress'. Nine percent of the common variance undefined by the primary-distress Rasch dimension is associated with this other, albeit minor dimension. This now provides empirical evidence for the existence of a separate subscale, and the researcher can decide if this is large enough and meaningful enough to measure separately from the main distress yardstick.

Now the original researchers can reflect on the costs/benefits of both including the social/physical anxiety items merely as part of the original Rasch dimension (potentially losing some sensitivity/validity of measurement) and excluding those items from the total score of the SCL-90-R and perhaps working toward assessing and interpreting the other dimension(s) separately. Even so, the structure revealed for this checklist by the combination of Rasch analysis and the PCA of the Rasch item residuals stands in considerable contrast to the originally claimed 9-factor structure: It is in vain to do with more what can be done with fewer (William of Occam).

It is important, when examining and ultimately identifying these extra dimensions, to remember that unidimensionality is always provisional, and a data set manifests one dimension so long as it is productive to think of it that way (Linacre, 1998 p. 268). This rather pragmatic approach to identifying unidimensionality is consistent with Ben Wright's reference to the yardstick—that is, any dimension is identified only to solve a problem at hand and is useful only if it remains current in what it is meant to help explain. Thus, measured dimensions must be monitored over time and recalibrated and adjustments made accordingly. Further, our measured dimensions, although representations of complex human phenomena, should never be confused as confirmed reifications of the construct under investigation.

One Dimension, Two Dimensions, Three Dimensions, More?

Multidimensional Rasch modeling is no longer as controversial as it was when it first entered the discussions of Rasch SIG members and participants of the

International Objective Measurement Workshops. Equally controversial were the early uses of Rasch factor analysis (PCA of Rasch residuals) for helping to determine the dimensionality of data sets. Now the role of PCA of Rasch residuals to check the distribution of the residuals of the data set not accounted for by the single Rasch dimension is regarded as a standard analytical procedure, but the idea of a multidimensional Rasch model still seems to deny the basic measurement principle espoused from the outset of this volume: Measurement should proceed one variable at a time.

For example, the focus of international achievement testing, such as OECD-PISA and TIMSS, is not the achievements of individual students but the performance profiles of large national and subnational groupings of students. Multidimensional item response model (MIRM) analyses combine the response information for different tests according to the size of the correlations between the latent variables. If the tests are really unrelated (i.e., have a correlation of 0), the multidimensional item response model, in effect, analyses the data from each test completely independently. If the correlation is perfect (1.0), then the data can be analyzed as one single Rasch dimension. However, if the correlation is high but not perfect, then the MIRM uses information from both tests to estimate of performances on each of the latent traits.

In the OECD international assessments of academic achievement (e.g., PISA, 2009), the estimated (unattenuated) correlations among reading, mathematics, and science were quite high (i.e., > 0.80) but not as high as a perfect correlation (1.0). (See Table 12.10 from OECD, 2012, p. 194.)

We could insist that *each* of mathematics, science, and reading be treated as a single achievement dimension in the Rasch measurement sense. Certainly our curriculum consultants would insist that mathematics, language, and science are actually separate dimensions. Some will go further and contend that the individual components of mathematics (or language) need to be tested, measured, and reported separately, especially for estimating those abilities for individual students. But the counterargument is also compelling: Treating each achievement test as separate and unrelated discards a lot of potentially important information about the ways in which, say, mathematics, language, and science might actually be related, especially at the population level.

The model applied to the PISA data is a generalized form of the Rasch model: the mixed coefficients multinomial logit model (MCMLM; Adams, Wilson, & Wang, 1997). It is implemented in the ConQuest software (Wu, Adams, & Wilson,

TABLE 12.10 Estimated Correlations Between Subject Areas for OECD Countries in PISA, 2009

	Reading	*Science*
Mathematics	0.82	0.88
Reading		0.87

1997) that has been used for the PISA analyses and is now also available as TAM (Test Analysis Modules; Kiefer, Robitzsch, & Wu), an IRT package written in R. By applying a variety of constraints in the control lines of these applications, researchers can use the variety of Rasch models already described in earlier chapters on a variety of data. While a review of the possibilities of the MCMLM and software is beyond the scope of this chapter, some points are worth noting.

Improving estimates for mathematics ability for individual students is best achieved by giving a longer test; but population estimates of math ability based on a shorter test can be improved by using information from responses to a reading test given at the same time. The extent of the improvement will depend on the extent of the latent correlation between the mathematics and reading variables. In the latter case, sample size rather than test length is the key. Sharing information *across* tests produces improved precision of estimates for *each* test but means that the reading result (say) contains information from the mathematics result. A possible downside of the improved precision might be that MIRM estimates on *each* test for some students might be biased toward their estimates across *all* tests.

Summary

The issue of dimensionality remains central to those interested in developing genuinely scientific measures in the human sciences. The benefits of the Rasch model for measurement, including interval-level person and item measurements, apply only to data that fit the model; but of course, no data ever can fit perfectly. Residual-based fit statistics and the PCA of those residuals remain rather imperfect ways to detect lack of adherence to the Rasch requirements for measurement. In spite of the requirements of journal editors and reviewers for unambiguous interpretation of indicators of misfit, the routine application of some cutoff criteria for acceptable fit statistics always risks undervaluing the theory-driven process of developing measures in the human sciences.

ACTIVITIES

Download and read:
   Wu, M., & Adams, R. (2007). *Applying the Rasch model to psycho-social measurement*. Melbourne: Educational Measurement Solutions.
   Richard Gershon's 1992 work motivated Mike Linacre to include the 'CUTLO=' command in Winsteps. Download and read Gershon's RMT research note, which is available at www.rasch.org/rmt/rmt62a.htm.
   To check on some of the potential impacts of guessing in multiple-choice testing, you can run the BLOT data file in Bond&FoxSteps:

1. For a simple check on the improvements to item characteristics, add the command line

   CUTLO=2

   and check the new item statistics table (Winsteps table 14) against the one you created in the Chapter 4 analysis. Any improvements in fit statistics? What happens to the SEs? Why? Did the item estimates change?

2. You could see a clearer picture of the impact of guessing on both the items and the persons by:
   (a) running the CUTLO=2 analysis. Output PFILE=pf.txt and IFILE=if.txt
   (b) rerunning the analysis without CUTLO=2 but include the commands PAFILE=pf.txt and IAFILE=if.txt

   The displacements in (b) would tell you the impact of any guessing in the data on the estimates.

   Using CUTLO=1 is closer to the criterion used by Andrich and colleagues: It eliminates more 'potential guessers'. Rerun the analyses with CUTLO=1 if you wish.

References

Adams, R. J., Wilson, M. R., & Wang, W. (1997). The multidimensional random coefficients multinomial logit model. *Applied Psychological Measurement, 21*, 1–24.

Andrich, D., & Marais, I. (2014). Person proficiency estimates in the dichotomous Rasch model when random guessing is removed from difficulty estimates of multiple choice items. *Applied Psychological Measurement, 38*(6), 432–449.

Andrich, D., Marais, I., & Humphry, S. (2012). Using a theorem by Andersen and the dichotomous Rasch model to assess the presence of random guessing in multiple choice items. *Journal of Educational and Behavioral Statistics, 37*(9), 417–442.

Bond, T. G. (2005a). Accountability in the academy: Rasch measurement of student feedback surveys. In R. F. Waugh (Ed.), *Frontiers in educational psychology* (pp. 119–129). New York, NY: Nova Science.

Bond, T. G. (2005b). Past, present and future: An idiosyncratic view of Rasch measurement. In S. Alagumalai, D. Curtis, & N. Hungi (Eds.), *Applied Rasch measurement: A book of exemplars. Papers in honour of John P. Keeves* (pp. 329–341). Dordrecht: Kluwer Academic.

Bond, T. G., & Fox, C. M. (2007). *Applying the Rasch model: Fundamental measurement in the human sciences* (2nd ed.). Mahwah, NJ: Lawrence Erlbaum Associates.

Clark, A., & Friedman, M. J. (1983). Factor structure and discriminant validity of the SCL-90 in a veteran psychiatric population. *Journal of Personality Assessment, 47*, 396–404.

Cliff, N. (1992). Abstract measurement theory and the revolution that never happened. *Psychological Science, 3*(3), 186–190.

Derogatis, L. R. (1975). *The SCL-90-R.* Baltimore, MD: Clinical Psychometric Research.

Derogatis, L.R. (1994). *SCL-90-R: Administration, scoring and procedures manual*. Minneapolis, MN: National Computer Systems.

Derogatis, L.R., & Savitz, K.L. (1999). The SCL-90-R, Brief Symptom Inventory, and matching clinical rating scales. In M.E. Maruish (Ed.), *The use of psychological testing for treatment planning and outcomes assessment* (2nd ed., pp. 679–724). Mahwah, NJ: Lawrence Erlbaum Associates.

Dinning, W.D., & Evans, R.G. (1977). Discriminant and convergent validity of the SCL-90 in psychiatric inpatients. *Journal of Personality Assessment, 41*, 304–310.

Elliott, R., Fox, C.M., Beltyukova, S.A., Stone, G.E., Gunderson, J., & Zhang, X. (2006). Deconstructing therapy outcome measurement with Rasch analysis: The SCL-90-R. *Psychological Assessment, 18*(4), 359–376.

Elliott, R., Watson, J.C., Goldman, R.N., & Greenberg, L.S. (2004). Accessing and allowing experiencing. In R. Elliott & J.C. Watson (Eds.), *Learning emotion-focused therapy: The process-experiential approach to change* (pp. 169–192). Washington, DC: American Psychological Association.

First, M.B., Spitzer, R.L., Gibbon, M., & Williams, J.B. (1995). The Structured Clinical Interview for DSM-III-R Personality Disorders (SCID-II). *Journal of Personality Disorders, 9*, 83–104.

Fischer, G.H., & Molenaar, I.W. (Eds.). (1995). *Rasch models: Foundations, recent developments, and applications*. New York, NY: Springer-Verlag.

Greenberg, L.S., Rice, L.N., & Elliott, R. (1993). *Facilitating emotional change: The moment-by-moment process*. New York, NY: Guilford Press.

Holcomb, W.R., Adams, N.A., & Ponder, H.M. (1983). Factor structure of the Symptom Checklist-90 with acute psychiatric inpatients. *Journal of Consulting & Clinical Psychology, 51*, 535–538.

Ingebo, G.S. (1997). *Probability in the measure of achievement*. Chicago, IL: MESA Press.

Kingsbury, G. (2003, April). *A long-term study of the stability of item parameter estimates*. Paper presented at the annual meeting of the American Educational Research Association, Chicago, IL.

Linacre, J.M. (1998). Detecting multidimensionality: Which residual data-type works best? *Journal of Outcome Measurement, 2*(3), 266–283.

Linacre, J.M. (2006). *A user's guide to Winsteps Ministep Rasch-model computer programs*. Chicago, IL: Winsteps.com.

Linacre, J.M., & Wright, B.D. (1994). Chi-square fit statistics. *Rasch Measurement Transactions, 8*(2), 360.

Luce, R.D. (1995). Four tensions concerning mathematical modeling in psychology. *Annual Review of Psychology, 46*, 1–26.

Luce, R.D., Krantz, D.H., Suppes, P., & Tversky, A. (1990). *Foundations of measurement: Vol. 3. Representation, axiomatization, and invariance*. San Diego, CA: Academic Press.

Michell, J. (1999). *Measurement in psychology: Critical history of a methodological concept*. New York, NY: Cambridge University Press.

OECD. (2012). *PISA 2012 assessment and analytical framework. Mathematics, reading, science, problem solving and financial literacy*. Paris: Author.

PISA. (2009). *Technical report, PISA*. Paris: OECD.

Schumacker, R.E., & Linacre, J.M. (1996). Factor analysis and Rasch analysis. *Rasch Measurement Transactions, 9*(4), 470.

Smith, R.M. (1991). The distributional properties of Rasch item fit statistics. *Educational and Psychological Measurement, 51*, 541–565.

Smith, R.M. (1994). Comparison of the power of Rasch total- and between-item fit statistics to detect measurement disturbances. *Educational and Psychological Measurement, 54*(1), 42–55.

Smith, R.M. (2000). Fit analysis in latent trait measurement models. *Journal of Applied Measurement, 1*(2), 199–218.

Smith, R.M., Schumacker, R.E., & Bush, M.J. (1998). Using item mean squares to evaluate fit to the Rasch model. *Journal of Outcome Measurement, 2*(1), 66–78.

Wright, B.D. (1984). Despair and hope for educational measurement. *Contemporary Education Review, 3*(1), 281–288.

Wright, B.D. (1996). Comparing Rasch measurement and factor analysis. *Structural Equation Modeling, 3*(1), 3–24.

Wright, B.D., Linacre, M., Gustafsson, J.-E., & Martin-Loff, P. (1994). Reasonable mean-square fit values. *Rasch Measurement Transactions, 8*(3), 370.

Wright, B.D., & Masters, G.N. (1981). *The measurement of knowledge and attitude* (Research Memorandum No. 30). Chicago, IL: University of Chicago, MESA Psychometric Laboratory.

Wright, B.D., & Masters, G.N. (1982). *Rating scale analysis.* Chicago, IL: MESA Press.

Wright, B.D., & Stone, M.H. (2004). *Making measures.* Chicago, IL: Phaneron Press.

Wu, M. (In press). *MIRT Book.* Melbourne: Educational Measurement Solutions.

Wu, M., & Adams, R. (2007). *Applying the Rasch model to psycho-social measurement.* Melbourne: Educational Measurement Solutions.

Wu, M.L., Adams, R.J., & Wilson, M.R. (1998). *ConQuest: Generalised item response modeling software* [Computer software]. Camberwell, Victoria: Australian Council for Educational Research.

13

A SYNTHETIC OVERVIEW

> Those who are enamored of practice without science are like a pilot who goes into a ship without rudder or compass and never has any certainty where he is going. Practice should always be based on a sound knowledge of theory.
> —Leonardo da Vinci (1452–1519, Notebooks)

The human condition is, by almost any definition, exceptionally complex. Although we remain amazed at the range of individual differences that distinguish each and every one of us from the others, one of the purposes central to the human sciences has been the generation of laws and theories to describe the common features of human existence. It seems as though those of us who try to understand the human condition must struggle to deal with the tension that exists between trying to describe, explain, measure, and predict the common attributes of human beings on the one hand and appreciating and accounting for idiosyncratic individual differences on the other.

Although many paradigms exist across the human sciences for studying and explaining the human condition, the work presented in this book is essential to the position that psychology, for example, is a rational science, and those aspects of it that we claim to be quantitative can be tested with measurement theory rather than simply asserted to be so. In spite of the many other paradigms that contribute to our understanding of human nature, social interaction, health, behavior, intellectual development, and school achievement, it is not unreasonable to claim that, in the 20th century, the social sciences have been dominated by those determined to quantify the important aspects of human behavior.

Latent trait theorists regard observable behavior (the manifest variable) as merely the outward indicator of human states that remain, for the most part, at least invisible and perhaps unknowable. The intention of the instrument developer, however, is to establish a clear picture in the researcher's mind of what is in the subject's mind; and the only potential bridge across that Kantian gulf is the administration of the instrument. This requires that the instrument be written as clearly and unambiguously as possible and that the respondent collaborate willingly with the investigator to use the instrument honestly and wittingly. In that case, the instrument is a vehicle for *communication* of shared meaning between investigator and respondent. To the extent to which the instrument fails to fulfil its purpose in providing clear two-way communication, our research endeavors are doomed. If we then fail to use the appropriate analytical tools to construct the invariant measurement properties and extract the qualitative meaning from these data, even the careful construction of the instrument will not suffice as a rigorous quantification of the latent variable.

In *Measurement in Psychology: A Critical History of a Methodological Concept*, Michell (1999) argued that measurement in psychology has failed because psychologists, unable to meet the stringent requirements of measurement as they exist in the physical sciences, invented their own definitions of what measurement in psychology would be. He maintained that these definitions ignore two fundamental steps in the measurement process. First, it is necessary to argue that the particular human trait under investigation is, in fact, quantifiable. Second, it then is necessary to construct a measure of this trait so that the numbers indicating the variety of values of the trait *may* be subjected lawfully to the mathematical computations that we routinely use in statistical analyses. It is not good enough, Michell claimed, to allocate numbers to events (e.g., responses, opinions, or behaviors) and then to assert that this is measurement.

Indeed, Michell argued that psychology must remain a mere pseudoscience if it does not deal with the almost complete absence of fundamental measurement from its discipline. On several occasions (e.g., Michell, 2000), he refers to psychology's resistance to this uncomfortable truth as pathological. (See "Is Psychometrics Pathological Science?" Michell, 2008, and the commentaries of Barrett, Kyngdon, and others in *Measurement, 6*, 78–123). It is not sufficient to allocate numbers to events merely on the basis of some accepted conventions such as the nominal, ordinal, interval, or ratio scales of Stevens (1946) that were designed to allow psychology to appear scientific when, in fact, it is not.

Axiomatic Conjoint Measurement—ACM

Duncan Luce and his colleagues have outlined the principles and properties of axiomatic conjoint measurement that would bring the same sort of rigorous measurement to the human sciences as the physical sciences have enjoyed for a considerable time (e.g., Luce, 1972; Luce & Tukey, 1964; Suppes, Krantz, Luce, & Tversky, 1989). But it seems that many psychologists are determined to avoid the work required to implement fundamental measurement as the cornerstone of a quantitative rational science of the human condition. They seem satisfied with Stevens's (1959) convention, peculiar to their own world, that measurement is the allocation of numbers according to a rule (p. 19) and to accept at face value his distinction among the nominal, ordinal, interval, and ratio scales.

In our experience, this occurs because psychologists and those in the other human sciences have not learned that there are any other tools to use. Academia is rather inbred, slow to change—and notoriously resistant to new ideas. So most doctoral students and new professors don't have a fighting chance of even learning about the mere existence of fundamental measurement (measurement isn't part of the standard undergrad or postgrad curriculum—only statistics is). This reliance on the persistence of the accepted practices is then reinforced by journal editors and reviewers who will not accept anything other than the standard formulaic ways of analyzing data.

These assertions, of course, are unwelcome news to those countless thousands who teach courses in measurement and statistics, who have spent lifetimes doing quantitative research based on the Stevens principles, or who have millions of dollars invested in testing procedures that produce mere numerals, not numbers, that is, the foundation of measures. The argument is that all the sophisticated statistical analyses conducted in psychology, in educational outcomes, in medical rehabilitation, for example, are likely to be wasted if the data that form the input for these analyses do not adhere to the measurement principles common in the physical sciences and described for us by Luce and Tukey (1964).

But here is the good news: We have often found that many of the instruments our colleagues have constructed and the data they have thereby collected do stand up quite well to the scrutiny of Rasch measurement. And this is because those instruments have been carefully constructed based on a deep understanding of the underlying variable or latent trait, augmented by a critical application of traditional statistical methods. These researchers usually learn more about their data when they adopt Rasch analysis—often it doesn't refute their past work but, rather, refines it. The BLOT test (the focus of Chapters 4 and 5) was the progeny of a deep commitment to operationalizing Piaget's work and the conventional statistical techniques of the era. It was only after the fact that it was subjected to the scrutiny of basic Rasch analyses (Bond, 2005, provides some anecdotal detail) that led to our first edition (Bond & Fox, 2001) and then to the invariance and fit analyses that later appeared in the second (Bond & Fox, 2007).

For those who have listened to Ben Wright from the University of Chicago as he made his expositions on Rasch analysis, Michell's critique of quantitative psychology is not news at all. Wright's ever-present teaching aid was a 1-foot ruler that he carried around in his back pocket and used as his model of what measurement in the physical sciences is like and what measurement in the human sciences must be like. It is clear that, at least for the present, the Rasch model is the only technique generally available for constructing measures in the human sciences. Andrich (1988), Fisher (1994), Perline, Wright, & Wainer (1979), Wright (1985, 1999), and others have demonstrated that the Rasch model can be used to produce the sort of measurements we expect in the physical sciences when it is applied to measurement construction in the social sciences. The claim is that the Rasch model instantiates the principles of *probabilistic* conjoint measurement (not ACM) to produce invariant interval-scale measures in which the principles of concatenation apply.

In 1992, however, Norman Cliff decried the much-awaited impact of Luce's work as "the revolution that never happened", although, in 1996, Luce was writing about the "ongoing dialogue between empirical science and measurement theory". But, the 'dialogue' between mathematical psychologists and the end users of data-analysis software continues to be like the parallel play that Piaget described in preschoolers: They talk (and play) in each other's company rather than *to* and *with* each other. But, at least, the attempts at discussion have continued: The collections in *Measurement*, volume 6 (2008), and *Theory & Psychology* volumes 18 (2008), 22 (2012), and 23 (2013) are testament to that (e.g., Borsboom & Zand Scholten, 2008; Kyngdon, 2008; Humphry, 2013).

Discussion among Rasch practitioners at conferences and online revealed that we thought we had something that no one else had in the social sciences—probabilistic additive conjoint measurement—a new kind of fundamental scientific measurement. We had long ago carefully and deliberately resiled from the S.S. Stevens (1946) view that some sort of measurement was possible with four levels of data—nominal, ordinal, interval, and ratio—a view, we held, that allowed psychometricians to pose (unwarrantedly) as scientists (Bond, 2005, p. 337).

This volume is then, in part, a small contribution to some sort of productive communication between theoreticians who study what measurement in the human sciences should be like and those involved in the foot slogging of day-to-day research who have heard whispers of a 'better way' or who have some suspicion that a better way must exist. The claim we are making is that the construction of fundamental measures via instrumentation (what is often called the Galilean task—see Trendler, 2009, and Saint-Mont, 2012) is the *primary* task in any of the human sciences in which real quantification is required. This is not to suggest that the Rasch model supersedes all that we learned in our statistics courses at college. Nor do we claim that Rasch measurement actually instantiates ACM. The use of the Rasch model is, however, the *precursor* of any other statistical analyses we want to conduct (see Chapter 10). It could be argued that the term 'psychometrics' is fatally flawed, that the current practices have a lot to do with the 'psycho' and very little to do with the 'metrics'. We can highlight the problem by looking at one of the classic texts used in postgraduate measurement classes, that of Hays (1994). In the introduction to his book, *Statistics*, he explains:

> Controlled experimentation in any science is an attempt to minimize at least part of the accidental variation or error in observation. Precise

techniques of measurement are aids to scientists in sharpening their own rather dull powers of observation and comparison among events. So-called exact sciences, such as physics and chemistry, thus have been able to remove a substantial amount of the unwanted variation among observations from time to time, place to place, observer to observer, and hence often are able to make general statements about physical phenomena with great assurance from the observation of limited numbers of events. . . . In the biological, behavioral, and social sciences, however, the situation is radically different. In these sciences, the variations between observations are not subject to the precise experimental controls that are possible in the physical sciences. Refined measurement techniques have not reached the stage of development that have obtained in physics and chemistry. . . . And yet the aim of the social or biological science test is precisely the same as that of the physical scientist—arriving at general statements about the phenomena under study.

(p. 4)

Hays then follows with the rest of his text, explaining how the statistics part is performed and relegating the measurement part to oblivion. His position seems to be that, because measurements of human phenomena are underdeveloped, we should drop that agenda and get on with the doable task of executing inferential statistical analyses. Of course, Hays is not peculiar in this regard. His approach to measurement, or his lack of approach to measurement, is quite typical in the field. Michell (1997) lists a large number of standard texts in the field in which the measurement aspect of research is so treated. The general approach is that because the sort of measurement taken for granted in the physical sciences is beyond the reach of the human sciences, psychology's own idiosyncratic view of what measurement is will have to suffice.

The relegation of measurement to the sidelines is lamented by Pedhazur and Schmelkin (2013):

Measurement is the Achilles' heel of sociobehavioral research. Although most programs in sociobehavioral sciences . . . require a modicum of exposure to statistics and research design, few seem to require the same where measurement is concerned . . . and it is, therefore, not surprising that little or no attention is given to the properties of the measures used in many research studies.

(pp. 2–3)

Unfortunately, even these authors do not seem to understand that the essential properties of useful measures are those of linearity, additivity, and invariance inherent in measures used in the physical sciences. Our claims are much stronger: Our instruments should produce interval-scale measures for items and persons (with error terms) on an interval-level scale that remain *invariant* across the intended uses of that instrument. Moreover, the construction of those measures is a necessary pre-requisite for meaningful statistical analyses. We harken back to the efforts of Galileo to build an instrument to measure temperature. His device was sensitive to two environmental attributes at the same time: temperature and pressure. Subsequent investigators refined that work until just one attribute, temperature, influenced the readings and those values were, eventually, located on invariant interval-level mea-surement scales. That is the standard for scientific measurement, which has been the servant of the physical sciences. We argue that those measurement principles can be *approximated* in the human sciences via probabilistic conjoint measurement. Currently, the Rasch model is the only model that is focused on providing for the construction of measures meeting these criteria. Using the Rasch model for the construction of invariant measures does not replace statistical analysis; it precedes it.

Therefore, those involved in the measurement of latent traits must deal with two difficulties. First, latent traits are not directly observable; only their conse-quent or manifest behaviors are. Second, measurement is not the mere allocation of numbers to events but the result of a deliberative process.

True Score Theory, Latent Traits, and Item Response Theory

It is at this point that we turn to distinguishing between the long-accepted True Score Theory (TST) and modern Item Response Theory (IRT). The traditional research practices we've discussed throughout the book, that is, those based on the Stevens principles, are deeply rooted in TST (also called Classical Test Theory, CTT). CTT/TST has as its basis the model, $X = T + e$. The value X is the actual observed score (N correct) of the examinee on the test. T, the true score, is a hypothetical (unknown) value of the true ability of that examinee. It can be thought of as the examinee's hypothetical average score calculated if the examinee were to take many repetitions of the same test without any learning effect. The value e represents the error. The model assumes that the value of T is constant and unknowable and that changes in the observed values of X are due to the error, e. As errors occur at random and are not related to T, or to each other, it follows that T and e can never be known.

In contradistinction, IRT is also referred to as latent trait theory or modern test theory.[1] The Rasch measurement approach shares features of the family of *latent trait models*. We hypothesize the existence of human traits, constructs, or attributes, which cannot be directly observed. The term *latent* is used to emphasize that the individual item responses are taken to be external or *observable manifestations* of these internal but unobservable human states. So the presence and amount of the *latent trait* must be inferred from those observed, manifest responses. Our measurement instruments, our tests, observation schedules, questionnaires, scoring rubrics, and so on are our attempts to operationalize those latent traits or variables.

Our temperature analogy still applies: Scientists *constructed* a scientific variable called temperature in order to explain certain observed phenomena, even though they could not observe temperature directly, merely the effects of temperature changes on certain classes of objects. Then they set about to measure temperature indirectly—by its systematic observable effects on thermometers (e.g., on the *volume* of mercury contained in a carefully constructed, calibrated space). When we use that thermometer, we actually read off the *length* of the mercury capillary and infer a particular *temperature* of, say, 37°C. And it is worth noting that many types of thermometers were constructed, calibrated, and used scientifically long before the all-encompassing scientific theory that explained their behavior was constructed.

Of the few textbooks that deal with the Rasch model, most tend to lump it together with two- and **three-parameter models** under the general heading, Item Response Theory or IRT. For our purposes, the idea of IRT models is virtually synonymous with the concept of latent trait models. They differ from True Score Theory, primarily for IRT's focus on each of the individual *items* of a test rather than TST's focus on the whole *test* or instrument as the unit. True Score Theory, for example, assumes that a test is composed of items that are all equally difficult. Our Chapter 6 analysis of Likert-type data reveals why the 'equally difficult' assumption for Likert scales, is, in fact, almost never met in practice.

IRT includes a number of models sharing common features that distinguish them from TST. These include the concept of a unidimensional underlying trait and the local independence of items used as indicators of that latent trait. Then the response of any person to any test item is modeled by a mathematical function. Most importantly, the estimated item characteristics are not dependent on any particular group for their values, and estimates of persons' abilities/attitudes are not dependent on the particular test/schedule administered. Each person ability estimate (and item difficulty estimate) has its own measure of precision (error term) for each ability score. Then it is possible to estimate probability of success for persons of any ability on items of any difficulty.

In this more general IRT context, the Rasch model is often referred to as the one-parameter Item Response Theory (IRT) model. Not unexpectedly, we claim that the Rasch model has attractive properties which advantage it over the other IRT models. Proponents of the Rasch model for measurement claim that it is a distinctly different IRT model, in spite of references to it as a 1-PL IRT model. The important distinction between the two is founded in Rasch's attempt to specify the rules of sound scientific measurement—using the measurement procedures of physical science as his reference point. Then sound human science measurement must follow Rasch's rules; if not, the measurement instrument/ practice must be reconsidered. Harking back to Stevens, interval-level measurement *can* be attained in the human sciences by the allocation of numbers to events according to certain rules; and *the rules are those encapsulated in Rasch measurement theory*.

But the 1-PL, 2-PL, 3-PL models are so called because the test items are characterized by one, two, or three parameters and the sample of persons by a distribution. The persons are not individually parameterized as in the Rasch model. This has important implications for the concept of measurement invariance, because those IRT models are not 'person–distribution free' (see Chapter 12). The two-parameter IRT model includes a parameter for item discrimination, and the three-parameter IRT model adds parameters for both item discrimination and guessing. Proponents of the two- and three-parameter models contend that data fit generally improves when these techniques are used. We should not be surprised that this is often, though not always, the case. The values of the second and the third parameters of these models are introduced or manipulated expressly for that purpose: to maximize the fit of the model to the data.

The Rasch model, however, is used for another purpose: the construction of fundamental measures. This is distinctly different from other IRT models and TST, where the observed data have primacy and the results of the analyses are descriptive of those data. In general, IRT and TST are *exploratory* and *descriptive* models; Rasch's model is *confirmatory* and *predictive*. Exploratory models must account for all the data; a confirmatory model requires the data to fit that model. In this context, ensuring fit to the model, by focusing on the size and structure of the residuals, indicates where the principles of probabilistic conjoint measurement have been sufficiently realized in practice to justify the claim that the results can be used as a measurement scale with invariant, interval measurement properties.

In this case, the Rasch model question is: How well do the empirical data fit to the measurement model requirements? Does the instrument yield invariant, interval-level measures for its intended purposes? For the two- and three-parameter IRT models, there is another focus: How can the additional parameters (discrimination and guessing) be manipulated to maximize the fit of the model to the data? How can the empirical data be most completely accounted for? Indeed, as we see later in this chapter, it is precisely the addition of the extra parameters that robs the data output of fundamental measurement properties. The 2- and 3-PL models are akin to statistical analyses in that additional parameters are added to the model to account for/explain the variability in the data rather than adhering to the properties of fundamental measurement and then questioning the data points that do not conform to those prescriptions.

To contrast succinctly the Rasch approach from the more general IRT approach, Panayides, Robinson, and Tymms (2010) claim:

> [I]t is important to distinguish between measurement and modeling. If the purpose is to construct a good measure then the items and the test should be constrained to the principles of measurement. If on the other hand the purpose is to model some test data then the model which fits the data best should be chosen. Rasch corresponds to the principles of measurement whereas other IRT models correspond to modeling.
>
> (Panayides et al., 2010, p. 10)

They then go on to quote from Fischer and Molenaar (1995), who state that:

> They (the 2-p and 3-p models) make less stringent assumptions (than the Rasch model), and are therefore easier to use as a model for an existing test. On the other hand, they typically pose more problems during parameter estimation, fit assessment and interpretation of results. Whenever possible, it is thus recommended to find a set of items that satisfies the Rasch model rather than find an IRT model that fits an existing item set.
>
> *(Fischer & Molenaar, 1995, p. 5)*

These differences in approach to data/model fit represent real differences in the conceptualizations of the role of the empirical human scientist. IRT theorists hold to their duty to investigate the facts—the empirical data that actually exist—and to use the appropriate (even if sophisticated) IRT to explain those data/facts. The Rasch approach we are advocating focuses on the Galilean task of the development and calibration of data collection instruments. The simple Rasch model focuses our attention on the failures of our attempts to do that, to investigate the sources and reasons for **anomalous** data. We cannot, we must not, blithely ignore, reject, or merely discard data we produce that do not fit our measurement model.

For guidance, we can hark back to the Galileo/thermometer example. Galileo's instrument was the best temperature indicator of its time. In spite of Galileo's preeminence as a scientist (after more than half a millennium, we still stand in awe of his scientific achievements), his instrument produced empirical data (scientific facts, if you like) that were anomalous. No change in the heat source, but the reading changed; heat source changed, but the reading remained the same. As would-be scientists, perhaps we should routinely ask, 'What would Galileo do?' We must learn from our shortcomings in instrument construction and improve on that in the next iteration.

In this context, the persistent comments of a long-time Rasch critic, Harvey Goldstein (1979, 2010, 2015; Panayides, Robinson, & Tymms, 2015), are both informative and illustrative: "'The (Rasch) criterion is that items should fit the model, and not that the model should fit the items'. This is an extremely radical proposal" (1979, p. 15). And, "This comes dangerously close to saying that the data have to fit the preconceived model rather than finding a model that fits the data. It is quite opposed to the usual statistical procedure whereby models (of increasing complexity) are developed to describe data structures" (2010, p. 2). Goldstein's comment presupposes that the sole objective of data analysis is to manipulate the data analytical procedures until the amount of variance that cannot be accounted for is reduced to a minimum. This approach to quantification is shared by many factor analytical techniques as well as the two- and three-parameter IRT models. From this perspective, the primacy of the empirical data is paramount. The task of data analysis is to account for the idiosyncrasies of the data. (See also Linacre & Fisher, 2012.)

From the fundamental measurement perspective, the requirements of the measurement model are paramount. The idiosyncrasies of the empirical data are of secondary importance. The measurement ideal, encapsulated in the Rasch model, has primacy. The researcher's task is to work toward a better fit of the data to the model's requirements until the match is sufficient for practical measurement purposes in that field. In other words, we monitor the measurement qualities of the data we collect. The anomalous data, those that do not meet the Rasch model's measurement requirements, provide the evidence that our instrument has failed somewhere and the motivation to act on that empirical evidence.

This is in contradistinction to Heene's (2013, p. 2) assertion that we are complicit in what he terms the resistance toward falsifiability in psychology: "the possibly best evidence of my claims comes from a logical argument: has anyone ever seen articles using SEM, IRT, or Rasch models in which the author admitted the falsification of his/her hypotheses? On the contrary, it appears that stringent model tests are mostly carefully avoided in favor of insensitive 'goodness-of-fit indices'" (cf. Heene, Hilbert, Draxler, Ziegler, & Bühner, 2011; Karabatsos, 2000). Many of the students in Ben Wright's MESA lab were obliged to acknowledge week after week the failure of the data of their test development to meet Rasch's specifications. Our students and colleagues routinely have their item-writing skills, based on their understanding of substantive theory, falsified by Rasch analysis as they undertake the iterative processes of test development and pilot testing of new instruments. Perhaps we have erred in regarding these trials and tribulations as routine and not newsworthy. Seems we should include them in our published research reports.

Heene's protest, however, is more substantial than that. Recall the IATA satisfaction survey that provided the data for Beltyukova's Rasch regression exemplar in Chapter 9: 29 of the 65 items did not satisfy the Rasch requirements for measurement. Now let's change the context a little so that a Rasch colleague has developed 65 items for measuring an important latent trait in one of the human sciences and s/he intends to use Rasch measurement criteria for refining the item set. Admirable intentions, but then 29 items fail on one or more of the key Rasch criteria: disordered thresholds, poor fit to the model, negative point–measure correlations, competing additional dimensions obvious in the PCA of residuals, and so forth. So our Rasch colleague is left with just 36 of the original 65 to form what is claimed as the 'fundamental measure of the underlying latent trait'—the omitted items are dropped without any further consideration of the substantive meaning.

Either of two consequences, which are rarely ever canvassed (thereby demonstrating the field's 'resistance toward falsification'), are obvious and damaging. The first is that the latent trait is now grossly underrepresented in the final test. If > 60 items were posited as necessary, but after Rasch analysis, < 40 are regarded as sufficient, either the length or the depth of the construct (or both) is sorely compromised. The second, more damaging conclusion, is that the Rasch colleague had a very inadequate conceptualization of the construct at the outset. (Others might not have conceived of the variable as necessarily unidimensional. For example, proponents of factor analysis often 'expect' multiple scales and dimensions within one instrument without ever specifying how these different dimensions should be combined—either conceptually or mathematically.) Our advice has been from the outset: If items do not fit the Rasch model, don't merely drop them; try to find out why. Item construction and testing encapsulate the implicit hypotheses we have about our latent trait and our measurement model; failing to face up to the evidence of falsification trivializes our data collection instruments and, consequently, those human sciences as well.

But, of course, it is the so-far-unresolved challenge for Rasch measurement to demonstrate that the procedures for determining whether the matrix of actual response frequencies (x_{ni}) that adheres sufficiently to the Rasch measurement prescriptions really does satisfy the requirements of fundamental measurement. Rasch measurement has not satisfied Michell and other measurement theorists yet, but proponents of Rasch measurement are addressing these issues—issues on which most psychometricians, both those from the CTT and general IRT fields, appear to remain silent. Just try raising these 'interval-level measurement' issues in a broader forum: Silence, dismissal, or being accused of dogmatic zealotry are regular responses.

Would You Like an Interval Scale With That?

No doubt a number of our learned colleagues will continue to regard our presentation of the ideas in this volume as parochial and tendentious rhetoric (e.g., van der Linden, 2001). Many in psychometrics subscribe to an alternative view: that many models (especially the other IRT models) have such features. Another pervasive view is that traditional statistical approaches in the social sciences provide all the techniques sufficient for understanding data quantitatively. In other words, the Rasch model is nothing special, and anything outside the scope of traditional statistics produces little or no extra for all the extra work involved: special software, Rasch workshops, and books such as this one.

In an influential large-scale empirical comparison of IRT (including Rasch) and CTT item and person statistics in mandated achievement testing, Fan (1988) concluded that the intercorrelations between person indicators and between item indicators across Rasch, 2PL, 3PL IRT, and CTT models were so high as not to warrant the extra effort of latent trait modeling.

> Because the IRT Rasch model (one parameter IRT model) assumes fixed item discrimination and no guessing for all items, the model only provides estimates for item parameter of difficulty. Because item difficulty parameter estimates of the Rasch model were almost perfectly related to CTT-based item difficulty indexes (both original and normalized), it appears that the one-parameter model provides almost the same information as CTT with regard to item difficulty but at the cost of considerable model complexity.

Unless Rasch model estimates could show superior performance in terms of invariance across different samples over that of CTT item difficulty indexes, the results here would suggest that the Rasch model might not offer any empirical advantage over the much simpler CTT framework.

(Fan, 1998, p. 371)

Novices to Rasch measurement might ask, 'How could that possibly be the case?' The explanation is really quite simple but goes to the very heart of the distinction canvassed in this volume between Rasch measurement on the one hand and general IRT– and CTT–based analyses on the other. Fan revealed, "As the tabled results indicate, for the IRT Rasch model (i.e., the one parameter IRT model), the relationship between CTT- and IRT-based item difficulty estimates is almost perfect" (p. 371). Of course, for both CTT and the Rasch model, N (number correct) is the **sufficient statistic** for the estimation of both item difficulty and person ability. However, for the Rasch model, there is a crucial caveat: To the *extent that the data fit the Rasch model* specifications for measurement, then N is the sufficient statistic.

In light of the attention paid to the issues raised about Rasch model fit requirements and unidimensionality in Chapter 11, it is not so easy then to glide over the telling feature of Fan's analyses: "Even with the powerful statistical test, only one or two items are identified as misfitting the two- and three-parameter IRT model. The results indicate that the data fit the two- and three-parameter IRT models exceptionally well" (Fan, 1998, p. 368). Or should that be the 2PL and 3PL models that were developed accounted for these data very well?

Fan went on to report, "The fit of the data for the one-parameter model, however, is obviously very questionable, with about 30 percent of the items identified as misfitting the IRT model for either test" (Fan, 1988, p. 368). Then, according to our approach to the fit caveat, only about 70% of the items might be used to produce a Rasch measurement scale in which N correct would be the sufficient statistic to produce linear person measures on an interval scale. Fan continued, "Because there is obvious misfit between the data and the one parameter IRT model, and because the consequences of such misfit are not entirely clear (Hambleton et al., 1991), the results related to the one-parameter IRT model presented in later sections should be viewed with extreme caution" (Fan, 1988, p. 368). Fan's advice that "the results . . . should be viewed with extreme caution" harks back to Stevens's (1946, p. 697) "we should proceed cautiously with our statistics, and especially with the conclusions." But neither Fan nor Stevens actually observed such caution. From our perspective, 'viewed with extreme caution' would be better written as 'dismissed as irrelevant to evaluating the value of the Rasch model'.

Given that the second and third item parameters (slope and guessing) are introduced into the 2PL and 3PL IRT models expressly for the purpose of reducing the variance not accounted for by the item difficulty parameter alone, we reasonably could expect (but do not always achieve) better fit of the 2PL and 3PL IRT models to the data. Let us not be equivocal about how proponents of the Rasch model rather than the authority cited by Fan regard the role of fit statistics in quality control of the measurement process: "Rasch models are the only laws of quantification that define objective measurement, determine what is measurable, decide which data are useful, and exposes which data are not" (Wright, 1999, p. 80). So what is the task of the scientific psychometrician, *ex post facto*? To explain all of the collected data, warts and all? *Or* to expose the failures of the data collection process and create interval measures from what's left?

In other words, in our view, results revealing the failure of items to fit the Rasch model should not merely be viewed with extreme caution, they should be dismissed out of hand for failing to meet the minimal standards required for measurement. Readers might wish to judge for themselves the extent to which Fan actually treated the Rasch results with extreme caution—but at the very minimum, unless the data for 30% of misfitting items were put aside from the data analyses adopting the Rasch model, the resultant Rasch versus IRT versus CTT comparisons remain misleading, invidious, or both.

There are two alternative investigative strategies from this Rasch perspective: one *a priori* and one *ex post facto*. For the latter, person measures would be constructed from the reduced (model-fitting) item set, and those person measures would be plotted against the CTT and then the IRT person estimates, and pass/ fail or cut-point decisions made. The similarities between the outcomes would delay us only little; investigating and seeking to explain the differences—the anomalous data—should contribute significantly to the understanding of the latent trait under investigation. *A priori*, of course, the Rasch model's instrument development and calibration team would have worked through several iterations to ensure the test was ready for data collection with the express purpose of creating interval-level person measures of the underlying latent trait. And then we would look to see what the CTT and IRT results could add to our understanding of the variable.

Because the controversy between the use of the Rasch model and of IRT models more generally persists in the literature and in reviews of articles (and even this book) for publication, it is relevant to understand the source of the original controversy. Andrich's paper (2004) does so by invoking Kuhn's studies in the history and philosophy of science, positing the Rasch data-to-model approach and traditional IRT and TST model-to-data approach as incompatible paradigms.

And would you like an invariant interval-level measurement scale with that? One along which both the person abilities and the item difficulties can be located simultaneously? Such that the estimation of item difficulties is independent of the distribution of the abilities of the persons in the sample and vice versa? Would you like inbuilt quality-control techniques to estimate the precision of each location as well as the adherence of each person and item performance to the requirements for measurement?

ACTIVITY

Please take the time to read Andrich's paper 'Controversy and the Rasch Model: A Characteristic of Incompatible Paradigms?'

1. Why does Andrich place general IRT practice and CTT/TST procedures in the same 'traditional' camp?
2. How did TST and then IRT practices become constituted as 'normal science' in the human sciences?
3. What are the potential dangers/problems Rasch researchers might face in having their dissertations/research proposals/publications accepted?
4. How might this issue of 'incompatible paradigms' for human science research be resolved? Is it already being resolved?

Model Assumptions and Measurement Requirements

Some bases of the Rasch model (e.g., unidimensionality, independence of items, equal item discrimination, and absence of guessing) are elsewhere described as model assumptions, and various critics hold those assumptions to be untenable. While IRT models all assert unidimensionality and independence of items, the existence of the 2PL model's discrimination parameter and the 3PL model's further parameter added for guessing clearly assert those two features of testing to be worthy of parameterization as well.

Our warning is that Rasch measurement users would ignore guessing at their own peril. Guessing is an important off-trait behavior, which, if present, creates measurement disturbances. Guessing is not an item parameter; it's the persons who guess. Although it is remotely possible that all persons taking a particular test might guess on all items, it is much more likely that *some* persons will guess on *some* items in *some* circumstances. And the patterns of such guessing, along with its impact on the measure quality, can be ascertained only by using the Rasch diagnostics. It is only by comparing data against a model of ideal measurement that we can observe such patterns of idiosyncrasies and systematic biases. Isn't it better to diagnose and rectify the situation instead of adding another parameter that sacrifices measure invariance? The evidence for BLOT Item 21 is illustrative: For students with very low probabilities of success on the most difficult BLOT items (when the $D - B$ discrepancy was > 1.5 logits), guessing seems to be the attractive strategy. So don't assume guessing has no impact on measures—look for the empirical indicators.

Equal discrimination of items—is that an assumption? In the absence of an item-discrimination parameter, the Rasch model implies a single (unused) value for the discrimination parameter. Indeed, the Rasch model requires that the discrimination is uniform, but software and users routinely overlook any specific reference to this feature. Again, we turn to goodness-of-fit indicators to help us out. But fit statistics merely indicate that *some* Rasch measurement requirement has not been met. They do not tell us *which* requirement or *why*. So, even if the scale is unidimensional, it is possible that an item might have a poor fit due to discrimination slope, which is either greater than or less that the slope expected from the model. Misfit could also be due to intersecting item characteristic curves. It might be the result of violating the Rasch requirement for local independence of items. But the fit statistics, in and of themselves, cannot tell us. It's the investigator's enquiring mind which must investigate all the evidence.

The Rasch assumption/requirement is that items should exhibit local independence. Clearly, the items in a single data collection instrument might all share the same format: (a) All items in a client satisfaction survey share a common Likert-type format; (b) ESL learners are required to provide a single-word answer to fill in the space in a sentence; and (c) nurses might be asked to record their actions in response to the symptoms of a 'standard case/patient'. The Rasch requirement for local independence is, however, that the *solution* to one item should not depend on the *solution* to another. So,

> 'Q1 Three boys each had four marbles; how many marbles altogether?' is okay;
> 'Q2 12 + 5 = □ ' is also okay;

But, if, instead, that question is:

> 'Q2 Another boy has five marbles; how many marbles altogether, now?' lacks local independence, because the *solution* to this Q2 *depends* on having the *solution* to another item, Q1. For the earlier examples, the following are also likely to lack local independence:
>
> (a) The final client satisfaction item that asks, 'Will you fly with this airline again?';
> (b) Single-word answers to fill a number spaces in a single paragraph; and
> (c) The correct treatment is a possibility only for the nurses who first detect cardiac arrhythmia in the 'standard case/patient'.

In each of these cases, the appropriate response to later item(s) *depends* on already having made the appropriate response(s) to earlier item(s).

The distinctive attractive features of the Rasch model—linear, additive, invariant values on an interval-level measurement scale—exist only to the extent that the data fit the Rasch model's requirements. Goodness-of-fit statistics seem, on the surface, to be our only salvation. Indeed, for many Rasch users, that's all that seems to count; the only reference to Bond & Fox in the article will be a citation from Chapter 12, claiming authority for fit statistics being between some 'usually acceptable values'. And that is the sort of authority that reviewers and editors want to see. But our advice is much more restrictive and nuanced: First, all items should work in the same direction (positive item–measure correlations); second, fit statistics should be interpreted intelligently; third, the PCA should reveal an unpatterned distribution of residuals; and fourth, invariance of measures should be demonstrated. Moreover, the investigator's use of Rasch measurement practice will be guided by an understanding of the substantive theory about how the latent trait under investigation will be revealed in measurement practice.

This latter but clearly important assertion has, for support, the position outlined in Kuhn's (1961) paper in which he described '[t]he function of measurement in modern physical science'. Given Rasch's own predilection to learn from measurement in the physical sciences measurement and our own adoption of thermometry as a model, extending the ideas of Choppin and other colleagues, Kuhn's ideas have particular salience for those aiming for fundamental measurement in the human sciences. Kuhn saw scientific measurement practice having its foundation in measurement theory. The hypotheses under investigation were related to a broader substantive theoretical framework. Then measurement practice was instrumental to detecting quantitatively the discrepancies between the measured outcomes and the theory-driven hypotheses.

Construct Validity

The foregoing discussion highlights a crucially important issue for our consideration. The primacy of empirical data over the theoretical model in the sphere of psychometrics often is accompanied by a parallel regard for the primacy of data over substantive theory. This perspective has its philosophical roots in positivism but often reveals itself in practice as analytical pragmatism. A personal expression of that alternative disposition might look like this: "I'm a pragmatist and empiricist . . . (and) would likely never choose to use a Rasch model in any applied measurement project that I'd be involved in. . . . Key to the scientific method is the view that *facts come first*, and if your theory doesn't fit the known facts, you *modify the theory* (not *ignore the pesky facts* that refuse to conform to it). From that perspective, it is senseless to advocate the IRT model that is arguably the *least consistent with the known empirical facts* (i.e., the Rasch one, which discards all items that don't fit its theoretical view)."

This deification of human sciences data remains influential in spite of Laing's admonition of almost half a century ago:

> The 'data' (given) of research are not so much given as *taken* out of a constantly elusive matrix of happenings. We should speak of *capta* rather than data. The quantitatively interchangeable grist that goes into the mills of reliability studies and rating scales is the expression of a processing we do *on* reality, not the expression of the processes *of* reality.
>
> *(Laing, 1967, p. 38f)*

Human sciences data do not exist in spite of us as do the shells on the shore or the stars in the heavens; they exist *because* of us. They are our own unique and very imperfect human creations: inadequately constructed questions not quite completely understood by partially motivated respondents who are coerced to construct the data we analyze. And we are meant to privilege those data over a conceptual, mathematical model of what good data should be like?

In this regard, Rasch practitioners often have been as guilty as any others. It frequently is the case that data have been collected in a relatively undisciplined manner, often using a poorly crafted instrument, and that Rasch measurement techniques are brought to bear on the assembled empirical data set, *ex post facto*, with the aim of making a silk purse out of a sow's ear. And herein lies a key bone of contention between groups of IRT practitioners. The Rasch approach adopts the quality-control mechanisms advocated herein to construct measures from only those data that fit the model. The more general IRT approach encompasses an obligation to use *all* the data and construct an IRT model (rarely the Rasch model) to account for all the empirical data. The Rasch analyst is seen to be guilty of cherry-picking the data to suit Rasch's 'impractical' theory; the 2-/3-PL approach is held to sacrifice interval measurement for data description. But the Rasch model's practicality is exactly what we emphasize. Because of its focus on *invariance*, it is actually useful—that is, it is predictive and inferential, unlike the 2-/3-PL models and SEM and G theory, which remain descriptive.

Although it has been possible to develop quite useful practical measurement outcomes from the *post hoc* use of Rasch techniques, that does not capitalize on the role that Rasch measurement can and should play, *a priori*, in instrument calibration and quality control as a tool of construct validity. From Bond (2005):

> Our research results . . . (see Bond, 2001; Bond, 2003; Endler & Bond, 2001) convince me that the thoughtful application of Georg Rasch's models for measurement to a powerful substantive theory such as that of Jean Piaget can lead to high quality measurement in quite an efficient manner. No wonder I publicly and privately subscribe to the maxim of Piaget's chief *collaborateur*, Bärbel Inhelder, "*If you want to get ahead, get a theory.*" (Karmiloff-Smith & Inhelder, 1975).
>
> *(p. 333)*

In his American Psychological Association (APA) presentation, "Construct Validity: A Forgotten Concept in Psychology?" Overton (1999) detailed the importance of Fisher's (1994) claim that the Rasch model is an instrument of construct validation. The term 'construct validity', introduced by Cronbach and Meehl (1955), according to Overton, is the "extent to which [a] . . . test [or score] may be said to measure a theoretical construct or trait". Construct validation should serve to focus our "attention on the role of psychological [or other guiding] theory" (Anastasi & Urbina, 1997, p. 126).

Therefore, given some theoretical claim about a construct, the Rasch model permits the strong inference that the measured behaviors are expressions of that underlying construct. Even in the text quoted earlier, construct validity then becomes a comprehensive concept that includes the other types: content validity, face validity, concurrent validity, and so on (Messick, 1989, 1995). In the research world, where empirical data have primacy, the process of validating tests involves showing their concurrence with already-existing data collection devices. It is the process of induction that leads us from the data we have collected to the summary statements or explanations we can make about them (Overton, 1998, 1999). But acting as specialist reviewers for a broad range of journals reveals that attention to construct validity is not as common as those involved in theory-driven enquiry might hope. It seems there is a whole approach to scale development that might be summarized thus: Poll a convenience sample of subjects for whom the scale under development has some personal relevance. Construct a large set of self-report indicators based on the list derived from the sample. Trial this with a broader relevant sample and discard the items with poor Rasch measurement credentials. Then assert success at developing a 'fundamental measure' of the condition under investigation.

The first edition of the current volume revealed that the Rasch-Messick link has been quite a rich source of ideas for those interested in the validity/measurement nexus (e.g., Fisher, 1994; Wilson, 1994; Wolfe & Smith, 2007a, 2007b). At the same time, Smith (2001) outlined a range of psychometric indicators of reliability and internal consistency from Rasch analysis in order to draw direct one-to-one correspondences between the eight facets of construct validity identified by Messick (1995) and inferences drawn directly from the theory and practice of Rasch measurement. The argument canvassed in Smith (2001) and Bond (2004) is that the Rasch measurement approach to the construction and monitoring of variables is directly amenable to the issues raised in Messick's broader conception of construct validity. Indeed, Rasch measurement instantiates an approach to assessment that can be described, borrowing Messick's own words, as a "comprehensive view of validity [which] integrates considerations of content, criteria, and consequences into a construct framework for empirically testing rational hypotheses about score meaning and utility" (Messick, 1995, p. 742; after Bond, 2004; see especially Wolfe & Smith, 2007a and 2007b for practical guidelines in demonstrating validity claims with Rasch evidence).

In the research situation positing a substantive theory about human behavior, educational achievement, or posttrauma rehabilitation, the role of the investigator is to identify or hypothesize an appropriate construct or latent trait and to use that construct as a guide in deciding which observable manifest aspects of the human condition should be operationalized as part of a data collection instrument. Following Kuhn, the investigator's understanding of the construct should provide for the prediction of the measurement outcomes to a considerable extent. Given that the measurement of the construct is the first goal, the investigator will ensure that the test items, prompts, observational checklists, or the like both validly represent the theoretical construct and meet the requirements for fundamental measurement. Attention will focus on detecting quantitatively the discrepancies between the measured outcomes and the theory-driven hypotheses.

We could use the illustration in Figure 13.1 to show the ongoing, dialectical nature of the theory–practice interface. As the left arrow (from theory, say) drives practice, then the right arrow (from practice) simultaneously drives theory. As theory tells the investigator how to go about the practice of the data collection process, the result of that practice informs about theory. The process of construct validation works at the interface between the development of a data collection instrument and the empirical data so collected. We have used a panopticon eye to show the supervisory role that Rasch measurement has so the investigator can determine the extent to which the data actually measure the latent trait or construct under examination.

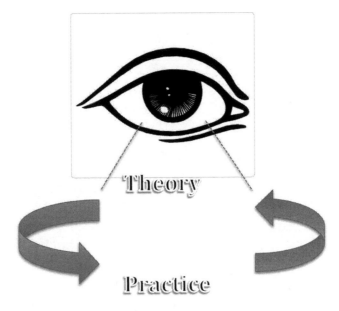

FIGURE 13.1 The iterative theory/practice loop conducted under Rasch model requirements.

The Rasch Model and Progress of Science

Michell (1999) asserted that it is the lack of attention to quantification and fundamental measurement in psychology that hampered its development as a science during the 20th century. It is not the case, however, that the construction of measures will, in and of itself, pave the way for progress in the human sciences. Too often, those working in research methods, data analysis, and even Rasch measurement are called on to give advice after the data have been collected, sometimes even after the first few attempts at data analysis have failed. Instead of being involved in the research methodology and instrument design process from the very beginning, number crunchers often are called in at the last minute to advise a soon-to-graduate doctoral student on how to analyze and present the results of the data already collected. In another scenario, a colleague, an external contracting agency, or a professional licensing board rushes in to take last-minute advice on how to save a project that, on reflection, looks rather poorly conceived from the start.

These one-shot research projects, it seems, are going nowhere. They are designed merely to satisfy some course requirement or to fulfill some institutional reporting obligation or the like and often are one-time research consultancies. We have Rasch measurement colleagues who insist that their nonnegotiable requirement for becoming involved in such *post hoc* situations is that Rasch measurement techniques will be used to see what sort of measures can be constructed (salvaged?) from the assembled data. This is a well-grounded but rather pragmatic approach to the situation. Indeed, much of the advice given in the preceding chapters is quite applicable under these circumstances, which involve knowing how to make something resembling a silk purse out of a sow's ear. We can note from the success of Yan's (Chapter 9) analyses of 6 years of already-existing fitness data in Hong Kong, such post-hoc investigations, often yield enlightening results, particularly if the data are based on strong theory and particularly when the items have been carefully designed. Such results should be encouraging to those readers who might want to explore the change to using Rasch measurement but fear losing a career's worth of data and analyses.

However, where researchers have a long-term commitment to a substantive area of research with human subjects, in which they are consulted at the conceptualization of the project, the approach can be somewhat different. In these circumstances, wherein researchers intend for their work to have some impact in the area under investigation, their understanding of the substantive (theoretical) area can work hand in hand with the Rasch models of fundamental measurement toward progress in that area of human science. Whereas Michell (1999) castigated psychologists for their persistence in avoiding the scientific measurement imperative, Mauran (1998) warned us that although measurement might be a necessary condition for scientific investigation, without a substantive theoretical orientation, it will never be sufficient.

But we must remember that all theory building starts, at some point, with observation. We both work with some (often early-career researchers) who are willing to venture forth with Rasch-guided data collection and analysis in the absence of existing theories in their discipline and often in the face of opposition by users of more conventional data analysis approaches. In those fields, it seems as though the standard procedure is to survey people to death in the absence of any guiding theory. Our approach is to encourage them use Rasch methods to try to build instruments and theory, and we have witnessed hundreds of researchers across the world and across disciplines who have succeeded in doing just that.

The contrast between the pragmatic use of the Rasch model and its incorporation at the very beginning of a research project became clear in the graduate measurement course we taught together in the College of Education at the University of Toledo. Most of our students had made considerable progress in doctoral programs. Some, in fact, were taking their last courses before writing and defending their dissertations. In our measurement course, they were required to demonstrate competency with appropriate use of Rasch analysis software and to demonstrate sufficient understanding of Rasch measurement principles for drawing reasonable conclusions and inferences from the data they had analyzed. For those students still at the stage of considering their dissertation proposals, we urged each to look at one small but important area of understanding and to work toward advancing the state of the field in that area.

For the measurement coursework assessment, any minimally satisfactory data set was fair game. As long as a modest-size item–person data matrix was available, Rasch modeling could be used to see the quality of the measures, if any, that could be constructed from the existing data. For the most part, practical considerations ruled while short timelines existed. For their dissertation purposes, however, students started consulting us about how fundamental measurement principles could be built into projects they already had in mind or how measures could be constructed in their particular fields of interest. Some students, of course, made the best of both worlds, using the measurement course assessment requirement as the trial for the investigative devices they were intending to develop in their doctoral research projects.

In a stark oversimplification, we could advise thus: If you merely want to finish your dissertation or fulfill the contractual obligations of your research funding, then whatever number crunching appeals to you will often suffice. But if you have a long-term commitment to your research topic, if you want to make a real difference, and if you are willing to undertake the iterations and reflection essential to the development of theory-driven measures, then choosing to use the Rasch model as your ideal for what measurement should be like in the human sciences is probably a very good start.

The contrast between past, present, and future can be more obvious in more traditional, perhaps patriarchal societies in which Rasch measurement is gaining ground over traditional techniques. PROMS—the Pacific Rim Objective Measurement Symposia—commenced life in 2005 to support Rasch measurement initiatives in Eastern Asian countries. In most participating countries, there are likely to be only very few senior academics who are open to such innovation. It's the doctoral students and early-career researchers who want to use what they hear of as a 'better way'—often in the face of stiff opposition of those in academic positions of influence and control. Interestingly, the Malaysian online Rasch measurement group alone has many hundreds of members, and a group of Chinese graduate students and early-career researchers now have a Chinese translation of Bond & Fox ready to go to the publishers.

Back to the Beginning and Back to the End

It was obvious to Ben Wright, in seeing some early presentations of Rasch measurement applied to Piagetian theory, that the apparent ease with which these developmentalists were able to develop a variety of data collection techniques to produce person and item measures was, in part, because of their reliance on a broad, thoughtfully constructed developmental theory expressed in thousands of Piagetian chapters and journal articles. To the developmentalists, it seemed as though the chief strength of the Rasch approach to data analysis came primarily from the role that ordinality played in the construction of item and person measures. Indeed, for developmentalists, Guttman scaling held out a promise for developmental assessment that was only ever rarely satisfied in empirical practice (Kofsky, 1966). With hindsight, we can see that the key problem of the Guttman ordering for developmental studies was its deterministic or true-score nature. Clearly the observation and recording of human performance is plagued by both systematic and random errors. A deterministic ordering model, like that of Guttman, has expectations that rarely can be met in empirical practice.

To developmentalists, the Rasch principles incorporate the attractive ordering features of the Guttman model and complement them with a more realistic probabilistic, or stochastic, framework. Indeed, this takes us back to our early work on the first edition of this volume, which was intended to be a sort of self-help book for developmental and educational psychologists who were trying to make some measurement sense of their data. However, a confluence of originally quite diverse circumstances shows that the value of the Rasch model is not coincidental. And the benefits have been felt much more broadly than just our intended audience of developmental and educational psychologists. The benefits to those who use Rasch modeling in constructing fundamental measures of some aspect of human existence derive from the model's expectation that good measurement should satisfy a probabilistic version of conjoint measurement (Luce & Tukey, 1964).

It is clear from the earlier work of Andrich (1988), Fisher (1994), Michell (1999), Perline, Wright, and Wainer (1979), and others that principles derived from conjoint measurement theory provide the only satisfactory prescription for scientific measurement and that, in terms of widespread application to the human sciences, Rasch measurement is the only game in town. In practical terms, it would be just as unexpected for any real data from the human sciences observation to satisfy the *deterministic* conjoint measurement axioms as it would be for them to attain a perfect Guttman structure. "However, because the axioms of additive conjoint measurement define measurement linearity, they should be considered as rules which data must statistically approximate" (Karabatsos, 1999, p. 12).

The question that we called 'fit' in the previous chapter could now be considered fruitfully in terms of the extent to which actual response probabilities in any Rasch-modeled data sets violate the conjoint measurement axioms. Details of the necessity and requirements of conjoint measurement are canvassed in several places (Cliff, 1992; Fisher, 1994; Michell, 1986, 1990, 1997, 1999; Narens & Luce, 1993). It appears that Luce's ongoing dialogue between empirical science and measurement theory splutters into life from time to time and then dies away. The issues of *Theory & Psychology* (Vols. 18, 22, & 23) and *Measurement* (Vol. 6) reflect the current state of that dialogue. Generally, the measurement case on behalf of the Rasch model and latent variable theory has made by Denny Borsboom (e.g., 2005, 2008; Markus & Borsboom, 2012).

One of the distinct pleasures of writing a volume such as this or of developing such widely used software as Winsteps, is the consequent invitations to conduct introductory Rasch measurement workshops or to speak to measurement-oriented colleagues at professional meetings. That often involves fielding questions about the Rasch model and, more particularly, fielding the objections that colleagues have about Rasch measurement and the claims of its proponents. Winsteps developer Mike Linacre reports that, in his lengthy experience, the objections to the Rasch model could be regarded as falling into three rather neat categories:

1. Rasch person and item estimates are forced to be linear and interval by the Rasch model;
2. The Rasch model has those properties but is an idealization that cannot work in the real world; and
3. The Rasch model might work sometimes in the real world, but it won't/can't work for my data.

So, in response:

1. The mathematical properties of Rasch estimates can be seen to parallel those of the three sides of Pythagorean right-angled triangles (Fisher, 1998). The values in each case (Rasch estimates and lengths of sides) are computed according to certain rules (those of Rasch and Pythagoras), and so the calculated values must meet the requirements set out in those rules.

So far as the laws of mathematics refer to reality, they are not certain. And so far as they are certain, they do not refer to reality.

—Albert Einstein, *Geometry and Experience*

2. This strikes to the very heart of the scientific endeavor, because, as in all science, there is a mismatch between theoretical results and empirical data:

> Science does not, so far as we know, produce theories which are true or even highly probable. Although rare, it sometimes happens that a theory exactly predicts an experimental outcome. When that desirable result is achieved, there is cause for general rejoicing. It is far more common for the predictions deduced from a theory to come close to reproducing the data which constitute a specific problem, but with no exact coincidence of results. Empirical problems are frequently solved because, for problem solving purposes, we do not require an exact, but only an approximate, resemblance between theoretical results and experimental ones.
>
> (*Laudan, 1977, pp. 23–24*)

3. This objection often masks a more personal claim: that the 'Rasch model will not work for *my* data'. Granted; but if the Rasch model won't work for your data, then neither will raw scores! This is precisely because the Rasch model can be derived from the requirement that raw scores (N) be the sufficient statistic for linear estimation.

> . . . for anyone who claims skepticism about 'the assumption' of the Rasch model, those who use unweighted scores are, however unwittingly, counting on the Rasch model to see them through. Whether this is useful in practice is a question not for more theorizing, but for empirical study.
>
> (*Wright, 1977, p. 116*)

Summary

Rasch measurement: Where do we go from here?

In an attempt to provide some answers to the question, 'So, what are we currently missing in published Rasch measurement research?' Bond's (2014) opening plenary address to the Pacific Rim Objective Measurement Symposium in Guangzhou attempted to diagnose common shortcomings in our research efforts and to provide guidelines for exemplary research practice into the future. In keeping with that theme, the following were posited:

A substantive theory about what it is we are trying to measure: Item development and selection should be driven by a deep knowledge of the underlying latent trait. Good theory should lead to improved practice and, ideally, for long-term measurement projects theory/practice, links would be iterative.

A hypothesis that the latent trait is actually quantitative: We are challenged at every turn concerning the 'assumptions of the Rasch model', but almost all of us in the human sciences, right across TST, IRT, SEM, and G-theory, remain completely blind to our far more fundamental assumption—that the latent traits we investigate are actually quantitative. The Rasch model is currently the only tool generally available for testing the hypothesis that we indeed are measuring a quantitative latent trait. We should report our results in terms of that hypothesis by detailing the extent and nature of our data's fulfillment of the requirements of that hypothesis.

A deeper understanding about the nature of residual based fit statistics: Rasch measurement requires that the data fit the model, but, of course, our empirical data never fit perfectly. Residual-based fit statistics detect violations of underlying Rasch measurement requirements. So residual-based fit statistics express the always-existing differences between the actual data set and the Rasch model's expectations, but they do not indicate *which* expectations have not been met, nor *why*. The PCA of residuals allows us to look for patterns in residuals in part, to help explain the *why*—when, of course, no pattern should exist among residuals. Rasch software detects misfit; interpretation of misfit remains our task.

Diagnosis of problem items: If you have a long-term commitment to your area of research, you probably care about your substantive theory and constructed instrument and measurement practice. Then misfit means: 'Find out why' not 'Throw it out'.

Attention to the measurement of persons: Often, most published initial work is about 'How I built a Rasch measurement scale of . . .' But more often than not, the instrument will be used to make decisions about persons. How do we establish cut points for decisions? What are the consequences of those decisions? Routinely, high item reliabilities are quoted, along with more modest person reliabilities. But our focus should be on person separation and the number of person strata generated by the instrument's use. This might be less important *only* if we are looking at group-level descriptions.

Evidence of measurement invariance: Genuine interval-scale measures of persons and items should remain invariant across uses of the instrument for its intended purpose. In that case, we are obliged to check the invariance of item measures by meaningful subgroups: male versus female or high versus low performers or by nationality, cultural group, and so forth—those that might reasonably be related to the variable of interest. Further, we need to check for the invariance of item estimates over time and across samples. Person measures should also be invariant across similar instruments; if not, as for all breaches of the invariance requirement, we need to diagnose and find out why.

Feedback to theory and to instrument: Last, the research circle is completed when the empirical evidence from the application of the instrument feeds back iteratively to further instrument refinement and to our understanding of the underlying substantive theory.

> ## ACTIVITY
>
> Find three or four research papers in which Rasch measurement techniques
> are applied to data in your area of interest in the human sciences. Examine
> them from the perspective of, 'So, what are we currently missing in pub-
> lished Rasch measurement research?' listed earlier.
>
> 1. Which of these features are present/missing in your chosen papers?
> 2. How could those features that are missing be introduced?

Note

1 Lovers of fine music and art are given friendly advice not to carry over the classical/
   modern distinctions from music to the use of these descriptors in test theory. Ben
   Wright would regularly quip, "There is nothing classical about classical test theory!"

References

Anastasi, A., & Urbina, S. (1997). *Psychological testing* (7th ed.). Upper Saddle River, NJ: Prentice Hall.

Andrich, D. (1988). *Rasch models for measurement*. Newbury Park, CA: Sage.

Andrich, D. (2004). Controversy and the Rasch model: A characteristic of incompatible paradigms? *Medical Care, 42*(1), 7–16.

Barrett, P. (2008). The consequence of sustaining a pathology: Scientific stagnation—a commentary on the target article "Is Psychometrics a Pathological Science?" by Joel Michell, *Measurement, 6*, 78–83.

Bond, T. G. (2001). Ready for school? Ready for learning? An empirical contribution to a perennial debate. *Australian Educational and Developmental Psychologist, 18*(1), 77–80.

Bond, T. G. (2003). Relationships between cognitive development and school achievement: A Rasch measurement approach. In R.F. Waugh (Ed.), *On the forefront of educational psychology* (pp. 37–46). New York, NY: Nova Science.

Bond, T. G. (2004). Validity and assessment: A Rasch measurement perspective. *Metodologia de las Ciencias del Comportamiento, 5*(2), 179–194.

Bond, T. G. (2005). Past, present and future: An idiosyncratic view of Rasch measurement. In S. Alagumalai, D. Curtis, & N. Hungi (Eds.), *Applied Rasch measurement: A book of exemplars. Papers in honour of John P. Keeves* (pp. 329–341). Dordrecht: Kluwer Academic.

Bond, T. G. (2014, August). *Rasch measurement: Where do we go from here?* Opening Keynote Address, Pacific Rim Objective Measurement Symposium, 2014, Guangzhou.

Bond, T. G., & Fox, C. M. (2001). *Applying the Rasch model: Fundamental measurement in the human sciences*. Mahwah, NJ: Lawrence Erlbaum Associates.

Bond, T. G., & Fox, C. M. (2007). *Applying the Rasch model: Fundamental measurement in the human sciences* (2nd ed.) Mahwah, NJ: Lawrence Erlbaum Associates.

Borsboom, D. (2005). *Measuring the mind: Conceptual issues in contemporary psychometrics*. Cambridge: Cambridge University Press.

Borsboom, D. (2008). Latent variable theory. *Measurement, 6,* 25–53.

Borsboom, D., & Zand Scholten, A. (2008). The Rasch model and conjoint measurement theory from the perspective of psychometrics. *Theory & Psychology, 18,* 111–117.

Cliff, N. (1992). Abstract measurement theory and the revolution that never happened. *Psychological Science, 3*(3), 186–190.

Cronbach, L. J., & Meehl, P. E. (1955). Construct validity in psychological tests. *Psychological Bulletin, 52,* 281–302.

Endler, L. C., & Bond, T. G. (2001). Cognitive development in a secondary science setting. *Research in Science Education, 30*(4), 403–416.

Fan, X. (1998). Item response theory and classical test theory: An empirical comparison of their item/person statistics. *Educational and Psychological Measurement, 58*(3), 357–381.

Fischer, G. H., & Molenaar, I. W. (Eds.). (1995). *Rasch models: Foundations, recent developments, and applications.* New York, NY: Springer-Verlag.

Fisher, W. P., Jr. (1994). The Rasch debate: Validity and revolution in educational measurement. In M. Wilson (Ed.), *Objective measurement: Theory into practice* (Vol. 2, pp. 36–72). Norwood, NJ: Ablex.

Fisher W. P., Jr. (1998). Do bad data refute good theory? *Rasch Measurement Transactions, 11*(4), 600.

Goldstein, H. (1979). The mystification of assessment. *Forum for the Discussion of New Trends in Education, 22*(1), 14–16.

Goldstein, H. (2010). *Rasch measurement: A response to Payanides [sic.], Robinson and Tymms.* www.bristol.ac.uk/cmm/hg/response-to-panayides.pdf.

Goldstein, H. (2015). Rasch measurement: a response to Payanides, Robinson and Tymms, *British Educational Research Journal, 41*(1), 176–179.

Hambleton, R. K., Swaminathan, H., & Rogers, H. J. (1991). *Item response theory: Principles and applications.* Newbury Park, CA: Sage.

Hays, W. L. (1994). *Statistics* (5th ed.). Fort Worth, TX: Harcourt Brace.

Heene, M. (2013). Additive conjoint measurement and the resistance toward falsifiability in psychology. *Frontiers in Psychology, 4*(246). doi:10.3389/fpsyg.2013.00246

Heene, M., Hilbert, S., Draxler, C., Ziegler, M., & Bühner, M. (2011). Masking misfit in confirmatory factor analysis by increasing unique variances: a cautionary note on the usefulness of cutoff values of fit indices. *Psychological Methods, 16,* 319–336.

Humphry, S. M. (2013). A middle path between abandoning measurement and measurement theory. *Theory & Psychology, 23*(6), 770–785.

Ingebo, G. S. (1997). *Probability in the measure of achievement.* Chicago, IL: MESA Press.

Karabatsos, G. (1999, July). *Axiomatic measurement theory as a basis for model selection in item-response theory.* Paper presented at the 32nd annual conference of the Society for Mathematical Psychology, Santa Cruz, CA.

Karabatsos, G. (2000). A critique of Rasch residual fit statistics. *Journal of Applied Measurement, 1*(2), 152–176.

Karmiloff-Smith, A., & Inhelder, B. (1975). If you want to get ahead, get a theory. *Cognition, 3*(3), 195–212.

Kingsbury, G. (2003, April). *A long-term study of the stability of item parameter estimates.* Paper presented at the annual meeting of the American Educational Research Association, Chicago, IL.

Kofsky, E. (1966). A scalogram study of classificatory development. *Child Development, 37*(1), 191–204.

Kuhn, T. S. (1961). The function of measurement in modern physical science. *Isis, 52,* 161–190.

Kyngdon, A. (2008). The Rasch model from the perspective of the representational theory of measurement. *Theory & Psychology, 18*, 89–109.

Laing, R. D. (1967). *The politics of experience.* New York, NY: Pantheon Books.

Laudan, L. (1977). *Progress and its problems.* Berkeley: University of California Press.

Linacre, J. M., & Fisher, W. P., Jr. (2012). Harvey Goldstein's objections to Rasch measurement: A response from Linacre and Fisher. *Rasch Measurement Transactions, 26*(3), 1383–1389.

Luce, R. D. (1972). What sort of measurement is psychophysical measurement? *American Psychologist, 27*(2), 96–106.

Luce, R. D., & Tukey, J. W. (1964). Simultaneous conjoint measurement: A new type of fundamental measurement. *Journal of Mathematical Psychology, 1*(1), 1–27.

Maraun, M. D. (1998). Measurement as a normative practice: Implications of Wittgenstein's philosophy for measurement in psychology. *Theory and Psychology, 8*(4), 435–461.

Markus, K. A., & Borsboom, D. (2012). The cat came back: Evaluating arguments against psychological measurement. *Theory & Psychology, 22*, 452–466.

Messick, S. (1989). Validity. In R. L. Linn (Ed.), *Educational measurement.* New York, NY: Macmillan.

Messick, S. (1995). Validity of psychological assessment. *American Psychologist, 50*(9), 74–149.

Michell, J. (1986). Measurement scales and statistics: A clash of paradigms. *Psychological Bulletin, 100*(3), 398–407.

Michell, J. (1990). *An introduction to the logic of psychological measurement.* Hillsdale, NJ: Lawrence Erlbaum Associates.

Michell, J. (1997). Quantitative science and the definition of measurement in psychology. *British Journal of Psychology, 88*(3), 355–383.

Michell, J. (1999). *Measurement in psychology: Critical history of a methodological concept.* New York, NY: Cambridge University Press.

Michell, J. (2000). Normal science, pathological science, and psychometrics. *Theory & Psychology, 10*(5), 639–667.

Michell, J. (2008). Is psychometrics pathological science? *Measurement: Interdisciplinary Research and Perspectives, 6*, 7–24.

Narens, L., & Luce, R. D. (1993). Further comments on the "nonrevolution" arising from axiomatic measurement theory. *Psychological Science, 4*(2), 127–130.

Overton, W. F. (1998). Developmental psychology: Philosophy, concepts, and methodology. In W. Damon (Series Ed.) & R. M. Lerner (Vol. Ed.), *Handbook of child psychology: Vol. 1. Theoretical models of human development* (5th ed., pp. 107–188). New York, NY: Wiley.

Overton, W. F. (1999, August). *Construct validity: A forgotten concept in psychology?* Paper presented at the annual meeting of the American Psychological Association, Boston, MA.

Panayides, P., Robinson, C., & Tymms, P. (2010). The assessment revolution that has passed England by: Rasch measurement. *British Educational Research Journal, 36*(4), 611–626.

Panayides, P., Robinson, C., & Tymms, P. (2015). Rasch measurement: A response to Goldstein. *British Educational Research Journal, 41*(1), 180–182.

Pedhazur, E. J., & Schmelkin, L. P. (2013). *Measurement, design, and analysis: An integrated approach.* New York, NY: Psychology Press.

Perline, R., Wright, B. D., & Wainer, H. (1979). The Rasch model as additive conjoint measurement. *Applied Psychological Measurement, 3*(2), 237–255.

Saint-Mont, U. (2012). What measurement is all about. *Theory & Psychology, 22*, 467–485.

Smith, E. V., Jr. (2001). Evidence for the reliability of measures and validity of measure interpretation: A Rasch measurement perspective. *Journal of Applied Measurement, 2*(3), 281–311.

Stevens, S. S. (1946). On the theory of scales of measurement. *Science, 103*, 667–680.

Stevens, S. S. (1959). Measurement, psychophysics and utility. In C. W. Churchman & P. Ratoosh (Eds.), *Measurement: Definitions and theories*. New York, NY: John Wiley.

Suppes, P., Krantz, D. H., Luce, R., & Tversky, A. (1989). *Foundations of measurement*. San Diego, CA: Academic Press.

Trendler, G. (2009). Measurement theory, psychology and the revolution that cannot happen. *Theory & Psychology, 19*, 579–599.

van der Linden, W. (2001). Book review *Applying the Rasch Model*. *International Journal of Testing, 1*(3&4), 319–326.

Wilson, M. (1994). Comparing attitude across different cultures: Two quantitative approaches to construct validity. In M. Wilson (Ed.), *Objective measurement: Theory into practice* (Vol. 2, pp. 271–294). Norwood, NJ: Ablex.

Wolfe, E.W., & Smith, E.V., Jr. (2007a). Instrument development tools and activities for measure validation using Rasch models: Part I—instrument development tools. *Journal of Applied Measurement, 8*(1), 97–123.

Wolfe, E.W., & Smith, E.V., Jr. (2007b). Instrument development tools and activities for measure validation using Rasch models: Part II—validation activities. *Journal of Applied Measurement, 8*(2), 204–234.

Wright, B. D. (1977). Misunderstanding the Rasch model. *Journal of Educational Measurement, 14*(2), 97–116.

Wright, B. D. (1985). Additivity in psychological measurement. In E. Roskam (Ed.), *Measurement and personality assessment* (pp. 101–112). North Holland: Elsevier Science.

Wright, B. D. (1999). Fundamental measurement for psychology. In S.E. Embretson & S.L. Hershberger (Eds.), *The new rules of measurement: What every educator and psychologist should know* (pp. 65–104). Mahwah, NJ: Lawrence Erlbaum Associates.

APPENDIX A

Getting Started

While many of our readers of the earlier editions told us that they found themselves off to a good start for understanding and applying Rasch analysis to their own data, some of our more experienced colleagues advised us to give our readers more detail about how actually to get started on that process. The steps to getting started are rather simple when one sits down with the owner of the data. The first step is to make a few simple checks to see that the data file is ready to run. Then import the data into Winsteps and run the analysis. After a quick flick through a few key data tables to make sure the output is displaying reasonable values (e.g., correct number of persons and items, reasonable ranges for measures and fit), we pull up the variable map—the Wright map we have used in almost every chapter to visually summarize some of the key aspects indicating how the data have performed under the scrutiny of the Rasch model.

Invariably it is the representation of the item and person performances along the same unidimensional continuum that attracts the most interest from the data owner. Then follow the questions: What is Item x? Should it be the easiest? Why would Item y be so much harder than all the others? Items w, x, and z all locate in the same place—is that right? Why? And is Person A really the smartest of all these kids on this test? So much smarter than all the others? Really? Why's that? And this group of respondents here, does it make sense for them all to be estimated at the same ability level? Did you think that your test would be too easy/difficult for this sample? Why's that? Looks like we need some more children (items) that are less/more able (difficult) than the children (items) you have in this data set. Is that possible? Why/not? Why's that? Keep those questions in mind for looking at your own Rasch analysis results. What did you expect to find, given your understanding of the latent trait you are trying to measure? Go back through those questions again; think about them in terms of the different variable maps you've seen in this text.

Data Input

One of the essentials for getting started is constructing the data file. One carryover from mainframe computing days has been a tendency, at least in early iterations of Rasch software, to allocate single data rows to individual cases and single data columns to individual items. In those times, data were read in from punch cards or magnetic tapes or large floppy discs, but in essence each data set was a rectangular text (or ASCII) file—cases horizontally and items vertically—with each cell containing just one ASCII character. The data files we provide on the book website for the analyses contained in Chapters 3 to 7 follow these same requirements. All of the data files in those chapters were either typed one character at a time by the researcher into word-processor files (the laborious way) or were saved as text-only files with. txt or. dat as the file extension. Here is that segment of the data file from the BLOT analysis in Chapter 4 again:

> rows = cases; columns = items (no ID and no empty cells in that file). That's the simple way to begin.

```
11111111110110101101011111111011111
11111111111111111111111111101111111
11010111111111011111011111101011111
11111111111111111111101111111111111
11111111111101111111011111111111111
11111111111110111101011111111111111
11111111111101111111011111111111111
11111111111111111111111111101011111
11111111111111111111111101111111111
11011110111110111110111110001110111
11111101111111111110110111111101111
11111101111111111111111111101001111
11111111111110111110101110101111111
11111111111101111101111111111111111
11111111111101111101111111111111111
11111111111101111110111111101110111  etc.
```

Many researchers now use spreadsheets (e.g., Excel) or other statistics packages (e.g., SAS, SPSS) for setting up data files. Perhaps they want to use parts of such files (say from a larger data set) to start the Rasch analysis process. Winsteps, for example, handles Excel and SPSS data files directly (see later in this Appendix).

Here are a few simple guidelines to help avoid some of the common problems:

1. Missing Data

    Text File: While leaving a space in a.txt file is no problem, exporting an .xls file with blanks to .txt format will often result in the blanks going missing, the data file conflating and the item columns losing their meaning (i.e., item data in the wrong columns). So a simple rule is: Don't leave blank cells at all. While many use '9' as a code for missing data now, in the future you might need '9' as valid in a RSM or PCM analysis. So use 'X' for missing; 'M' for multiple responses or other invalid response codes (ticked two response boxes or response made but unscorable); '0-zero (not 'O'- 'oh') for incorrect or the lowest valid response value. So, 0–9 (numeric) codes for valid responses and a–z (alphabetic) codes for invalid responses.

    Spreadsheet: The approach for text files will not work for Excel or SPSS, because alphabetic codes are a different data type from numeric codes and cannot be accepted in the same field/cell. Thus, it is best to leave blank cells for missing data when using SPSS or saving SPSS or Excel to a .csv format.

2. Font

    Text File: Use a nonproportional (i.e., fixed-pitch) font such as Courier for the .txt file so data columns remain in line. A check of the row length well help to confirm the integrity of the data row for each case. With a little practice and concentration, it is possible to scan thousands and thousands of cases in a data.txt file by fast scrolling and watching the vertical columns and the row lengths flash by. A few minutes of tedium now can save hours of frustration later.

    Spreadsheet: Font is not an issue with spreadsheet data entry.

However, once your Winsteps output is saved into word-processing software, you will need to use the Courier font mentioned (or something similar) to maintain best alignment.

Software

Each of the major software packages for Rasch analysis has its adherents, and some colleagues are just as passionate about a particular software package as we are about the Rasch model itself. But beginners often have the same difficulty 'getting into' a new Rasch software package as they had getting started in understanding Rasch measurement in the first place. So instead of trying to be all things to all Rasch analysts, we have restricted this introduction to one piece of Rasch software: Bond&FoxSteps is a *full-size* version of Winsteps, which is provided free of charge as a download from the book website. The choice of software for this purpose has been made very easy for us. As we mentioned previously, Mike Linacre,

Winsteps developer, has been very proactive in collaborating with us: Just months after the first edition of Bond & Fox was released, Winsteps contained the output option of 'Bubble Maps' in the form of the pathway analogy that we had just introduced in that first edition.

Bond&FoxSteps installation instructions are included on the website, so download and install it now on your PC if you do not already own a full copy of the Winsteps program. The free online version of Bond&FoxSteps contains the full-size software (9,999,999 persons, 60,000 items, and 255 categories per item) and is preloaded with the data files and control files for running the analyses for Chapters 4, 5, 6, and 7. Additionally, PDF files provide step-by-step instructions for analyzing and interpreting each of those data sets.

Mike Linacre's free student-version download, Ministeps, has data size restrictions, so it does not allow all the BLOT items or all the CEAQ cases to be run at once. You will need to use Winsteps (or Ministeps) for the Extended Understanding section of Chapter 6. Most Winsteps functions perform very well on a Mac platform running PC-emulation software (e.g., Virtual PC; vbox; etc.). Please copy the data files we have provided for your practice onto your hard drive as well. The Facets folder, containing Bond&FoxFacets (a free copy of Minifac) and the data and control files for the Guilford many-facets analysis from Chapter 8 can wait until later if you like.

Moreover, on the website, we have added extra data files that follow the Chapter 4, 6, 7, and 8 techniques, so you can practice those techniques and confirm that you have implemented them correctly.

Please follow the ReadMe.txt files on the website for the latest instructions.

First Analysis

We are going to take you through the first analysis and interpretation steps that we might use with a newcomer and new data set. Once you've worked through this, you should be able to repeat the steps with your own file for dichotomous data. If you open the BLOT instructions file (BLOTinst.doc) that you downloaded from the book website, you will find details of how to enter the BLOT.txt data into (or Winsteps):

Follow the instructions:

Highlight with your mouse from here >
```
Title = "B&F BLOT data: 35 items"

156 011011100111001101010110011001101100101
158 110011011111011101111001101011111111
```
< to here. Then Copy.

Start WINSTEPS.
Do not answer the "Control File Name?" question. Go immediately to "Edit" pull-down menu.

Click on "Edit/Create File with WordPad"
WordPad screen opens.
"Paste Special" as "Unformatted Text" what you just copied above.

It should look exactly like the block in the instruction file.
"Save as"
Go to the C:\WINSTEPS directory
File Name: BLOT.txt
Save as type: Text document
"Save"
You are about to save the document in a Text-Only format

Click "Yes"

Click on WINSTEPS or BOND&FOXSTEPS on the bottom of your screen
"Control File Name?" displays.
Press the Enter key
Find BLOT.txt in the file list. Click on it.
Click "Open"

"Report output file name"
Press the Enter key

"Extra specifications"
Press the Enter key

WINSTEPS runs.
WINSTEPS reports "Measures constructed"

Output

Winsteps provides 36 sets of tables and figures, and has the option of producing journal quality graphs for many of the crucial figures. The downside of this provision is that beginners can be left wondering where to look to get the basic crucial information to determine whether the analysis was successfully executed and how well the data stood up to the scrutiny of the Rasch model. Bond&FoxSteps greys out many of the options relevant to only experienced analysts.

What to Look For

Throughout this book, we have emphasized two crucial and interrelated aspects of the Rasch approach to genuine scientific measurement: 'quantitatively defensible' and 'qualitatively meaningful'. The 'quantitatively defensible' aspect focuses on the adequacy of the Rasch output, that is, estimates of person ability and item difficulty (and their associated measurement errors), fit indicators (and PCA of residuals) that we use for quality control, reliability, and dimensionality. And while we might look at the Rasch output maps and tables one by one, it's the *interrelationships* among all the components that will help inform the decision as to whether any attempt at measurement is good enough for its intended purpose—that is, is it 'qualitatively meaningful'? So when we look at estimates, we keep fit in the back of our minds; when we look at fit, we know that the estimates must be where we need them to be. And all of this must be contextualized within our construct theory.

Where to Look

In this Bond&FoxSteps version of the Winsteps Rasch analysis software, we have greyed out the parts of the pull-down menus that we think are of more direct benefit to experienced users in order to focus your attention on the more crucial aspects of the output. Experience at workshops suggests that some new users get so carried away with all the different aspects of the program output (all those pull-down menus) that they find it hard to decide which bits really matter. This might not be as important when you are just looking over someone else's data, but it can be a bit distracting when you really want to know whether your own data are good enough.

The following are the basic steps we would take with a new data set to see if we have created 'something' or 'nothing' or, at least, whether we are approaching that magic 'something'.

The Wright Map

A picture paints a thousand words, so:

> Clicking on "12. ITEM Map" in the Output Tables pull-down menu displays the Wright map.

Here the 'quantitatively defensible' and 'qualitatively meaningful' aspects come together more completely: On the right-hand side of the variable map, the items are located against the logit scale in the same location as they would be found in the pathway map, but the locations of person performances tells us something about the existence of this ability in the sample of high school children who faced the test. They are represented by the Xs on the left hand side of the map. Each number represents two students on this map. They are nicely spread out over about 6 logits, with more students toward the top of the map and a bit of a tail toward the bottom. By looking at the person distribution against the item distribution, we learn more about the item–person relationships in relation to the underlying variable. Most of the persons are located opposite the items—so they seem well targeted by these items. However, there is a sizable group of person locations above the hardest item (21)—the test can't tell much about students with that much ability. Thus, this test will work better with kids who are less able than those at the top of the Wright map.

The Item Statistics Table

This table summarizes the information provided for each item in the test. The 'How much?' question is answered by looking at the 'MEASURE' column, where item difficulty estimates are located, and column 'S.E.', where the precision of the estimate is indicated by its error term.

> Still *in* the "Output Tables" pull-down menu, click on "14. ITEM Entry".

First, check to see that all items are 'heading in the right direction'. Look at the PTMEAS column for item to measure correlations that are negative or near zero. No problems. In order to interpret the item fit statistics, Bond&FoxSteps uses ZSTD, which corresponds to *t with* ∞ degrees of freedom. ZSTD means 'standardized as a Z-statistic'. For the practical purpose of monitoring fit in these outputs, *t* and *z* statistics are equivalent. 'Table 14: Item Entry' gives the item information in the order the questions are on the test, 1 through 35. There is a one-to-one correspondence between item locations on the Wright and pathway maps and the numerical values in 'Output Table: 14' representing item difficulty estimates. 'Output Table: 13.1 Item measure' provides that information in a table in which the items are ordered (as they are on both maps) by their difficulty estimates—not by their item numbers: The matching of item values to map locations can be done by eye.

A scan down the columns containing the fit statistics should reveal any major quality-control problems. You might like to keep an eye on the standardized infit statistic on the first go-through; just scan the first digit and look for '2' or greater—slide past any starting with '0' or '1'. The Infit ZSTD statistics for Items 21 and 30 catch the eye here (notice the '2'), so look at the complete fit information for each more closely:

#21	1.27	2.6	1.76	3.7
#30	1.19	2.3	1.15	1.0

Now, on three out of four fit indicators, Item 21 doesn't look good (only infit mnsq of 1.27 is okay); we'll need to find out what went wrong there. Item 30, on the other hand, does well enough on three out of four fit indicators (only one statistic, the infit Zstd of 2.3, seems a bit too erratic), so let Item 30 go for now.

Case Statistics Table

It's not much use that the test's items' performance is okay if the person measures don't stand up to scrutiny, so:

> Click on the "Output Tables" pull-down menu and click on "18: Person Entry".

But with 150 cases to inspect (and often many, many more), running your eye over the fit statistics can be a bit daunting. Again, just scan the Infit Z and note those starting with the digit '2' or higher for starters.

Alternatively, 'Output Table: 6 Person Fit Order' is more user friendly, especially for large data sets, because it orders the most pertinent persons by the *size* of misfit. Seems that the top three or four cases could cause some concern. But that makes about only 2% of our 150 candidates with performances that should not be judged just on the basis of the ability estimate alone: A bit of detective work is needed here. For example, Student 4 is a high-ability candidate (est. = 3.96), but the fit stats indicate erratic performance by that candidate. The fit statistics (1.12, 0.4, 4.48, and 1.8) show poor *outfit*, so unexpected off-target performance is diagnosed. That suggests that this very *capable* student *missed* a very *easy* question; that could be confirmed by looking at Output Table: 6.6 (or 7.2.1 in the purchased version of Winsteps).

Next Steps

Clearly, the test has a couple of items that need some attention. Bond&FoxSteps allows you to see the *empirical* versus *theoretical* ICCs for each item. Pull up 'Expected Score ICC' in the 'Graphs' menu, and find graphs 21.21 and 30.30 by clicking on 'Next Curve' for a few more hints about what went wrong with Items 21 and 30. The Item 30 curves confirm what the fit statistics indicated: Apart from a few blips to the left of the red ICC curve, the jagged empirical line stays close enough to the smooth theoretical curve. Again, there is no cause for alarm. The graph for Item 21 shows that on-target students (between, say, 2 logits above and 1 logit below the item's difficulty—0.0 in this figure) perform close to expectations, but those more than 1 logit *less able* than the item difficulty have surprisingly (unpredictably) high success rates (i.e., much higher than expectation). What did the item table say for Item 21? Hardest item, on-target students perform close to expectations (the infit is marginal), but off-target students (they must be in the less-able part of the distribution to be off target for the hardest item) performed erratically. This implies that we should find a few of those kids (low estimate, but a tick for Item 21) and ask them to describe how they solved that item. Did those children guess? Did they see another child's answer? Was there a giveaway use of words that was somehow attractive to these children? From all information we have about persons and items, the practical summary is that the model correctly predicts the performance of 69% of this sample of children on Item 21 (see pp. 277–278).

The Pathway Map

The pathway map gives an elegant pictorial summary of how the test performed (i.e., item information but no person information). In response to participants who turned up at Winsteps workshops armed with Bond & Fox (2001), Mike Linacre developed the 'Bubble Chart' in the 'Plots' menu to report the basic item indicators in the form of the pathway introduced in the first edition. So,

> Click on the "PLOTS" pull-down menu.
> Click on "Bubble Chart". The Dialog Box displays. Tick Items (not Persons); Measures vertically; Infit; Standardized. OK. Data point label = Entry Number. The Excel graph displays as a Pathway.

The items are in measure-order along the pathway, and they spread across the pathway in the Infit Standardized central column. You will need to manually adjust the size of the Bubbles so they accurately reflect the SE of the measures. (See the Chapter4Tutorial.pdf.)

Interpretation

In answer to the questions about how much was measured and how well it was measured, the pathway map gives the following summary: Most of the 35 items fall on the pathway, so it seems like this quality-control aspect of item performance is satisfactory. Performance on Item 21 is a bit too erratic (off the pathway to the right), and so is Item 30; two erratic items out of 35 isn't so bad. So the item locations (how much) might be worth taking seriously; their fit seems okay at first glance. Thirty-five locations are calibrated with a default mean difficulty set at 0.0. Although from top to bottom they cover more than 4 logits, most of them are located within a band of just over 2 logits, spread around the zero origin. A more even spread of item locations from top to bottom would have been better (a) to fill up the holes in the variable and (b) to reduce the number of items where the test seems to have more than enough.

Extended Understanding

While the test characteristics alone for this analysis suggest future directions for test development, the purposes and theoretical background of the original test development should be the bases on which to choose between the options. Whatever happens, Item 21 needs a thorough reappraisal based, first, on a qualitative investigation of the strategies and processes used by some of the low overall test performers who were unexpectedly successful on Item 21. Any new wording would need to be trialed. Is the stem okay? Is there a giveaway in one of the distracters? The output can't tell you that. You'll need to interview some of those children.

As for the problem of the clustering of many items between −1 and +1 logits and the gaps in the item distribution above and below that zone, the purposes of the test must be considered. If the role of the test is to measure *progress* along the variable, that is, to provide accurate measures all along the variable, then development of both harder and easier BLOT items is required. It's back to the drawing board, starting with the theoretical blueprint (Inhelder & Piaget, 1958) that gave rise to the test in the first place. On the other hand, if the test is to be used to distinguish those who *can* from those who *can't* (or, more pedantically, those who *did* from those who *didn't*), the concentration of items around the cutoff will be helpful, and the gaps in the variable will not prove a hindrance. Theory and purpose will guide practice; the empirical results are then used to shine a light back on the theory.

Working With Excel and SPSS Data Files

Recent versions of Winsteps have made it simple to go directly from an SAS, SPSS, or Excel file straight into developing a control file. The original screen for constructing the file might be a little confusing at first, so the following series of step-by-step screen shots should help smooth out that bumpy start. Upon launching Winsteps, click on the link third from the right titled 'Excel/RSSST' to see the options in the window below.

FIGURE A.1 Select 'Excel/RSSST'.

Because the CEAQ data are in an SPSS file (available on the book website), click on the purple SPSS link and get this window:

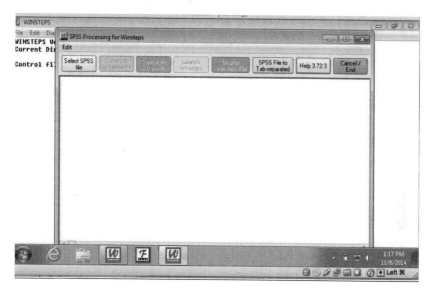

FIGURE A.2 Select SPSS link.

Click on the leftmost grey bar 'Select SPSS file' to access the desktop and document folders and scroll through to find the appropriate SPSS file.

FIGURE A.3 Select SPSS file.

Choose the file from the hard drive and a very 'wordy' screen pops up:

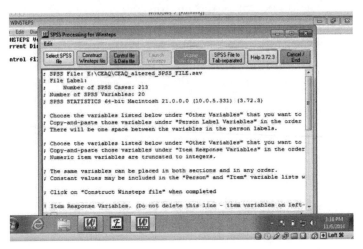

FIGURE A.4 SPSS processing for Winsteps.

Scrolling down a bit will reveal the variables at the bottom of the file. The notations in red font are important place markers that indicate where to place the 16 CEAQ items '**Item Response Variables**' and where to place the person identification variables '**Person Label Variables**' such as ID, age, grade, and gender. This simply requires scrolling down to cut and paste the variable names under the appropriate heading as shown in Figure A.5.

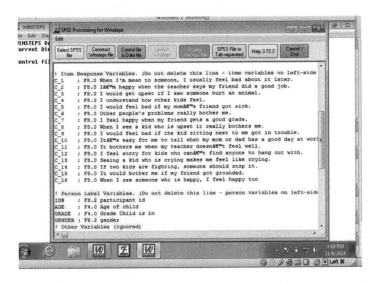

FIGURE A.5 Construct Winsteps file.

To finish, simply click on the light-green 'Construct Winsteps File' button and name the file when prompted. Winsteps will create a control file by that name and place it in the same directory as the original SPSS file. (The same procedure is followed when choosing an Excel or SAS file.) Launch Winsteps from that same screen once the control file is constructed.

Further Analyses

The researcher committed to excellence in measurement won't stop at this point in the test refinement or data analysis process. Throughout this book, we have posited the central roles of unidimensionality and invariance as the hallmarks of genuine scientific measurement in the human sciences. Two early checks on these features are available in software such as Winsteps. The factor analysis of Rasch measurement residuals seems a good place to start for examining whether what's left over in a data set after the Rasch dimension has been removed indicates the possibility of a second dimension or is likely to be mere noise. Invariance checks at the item-by-item level are carried out using the DIF plots to compare the performances of two meaningful divisions in the sample: male and female; old and young; healthy and unhealthy; and so forth. Of crucial importance is the performance of your developed test with other suitable sample: The *invariance* of the item measures is the key here.

Next Steps

This book was designed to introduce Rasch measurement in the context of the larger and more important theoretical issues about the nature of genuine scientific measurement for the human sciences. While many readers will be kept busy enough accommodating to the demands of the arguments and rehearsing the techniques elucidated in this volume, we expect that sooner or later, most will want to venture further than the confines of these ideas. Readers who take seriously the ideas herein will have little trouble participating in Rasch-based discussions or moving on to the ideas contained in the classic Rasch measurement texts.

The Classic Reference Texts

The following texts have been indispensable to the progress of Rasch measurement and to the writing of this book. Inevitably, each should become part of the serious Rasch practitioner's reference library.

The foundation stone of the Rasch family of models:

Rasch, G. (1980). *Probabilistic models for some intelligence and attainment tests* (Expanded ed.). Chicago, IL: University of Chicago Press. (Reprinted 1992, Chicago: MESA Press)

This is Georg Rasch's seminal work on measurement that describes the theory, simple applications, and mathematical basis of the model. Many claim that in that prescient work, Rasch outlined the problems and principles that underlie even recent developments in Rasch measurement.

The dichotomous model reference:

Wright, B.D., & Stone, M.H. (1979). *Best test design.* Chicago, IL: MESA Press. (Also available in Spanish)

In *Best Test Design,* Wright and Stone outline the principles of Rasch measurement and apply the analytical techniques to dichotomous data. This instructional text on Rasch measurement introduces very straightforward estimation procedures as well as more complex estimation methods. Chapter 1: 'What Is Measurement?' and Chapter 2: 'How to Measure?' show how to perform by hand a Rasch analysis of the Knox Cube Test. The chapter on 'How Well Are We Measuring?' introduces the concept of data-to-model fit.

The polytomous model reference:

Wright, B.D., & Masters, G.N. (1982). *Rating scale analysis.* Chicago, IL: MESA Press.

In *Rating Scale Analysis,* Wright and Masters discuss the philosophy behind linear, interval measurement and extend the application of the Rasch model to rating scales as part of the family of Rasch models for different polytomous applications, including Poisson counts, binomial, Bernoulli trials, and partial credit responses. In keeping with the principles behind *Best Test Design, Rating Scale Analysis* derives the major estimation methods and investigates data-to-model fit.

The many-facets Rasch model:

Linacre, J.M. (1989). *Many-facet Rasch measurement.* Chicago, IL: MESA Press.

Judges, tasks, time points, and other facets of the measurement situation can be parameterized with the many-facets Rasch model. Because these extensions are hard to conceptualize and difficult to manage, they are usually avoided whenever possible. But these extensions can be crucial, for instance, in the adjustment of candidate measures for the severity of the judges they encountered. This book outlines the theory and application of this methodology.

The most accessible account of the many European contributions to the development is found in:

Fischer, G.H., & Molenaar, I.W. (Eds.). (1995). *Rasch models: Foundations, recent developments and applications.* New York, NY: Springer-Verlag.

A succinct account emphasizing Rasch measurement properties:

Andrich, D. (1988). *Rasch models for measurement.* Newbury Park, CA: Sage.

How psychologists willfully ignored the requirements for fundamental measurement and why the delusion continues to the present:

Michell, J. (1999). *Measurement in psychology: Critical history of a methodological concept.* New York, NY: Cambridge University Press.

A succinct account of the Rasch family of measurement models:
Wright, B., & Mok, M. (2000). Rasch models overview. *Journal of Applied Measurement, 1,* 83–106.

Other Rasch-Based Texts

Applying Rasch measurement to measuring language performance:
McNamara, T.F. (1996). *Measuring second language performance.* New York, NY: Longman.

George Ingebo contrasts the results of Rasch methods with conventional statistics for assessing student responses to basic skills testing and shows the advantages of Rasch measurement for school-district testing programs. It details linking strategies behind building large item banks:
Ingebo, G.S. (1997). *Probability in the measure of achievement.* Chicago, IL: MESA Press.

Key papers from the International Objective Measurement Workshops have been issued in an important series of reference texts.

The first series of five volumes was published as:
Objective measurement: Theory into practice from 1992, by Ablex.

The current series from JAM Press:
Advances in Rasch measurement commenced in 2006.

The selection of papers includes interesting applications and themed sections exploring topics such as rating scale analyses, facets-type analyses, and multidimensional measurement.

An edited volume that explores diverse applications of Rasch measurement in the health sciences:
Bezruczko, N. (Ed.). (2005). *Rasch measurement in health sciences.* Maple Grove, MN: JAM Press.

The Smith and Smith edited volumes are based on the Understanding Rasch Measurement series that appeared in the *Journal of Applied Measurement.*
Smith, E., & Smith, R. (2004). *Introduction to Rasch measurement.* Maple Grove, MN: JAM Press.

Smith, E., & Smith, R. (2007). *Rasch measurement: Advanced and specialized applications.* Maple Grove, MN: JAM Press.

A collection of exemplary applications of Rasch models in science education.
Liu, X., & Boone, W. (2006). *Applications of Rasch measurement in science education.* Maple Grove, MN: JAM Press.

Seminal Papers

Physicist Norman Campbell's theory of fundamental measurement as described for psychologists by Thomas Reese (1943) is available at www.rasch.org/m8.htm.
Wright, B. (1967). *Sample-free test calibration and person measurement.*

This presentation at the 1967 Educational Testing Service Invitational Conference launched Rasch measurement in the United States. Available at www.rasch.org/memo1.htm.
Linacre, J.M., Heinemann, A.W., Wright, B.D., Granger, C.V., & Hamilton, B.B. (1994). The structure and stability of the Functional Independence Measure (FIM)™. *Archives of Physical Medicine and Rehabilitation, 75*(2), 127–132.

This paper demonstrated the efficacy of Rasch measurement in clarifying and solving measurement problems in survey and diagnosis situations. Available at www.rasch.org/memo50.htm.

Ben Wright (1997). *A history of social science measurement.*

This paper addresses the main threads in the conceptualization of measurement (as opposed to mere numeration) in the social sciences and relates them to the Rasch model. Available at www.rasch.org/memo62.htm.

Other Rasch Publications

Journal of Applied Measurement. P.O. Box 1283, Maple Grove, MN 55311

Under the senior editorial hand of founder Richard Smith, *JAM* publishes refereed scholarly works from all academic disciplines that relate to measurement theory and its application to constructing variables. We must concur with Mike Linacre, who describes it as it the "most authoritative journal for Rasch research".

Start Reading Rasch Research and Methods for Free

The complete set of the earlier *Journal of Outcome Measurement*, also founded by Richard Smith, is now available for *free download* as PDFs from www.jampress.org.

Rasch Measurement Transactions, due to the inspiration and work of Mike Linacre, is a quarterly publication of the Rasch Measurement Special Interest Group of the American Educational Research Association. *RMT* contains short research notes addressing many of the key issues and questions raised in the theory and practice of Rasch analysis. A *must* for newcomers to Rasch measurement; many of your questions have been asked—and answered—before. It is available free in PDF form at www.rasch.org/rmt.

Rasch Research Papers, Explorations & Explanations: Books, papers, audio, and video available for *free download* at www.rasch.org/rasch.htm.

Wu, M., & Adams, R. (2007). *Applying the Rasch model to psycho-social measurement: A practical approach.* Available for *free download* as PDF at http://www.edmeasurement.com.au/resources.

MESA Research Memoranda by Ben Wright and several others form a collection of many of the foundational papers in Rasch measurement. The entire text of the pivotal *MESA Research Memoranda* is available at www.rasch.org/memos.htm.

Computer Software for Rasch Measurement

Each of the software packages that follows implements estimation and fit procedures for more than one of the Rasch family of measurement models. Each of the estimation procedures has its own band of rather devoted adherents, but each has its shortcomings as well.

JMLE: Joint Maximum Likelihood Estimation (sometimes called UCON)
MMLE: Marginal Maximum Likelihood Estimation
PAIR: Pairwise Estimation

Similarly, each of the Rasch software programs has its own disciples, but no single program incorporates the advantages of all the packages or avoids the tolerable shortcomings of its own particular estimation procedure. For the members of the Rasch family of models dealt with in detail in this textbook—the models for dichotomous, partial credit, and rating scale data—the usual Rasch analytical procedures, as they are implemented in the software packages listed here, produce estimates that are generally equivalent, for all practical analytical purposes. Sometimes pragmatic considerations are foremost in the practitioner's mind:

RUMM and Winsteps take full advantage of the Windows platform; Winsteps has lots of diagnostics and is the software available free on the book website as Bond&FoxSteps; Bigsteps is free; ConQuest and TAM have more analytical potential than most mere mortals can imagine; and so on. (Mac users can run most Rasch analyses using PC emulation software.)

Quest—The Interactive Test Analysis System (Adams & Khoo):
Joint Maximum Likelihood Estimation

Quest claims to offer a comprehensive test- and questionnaire-analysis environment by providing access to Rasch measurement techniques as well as a range of traditional test-analysis procedures. It combines a rather easy-to-use control language with flexible and informative output. Quest can be used to construct and validate variables based on dichotomous and polytomous observations.

The Rasch analysis provides item estimates, case estimates, and fit statistics; the results from this analysis can be accessed through a variety of informative tables and maps. Traditional analyses report counts, percentages, and point biserials for each possible response to each item and a variety of reliability indices. Quest runs in batch mode and/or interactive mode. In interactive mode, Quest allows analysis results to be viewed on the screen as the analysis proceeds.

Quest allows the user to define subgroups and subscales so that analyses can be performed for any combination of subgroup and subscale. It has the usual Rasch flexibility for dealing with missing data and allows for item and case estimate anchoring to facilitate test equating and item banking. The software supports export of results to facilitate importation into database, analysis, and spreadsheet programs. The Quest Compare command provides Mantel-Haenszel and Rasch tests of differential item functioning.

Quest has been implemented on several platforms. In its desktop form, it handles up to 10,000 cases and 400 items with up to 10 response categories per item. A total of 10 subgroup–subscale combinations are permitted.

ConQuest (Adams, Wu, & Wilson):
Marginal Maximum Likelihood Estimation

ConQuest is able to fit a much more extensive range of item-response models than any of the other programs described here. Perhaps it is easiest to describe this package at two levels. First, at the level of Rasch analysis software, it can not only fit the standard dichotomous and polytomous Rasch models but can be used for facets-type analyses and what ConQuest refers to as LLTM-type item response models as well. ConQuest does most of what Quest does, offering access to Rasch measurement techniques as well as a range of traditional test-analysis procedures. At this level, it is directly related to the content of this textbook and is suited to the entry-level Rasch measurement practitioner.

At the next level, directed specifically to those with more advanced analytical needs, ConQuest is a very versatile and powerful general modeling program that can also fit multidimensional item-response models and both unidimensional and multidimensional latent regression models (i.e., multilevel models) as well as generate plausible values for the solution of difficult measurement problems. It uses a special keyword syntax to define the very wide range of item-response models just described. Beyond that, it includes a method of defining special models using a design matrix approach, which makes it extremely flexible for more experienced users.

ConQuest is available for standard Windows and UNIX operating systems. It can be run from either a GUI (Windows) interface or a console interface. It combines a rather easy-to-use control language with flexible and informative output. In terms of output from Rasch and traditional analyses, as well as operation modes, ConQuest provides the same features detailed for the Quest package.

TAM—Test Analysis Modules (Kiefer, Robitzsch, & Wu):
Joint Maximum Likelihood Estimation &
Marginal Maximum Likelihood Estimation

TAM (Test Analysis Modules; Kiefer, Robitzsch, & Wu) is an IRT package written in R. As with all R packages, TAM is free for download from the R CRAN website. TAM can fit the Rasch model using JML estimation for dichotomous and polytomous item responses. It provides item-fit statistics, weighted likelihood estimates (WLE) for ability, item characteristic curves, and classical test theory item point-biserial correlations. TAM can also fit Bayesian IRT models in which a population distribution model is incorporated with the item-response model (MML estimation). Under the MML estimation method, TAM can fit the one-parameter Rasch dichotomous and partial credit models, two-parameter generalized partial credit models, facets models, and latent regression models. TAM can fit both unidimensional and multidimensional models with between- and within-item dimensionality. TAM can produce plausible values for secondary data analysis. As an R package, TAM results can be seamlessly integrated in other R codes for additional analysis or for reporting.

Winsteps (Linacre):
Joint Maximum Likelihood Estimation

Winsteps constructs Rasch measures from simple rectangular data sets, usually of persons and items, with up to 9,999,999 cases and 60,000 items. Winsteps is the basis of the Bond&FoxSteps software provided on the book website for this edition. In Winsteps, each item can have a rating scale of up to 255 categories; dichotomous, multiple-choice, and multiple-rating-scale and partial credit items can be combined in one analysis. The developers of Winsteps use the program daily in their own work and are continually adding new features as a result of their own experience and feedback from users. The inclusion of the pathway chart is but one example of responsiveness to user feedback. Winsteps is designed as a tool that facilitates exploration and communication.

Winsteps provides for powerful diagnosis of multidimensionality, using principal components analysis of residuals to detect and quantify substructures in the data. The working of rating scales can be examined thoroughly, and rating scales can be recoded and items regrouped to share rating scales as desired. Measures can be anchored at preset values. A free student/evaluation version, limited to 75 cases and 25 items, is available at www.winsteps.com. An earlier DOS–based Rasch program, Bigsteps, with a capacity of 20,000 persons and 1,000 items, can also be downloaded free. The Bond&FoxSteps version of Winsteps designed to support readers of this text is available on the book website with the data files for analysis.

Facets (Linacre):
Joint Maximum Likelihood Estimation

Facets is designed to handle the more complex applications of unidimensional Rasch measurement and performs many-facets Rasch measurement handling more than 250 million observations for over 1.6 million examinees + items + raters + tasks + . . . and up to 255 response categories for each item. Facets constructs measures from rectangular and nonrectangular datasets involving heterogeneous combinations of examinees, items, tasks, and judges along with further measurement and structural facets. All facet summary 'rulers' are provided so the user can view all facets in the same frame of reference. It is designed to flexibly handle combinations of items of different formats in one analysis. Measures can be fixed or anchored individually or by group means, facilitating equating and linking across test sessions. Quality-control fit evaluation of all measures is provided, and bias, differential item functioning, and interactions can be estimated. Weighting schemes can be implemented.

Since organizing the data for input to Facets and then interpreting its output can be challenging, it is recommended that simpler rectangular approaches be tried first, such as those implemented in Winsteps. Minifac, a free student/ evaluation version of Facets, can be downloaded from www.winsteps.com. The Bond&FoxFacets version is available on the book website with the data files for analysis.

RUMM2030: Rasch Unidimensional Measurement Models
Pairwise Conditional Estimation & Maximum Likelihood or Weighted Likelihood
Estimation.

RUMM2030 is an interactive Rasch software application package for Windows XP and Windows 7 platforms and operates on Windows 8. Output from a large range of analyses is provided in both tabular displays and graphical displays, which can be edited in other applications.

RUMM2030 is entirely interactive, from data entry to the various analyses. It permits rerunning analyses based on diagnosis from a previous analysis, by rescoring items, eliminating items, resolving DIF items, forming subtests (testlets), and so on. Test equating in both raw-score and latent-trait metrics can be carried out interactively.

RUMM2030 can handle 5,000 or more items, with the number of persons limited by available memory. It allows up to nine distracter responses for multiple-choice items, a maximum of 100 thresholds per polytomous item, and up to at least seven person factors such as gender, grade, age groups for group comparisons, DIF detection, and so on.

RUMM2030 implements the Rasch model for dichotomous and polytomous items using pairwise conditional estimation of item parameters, while all person parameters are eliminated. The procedure provides consistent estimates of the item parameters and generalizes naturally to handle structural and random missing data. Given the item parameter estimates, the person parameters are estimated optionally by direct maximum likelihood or weighted likelihood to minimize the bias for persons with extreme responses. Estimates for persons with extreme responses are extrapolated.

Currently, RUMM2030 comes in two editions: the Standard Edition contains essential Rasch analysis options, and the Professional Edition provides additional options for advanced analyses.

With RUMM2030 comes a *Getting Started Manual* together with three other manuals that describe the input and output. In addition, there are *Interpreting Documents* with extensive descriptions of Rasch measurement theory, the equations used in the software, and for interpreting the output.

For further information, including ordering options, please visit www. rummlab.com.

The Institute for Objective Measurement maintains the website www.rasch. org, which is an up-to-date portal for accessing Rasch measurement information.

APPENDIX B

Technical Aspects of the Rasch Model

Rasch Family of Models

Dichotomous Model

Georg Rasch developed a mathematical model for constructing measures based on a probabilistic relation between any item's difficulty and any person's ability. He argued that the difference between these two measures should govern the probability of any person being successful on any particular item. The basic logic is simple: All persons have a higher probability of correctly answering easier items and a lower probability of correctly answering more difficult items. For example, the simplest member of the Rasch family of models, the dichotomous model, predicts the conditional probability of a binary outcome (correct/incorrect) given the person's ability and the item's difficulty. If correct answers are coded as 1 and incorrect answers are coded as 0, the model then expresses the probability of obtaining a correct answer (1 rather than 0) as a function of the *size* of the difference between the ability (B) of the person (n) and the difficulty (D) of the item (i).

The starting point for creating measures begins with a calculation of the percentage correct for each person (the number of items successfully answered divided by the total number of items) and each item (the number of persons successfully passing the item divided by the total number of persons) when the test is administered to an appropriate sample. These raw score totals are ordinal level data, yet they are both necessary and sufficient for estimating person ability (B_n) and item difficulty (D_i) measures as shown by Andersen (1973), Douglas and Wright (1986), and Wright and Douglas (1986).

The first step in estimating B_n (the ability measure of person n) is to convert the raw score percentage into odds of success, which are estimated by calculating the ratio of each person's percentage correct (p) over the percentage incorrect

$(1 - p)$. For example, a raw score of 40% correct is divided by the percentage incorrect $(1 - p)$, that is, 60%, to obtain the ratio $40/60$. The natural log of these odds (ln $40/60 = -0.4$) then becomes the person ability estimate. The procedure is exactly the same for items, estimating D_i (the difficulty measure of item i); that is, dividing the percentage of people who answered the item correctly by the percentage of people who answered the item incorrectly and taking the natural log of that value.

These item difficulty (D_i) and person ability (B_n) estimates then are expressed on a scale of log odd ratios, or logits. The average logit is arbitrarily set at 0, with positive logits indicating higher-than-average probabilities and negative logits indicating lower-than-average probabilities. The Rasch model calculations usually begin by ignoring, or constraining, person estimates, calculating item estimates, and then using that first round of item estimates to produce a first round of person estimates. The first rounds of estimates are then iterated against each other to produce a parsimonious and internally consistent set of item and person parameters, so that the $B - D$ values will produce the Rasch probabilities of success described more fully later. The iteration process is said to converge when the maximum difference in item and person values during successive iterations meets a preset **convergence** value. This transformation turns ordinal-level data (i.e., correct/incorrect responses) into interval-level data for both persons and items, thereby converting descriptive, sample-dependent data into inferential measures based on probabilistic functions.

Once we have estimated ability (B_n) and difficulty (D_i), the probability of correctly answering an item can be expressed mathematically as the general statement:

$$P_{ni}(x = 1) = f(B_n - D_i) \tag{1}$$

where P_n is the probability, x is any given score, and 1 is a correct response. This equation therefore states that the probability (P_n) of person n getting a score (x) of 1 on a given item (i) is a function (f) of the difference between a person's ability (B_n) and an item's difficulty (D_i).

By using the Greek symbols commonly used in statistics to indicate the parameters being estimated as opposed to the values calculated, the formula is expressed as follows:

$$\pi_{ni}(x_{ni} = 1) = f(\beta_n - \delta_i) \tag{2}$$

where π (pi) represents response probability, β (beta) denotes person ability, and δ (delta) stands for item difficulty.

Given B_n and D_i, we then can expand upon equation 1 to demonstrate that the function (f) expressing the probability of a successful response consists of a natural logarithmic transformation of the person (B_n) and item (D_i) estimates. This relationship can be expressed mathematically as follows:

$$P_{ni}\left(x_{ni} = 1 / B_n, D_i\right) = \frac{e}{1 + e^{(B_n - D_i)}} \qquad (3)$$

where $P_{ni}\left(x_{ni} = 1 / B_n, D_i\right)$ is the probability of person n on item i scoring a correct $(x = 1)$ response rather than an incorrect $(x = 0)$ response, given person ability (B_n) and item difficulty (D_i). This probability is equal to the constant e, or natural log function (2.7183) raised to the difference between a person's ability and an item's difficulty $(B_n - D_i)$ and then divided by 1 plus this same value. Therefore, for example, if a person's ability is estimated at 3 logits and the difficulty of the item at 1 logit, then

$$P_{ni}\left(x = 1 / B(3), D(1)\right) = \frac{2.7183^{(3-1)}}{1 + 2.7183^{(3-1)}} = \frac{2.7183^2}{1 + 2.7183^2} = 0.88 \qquad (3.1)$$

and the person has an 88% probability of successfully passing the item.

If that same person $(B = 3)$ were given an item with a difficulty estimate of 2 logits $(D = 2)$, the expected probability of correctly answering that item would necessarily be lower than 0.88:

$$P_{ni}\left(x = 1 / B(3), D(2)\right) = \frac{2.7183^{(3-2)}}{1 + 2.7183^{(3-2)}} = \frac{2.7183^1}{1 + 2.7183^1} = 0.73 \qquad (3.2)$$

(i.e., the probability would be 73%).

By following the same procedure in equations 3.1 and 3.2, we can see how an item perfectly targeted for that person, (i.e., an item with a difficulty estimate [e.g., $D = 3$] equal to the ability estimate of the person [$B = 3$]), results in a 50/50 likelihood of that person successfully passing that item:

$$P_{ni}\left(x = 1 / B(3), D(3)\right) = \frac{2.7183^{(3-3)}}{1 + 2.7183^{(3-3)}} = \frac{2.7183^0}{1 + 2.7183^0} = 0.50 \qquad (3.3)$$

Similarly, encountering a more difficult item (e.g., $D = 4$) would result in a less than 50/50 probability of passing:

$$P_{ni}\left(x = 1 / B(3), D(4)\right) = \frac{2.7183^{(3-4)}}{1 + 2.7183^{(3-4)}} = \frac{2.7183^{-1}}{1 + 2.7183^{-1}} = 0.27 \qquad (3.4)$$

Table B.1 shows the probabilities of passing an item for a variety of difference values between B_n (in rows) and D_i (in columns). If the values for ability (B_n left-hand column) and difficulty (D_i heading row) column are placed in equation 3, the probabilities of success will match the corresponding values in

TABLE B.1 Probability of Agreeing With an Item for Various Differences Between Item Difficulty (column) and Person Ability (row)

Di	3.00	2.50	2.00	1.50	1.00	0.50	0.00	-0.50	-1.00	-1.50	-2.00	-2.50	-3.00
Bn													
3.00	0.50	0.62	0.73	0.82	0.88	0.92	0.95	0.97	0.98	0.99	0.99	1.00	1.00
2.50	0.38	0.50	0.62	0.73	0.82	0.88	0.92	0.95	0.97	0.98	0.99	0.99	1.00
2.00	0.27	0.38	0.50	0.62	0.73	0.82	0.88	0.92	0.95	0.97	0.98	0.99	0.99
1.50	0.18	0.27	0.38	0.50	0.62	0.73	0.82	0.88	0.92	0.95	0.97	0.98	0.99
1.00	0.12	0.18	0.27	0.38	0.50	0.62	0.73	0.82	0.88	0.92	0.95	0.97	0.98
0.50	0.08	0.12	0.18	0.27	0.38	0.50	0.62	0.73	0.82	0.88	0.92	0.95	0.97
0.00	0.05	0.08	0.12	0.18	0.27	0.38	0.50	0.62	0.73	0.82	0.88	0.92	0.95
-0.50	0.03	0.05	0.08	0.12	0.18	0.27	0.38	0.50	0.62	0.73	0.82	0.88	0.92
-1.00	0.02	0.03	0.05	0.08	0.12	0.18	0.27	0.38	0.50	0.62	0.73	0.82	0.88
-1.50	0.01	0.02	0.03	0.05	0.08	0.12	0.18	0.27	0.38	0.50	0.62	0.73	0.82
-2.00	0.01	0.01	0.02	0.03	0.05	0.08	0.12	0.18	0.27	0.38	0.50	0.62	0.73
-2.50	0.00	0.01	0.01	0.02	0.03	0.05	0.08	0.12	0.18	0.27	0.38	0.50	0.62
-3.00	0.00	0.00	0.01	0.01	0.02	0.03	0.05	0.08	0.12	0.18	0.27	0.38	0.50

the matrix in Table B.1. Note that when item difficulties are greater than person abilities (negative $B_n - D_i$ values), persons have a lower than 50% probability of correctly answering the item. Likewise, when item difficulties are lower than person abilities (positive $B_n - D_i$ values), persons have a higher than 50% probability of correctly answering the item.

Parameter Separation

Parameter separation implies that one set of parameters (e.g., the items) can be estimated without knowing the values for the other set (e.g., the persons). This is taken advantage of in the estimation procedure known as Conditional Maximum Likelihood Estimation. To demonstrate the calculation of the relationship between the abilities of two persons (i.e., B_n and B_m) independent of the actual difficulty value for an item (D_i):

Now

$B_n - D_i \cong \log\left(F_{ni} / F_{in}\right)$ where F_{ni} is the count of successes by person n on item i; and

$B_m - D_i \cong \log\left(F_{mi} / F_{im}\right)$

So

$$B_n - B_m \cong \log\left(F_{ni} / F_{in}\right) - \log\left(F_{mi} / F_{im}\right) \tag{4}$$

So that the relationship between B_n and B_m can be estimated without knowledge of the difficulty of item D_i.

The capacity of the Rasch model to compare persons and items directly means that we have created person-free measures and item-free calibrations, as we have come to expect in the physical sciences—abstract measures that transcend specific persons' responses to specific items at a specific time. This characteristic, unique to the Rasch model, is called *parameter separation*. Thus, Rasch measures represent a person's ability as independent of the specific test items and item difficulty as independent of specific samples within standard error estimates. Parameter separation holds for the entire family of Rasch models.

Rating-Scale Model

The rating-scale model is an extension of the dichotomous model to the case in which items have more than two response categories (e.g., Likert-type scales). For example, if an item has four response choices (0 = strongly disagree, 1 = disagree, 2 = agree, 3 = strongly agree), it is modeled as having three thresholds. Each item threshold (k) has its own difficulty estimate (F), and this estimate is modeled as the threshold at which a person has a 50/50 likelihood of choosing one category over another. The first threshold, for example, is modeled as the probability of choosing a response of 1 (disagree) instead of a response of 0 (strongly disagree), and is estimated with the following formula:

$$P_{ni1}\left(x = 1 / B_n, D_i, F_1\right) = \frac{e^{\left(B_n - [D_i + F_1]\right)}}{1 + e^{\left(B_n - [D_i + F_1]\right)}} \tag{5}$$

where P_{ni1} is the probability of person n choosing "disagree" (category 1) over "strongly disagree" (category 0) on any item (i). In this equation, F_1 is the difficulty of the first threshold, and this difficulty calibration is estimated only once for this threshold across the entire set of items in the rating scale. The threshold difficulty F_1 is added to the item difficulty D_i (i.e., $D_i + F_1$) to indicate the difficulty of threshold 1 on item i. Given that $B_n - (D_i + F_1)$ has the same value as $B_n - D_i - F_1$ and helps to show more easily the shared bases of the Rasch models, the latter is used in the following explanations of the rating-scale model.

Modeling subsequent thresholds in the rating scale follows the same logic. The difficulty of endorsing category 2 (agree) instead of category 1 (disagree) is modeled as follows:

$$P_{ni2}\left(x = 2 / B_n, D_i, F_2\right) = \frac{e^{\left(B_n - [D_i + F_2]\right)}}{1 + e^{\left(B_n - [D_i + F_2]\right)}} \tag{6}$$

where B_n is the person ability, D_i is the difficulty of the entire item, and F_2 is the difficulty of the second threshold, estimated across all items. Thus the general form of the rating-scale model expresses the probability of any person choosing any given category on any item as a function of the agreeability of the person n (B_n) and the endorsability of the entire item i (D_i) at the given threshold k (F_k; Wright & Masters, 1982).

$$P_{nik} = \frac{e^{\left(B_n - D_i - F_k\right)}}{1 + e^{\left(B_n - D_i - F_k\right)}} \tag{7}$$

Furthermore, if these probabilities are converted to odds, parameter separation can be demonstrated for the rating-scale model as well:

$$\ln\left(\frac{P_{nik}}{1 - P_{nik}}\right) = B_n - D_i - F_k \tag{8}$$

By using the Greek symbols commonly used in statistics to indicate the parameters estimated (as opposed to the values calculated), the formula is expressed as:

$$\ln\left(\frac{\pi_{nik}}{1 - \pi_{nik}}\right) = \beta_n - \delta_i - \tau_k \tag{9}$$

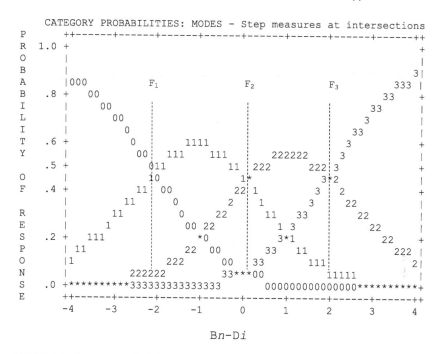

FIGURE B.1 Category probability curves for a rating-scale item with three thresholds.

where β_n is the person ability, δ_i is the item difficulty and τ_k is the difficulty of the kth threshold.

The thresholds for a set of rating-scale items can be depicted as the intersection of category probability curves for each response option (see Figure B.1). Figure B.1 shows F_1 as the threshold for choosing category 1 over category 0, F_2 as the threshold for choosing 2 over 1, and F_3 as the threshold for choosing 3 over 2. The x-axis expresses the difference between person ability (B_n) and item difficulty (D_i). So, for example, a person whose agreeability is 3 logits lower than the endorsability of the item as a whole $(B_n - D_i = -3)$ has a greater than 70% chance of choosing category 0. If, however, a person's agreeability is, for example, 3 logits higher than the endorsability of the item $(B_n - D_i = 3)$, category 3 is clearly the one most likely to be endorsed.

Partial Credit Model

The partial credit model can be seen as a version of the rating-scale model in which the threshold estimates, including the number of thresholds, are not constrained, that is, they are free to vary from item to item. When the partial credit model is used to model rating-scale data, it allows each item to vary in its threshold estimates. Whereas the rating-scale model used one set of threshold estimates that applies to the entire set of items (an example was depicted in Figure B.1), the partial credit model provides a set of individual threshold (k) estimates for each item (i):

$$\ln\left(\frac{P_{nik}}{1 - P_{nik}}\right) = B_n - D_{ik} \tag{10}$$

Therefore, the D_{ik} replaces the $(D_i + F_k)$ from equation 8, signifying that in the partial credit model, each set of threshold estimates is unique to its own individual item (i.e., threshold k for item i), instead of being estimated as a separate set of threshold estimates (F_k) for the entire set of items.

The partial credit model allows not only for an empirical test of whether the distances between response categories are constant for each item, but, more importantly, it allows the option for each item to vary in its number of response categories. A test or survey, for example, could comprise a mix of response formats, with some questions having two response options, some five, and some seven. This model could be ideal for situations in which partial marks are awarded for answers, such as essay examinations.

Many-Facets Rasch Model

The many-facets Rasch model adds yet more flexibility for estimating fundamental aspects of the measurement process. If we can imagine another aspect of the testing process (in addition to person ability and item difficulty) that might systematically influence persons' scores, for example, individual raters, specific tasks within an item, time of day the test is given, and method of testing (paper and pencil versus computer), we can estimate the impact of each facet on the measurement process. A difficulty estimate for each facet is calibrated, for example, the severity (C) of rater j. This severity is considered in the probability estimate of any person (n) responding to any item (i) for any category threshold (k) for any rater (j):

$$P_{nik} = \frac{e^{\left(B_n - D_i - F_k - C_j\right)}}{1 + e^{\left(B_n - D_i - F_k - C_j\right)}} \tag{11}$$

and is a function of the ability of the person (B_n), the difficulty of the item (D_i), the difficulty of the threshold (F_k), and the severity of the rater (C_j).

This model adheres to the principles of parameter additivity:

$$\ln\left(\frac{P_{nikj}}{1 - P_{nikj}}\right) = B_n - D_i - F_k - C_j \tag{12}$$

The symbols for the Rasch family of models are summarized in Table B.2.

TABLE B.2 Notation for the Rasch Family of Models

Values Calculated	Parameter Estimated	Definition
B	β (beta)	Person ability/measure
D	δ (delta)	Item difficulty/ calibration
F	τ (tau)	Category threshold/ calibration
C	λ (lambda)	Facet difficulty
P	π (pi)	Probability
n		Person
i		Item
k		Threshold
j		Facet
x		Response

Rasch Model Assessment

Reliability Indices

In the Rasch model, reliability is estimated both for persons and for items. The *person separation reliability* (R_p; Wright & Masters, 1982) is an estimate of how well one can differentiate persons on the measured variable. That is, it estimates the replicability of person placement across other items measuring the same construct. The estimate is based on the same concept as Cronbach's alpha. That is, it is the fraction of observed response variance that is reproducible:

$$R_p = \frac{SA_p^2}{SD_p^2} \tag{13}$$

The denominator $\left(SD_p^2\right)$ represents total person variability, that is, how much people differ on the measure of interest. The numerator $\left(SA_p^2\right)$ represents the reproducible part of this variability (i.e., the amount of variance that can be reproduced by the Rasch model). This amount of variance that is reproducible with the Rasch model is called the *adjusted person variability* $\left(SA_p^2\right)$. The adjusted person variability is obtained by subtracting error variance from total variance $\left(SD_p^2 - SE_p^2 = SA_p^2\right)$. This reproducible part then is divided by the total person variability $\left(SD_p^2\right)$ to obtain a reliability estimate for persons (R_p), with values ranging between 0 and 1 (Wright & Masters, 1982).

An alternative index for estimating the spread of persons on the measured variable is the *person separation index* (G_p). This is estimated as the adjusted person standard deviation (SA_p) divided by the average measurement error (SE_p), where measurement error is defined as that part of the total variance that is not accounted for by the Rasch model:

$$G_P = \frac{SA_P}{SE_P} \qquad (14)$$

Person reliability is expressed in standard error units (Wright & Masters, 1982, p. 92).

Reliability is estimated in the same manner as for persons, with item variance being substituted for person variance:

$$G_I = \frac{SA_I}{SE_I} \qquad (15)$$

The formula that follows converts the (person *or* item) separation index (G) into a strata index:

$$\text{Strata} = \frac{4G - 1}{3} \qquad (16)$$

which represents the number of measurably distinct strata (of persons or items) that can be supported by the data.

Test Information

Test information is routinely reported in graphical form and shows the Fisher information (y-axis) for a test at each point along the latent variable (in logits on the x-axis). The information is the inverse square of the person measure at that location of the variable (see Figure B2).

Test information is the amount of information provided by all of the items as it relates to any person parameter. The test information function is the sum of all the item information functions. Well-targeted persons have more information (and less error) than do poorly targeted persons.

Fit Statistics

Because the Rasch model is a strict mathematical expression of the theoretical relation that would hold among all items and all persons along a single underlying continuum, no items and persons will ever fit the model perfectly. We are interested, however, in identifying those items and persons whose patterns of responses deviate more than expectation, resulting in fit statistics for all persons and all items in the data matrix.

The estimation of fit begins with the calculation of a response residual (y_{ni}) for each person n when each item i is encountered. That is, how far does the actual response (x_{ni}) deviate from Rasch model expectation (E_{ni}; Wright & Masters, 1982)?

$$y_{ni} = x_{ni} - E_{ni} \qquad (17)$$

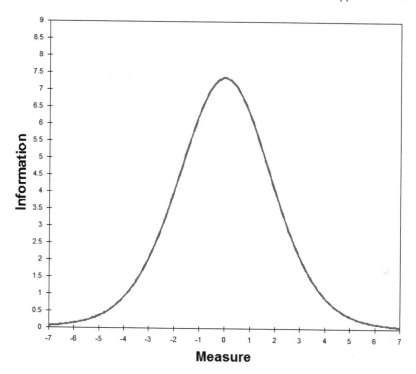

FIGURE B.2 Test information curve.

Because there are too many person–item deviations, or residuals (y_{ni}), to examine in one matrix, the fit diagnosis typically is summarized in a fit statistic, expressed either as a mean square fit statistic or a standardized fit statistic, usually a Z or t distribution. Additionally, these two fit statistics are categorized further into (a) those that have more emphasis on unexpected responses far from a person's or item's measure (outfit statistics) and (b) those that place more emphasis on unexpected responses near a person's or item's measure (infit statistics).

The outfit statistic is simply an average of the residual (z_{ni}) variance across both persons and items. This average is unweighted. That is, it is not influenced by (multiplied by) any other information. This results in an estimate that gives relatively more impact to unexpected responses far from a person's or item's measure (Wright & Masters, 1982):

$$\text{outfit} = \frac{\Sigma Z_{ni}^2}{N} \tag{18}$$

The infit statistic, on the other hand, is a weighted residual, in which relatively more impact is given to unexpected responses close to a person's or item's measure. Residuals are weighted by their individual variance (W_{ni}) to lessen the impact of unexpected responses far from the measure:

$$\text{infit} = \frac{\Sigma Z_{ni}^2 W_{ni}}{\Sigma W_{ni}} \qquad (19)$$

When these infit and outfit values are distributed as mean squares, their expected value is 1. Guidelines for determining unacceptable departures from expectation include flagging items or persons as misfits when mean square infit or outfit values are larger than 1.3 for samples less than 500, 1.2 for samples between 500 and 1,000, and 1.1 for samples larger than 1,000 (Smith, Schumacker, & Bush, 1995).

When reported simply as standardized Z or t values, the fit statistics have an expected mean of 0 and a standard deviation of 1. Note that t is a Student's t-statistic, which needs its accompanying df. So the Z statistic used for fit statistics is actually t with infinite degrees of freedom. Technically, $Z = t_\infty$. Here the recommended cutoff for flagging misfits includes Z or t values outside of ± 2.0 (Smith, 1992).

The four types of fit statistics (mean square, Z or t, infit, outfit) can be used separately or in combination for making fit decisions. Generally speaking, more emphasis is placed on infit values than on outfit values in identifying misfitting persons or items. The issues surrounding the estimation and interpretation of misfit are more thoroughly canvassed in Chapter 12. Table B.3 provides a summary of symbols and definitions for the model assessment formulas.

TABLE B.3 Notation and Definition for Model Assessment

Notation	Definition
R_p	Person reliability index; bound by 0 and 1
SA_p^2	Person variance, adjusted for measurement error
SD_p^2	Person variance, unadjusted
SE_p	Standard error for persons
SA_p	Standard error for persons, adjusted for measurement error
G_p	Person separation index; in standard error units
R_I	Item reliability index; bound by 0 and 1
SA_I^2	Item variance, adjusted for measurement error
SD_I^2	Item variance, unadjusted
SE_I	Standard error for items
SA_I	Standard error for items, adjusted for measurement error
G_I	Item separation index; in standard error units
γ	Residual
x	Observed score
E	Expected score from the Rasch model
Z_{ni}	Standardized residual for each person on each item
W_{ni}	Variance for an individual across a given item

GLOSSARY

aberrant	Departing from the expected standard.
ability	See *person measure*.
ability estimate	The location of a person on a Rasch measurement scale, calculated from the collected observations.
anchor	The process of using fixed (invariant) item values to ensure that different analyses produce directly comparable results.
anchor value	Preset values (in logits) assigned to particular items, persons, or thresholds used as invariant values for calibrating the measurements of other items, persons, etc.
Angoff method	A person-performance–based, criterion-referenced model for standard setting introduced by William Angoff in 1971.
anomalous	Deviating from what is expected.
average measure	In the RSM, is the average of the ability estimates for all persons in the sample who chose that particular response category. Higher response categories should have higher average measures.
bookmark method	An item-centered, criterion-referenced model for standard setting in which items are arranged in difficulty order from easiest to

hardest and subject matter experts place a bookmark at the location where the cut score should be constructed.

calibration

The procedure of estimating person ability or item difficulty by converting raw score odds to logits on a Rasch measurement scale.

classical test theory (CTT)

True score theory is classical in the sense that it is traditional. See also *true score model* and *traditional test theory*.

common-item linking

The procedure that allows the ability estimates of two different samples of persons to be plotted on a single scale when they have been measured on a common test.

common-person linking

The procedure that allows the difficulty estimates of two different sets of items to be plotted on a single scale when the two tests have been used with a common sample of persons.

common scale

A measurement scale along which all items, persons, etc. can be located.

concurrent validity

The validity of an instrument determined by how well it performs in comparison with another instrument that focuses on the same latent trait.

construct

The single latent trait, characteristic, attribute, or dimension held to be underlying a set of items.

construct validity

The theoretical argument that the items are actual instantiations or operationalizations of the theoretical construct or latent trait under investigation—that is, that the instrument assesses exactly what it claims to assess.

convergence

The point at which further improvement of the Rasch item and person estimates makes no practical difference to the results. The Rasch estimation iterations end at convergence.

counts

The simple attribution of numerals to record the number of observations. In the Rasch model, raw scores for items or persons are regarded as counts. Counts are merely ordinal.

data/model fit

The Rasch model is a confirmatory model and requires that the *data fit the model* in order to create interval measures from the data set. Exploratory models (e.g., other IRTs, SEM, G theory) require that the *model fit the data* in order to account for as much variance in the data set as possible.

dependent variable (DV)

The outcome variable, the variable being studied. The DV is expected to change in concert with changes to the independent variable(s). The DV might also be called the output variable, explained variable, or experimental variable, etc. See also *independent variable (IV)*.

deterministic

Characteristic of a model that implies the exact prediction of an outcome. Deterministic models explicate the relation between the observed responses and person ability as a causal pattern; for example, Guttman scaling is deterministic—the total score predicts exactly which items were correctly and incorrectly answered (cf. *probabilistic*).

dichotomous

Dichotomous data have only two values such as right/wrong, pass/fail, yes/no, mastery/fail, satisfactory/unsatisfactory, agree/disagree, male/female, etc.

DIF (differential item functioning)

The loss of item estimate invariance across subsamples of respondents. DIF is often called item bias.

difficulty

See *item difficulty*.

endorsability

A term used to represent the difficulty of endorsing a Likert-type items for attitude, satisfaction scales, etc.

error

The difference between an observation and a prediction or estimation; the deviation score.

error estimate

The difference between the actual observed and the expected response associated with item difficulty or person ability.

essential(ity) in objective standard setting

The quality of the item in which it is considered to be core content for the passing test taker to have mastered in order to successfully challenge the examination. Essentiality may be described as *very important, key, core, critical,* and by other descriptors appropriate for the group. Word choice for the group is critical to understanding that while all content on an assessment should be relevant and important, not all can or should be *essential*.

estimation

The Rasch process of using the obtained raw scores to calculate the probable values of person and item parameters.

expected response

The response predicted for a person according to the Rasch model.

facet

An element of the measurement condition. In Rasch measurement, the two key facets are person ability and item difficulty. Other facets in performance measurement might include judge, prompt, etc.

fair average

The "fair average" transforms the estimated MFRM person measure back into an expected average raw response value. It is "fair" to all elements in that it adjusts raw ratings for severe and lenient raters.

fit

The degree of mismatch between the pattern of actual observed responses and the Rasch modeled expectations. This can express either the pattern of responses observed for each candidate across items (person fit) or the pattern for each item across persons (item fit).

fit statistics

Indices that estimate the extent to which actual empirical responses differ from the Rasch-modeled theoretical expectations. Outfit statistics are unweighted; infit statistics are weighted. High fit values are regarded as misfitting (noisy, erratic) and low values as overfitting (muted).

fundamental measurement

Physicist Norman Campbell claimed that what physical scientists mean by measurement requires an ordering system and the kind of additivity illustrated by physical concatenation. He called this 'fundamental measurement'. The Rasch model is held to be a special (probabilistic) case of additive conjoint measurement, a form of fundamental measurement.

Guttman
See *Guttman pattern.*

Guttman pattern
A Guttman scale consists of a unidimensional set of items that can be ranked in order of difficulty, such that any person's entire set of responses to all items can be determined from that person's total score on the test. For a true Guttman pattern, the response pattern for person scoring, say 6 on a 10-item Guttman scale, will show success on items 1–6 and failure on items 7–10 when those responses are ordered by item difficulty, e.g., 1111110000.

identity line
A line with slope $= 1$, plotted through the means of two sets of calibrations for the purpose of linking them and testing their invariance. The identity line is the Rasch-modeled expected relation between the two sets of calibrations.

independent variable (IV)
The input variable(s). The researcher attempts to determine whether changes or differences in IV values are related to changes in the dependent variable (DV). Independent variable(s) might also be called predictor variable(s), regressor(s), or controlled or explanatory variable(s). See also *dependent variable (DV).*

inference
A conclusion reach on the basis of empirical evidence augmented by reasoning.

infit
See *infit statistics.*

infit mean square
One of two alternative weighted fit indices that indicate the degree of misfit of an item or a person (the other being standardized infit t/Z). Infit mean square is a transformation of the weighted residuals, the difference between the predicted and the observed, for easy interpretation. Its expected value is 1.

infit statistics
Residual-based statistics that indicate the degree of misfit of observations to the Rasch

modeled expectations. Squared residuals are information weighted, thereby giving more impact to on-target observations (cf. outfit statistics, which are unweighted). Infit statistics, then, are more sensitive to irregular *in*lying (on-target) response patterns and are usually expressed in two forms: (unstandardized) infit mean squares and (standardized) as a *t* or *Z* distribution.

infit *t/Z*

One of the two alternative infit indices that indicate the degree of fit of an item or a person to the Rasch model (the other being infit mean square). The infit *t* or *Z* (also called standardized infit) is the result of a transformation of information weighted mean square values to a distribution with a mean of 0 and *SD* of 1. Its expected value is 0.

interrater correlation

Also termed interrater reliability or interrater agreement, estimates the degree of agreement of scores provided by raters. It indicates the correlation between, there is in the ratings given by judges when evaluating performance assessments.

interval scale

A measurement scale in which the value of the unit of measurement is maintained throughout the scale so that equal differences between points on the scale have equal values, regardless of location. The 0 point on an interval scale is often regarded as arbitrary or pragmatic (e.g., 0 degrees Celsius) rather than absolute, as in a ratio scale (e.g., 0 Kelvin).

invariance

The maintenance of the value of an estimate across measurement contexts. For example, item estimates remain stable (within error) across samples and subsamples of suitable persons; person estimates remain stable (within error) across suitable tests and subtests.

IRT models

IRT (item response theory) models are based on the modern test theory concept that the probability of a correct response to an item is a mathematical function of person and item parameters. The name *item response theory* is due to its focus on the item, rather than the test-level focus of classical test theory.

item characteristic curve (ICC)
An ogive-shaped plot of the probabilities of a correct response to an item for any value of the underlying trait in a respondent.

item difficulty
An estimate of an item's underlying difficulty calculated from the total number of persons in an appropriate sample who succeeded on that item.

item fit statistics
Residual-based indices that show the extent to which each item performance differs from the Rasch-modeled expectations. A unidimensional variable requires sufficient fit of the items to the model.

item measure
The Rasch estimate of item difficulty in logits.

item reliability index
The estimate of the replicability of item placement within a hierarchy of items along the measured variable, if these same items were to be given to another sample of comparable ability. Analogous to Cronbach's alpha, it is bounded by 0 and 1.

item response theory (IRT)
The central postulate of IRT is that the probability of a person's expected response to an item is a mathematical function of that person's ability and one or more parameters characterizing the item. The response probability is displayed in the form of an item characteristic curve as a function of the latent trait.

item separation index
An estimate of the spread or separation of items along the measured variable. It is expressed in standard error units, that is, the adjusted item standard deviation divided by the average measurement error.

item strata
The number of item or person strata reflects the measurably distinct groups of items or persons from the Rasch analysis.

iteration

A repetition. In Rasch analysis computation, the item-estimation/person-estimation cycle is repeated (iterated) until a specified condition (convergence criterion) is met.

iterative process (standard setting)

Any process wherein the group members are required to discuss and reconsider their original ratings or markings. For example, in Angoff, group predictions might be rethought after the presentation of actual item difficulties or after group discussion of what other experts had predicted. Iterative processes largely norm the expert group data to group consensus.

latent trait

A human characteristic or attribute of a person inferred from the observation of person behaviors. Observable behaviors might display more or less that characteristic, but no one observation can cover all of the trait.

latent trait theory/models

IRT models are often referred to as latent trait models. Latent traits are hypothesized traits, constructs, or attributes that cannot be directly observed.

Likert scale

(after Rense Likert) A style of questionnaire format used widely in human science research, especially in the investigation of attitudes. Respondents to Likert-style instruments are given statements or prompts and asked to endorse a response from the range of ordered response options, such as 'strongly agree', 'agree', 'disagree', or 'strongly disagree'. Rense Likert's own scale requirements were much more stringent than most of those that now invoke his name.

limen

Threshold.

link

Relating the measures derived from one test with those from another test so that the measures can be directly compared.

logit

The unit of measurement (*log* odds un*it*) that results when the Rasch model is used to transform raw scores obtained from ordinal data to log odds ratios on a common interval scale. The value of 0.0 logits is routinely allocated to the mean of the item difficulty estimates.

logit scale — An interval level Rasch measurement scale adopting the *logit* as its iterative unit.

log odds — A logarithmic transformation of the odds or probability of success.

many-facets Rasch model (MFRM) — A version of the Rasch model developed by Mike Linacre of Chicago (esp.), in which facets of testing situation in addition to person ability and item difficulty are estimated. Rater, test, or candidate characteristics are often-estimated facets in performance assessments.

matrix — A rectangular table of responses (i.e., a data set) with rows (usually) defined by persons and columns (usually) defined by items.

mean squares — Rasch measurement fit statistics are reported as mean-square residuals, which have approximate chi-square distributions.

measurement — The location of objects (esp. persons and items) along a single dimension on the basis of scale intervals that add together.

measurement accuracy — The validity of the measurement; its trueness. Does the test measure what it is supposed to measure?

measurement error — Inaccuracy resulting from a flaw in a measuring instrument—as contrasted with other sorts of error or unexplained variance.

measurement precision — The amount of error or variation associated with any measurement.

misfit — Item and person performance patterns that are too erratic to meet the Rasch model probabilistic expectations are misfitting. Misfitting item and person performances degrade measures.

missing data — One or more values that are not available for a person or item for which other values are available; for example, questions in a survey that the respondent does not answer, the item(s) skipped by a child in a mathematics test. Rasch model procedures are robust in the face of missing data.

model

A mathematical model is used to estimate person and item parameters from discrete observations. Conversely, the probability of any response is a mathematical function of person and item parameters.

muted

Items or persons with unexpectedly low misfit values are considered muted or over-fitting. This indicates less variability in the data than the Rasch model predicts and generally reflects dependency in the data.

natural logarithm (ln or log$_e$)

The logarithm of a number to the base e, where e is a constant (≈ 2.718281828).

95% confidence band

In item or person linking, the interval within the control lines set by the investigator (at $p < .05$) requiring that 95% of measured items or persons should fit the model.

noisy

Items or persons with unexpectedly high misfit values are considered noisy or misfitting. This indicates more erratic or haphazard performance than the Rasch model predicts.

nominal scale

A scale in which numerals are allocated to category values that are not ordered (e.g., 1 = male, 2 = female; 1 = US, 2 = UK, 3 = Aust., etc.). Although allocations to categories are necessary for measurement, a nominal scale is not sufficient for any form of scientific measurement (cf. Stevens).

normal

The random distribution of an attribute, graphically represented as a bell curve. The distribution has a mean of 0 and a standard deviation of 1.

normalized

the transformation of the actual statistics obtained so that they theoretically approximate a normal distribution.

objective standard setting (OSS) method

A content-based family of criterion-referenced, Rasch-based standard-setting models, including OSS for objective examinations and OSS for judge-mediated examinations, introduced by Gregory Stone in 1996.

observed response
The actual (empirical) response by a person to an item or prompt.

OECD-PISA
The Programme for International Student Assessment is a triennial survey that aims to evaluate education systems worldwide by testing the skills and knowledge of 15-year-old students.

one-parameter item
response model (1PL-IRT)
The Rasch model is *a* 1PL-IRT, not *the* 1PL-IRT. This description of the Rasch model highlights the Rasch focus on just one item parameter—difficulty—along with the model's membership in the IRT family of latent trait models. Such a description usually ignores the Rasch model focus on fundamental measurement.

order
The transitive relationship between values A, B, C, etc., of a variable such that A > B, B > C, and A > C, etc.

order effect
When persons receive more than one test, survey, treatment, or intervention, the order in which they receive those treatments or interventions might affect the result. To avoid this potential problem, researchers often use a design of counterbalanced testing or treatments.

ordinal scale
A method of comparisons that ranks observations (puts them in an order) on some variable and allocates increasing values (e.g., numerals 1, 2, 3 or letters a, b, c, etc.) to that order. The size of differences between ranks is not specified. Although this is necessary for measurement, it is not sufficient for any form of scientific measurement (cf. Stevens).

outfit
See *outfit statistics*.

outfit mean square
One of the two alternative outfit indices that indicate the degree of misfit of the performance of an item or a person to the model (the other being standardized infit t/Z). Outfit mean square is a transformation

of the unweighted residuals, the difference between the predicted and the observed, for easy interpretation. Its expected value is 1.

outfit statistics

Residual-based statistics indicating the degree of misfit of observations to the Rasch modeled expectations. Unweighted squared residuals are summed and averaged (cf. weighted infit statistics). Outfit statistics, then, remain more sensitive to irregular *out*-lying (or off-target) response patterns and are usually expressed in two forms: (unstandardized) outfit mean squares and (standardized) as a t or Z distribution.

outfit t/Z

One of the two alternative outfit indices that indicate the degree of misfit of an item or a person to the Rasch model (the other being outfit mean square). The outfit t or Z (also called standardized outfit) is the result of a transformation of unweighted mean square values to a distribution with a mean of 0 and SD of 1. Its expected value is 0.

overfit

Item or person performances that are more determined than expected by the Rasch model, so that misfit is so low as to be 'too good to be true'. Generally, overfit does not contribute to good measurement, but does not degrade it. See also *muted*.

partial credit model (PCM)

An unconstrained Rasch model for polytomous data, developed in the work of Geoff Masters (esp.), which allows the number of ordered response categories and/or their threshold values to vary from item to item.

pathway variable map

A Rasch item/person or variable map which incorporates measures, SEs and fit in one figure. The Pathway variable map was original with Bond & Fox (2001).

Pearson's r

The Pearson product-moment correlation coefficient is an estimation of the linear relationship between two (interval data) variables. Values range from -1 to $+1$.

perfect score	The maximum possible score a respondent can achieve on a given test by answering all items correctly or endorsing the highest-level response category for every survey prompt.
person ability	See *person measure*.
person fit statistics	Residual-based indices that show the extent to which each person performance differs from the Rasch-modeled expectations. A unidimensional variable requires sufficient fit of the persons to the model.
person measure	An estimate of a person's underlying ability based on that person's performance on a set of items that measure a single latent trait. It is calculated from the total number of items to which the person responded successfully in an appropriate test.
person reliability index	The estimate of the replicability of person placements that can be expected if a particular sample of persons were to be given another set of suitable items measuring the same construct. Analogous to Cronbach's alpha, it is bounded by 0 and 1.
person separation index	An estimate of the spread or separation of persons on the measured variable. It is expressed in standard error units, that is, the adjusted person standard deviation divided by the average measurement error.
polytomous	Polytomous data have more than one value. As dichotomous data are a special case, having two values (usually 0,1), the term polytomous is usually reserved for data with more than two values (e.g., 0,1, 2, 3; 0,1, 2, 3 *etc.*)
probabilistic	The outcomes of the Rasch model (and IRT models in general) are expressed mathematically as probabilities. The Rasch model is probabilistic (in contrast to the Guttman model, which is deterministic) in that the person measure predicts with varying degrees of uncertainty which items were

correctly answered. See also *stochastic* and *Guttman*.

Rasch model

A mathematical formula for the probability of success (*P*) based on the difference between a person's ability (*B*) and an item's difficulty (*D*).

rater severity

See *severity (rater)*.

raters

Judges who assess candidates' test performances in terms of performance criteria. The MFRM estimates rater severity (leniency) in applying those performance criteria.

rating scale

A format for collecting responses in which the categories increase in the level of the variable, and this increase is uniform for all items/prompts.

rating scale model (RSM)

A constrained Rasch model for polytomous data, developed in the work of David Andrich (esp.) and Earling Andersen, now routinely used for the sort of polytomous data generated by Likert-type scales. The RSM constraint requires that every item in a test have the same number of response options and applies the one set of response threshold values to all items on the test.

ratio

Ratio measurement is the estimation of the ratio between a magnitude of a continuous quantity and a unit magnitude of the same kind. A ratio scale has non-arbitrary zero value.

raw scores

Scores or counts in their original state—that is, that have not been statistically manipulated.

reliability

The ratio of sample or test variance (corrected for estimation error) to total observed variance.

residual

A residual represents the difference between the Rasch model's theoretical expectation and the actual performance. Because Rasch probabilities are expressed as fractions and actual responses are recorded as whole numbers, *every* item/person interaction in a data set will yield some residual value. Large residuals are the result of unexpected performances and, so, contribute to misfit.

scalogram   A tabular display of person/item responses in which items are ordered by difficulty and persons by ability. See also *Guttmann pattern* and *matrix*.

segmentation   When tests with items at different developmental levels are subjected to Rasch analysis, items representing different stages or levels should be contained in different segments of the scale with a nonzero distance between segments. The items should be mapped in the order predicted by the underlying substantive theory.

separation   The ratio of sample or test standard deviation (corrected for estimation error) to average estimation error.

severity (rater)   The MFRM term which represents the severity or leniency of any judge or rater who awards performance ratings to persons on items when applying the judging criteria. Each of the raters is modeled to exhibit a specific amount of leniency or severity, and to act as an independent expert, not as a "scoring machine". Each rater is expected to judge consistently, but not identically to other raters.

Spearman's *rho*   Spearman's rank correlation coefficient is a nonparametric estimate of the relationship between two (ordinal data) variables. Values range from -1 to $+1$.

specific objectivity   The measurement of any person's trait is independent of the dispersion of the set of items used to measure that trait (i.e., item-distribution free) and, conversely, item calibration is independent of the distribution of the ability in the sample of persons who take the test (i.e., person-distribution free).

standard deviation   The root mean square of the differences between the calculated logit values and their mean.

standardized fit statistics

Usually expressed as t/Z, standardized fit statistics are the result of a Wilson-Hilferty transformation of mean squared residuals to a distribution with mean of 0 and an SD of 1. Following the traditional interpretation of t/Z statistics, values between -2 and $+2$ are interpreted as fitting (at $p < .05$). Mean square fit statistics indicate the *amount* of misfit; standardized fit statistics indicate the *likelihood* of that misfit.

standardized infit

See *infit t/Z*.

standardized outfit

See *outfit t/Z*.

step

See *threshold*.

stochastic

Characteristic of a model that expresses the *probabilistic* expectations of item and person performance on the construct held to underlie the observed behaviors. See also *deterministic*.

sufficient statistic

A statistic is *sufficient* for a statistical model and any parameter if no other statistic calculated from that sample yields more information as to the value of the parameter. In Rasch measurement, 'N correct' is the sufficient statistic for estimating item difficulty and person ability.

t_∞

See *t statistic*.

targeted

A well-targeted instrument has a distribution of items that matches the range of the test candidates' abilities. Ideally, the means and SDs of items and persons would match closely, too.

test equating

(is often used to describe) the process of equating the units and origins of two scales on which abilities have been estimated from different tests. In the strictest sense, it is the process of producing psychometrically identical tests with different contents (items), e.g., Form A and Form B (requiring no *post hoc* adjustment).

three-parameter item response model (3PL-IRT)

An item response model that estimates three item parameters—item difficulty, item discrimination (or slope), and a (pseudo-)

guessing parameter—to better fit the resultant model to the empirical data.

threshold

The level at which the likelihood of failure to agree with or to endorse a given response category (below the threshold) turns to the likelihood of agreeing with or endorsing the category (above the threshold).

traditional test theory

See *true score model* and *classical test theory*.

true score model

A traditional psychometric model that posits that any observed test score is the composite of two hypothetical components: a (unknowable) true score and a random error component. True score theory focuses on the level of the whole test (cf. *item response theory*).

t **statistic**

This is a student's *t*-statistic, which needs its accompanying *df*. The *Z* statistic is actually *t* with infinite degrees of freedom. Some Rasch software packages show *t* even when they are reporting *Z*. Technically, $Z = t_\infty$.

two-parameter item response model (2PL–IRT)

An item response model that estimates two item parameters—item difficulty and item discrimination (slope)—to better fit the model to the empirical data.

underfit

Item or person performances that are more erratic than expected by the Rasch model, so that misfit is so high as to degrade measurement. See also *noisy*.

unidimensionality

A basic concept in scientific measurement that only one attribute of an object (e.g., length, width, weight, temperature, etc.) be measured at a time. The Rasch model requires a single (i.e., unidimensional) construct to be underlying the items that form a hierarchical continuum.

unweighted

The calculation of fit in which all residuals are given equal impact in fit analysis, regardless of the amount of the information contained in them.

validity	Evidence gathered to support the inferences made from responses to explicate the meaningfulness of a measured construct through examining person fit, item fit, and item and person ordering and the like. Validity is an argument, not any statistic.
variable	An attribute of the object of study that can have a variety of magnitudes. The operationalization of a scale to measure these values is termed variable construction. Any variable is necessarily unidimensional.
visual analog scale (VAS)	Scale designed to present to the respondent a rating scale with minimum constraints. Usually respondents are required to mark the location on a line segment corresponding to the amount to which they agree or the amount of pain they feel, etc. The score is routinely read from the scale in millimeters. VAS data are ordinal, *not* interval level data.
weighted	The adjustment of a residual for fit calculation, according to the amount of information in the residual.
Wright map	A representation of the relationship between the distributions of person and item measures plotted along a vertical logit scale. An item/person or variable map.
Z statistic	This is a t statistic with infinite degrees of freedom. Technically, $Z = t_\infty$.
Zstd	See *Z statistic.*

AUTHOR INDEX

SUBJECT INDEX